Stonewall's Prussian Mapmaker

CIVIL WAR AMERICA

Gary W. Gallagher, Peter S. Carmichael,
Caroline E. Janney, and Aaron Sheehan-Dean, *editors*

Stonewall's
Prussian Mapmaker

The Journals of
CAPTAIN OSCAR HINRICHS

Edited by
RICHARD BRADY WILLIAMS
Foreword by Robert K. Krick

The University of North Carolina Press *Chapel Hill*

This book was published with the assistance of the Fred W. Morrison Fund for Southern Studies of the University of North Carolina Press.

© 2014 THE UNIVERSITY OF NORTH CAROLINA PRESS

Cover illustration of Oscar Hinrichs and title page illustration of Hinrichs after the Civil War both from the Henson Family Properties; courtesy of the Jim Henson Company Archives.

Library of Congress Cataloging-in-Publication Data
Hinrichs, Oscar.
Stonewall's Prussian mapmaker : the journals of Captain Oscar Hinrichs / edited by Richard Brady Williams ; foreword by Robert K. Krick.
pages cm. — (Civil War America)
Includes bibliographical references and index.
ISBN 978-1-4696-1434-2 (cloth : alk. paper)
ISBN 978-1-4696-5910-7 (pbk. : alk. paper)
ISBN 978-1-4696-1435-9 (ebook)
1. Hinrichs, Oscar—Diaries. 2. United States—History—Civil War, 1861–1865—Personal narratives, Confederate. 3. Confederate States of America—Army—Officers—Diaries. 4. Cartographers—Confederate States of America—Diaries. 5. German American soldiers—Confederate States of America—Diaries. 6. Soldiers—Confederate States of America—Diaries. 7. United States—History—Civil War, 1861–1865—Cartography. 8. United States—History—Civil War, 1861–1865—Maps. I. Williams, Richard Brady, editor. II. Title.
E605.H63 2014
973.7′82092—dc23
[B]
2014010105

Thanks to the descendants of Oscar Hinrichs who have preserved his legacy; Rosanne Thaiss Butler, a researcher extraordinaire; and Mary Jo Williams, my wife and best friend

Contents

Figures and Maps

Maps

Foreword

European officers who served in the Army of Northern Virginia, or who visited it at length, afford a valuable perspective on the famous army and its leaders and campaigns. With the publication of his wonderful contemporary account, Oscar Hinrichs moves to the head of that foreign legion.

Justus Scheibert, Fitzgerald Ross, Heros von Borcke, and others of similar origin sometimes enjoyed a vantage point as useful as Hinrichs's, but none of them remained in place for anything remotely like his tenure. The combination of an assignment at important headquarters and service that covered several years gave the Prussian cartographer a unique advantage as narrator. His smart and literary sensibilities, and his diligent attention to his record of events almost every day, augment the other attributes to constitute an enormously important primary source.

Oscar Hinrichs spent virtually his entire Confederate career on duty at the headquarters of some component of the Second Corps of the Army of Northern Virginia—then eventually in the corps commander's establishment itself. That brings to mind the classic contemporary accounts by Jedediah Hotchkiss and G. Campbell Brown. The Hinrichs narrative deserves as much attention as those fine sources have earned and makes with them an invaluable trilogy of spotlights illuminating the corps and its officers.

Fascinating descriptions, opinions, and analyses brighten almost every page of the journals. The European undertones in the language, and in some opinions, spice Hinrichs's observations.

Some passages address important military operations, widely reported and discussed elsewhere. Hinrichs also remarks at length on some engagements less well known. His thoughtful summary of Mine Run (Hinrichs calls the engagement "Paynes Farm"), for instance, deserves attention.

Entries in the diary and journal provide details on temporary organizational adjustments. Hinrichs describes, for one example, the shuffling within the Second Corps in mid-May 1864, necessitated by dire losses at Spotsylvania's East Angle and Bloody Angle. The ad hoc organizations that resulted are not well explained anywhere else.

Amusing and whimsical anecdotes intervene between deadly serious portions of the journals. The day before the Third Battle of Winchester, Hinrichs watches the renowned memoirist Henry Kyd Douglas ride away for an outing "with his sweetheart." Douglas had hopes of "having a good start" over the corps commander, the sometimes outspokenly misogynist General Jubal A. Early, "who is also crazy about that woman." Douglas was doomed to disappointment, Hinrichs prophesies, "because old Early has already too great an advantage."

The journals provide ample evidence that Captain Hinrichs quickly engaged his comrades, whether positively or not. A great strength of his work is how many individuals he describes without inhibition. He likes more than he dislikes among the people with whom he interacts. In neither category did Victorian conventions prompt him to be discreet in his private forum. That attitude redounds decidedly to the benefit of modern readers. The reticence to criticize that impairs many narratives from that era did not afflict Oscar Hinrichs.

Although much more in these pages is salutary than hostile, negative comments in the journal probably will be those most often quoted because of their frankness. Braxton Bragg "is an old woman." General Edward Johnson, freshly captured at Spotsylvania, "the Yankees may keep." General George H. Steuart's reputation is "a very poor one. . . . [H]e was not the man for this division." General William B. Taliaferro is a "man lacking much. . . . Thus wags the world." And a Tar Heel colonel is "like most N.C. officers not worth much."

In a number of cases, Hinrichs judges an officer positively and then gradually retrenches—or, on the other hand, offers an early negative opinion that he reverses over time. Observing those evolutions, and the reasons for them, makes for entertaining reading. General Isaac Ridgeway Trimble did not impress Hinrichs at first: "As a fighting man, I did not think much of him," he reports. The fiery Marylander, though—one of the oldest general officers in the army—gave Hinrichs occasion to repent of that judgment: "these first impressions have been materially changed since then. I have seen him stand cool and quiet among a shower of balls that might have excused anyone from desiring more of them."

Men who earned Hinrichs's firm respect usually retained it, even when public opinion turned against them. He remained confident of generals William H. C. Whiting, Williams C. Wickham ("short and bowlegged," in deft description), and Jubal A. Early when animadversions against them appeared in the public press. In a spirit familiar to warriors in many American wars, Oscar suggests disgustedly: "I wish that all these damned newspapermen would be put into the service."

Hinrichs dismisses emphatically and amusingly a lesser figure, clergyman Beverley Tucker Lacy, who had been Stonewall Jackson's favorite preacher.

Despite the perfervidly pious Jackson's high opinion, some observers thought Lacy a fraud. Captain Hinrichs declares bluntly: "a wretched fellow and a still more wretched soul. . . . I did not like his ways."

Among the most memorable phrases in the journals is the captain's colorful usage about Jubal Early's voice. Contemporaries wrote of an annoying nasal whine. Hinrichs's version will be the quote of choice henceforth. He describes the general's "cracked chinese fiddle voice."

Editor Rick Williams amassed this document by carefully integrating an olio of original pieces: diaries and journals, some in German and some in English, some in unadulterated original format and some transcribed by Hinrichs from original versions. Careful editing and annotations by Williams smooth and enrich the resulting text.

Civil War seminars and symposiums often include as a staple feature a session in which the speakers form a panel to discuss the best (and sometimes the worst) recent publications in the field. In conclusion, such panels often look eagerly forward to the best new books known to be on the horizon. For a decade—while Oscar Hinrichs labored through a lengthy gestation period—I have been saying on such panels that when Oscar reaches print, his memoir will be a candidate for nomination as Confederate Memoir of the Decade and among the dozen best ever to reach print. Here is Oscar Hinrichs at last, and in splendid form.

Robert K. Krick

Preface

In the spring of 2000, Colonel Kenneth X. Lissner was stationed at the Quantico Marine base and contacted Dave Zullo, a Civil War dealer, to assess the historical importance of his great-great-grandfather's journals. Dave determined that the Civil War account of Oscar Hinrichs, a staff officer in Robert E. Lee's army, ranked among the top unpublished Confederate manuscripts known to exist. Colonel Lissner asked him to find a museum or private collector to edit and publish these rare journals. Although living in the San Francisco area, I was on an East Coast business trip and stopped to see Dave in search of a letter or diary collection for my next book project. (I was in the process of completing research on *Chicago's Battery Boys: The Chicago Mercantile Battery in the Civil War's Western Theater* (2005), which was based on another collection I had acquired from Dave.)

The Oscar Hinrichs journals fulfilled my criteria for editing firsthand accounts: (1) the writer was well educated, articulate, and observant; (2) he had been involved in major events and could provide an insider's view; and (3) the diaries were a truthful, compelling record of the war and provided fresh insights for today's readers.

I acquired the Confederate diaries but decided first to establish their veracity before I began to edit them. After procuring Oscar Hinrichs's service records from the National Archives in Washington, D.C., I validated some important assertions that he made in his journals.

Oscar indeed wrote a letter to President Jefferson Davis on April 8, 1861, volunteering his services as a topographical engineer and, as noted, did not get a response. He later received support from influential North Carolinian politicians—including the Confederate States of America (CSA) attorney general—and respected military officers who helped him to obtain a commission in the elite Engineer Corps. He served on the staffs of Major General Thomas J. "Stonewall" Jackson and other prominent Confederate generals.

Next, I visited the National Archives facility in College Park, Maryland, where I reviewed records from the U.S. Coast Survey, a prestigious scientific organization that Oscar worked for prior to the war. My son, Richard Williams Jr., conducted more onsite research there. The correspondence we reviewed from 1856 to 1861 corroborated what Oscar had written regarding his surveys of the Carolina coasts—and that the head of the agency had tried to prevent him from leaving the Union to assist the Confederacy.

As part of my preliminary research, I also found Oscar Hinrichs's name listed in the *The War of the Rebellion: A Compilation of the Official Records of the Union and Confederate Armies* and in other books, such as Jed Hotchkiss's journals (the renowned cartographer mentioned Oscar sixteen times, usually related to maps they were working on together), John Beauchamp Jones's *A Rebel War Clerk's Diary*, Henry Kyd Douglas's *I Rode with Stonewall*, and William H. Parker's *Recollections of a Naval Officer*. During my extensive research and fieldwork, I substantiated nearly everything that Oscar chronicled during his service in Lee's army.

Being interested in "walking in Oscar's footsteps," I attended more than fifteen multiday battlefield tours conducted by leading historians such as Michael Andrus, Edwin C. Bearss, Arthur W. Bergeron Jr., Mark L. Bradley, Chris M. Calkins, Peter S. Carmichael, Gary L. Ecelbarger, Chris E. Fonvielle Jr., Gary W. Gallagher, Robert E. L. Krick, Robert K. Krick, Brooks D. Simpson, and Joseph W. A. Whitehorne. In discussions with the Kricks, I learned more about their assessment of Oscar's diaries, which they believed had significant historical value. Without the support and guidance of Robert K. Krick, this project would not have been completed.

Additionally, I visited numerous other relevant battlefields and historical sites on my own. One of the highlights of my battlefield trips was seeing the extant earthworks along White Oak Road southwest of Petersburg, which Oscar helped to construct near the end of the war. The Civil War Trust, a preeminent organization I have supported for twenty years, incorporated these fortifications into a small regional park.

Rosanne Thaiss Butler, my research partner, spent a year and a half compiling an impressive thirty-page history of the Hinrichs family, starting only with the names of Oscar, his father Carl E. L. Hinrichs, and the Reverend Harvey Stanley. She accomplished most of the initial work over the Internet and by accessing her network of archivist contacts in the historical-research community. After qualifying leads, Rosanne and I visited key repositories such as the Surratt House Museum and Research Center in Clinton, Maryland.

We continued to develop hypotheses, which we proved or disproved by conducting additional research, much as a scientist approaches a series of experiments. The discovery of information on the Reverend Harvey Stanley and his family, the 1892 *Washington Post* article on Oscar's death, Chris Klasing's history of the Ehringhaus family, and records from Holy Trinity Episcopal Church and Christ Episcopal Church were among our early research breakthroughs. Robert K. Krick also introduced me to author Gregg Clemmer, who provided surprising new information: Federal authorities had imprisoned Major General Edward Johnson, Henry Kyd Douglas, and Oscar Hinrichs to question them about the assassination of President Abraham Lincoln. Douglas wrote about this episode at the end of his memoir *I Rode with Stonewall*. (The Confederate officers were detained but exonerated.)

With the genealogical assessment nearing completion, we were ready to track down Oscar Hinrichs's direct descendants. At the time, Robert K. Krick was assisting the Marine archives at Quantico on a project and obtained the e-mail address for Colonel Lissner. I contacted the officer—not knowing that he was serving our country in Afghanistan—and he arranged for me to meet his mother, Adrienne "Addie" Lissner.

Colonel Lissner's grandmother, Dr. Mary Stanley Hessel, had given him the Civil War journals for which she had done some preliminary research. She was the daughter of Stanley Hinrichs, Oscar's eldest son, and an author and historian. I visited Addie in St. Louis and learned more about her family history and memorabilia. She showed me Dr. Hessel's oral-history notes; family photos; the Reverend Harvey Stanley's diary; her Revolutionary War book for Tryon Palace in New Bern, North Carolina; and Oscar Hinrichs's artwork (including an intricately drawn coat-of-arms and a Confederate flag drawing).

From Addie Lissner, I learned that family members of her cousin, Jim Henson, might also have Hinrichs information and memorabilia since they represented a different branch in the genealogical tree. I therefore sent an overview of the Hinrichs project to Cheryl Henson, a daughter of Jim Henson, who was one of Oscar's great-grandsons and the creative genius behind the Muppets.

Cheryl and her sisters, Heather and Lisa, supported this project, arranging for me to meet Barbara "Bobby" Miltenberger Henson. Bobby's mother was Sarah Hinrichs Brown, the only daughter of Oscar and Mary Stanley Hinrichs.

Although ninety-two years of age when I met her, Bobby Henson was extraordinarily sharp. She had retained her joie de vivre and lifelong passion for learning. I treasure those visits with Bobby—I am still amazed I got to speak with Oscar's granddaughter—and savor the stories she passed down from her mother, Sarah Hinrichs Brown. At the end of the interviews, Bobby presented me with a gift: a watercolor painting that Sarah Hinrichs Brown had created of her mother, Mary Stanley Hinrichs. For me, Addie Lissner and Bobby Henson exemplify many of Oscar Hinrichs's chief attributes, such as self-sufficiency, generosity, integrity, and a commitment to family and education.

Addie Lissner also provided another new lead: she recalled her mother saying that Oscar was involved with New York City's Central Park after the Civil War. Rosanne Thaiss Butler delved into this family story and, in the Library of Congress, found a *Guide to the Central Park*, which Oscar published in 1875, as well as an exquisite map he developed of the park. (It is not known whether Oscar drew the map from an existing version or if he conducted his own survey to produce it.) While it was exciting to find another *postwar* map that Oscar had drawn besides the one he produced of Mexico in 1888, Rosanne and I were nonetheless frustrated that we could not locate an extant Civil War map with Hinrichs's name on it—especially since there was irrefutable evidence that Oscar had worked on maps either alone or with Jed Hotchkiss.

After a thorough search of archives and museums, we had also been unable to find a photo of Oscar Hinrichs "to put a face to the story." We were thrilled when Cheryl Henson informed us that there were two of photos of Oscar in the Henson Family Properties. When Karen Falk, archivist for The Jim Henson Company, sent me the photos—one of Oscar in his Confederate uniform and the other an image of him after the war—she also provided a map of the Civil War. The latter was a detailed drawing of rebel fortifications, which Oscar had helped to construct, along the southern bank of the Rappahannock River near Germanna Ford and Chancellorsville. Bobby Henson furnished another image of Oscar Hinrichs as well as photos of his children (her mother and uncles).

Cheryl Henson also found out that one of her brothers, Brian Henson, had received other memorabilia from their father. First, there were copies of two letters—probably transcribed by Elizabeth Brown Henson—which Oscar's stepmother Amalia Ehringhaus Hinrichs had written to her step-grandson, Stanley Hinrichs, in 1902 and 1903. These letters contained compelling genealogical information about Oscar, his parents, and Amalia.

In addition to these wonderful family letters, there was an essay, "From Maine to Dixie: In the Early Days of the War," which Oscar had written in his middle age. It offered a more detailed account of the mapmaker's escape from the North into the Confederacy than what was found in his journal. He evidently had hoped to get the essay published, but that never occurred. Oscar's granddaughter, Agnes Brown Jenkins, typed the Hinrichs essay in 1968, a year after the death of her mother, Sarah Hinrichs Brown. (There are scraps of Oscar's original handwritten version of this essay in his collection.)

Other family members, such as Oscar's great-grandchildren Dr. Stanleigh Jenkins, William Hinrichs Jenkins, Fred Miltenberger, and Barbara Miltenberger Erwin, shared their family's information and memorabilia with me as well. A great-great-granddaughter, Cindy Lissner Hartley, provided a copy of Oscar's only known watercolor painting—a riverfront city, possibly Holzminden in Germany, where he studied as a young man. (Cindy's son Donald has "Hinrichs" as his middle name, as does William Jenkins's daughter and grandson.)

Copies of the Hinrichs family's memorabilia are preserved in the Henson Family Properties of the Jim Henson Company Archives. I have also incorporated them into my book and website (www.civilwarlegacy.com). I am grateful that archivists from the University of North Carolina at Chapel Hill's Southern Historical Collection have agreed to accept my donation of the Oscar Hinrichs journals so that future historians can further study this collection.

Using the research that Rosanne and I conducted and everything the family shared with us, we answered all of the major questions about Oscar Hinrichs, except for burial information. While records in the Maryland State Archives and the Vital Records Division of the Government of the District of Columbia indicate that Oscar and his wife were buried at Holy Trinity Episcopal Church in Bowie, Maryland, we could not find any Hinrichs gravestones on the church property. We are hopeful that someone will solve this mystery about the Hinrichs burial sites.

The remarkable "Oscar Hinrichs discoveries" continued up until my last week of conducting research for this project. Now living near the University of North Carolina, I decided to return for one final examination of the Southern Historical Collection to review the papers of Colonel William F. Martin from Elizabeth City and Major General Jeremy F. Gilmer. The former had helped Oscar to enter the Confederacy; the latter was in charge of the Confederate Engineer Corps. After looking at those documents, I examined the collection of Lenoir Chambers, a Pulitzer Prize–winning newspaper editor from Norfolk who had written a two-volume book on Stonewall Jackson in 1959.

In Chambers's miscellaneous files, I found a "second-generation typescript" of Oscar Hinrichs's narrative from November 1860 to December 1863. On page seventy-nine there is a handwritten note from H. Stanley Hinrichs, Oscar's attorney son who kept the original journals, regarding a commendation his father received at Chancellorsville. Initials from his brother Frank, plus the date "10/23/05," appear at the end of the typescript. Frank worked at the White House as a clerk and was proficient at typing. (The paper he used for the typescript might have been outdated White House stationary since each sheet contains a 1903 watermark by Crane, which at that time was the premier producer of high-quality paper for important government documents, stocks, and bonds.)

Early in the process of transcribing and editing the Hinrichs journals, I realized how confusing this project was going to be. It is actually a combination of a *contemporaneous* wartime narrative—written by Oscar Hinrichs when his November 1860–September 1863 notebooks fell apart—and a traditional journal, which he started out writing in English and then switched to German.

At the end of 1862, Jackson's army went into winter camp south of Fredericksburg. During the month of February, Oscar transcribed the journal entries from his damaged notebook into a narrative form. He began his chronicle of the war with the following explanation: "My note-book being on the point of giving out, I transcribe and make addition to the notes therein contained, being notes public and private of my own personal feelings and experience during the war, and with persons with whom the fortunes of war has brought me in contact. I also relate my opinion at the time of measures and affairs as they occurred to me."

Oscar Hinrichs repeated the same transcription process during the following 1863–1864 winter camp. In September 1863, however, he switched from notebooks to standard journal books, keeping concurrent records for four months.

Using the narrative-journal overlap, I verified that Oscar adhered to his original diary entries—other than adding a few additional observations, mainly an elaboration of battles in which he participated. For example, Oscar wrote very little in his journal about the Battle of Payne's Farm during Lee's Mine Run Campaign, probably since he was wounded there. A couple of months later, the staff officer added information on the events leading up to the engagement and what transpired on the battlefield. Before he died, Oscar either typed the narrative himself, as well as his English and German diaries from September 1863 to April 1865, or arranged for someone else to produce a copy. According to his family, he hoped to get his Civil War account published. Family members kept the project alive by transcribing and preserving the journals.

In developing this book, I have included the following:

- November 1860 to September 1863—a wartime transcript of Oscar's narrative
- September 1863 to April 1865—Oscar's *verbatim* English journal and translation of his German journal
- September to December 1863 overlap—both the mapmaker's commentary and diary entries covering the same period

I also hired an expert in Old German, Jeannette Norfleet, to review approximately one-third of the German portions of Oscar's diaries. She validated that they were translated without embellishment.

My strategy for this project has been to exercise a "light editorial touch." Therefore, I have transcribed Oscar's journals just as he wrote them. Based on my study of his wartime accounts, however, I believe that many errors occurred during the typing of the manuscript. For example, Major General

Chase Whiting was one of Oscar's friends, yet his name is misspelled in the narrative but not in the journals. Some of the other misspellings, such as "accross," "encampt," "undoubtably," and "decissive," simply reflect the mapmaker's personal writing idiosyncrasies.

Wherever I had the original diaries to consult, I corrected the transcription errors pertaining to the names of people and geographical sites. I did not change mistakes that were made by Oscar himself but added a bracketed correction—for example, "Sumpter [Sumter]" or "Rapidam [Rapidan]"—following the first appearance of the error. I have only used the standard editorial denotation *sic* in my introduction, epilogue, and endnotes when there is a misspelling within a quote from someone other than Oscar. I did not otherwise alter any of the narrative or diaries—with the exception of correcting minor punctuation and typographical errors like "mne," "gor," and "fro," which were changed to "men," "got," and "for," respectively. I kept intact Oscar's mistakes involving verb tense, syntax, run-on sentences, point of view, and the like.

By only correcting some superficial typographical errors, I have preserved the integrity of Oscar Hinrichs's chronicle of the Civil War. My estimate is that 99 percent of the text is exactly as it appeared in the narrative transcript and his original diaries. Any criticism of this editing strategy should be directed at me and not the publisher, researchers, or historians who assisted with this project. I take full responsibility for how I have reproduced and edited the Hinrichs manuscript.

To assist readers in gaining a better understanding of Oscar Hinrichs and the challenges he faced before and during the war, I have provided an introduction that contains salient information on his Prussian background, his Coast Survey work, the southern Maryland underground, and the Confederate Engineer Corps. I also added an epilogue to cover what happened to Oscar and his family after the war, including extensive footnotes that contain essential genealogical information.

Acknowledgments

I noted in my first book, *Chicago's Battery Boys: The Chicago Mercantile Battery in the Civil War's Western Theater*, that writing an academic-quality Civil War book is like participating in the Tour de France. In that marathon cycling race, the winner does not cross the finish line alone but achieves the victory on behalf of all those team members supporting the athlete behind the scenes. This book project has been another long journey, and many people have collaborated behind the scenes to bring it to fruition. Their knowledge, inspiration, and encouragement have been invaluable.

Robert K. Krick played a vital role in confirming the historical significance of Hinrichs's diaries and provided guidance as I edited and published them. What a thrill for me to receive assistance from one of the foremost authorities on Stonewall Jackson and Lee's Army of Northern Virginia.

I appreciate the continued support and encouragement I receive from Edwin Cole Bearss, a preeminent expert regarding all aspects of American history whom *Smithsonian Magazine* honored in its special thirty-fifth anniversary edition. He is a great role model for those of us who support Civil War battlefield preservation. It was an honor to work with Ed and my publisher on the trade paperback edition of *Chicago's Battery Boys*, Ted Savas; we donated signed copies of the book to raise funds for the Civil War Trust. I'm hopeful that *Stonewall's Prussian Mapmaker* can likewise be used to protect our American heritage.

In my quest to "walk in Oscar Hinrichs's footsteps," I visited over 100 Civil War–related sites as part of tours conducted by Ed Bearss. I cannot imagine having had a better guide to teach me about the military engagements and places described in the Hinrichs journals. I am also grateful that Ed reviewed portions of the manuscript, shared his insights throughout the development of this project, and validated my approach to editing firsthand Civil War accounts by extending his imprimatur to *Chicago's Battery Boys*.

I am fortunate to have had Rosanne Thaiss Butler, a gifted archivist, as my writing partner for this project. She provided sage editorial input and spent many hours playing "history detective" and strategizing with me. Her contributions to *Stonewall's Prussian Mapmaker* have been invaluable. As I handled the Civil War–related research, she focused on compiling genealogical information on Oscar Hinrichs and his immediate and extended family while investigating an assortment of unresolved topics.

Rosanne is eminently qualified to conduct research, having worked at the National Archives for twenty-six years and more recently as director of the Colonial Williamsburg Foundation Archives. Her husband, Stuart L. Butler, and daughter, Elisabeth Frederick Butler, both of whom are archivists, also assisted with this project. In addition to tracking down documents and reviewing the manuscript, Stuart accompanied Rosanne on two trips to Elizabeth City to conduct research on the family of Oscar's stepmother, Amalia Hinrichs, and her father, John C. Ehringhaus.

On their second trip to Elizabeth City, Rosanne and Stuart met with James MacNeill (Mac) Duff and his wife, Patty Duff. Mr. Duff shared information about his Ehringhaus ancestors and showed them a painting of his great-great-grandfather, John C. Ehringhaus, who had been one of the most influential businessmen in Elizabeth City at the time of the Civil War. At the end of this project, we benefited from the time Stuart spent living in Germany as he deduced that Oscar's watercolor painting probably depicted the town of Holzminden. Elisabeth Frederick Butler joined her mother on a research trip to Holy Trinity Episcopal Church and the John Surratt House Museum and Research Center, and she also obtained information from the Library of Congress and Fairfax County Public Library's Virginiana Room.

The following is a list of other people, along with museums and archives, who made this project possible: Elmer S. Biles; Christ Episcopal Church, Elizabeth City, North Carolina; Church of St. Stephen and the Incarnation, Washington, D.C.; Gregg Clemmer; Karen Falk, archivist for the Jim Henson Company; Chris E. Fonvielle Jr.; Sharon Gable, Family Research Society of Northeastern North Carolina, Elizabeth City; David W. Gaddy; the Geheimes Staatsarchiv Preussischer Kulturbesitz, Berlin, Germany; Donald Hinrichs Hartley; John Hennessy, Fredericksburg and Spotsylvania National Military Park; Ann Hentschel, who helped with research in Germany; Jane Henson; the Reverend Tom Andrews, the Reverend Mariann Babnis, Curt Reiber, and Sherrill Bower of Holy Trinity Episcopal Church, Bowie, Maryland; Fritz Hopfgarten of Die Maus, Gesellschaft fuer Familienforschung e. V., Bremen, Germany; Chris Klasing and his online monograph, *The Ehringhauses*; Robert E. L. Krick; the Reverend Christopher Lehnert, Marienkirche, Stralsund, Germany; the Library of Congress; A. K. Lorenz, Thueringisches Staatsarchiv, Altenburg, Germany; Timothy Mulligan, Captured German Records, the National Archives and Records Administration (NARA), College Park, Maryland; Eric Bittner and Eileen Bolger, NARA, Rocky Mountain Region, Denver, Colorado; Bill Seibert and Rosanne Mersinger, NARA, National Personnel Records Center, St. Louis, Missouri; Jeannette Norfleet; NARA, Washington, D.C.; North Carolina State Archives, Raleigh, North Carolina; Arthur Novell, the Jim Henson Legacy; Prince George's County Genealogical Society, Bowie, Maryland; Susan G. Pearl, Prince George's County Historical Society, Bowie, Maryland; the John D. Rockefeller Jr. Library, Colonial Williamsburg Foundation, Williamsburg, Virginia; Jane Singer; John Stanton; Stralsund, Germany, city archives; Swem Library, the College of William and Mary, Williamsburg, Virginia; Jeffries Thaiss, who conducted research at the New York City Municipal Archives; Laura C. Brown and Matt Turi, Southern Historical Collection, University of North Carolina at Chapel Hill; Laurie Verge, Sandra Wahlia, and Julia Cowdery, James O. Hall Research Center, Surratt House Museum and Research Center, Clinton, Maryland; Jayne Wheeler; and Steve Zerbe.

I would like to thank the following people who have provided timely encouragement as I have continued on my writing journey: Bill Bernhardt, Liz Berry, Dr. Naina Bhasin, Kirk Bradley, Mark Bradley, Louis Breton, Carrie Browning, Carol Williams Castelli, James Coon, Dr. Margaret Dardess, Clay Feeter, Lisa Gardner, Dr. Wolfgang Gilliar, Dr. Geraldine Hamilton, Dr. Charles Hamner, Helen Hannon, Peyton Howell, Lucas Johnson, Bob Menges, Mark Mitchell, Randy Perry, Len Riedel, Ted Savas, Sam Small, Wes Small, Adam Smith, Dr. David Stump, Taylor Poole, David van Doren, Greg Vontz, and Dr. Yang Yunsong.

There are two people from my youth and early adulthood that I want to recognize. Mrs. Mildred Dunham, my Advanced Placement English teacher at Penn Hills High School in Pittsburgh, Pennsylvania, taught me a lot about the principles of sound writing. Morris Fockler, who gave me my first opportunity to work at a bioscience corporate headquarters, generously shared his knowledge about effective written communication.

Most recently, I have had a unique opportunity to become friends with Dr. Richard Cox, who at age eighty-five recently published two books. He has been a great mentor and adviser. I'm blessed to have spent so much time in the past few years learning from him.

Gary Gallagher, renowned historian from the University of Virginia, and David Perry, retired editor in chief of the University of North Carolina Press, played key roles in getting the Oscar Hinrichs manuscript ready for publication. David's understudy, editorial director Mark Simpson-Vos, received the baton and took the project across the finish line. Thanks to George Skoch for again adding his masterful mapmaking touch to this latest project and to Paul Betz and Jay Mazzocchi for their editing insights.

I would also like to extend a special thanks to the following members of

Oscar Hinrichs's family who enhanced this project by diligently preserving his journals, essay, photographs, artwork, and other memorabilia: Sarah Hinrichs Brown (daughter); Cindy Lissner Hartley (great-great-granddaughter); Brian, Cheryl, Heather, John, and Lisa Henson (great-great-grandchildren); Barbara Miltenberger Henson (granddaughter); Elizabeth Brown Henson (granddaughter); Jane Henson; Dr. Mary Stanley Hessel (granddaughter); Frank Stanley Hinrichs (son); H. Stanley Hinrichs (son); Agnes Brown Jenkins (granddaughter); Dr. Stanleigh Jenkins (great-grandson); William Hinrichs Jenkins (great-grandson); Adrienne Hessel Lissner (great-granddaughter); Colonel Kenneth X. Lissner (great-great-grandson); Fred Miltenberger (great-grandson); and Barbara Miltenberger Erwin (great-granddaughter). Oscar and Mary Stanley Hinrichs would no doubt be pleased that this project has created new opportunities for their descendants to communicate with one another.

While doing the final editing of this book, I read Brian Jay Jones's *Jim Henson: The Biography*, which offered further insights into the broad scope of Jim Henson's artistic gifts and pursuits—and reinforced the legacy of Oscar Hinrichs. The artistic lessons handed down by Oscar and his only daughter (Sarah Hinrichs Brown) are seen by their family as providing the creative impetus for Jim Henson to become an innovator in visual-art entertainment. The biography also reminded me of the breadth and depth of Oscar's "Renaissance Man" interests, which ranged from ink drawing, painting, and map-making to music, poetry, and the theater.

I have also been blessed to be part of a family dedicated to lifelong learning. Beginning with my parents, Charles Brady and Josephine Nancy Williams, and continuing with all of the aunts, uncles, nieces, nephews, and spouses in the Castelli, Johnson, Myers, Tomashewski, and Williams families, there has been a strong commitment to books and education. Special thanks to Katie Winjammer, who shares her love of American history in the classroom and uses the Civil War memorabilia she has inherited from me in her lectures.

I especially appreciate the ongoing support I receive from Richard Jr. (son), Elizabeth (daughter), Megan (daughter-in-law), Mary Jo (wife), and Stephen (son-in-law) to pursue my writing quests. For this book, Richard conducted research at the NARA and uncovered a treasure trove of correspondence between Oscar Hinrichs, Carl Hinrichs, and the superintendent of the U.S. Coast Survey. His wife, Megan, supported the launch of this book project. Elizabeth offered constructive input throughout the process—and patiently listened to my litany of stories about the amazing Hinrichs research discoveries. Mary Jo was kind enough to spend many hours transcribing Oscar's narrative and journals as well as editing the manuscript. My life has been enriched by having such a wonderful son, daughter-in-law, daughter, son-in-law, and wife—along with two grandsons (Brady and Caleb), whom I hope will also carry on the Williams legacy of honoring our American heritage.

Ultimately, *Stonewall's Prussian Mapmaker* is about Captain Oscar Hinrichs. From the beginning, my goal has been to create awareness about a confident, ambitious, and idealistic man who, as an outsider, risked his career and life to join a cause that had a low probability of success. One might argue that the mapmaker's adventurous decision to join the Confederacy sent the trajectory of his life in the wrong direction—perhaps a misstep from which his career never recovered.

During the years I spent studying Oscar Hinrichs, I gained many new personal insights as I learned more about his courage, integrity, and intensity of purpose. I am confident that readers will also benefit from gaining access to Oscar's narrative and journals.

Stonewall's Prussian Mapmaker

Introduction

I found much pleasure in writing [in] my diary.

—Oscar Hinrichs

As the Civil War sliced the American nation in two, Oscar Hinrichs struggled with his own divided loyalties. Although working for the past five years charting the coast of North and South Carolina, he resided offseason in New York City, where his parents and siblings lived. He had a promising career in the U.S. Coast Survey, which was the preeminent scientific organization of its time. By the end of 1861, most of his mapmaking colleagues had already opted to remain with the Union and were poised for rapid advancement in the army and navy.

Alexander Dallas Bache, head of the Coast Survey and a member of the president's Blockade Commission, dangled promotional opportunities and pay increases in front of Oscar as he enticed him to stay in his agency. Keeping Oscar within his Federal grasp became a priority for Bache: as the only remaining expert mapmaker for the North Carolina coast, Oscar represented a threat to the planned blockade of the Confederacy if he abandoned the Union.

However, Oscar could not shake his allegiance to the South, where he had so many friends. If he wanted to join the rebels, he had to outmaneuver the Federal agents who monitored his mail and followed him around New York City. The most direct route passed through Baltimore to the Potomac River, where the U.S. government controlled the Union-Confederacy border.

Yet it would not be easy to penetrate the Union gauntlet in Maryland since the Lincoln administration exerted fierce control over the area that surrounded its capital. Blue-coated horse soldiers patrolled the plantation roads and forests of southern Maryland. Local Unionists kept an eye out for strangers. Even if he could reach the Potomac River, Oscar would have to cross at night to avoid enemy gunboats.

Oscar Hinrichs's stepmother grew up in Elizabeth City, North Carolina. She arranged for him to travel with the identification papers of her deceased brother. Reaching Baltimore, Oscar donned a disguise, eluded the detective following him, and headed for southern Maryland. His mother's best friend from her hometown, Mary Anne Kinney Stanley, promised to help. She now lived outside Washington, and her North Carolinian husband, Harvey Stanley, served as rector of Holy Trinity Episcopal Church in Collington. (After the war, Oscar designed the stained-glass window behind the altar of their church.) The authors of *Come Retribution: The Confederate Secret Service and the Assassination of Lincoln* (1988) conducted an extensive study of the rebel secret service and noted that Reverend Stanley "was a strong supporter of the southern cause and helped many Confederates traveling through Maryland."[1]

Reverend Stanley introduced Oscar to a small band of intrepid young men who traveled along the "Secret Line," which was like the Underground Railroad except that it facilitated the back-and-forth flow of rebels and materials between the Union and the Confederacy. Stanley's son Charles (Oscar's future brother-in-law) was on a winter leave from Maryland's 1st Infantry Regiment in search of new recruits for General Joe Johnston's army, quartered near Manassas.

Some of Reverend Stanley's congregation and neighbors, like Wat Bowie, were rebel spies and couriers; others used their homes as safe houses. Familiar with what became known as the "John Wilkes Booth escape route" through Port Tobacco, Bowie served the Confederacy as a secret agent and later became a Mosby Ranger. His knowledge of the rebel network in southern Maryland—including contacts to facilitate his crossing of the Potomac River—led to his fatal attempt in 1864 to kidnap the Maryland governor.[2]

After dark on December 29, 1861, Oscar and his new friends departed in an overloaded wagon for the way station run by John Surratt Sr. in southeastern Maryland. Surratt and his wife, Mary—later hanged for her alleged role in the assassination of President Abraham Lincoln—helped them to avoid being captured by Union cavalry patrols. Oscar took the lead to commandeer a Federal schooner and escaped with his comrades across the Potomac River to deliver their smuggled shipment, which included weapons, medical supplies, and secret dispatches for Confederate officials.

After the surrender of General Robert E. Lee's army at Appomattox Court House in April 1865, Oscar used his Guards and Patrols Pass to make his way from the Virginia battlefields to his home in New York City. Stopping in Washington, D.C., with his Confederate uniform acting as a lightning rod in the aftermath of President Lincoln's assassination, he visited a tailor to have new inconspicuous clothes made, but provost officials arrested him.

No. Provost Marshal's Office.

PETERSBURG, VA., Apl 16 1865.

Guards and Patrols Pass

Oscar Hinrichs. Paroled Prisoner

To City Point By R.R.

This Pass expires Apl 17 1865.

[illegible]

Lieut. 10th N. Y. Art. and Asst. Provost Marshal.

PROVOST MARSHAL'S OFFICE

Oscar Hinrichs's Guards and Patrols Pass, dated April 16, 1865

Henry von Steinecker, a draftsman who worked on maps in the Army of Northern Virginia before deserting, made false charges against Oscar, Major Henry Kyd Douglas, and Major General Edward Johnson, pulling them into the vortex of Lincoln's assassination. He testified that the Confederate officers, along with members of the 2nd Virginia Infantry in the Stonewall Brigade, met with John Wilkes Booth during the summer of 1863 in the Shenandoah valley.[3]

Besides being implicated in a conspiracy that dated back to his service under Stonewall Jackson, Oscar Hinrichs had other issues to worry about as Federal officials interrogated him. Mary Surratt, held in the same Old Arsenal prison, would soon be found guilty in the assassination conspiracy and hanged. She could have easily implicated him for colluding with southern Maryland blockade-runners. His confiscated journal contained entries from December 1861 to connect him with the Surratts—unless he had sent the first two years of his chronicle back to his parents. With the U.S. Coast Survey headquartered nearby, his former colleagues could also have worsened his situation by notifying authorities of his defection from the Union after signing an oath of allegiance.[4]

Additionally, Oscar had learned about covert rebel communication while traveling along the Secret Line. After Federal officials found a cipher in the

Oscar Hinrichs's wartime journals (Richard Brady Williams Private Collection)

Washington, D.C., hotel room of John Wilkes Booth, they sought to identify any Confederate loyalist who might be familiar with similar communication techniques. During the war, Oscar corresponded with fellow Confederate officer Charles Stanley and received at least one cipher letter from him. In *Come Retribution*, the authors stated that "personnel who enciphered or deciphered the messages had to be trained, and a procedure had to be developed to keep them apprised of changes in the cipher systems."[5]

Worse yet, near the end of the war, Oscar submitted a proposal to generals Robert E. Lee and John Gordon regarding a plot he developed to destabilize the Federal government. He planned to return to his family and friends in New York City as a secret agent to incite an insurrection (like the draft riots in July 1863) among the German residents there. An earlier scheme to wreak havoc in New York City had failed: Confederates tried to burn a dozen hotels on November 25, 1864, but the plot fizzled out.[6]

Despite switching to German for his journal entries starting in July 1864, Oscar ran the risk of having someone translate his incriminating diary into English. With suffocating circumstantial evidence mounting up against him, Oscar might not have escaped from being squeezed in the Federal vise that implicated Confederate officers and government officials in the conspiracy. His fate would likely have been the same as that of his comrade from the 2nd Virginia Infantry, John Y. Beall, who became a dangerous privateer and guerrilla warrior behind enemy lines; Federal officials convicted Beall of being a spy and hung him on February 24, 1865.[7]

Oscar Hinrichs had grown up in New York City among a burgeoning population of immigrants, which, at the beginning of the Civil War, included 120,000 Germans. His parents, Carl and Fanney Bettie Klaner Hinrichs, arrived in New York from Prussia in the spring of 1836 when Oscar was one year old. Fanney was "well educated and quite a talented musician." She came from Bremen, where her mother owned the largest hotel in town. Carl's birthplace was Stralsund, located in Pomerania on the Baltic coast. His father served as a "captain of the Guard of the King of Sweden."[8]

According to immigration records, Carl Hinrichs became a U.S. citizen in 1843; Oscar was probably naturalized at the same time. In America, the elder Hinrichs set up a successful importing business. He served for about twenty years as consul for the dukedoms of Saxe-Altenburg and Saxe-Coburg-Gothe, representing their business interests in America, and he also owned a chemical factory. Fanney died in March 1839 when Oscar was four years old.[9]

Carl Hinrichs married Amalia Matilda Gregory Ehringhaus, the granddaughter of a Revolutionary War general, in March 1841. His father-in-law, John C. Ehringhaus, had immigrated to the United States approximately fifty years before the Civil War. He served as a legislator (1819 and 1820) and Pasquotank County's registrar of deeds. A successful commission merchant, he owned real estate, opened a branch of the Bank of North Carolina (1835), and later started Ehringhaus Bank. Amalia treated Oscar as her own son and took him on visits to Elizabeth City, where he became immersed in Southern culture.[10]

Upon Amalia's request, John Ehringhaus paid for Oscar to study in Holzminden, which had been "a seat of learning for years." At that time, educators regarded Prussia's school system as the best in the world. Oscar traveled to Europe when he was twelve and stayed with an Ehringhaus niece. The niece's husband, Mr. Schiber, was "a professor in the Institution, where Oscar remained for 6 years receiving every benefit money could give him."[11]

Oscar studied French and other languages as well as the disciplines—science, mathematics, drawing, and mapmaking—that prepared him for a career in civil engineering. He had a variety of other talents and interests that included music, writing, and poetry. A skillful artist, he passed on that knowledge to his only daughter, Sarah. She also became an artist, and two of her daughters became pianists. Sarah, known in the family as "Dear," encouraged her grandson, Jim Henson, to develop his artistic skills and pursue his passion for entertainment and media, which led to the Muppets, *Sesame Street characters*, family-oriented movies, and other innovations in the visual arts.

His biographer wrote that "Jim Henson could trace his artistic ability, in a straight and colorful line" that ran directly from "his mother and grandmother back to his maternal great-grandfather, a talented Civil War–era mapmaker named Oscar." [12]

Well educated and highly confident in his abilities, Oscar left Prussia and returned to America in 1853. Using family connections, he received a job offer from the U.S. Coast Survey in December 1856 and traveled to North Carolina for his first assignment. Working on maps of the Atlantic coast from Virginia to Georgia, he spent considerable time in Wilmington, North Carolina, and Charleston, South Carolina, where he got to know rebel "fire eaters." Oscar respected the Southern gentleman code of honor—he once threatened to fight a Richmond newspaperman who insulted him—and supported the creation of a separate government. He believed secession would be "most conducive to the prosperity of the Southern States." In his postwar essay, Oscar wrote: "My sympathies were with the people of the South, among whom I had lived so long, and where I had many warm friends." [13]

Additionally, the close relationship Oscar had with his stepmother influenced his decision to join the Confederacy. Years later, Amalia Ehringhaus Hinrichs recalled that Oscar cared for her "truly as a child could love his mother." Upon leaving his position with the Coast Survey, he told his father: "the South has given me my mother and all [my] talent and strength I will give fully to the South." [14]

Oscar wrote a letter to President Jefferson F. Davis on April 8, 1861, four days before the bombardment of Fort Sumter. He sought an appointment in the Engineer Corps, knowing that his supervisor, Charles P. Bolles, planned to join the rebel cause. Bolles resigned from the Coast Survey on April 20, 1861, returning home to Wilmington. By default, Oscar became one of the Union's only remaining surveyors of the Atlantic Coast. [15]

Taking a lead role to establish the Union's "Anaconda Strategy," Alexander Dallas Bache feared that Bolles—and possibly Oscar—might thwart the secret Federal plan to assault the Carolina coast. In his annual Coast Survey report for 1861, Bache noted that Bolles resigned and took a "small vessel, the instruments that had been in the use of his party, and other property belonging to the government . . . and the sheets containing the topography executed by Mr. Hinrichs in the working season of 1859–'60." Bache's concerns became real as Bolles started to construct what would become Fort Fisher, the massive sand bastion between the Atlantic Ocean and the Cape Fear River. [16]

When Oscar did not receive a reply from President Davis, he decided to remain with the Coast Survey based on recommendations from his family, who thought the North-South conflict would soon be resolved. He obeyed orders from Bache to survey the wilderness of Maine and was working there when news from the Battle of First Manassas, fought on July 21, 1861, reached the remote parts of New England. "Surrounded by strangers," he hid his jubilation about the Confederate victory, recognizing "it was incumbent upon me to walk circumspectly."[17]

Coast Survey officials pressured employees to document their loyalty to the Union. Oscar conceded to see a notary public in Maine and signed an agreement, under protest, not to bear arms against the Federal government. In October he returned to his family in New York City, where detectives prevented him from leaving until he boarded a train on November 20: Bache had sent instructions for him to support Ambrose Burnside's North Carolina expeditionary force.[18]

When he reached Baltimore, Oscar spotted the detective who had shadowed him in New York City. He visited a barber to alter his appearance, changed clothes to make it seem like he was going on a hunting trip, and began to use his alias. Boarding a train for Bladensburg, he met a Confederate loyalist who agreed to transport him by wagon to "the heart of the 'Forest,' the richest and wealthiest portion of Prince Georges County." They avoided Union horse soldiers and reached the town of Collington, which today is part of Bowie. His mother's friends, Reverend Harvey and Mary Anne Stanley, pretended he was their cousin.[19]

The Reverend Harvey Stanley came from New Bern, North Carolina. His grandfather, a Revolutionary War privateer, helped to fund General Nathanael Greene's army in its 1781 fight against British Lord Charles Cornwallis, which culminated in the colonists' victory at Yorktown. Initially trained to be an attorney, Harvey Stanley started his ministerial career as the rector of Christ Episcopal Church in Elizabeth City. There, he met and married Amalia's best friend, Mary Anne Kinney, whose father sat on the board of Ehringhaus Bank. Many years later, Amalia wrote that she and Mary Anne "were as near to each other as any sisters could be."[20]

Oscar regarded Reverend Stanley as "a man of more than ordinary culture" who read widely and studied astronomy as a hobby. He also admired his passion for the South and observed that the rector and his friends were "in daily communication with Dixie." However, he recognized the danger associated with their deep convictions. For example, it was "a difficult matter to visit any house after dark" since local slaves would communicate the rebels' whereabouts to Union officials. Oscar nevertheless attended local clandestine meetings and learned how the secessionists used signals, whistles, and signs to avoid detection—including "two sticks left crosswise in a manger" to designate if a horse had been borrowed for an escape.

During his short stay, Oscar got to know the Stanleys' daughter Mary (or Mamie), who had attended St. Mary's School in Raleigh. They corresponded during the war and would get married in 1868.[21]

In late December 1861, Oscar Hinrichs prepared to complete his odyssey. He left behind an undated letter of resignation for the Coast Survey, which he advised the Stanleys to mail from another location in Maryland. His caution was warranted. An agent from Bache's organization showed up in Collington looking for Oscar after he left to meet John Surratt Sr. and his wife, Mary, who had opened their tavern in 1853. When necessary, Surratt converted the tavern, located at the busy intersection of Marlboro-Piscataway Road and New Cut Road, into a rest station for secessionists. He also used his post office as a mail drop. In his journal, Oscar wrote: "Mr. Surrat[t] was a friend to the cause, and had been made acquainted with our intentions."[22]

Under cover of darkness, Oscar and his companions—Walter "Wat" Bowie and George Lemmon—used bound strands of hay to cushion their wagon wheels as well as the mules' hooves. They drove along the back roads and across fields to avoid capture. They arrived in Surrattsville around two in the morning, transferring their cumbersome baggage to the Surratts' home, where they hid in the room above the tavern/post office until the following night. The Surratts covered the floor of the bedroom with straw to deaden the sound of the visitors hiding upstairs as Union soldiers stopped for whiskey and information. This precaution proved to be fortuitous since one of Oscar's comrades dropped his sword on the floor during the day.[23]

After dark on December 30, Oscar and his friends gathered their belongings to leave. The sound of a bugle and horse hooves broke the silence of the night. Yankee cavalrymen burst into the tavern in search of Wat Bowie and George Lemmon. Mr. and Mrs. Surratt "were questioned and cross questioned, at times in no moderate terms," but the soldiers left without finding the young men concealed in the upstairs guest room. A couple of teamsters lingered behind, and John Surratt plied them with liquor to distract them. His guests eased out the back door.[24]

Equipped with "a bountiful supply of provisions" from the Surratts, the band of rebels drove the overloaded wagon to the Potomac River. Along the way, they discovered horses of Union cavalrymen and released them to delay pursuit. Upon crossing the border from Prince George's County into Charles County, they encountered a new problem: the boats hidden for them along the river were decrepit and leaked.

Stranded and weighed down by a huge load of baggage—consisting of not only their own belongings but also large trunks filled with uniforms, weapons, drugs, horse equipment, clothing, and personal letters—they expected blue-coated horse soldiers to show up at any moment to seize them. Always resourceful, Oscar explored the area and found two flat-bottomed boats, which he and his friends used to approach and commandeer a Federal schooner on Mattawoman Creek.

Drawing upon his Coast Survey skills, Oscar sailed the captured schooner past enemy gunboats at the mouth of Occoquan Creek and landed at Hallowing Point on Mason's Neck, south of Mount Vernon. During the evening of New Year's Day, the young men stumbled upon a Confederate camp. The commander, Wade Hampton, helped them to reach the 1st Maryland Infantry, encamped with the rest of Johnston's army near Centreville, to deliver their smuggled goods. At Manassas, Oscar took a train to Richmond.[25]

As the war escalated, Confederate secretary of war Judah Benjamin decided that additional engineers would be required to sustain his army. In response to his request in December 1861 for experienced engineers, Congress approved formation of an engineer corps within the Provisional Army. This led to the hiring of fifty new engineers in February 1862. Oscar hoped to become one of the initial eight engineers assigned to Virginia, which was the war's hotspot. Arriving in Richmond on January 4, 1862, he solicited the assistance of Attorney General Thomas Bragg, with whom Reverend Stanley had gone to school in New England. He also approached North Carolina congressman William N. H. Smith, a friend of the Ehringhaus family.[26]

Besides performing standard engineering duties, such as construction of bridges, roads, and fortifications, Oscar anticipated getting involved in the fighting. Engineers on the staffs of division commanders often had an opportunity to lead expeditions and reconnaissance teams. He knew that more aggressive engineers served as couriers and temporary aides-de-camp during combat, rounding up prisoners or selectively commanding soldiers. He longed to prove himself in battle. As leaders like Jeremy F. Gilmer enhanced the professionalism of the engineer bureau, he also sought to advance in its administrative positions.[27]

While awaiting his appointment, Oscar wanted to travel to Elizabeth City, but Confederate officials detained him for questioning. Convinced he was not a spy, they yielded and gave him a pass. In Elizabeth City, he volunteered to evaluate the forts that had been built to protect the town. John B. Jones, a clerk in the War Department under Benjamin, commented on Hinrichs's trip in his diary on January 17, 1862. "Mr. O. Hendricks [*sic*], very lately of the U.S. Coast Survey, has returned from a tour of the coast of North Carolina," wrote Jones, "and has been commissioned a lieutenant by the Secretary of War."[28]

Returning to Elizabeth City at the beginning of February, Oscar received a request from Colonel William F. Martin, who was a well-respected Elizabeth

City attorney and plantation owner, to help in defending the city. As a close friend of the Ehringhaus family, Martin supported Oscar's application to the Engineer Corps. Worried about his hometown's defense, Martin had collaborated with a friend and funded the building of three gunboats to operate on the Pasquotank River. Oscar discovered it was too late: Burnside's naval force had already entered the Albemarle Sound.[29]

After being forced to retreat from Elizabeth City, a Confederate naval officer included Oscar Hinrichs in his after-action report. He commended Oscar for his valor in manning the city's main fort after the local militia ran off: "I must not forget to say that the engineer officer who had been sent from Richmond for service in the fort remained bravely at his post. He asked me to report this fact in case he was killed. He was Prussian, and I think his name was Heinrich [Hinrichs]. He was not the engineer who built the fort."[30]

Upon receiving his commission—one of only two new lieutenants appointed from North Carolina—Oscar reported to General Joe Johnston, who sent him to conduct a reconnaissance from Centreville-Manassas to a position behind the Rappahannock River. Johnston incorporated the young lieutenant's recommendations into his plan and executed a retrograde movement from northern Virginia. Utilizing his survey experience again in May, Oscar provided Johnston with an objective assessment of the suboptimal fortifications at Yorktown.[31]

After the May 15 engagement at Drewry's Bluff, Oscar wrote that he was "ordered to Gen. T. J. Jackson in the Valley of Virginia." He reached Stonewall Jackson in time to participate in stunning victories at Cross Keys and Port Republic. Jackson and his chief mapmaker, Jedediah Hotchkiss, welcomed him. Hotchkiss continued to collaborate with Oscar on mapmaking projects, mentioning him sixteen times in his acclaimed chronicle of the war.[32]

After the death of Jackson following the Battle of Chancellorsville, Oscar worked for a number of generals from the Second Corps. He soon realized, however, that few were committed to "a quick and vigorous prosecution of the war, on the style of the lamented Chief Jackson, whose loss the Confederacy has not yet fully comprehended."

Oscar played an active role in Lee's army during most of its subsequent engagements. Promoted to captain in the fall of 1864, he served under a series of Army of Northern Virginia generals.

Transferred to the siege lines around Petersburg in December 1864, Captain Oscar Hinrichs grew despondent. The capture of Wilmington, where he had spent so much time, weighed heavily upon him. Oscar's hopes further plummeted when he learned about the death of newly wed Brigadier General

John Pegram at Hatcher's Run. Returning to camp at midnight, he discovered his commander's body on his bed.

Desperate for a Confederate turnaround, Oscar approached his superior, Major General John B. Gordon, about a plan to turn Northern public opinion against the Lincoln administration. He volunteered to go to New York City to foment some kind of public demonstration—or rebellion—among the German population. He would likely be hanged if caught.[33]

Before Lee could approve the plan, his troops suffered a loss at Fort Stedman, and the Yankees broke through Confederate lines at Five Forks on April 2, 1865. The Army of Northern Virginia began to cross the Appomattox River. Oscar, who played a vital role in the retreat, wrote in his journal: "I remained in our lines until about 3 o'clock in the morning, at which time I withdrew the outpost to follow the infantry, and set fire to the [Pocahontas] bridge. My sharpshooters covered the retreat and the bridge until it burned down."

Blocked from reaching North Carolina and prevented from receiving food supplies and fodder, Lee's army marched farther west toward Lynchburg. On April 7, the day after disastrous losses around Sailor Creek, Oscar Hinrichs suffered a serious bullet wound near Cumberland Church a few miles north of Farmville. He had to travel in an ambulance to Appomattox Court House. At daybreak on April 9, however, he struggled to get back on his horse. He led sharpshooters in one last, futile charge against the Yankees. Lee surrendered the remnant of his haggard army that afternoon.

Oscar suffered through the agonizing April 12 ceremony during which Lee's infantrymen turned over their arms and laid down their bullet-riddled flags. Some Yankees felt sorry for the wounded captain and allowed him to ride in an ambulance that left Appomattox Court House later in the day. Reaching Farmville, he took a train to Petersburg and received a pass to City Point, the sprawling Federal supply depot along the James River. After pausing at Fort Monroe, he continued by steamboat to Washington, where he planned to take a train to Baltimore for the final stage of his return trip to New York City. A lot had happened to him since he left his family on November 20, 1861. His ordeal, however, was not yet over.

Captain Oscar Hinrichs's last entry in his diary on April 19, 1865, provided a cryptic revelation about being detained in Washington, D.C.: "Remain in this prison today."

1. Leaving the Country

Upon the secession of South Carolina, Mr. Bolles had resigned and had carried with him the manuscript charts and archives of our joint work at the South. I was the only person then at the North who was acquainted with the latest surveys.

—Oscar Hinrichs

Editor's note: Oscar Hinrichs wrote the following contemporaneous narrative during Stonewall Jackson's winter quarters in 1862–63 near Fredericksburg, Virginia. It was a transcription of his diary, which began to fall apart as he ended his first year of service (1862) as an engineer for the Confederacy.

Headquarters 1st Division 2nd Army Corps. Army of Northern Virginia
Engineer Department, February 1863
by
Oscar Hinrichs, C. E.

My note-book being on the point of giving out, I transcribe and make addition to the notes therein contained, being notes public and private of my own personal feelings and experience during the war, and with persons with whom the fortunes of war has brought me in contact. I also relate my opinion at the time of measures and affairs as they occurred to me, hoping that at some future time they may become useful references and also records which have mostly been verified by subsequent events.[1]

To make this narrative more plain let me write about affairs preceding the breaking out of the war.

During the month of November, 1860, I received orders from the [U.S. Coast Survey] Department at Washington to proceed to North Carolina and continue the survey as it then stood on the coast under Assistant C. [Charles] P.

Bolles. This man, whose name will perhaps frequently occur in these pages, had by a uniform kindness won my highest regards both in his official and private intercourse with me, and during the several years which I had served under him, made frequent allusions to the state of the country.[2]

I had also by systematic attention to my duty, and uniform respectfullness of manner and speech, won his esteem and respect and subsequently his good will and friendship. In conversations above alluded to, with him as also with others whose names will appear, I had always advocated the separation of the Northern States from the Southern, as being most conducive to the prosperity of the Southern States, as also to their best interest to make a sovereign and independent power. . . .

Affairs of an intirely private nature called me on a visit to Charleston, South Carolina, during November, 1860. While there and while attending to my private affairs, public affairs were brought to bear upon me; the uncertain condition of the country, all combined against me, and while being compelled to leave my private matters "in states quo ante bellum" I nevertheless learned that a great revolution was impending and would soon break out in open flames.

I saw that as far as South Carolina was concerned the feeling of animosity to the North was only increasing in force, and needed but the opportunity of showing itself in full force. A procession and torch-light affair passed my hotel, carry[ing] illumination, which tought the destruction of the American Union. "Born July, 4th, 1775 [1776] and Died November, 18th, 1860," was one of the mottos marked on an illumination representing a tombstone. It was greeted with frantic cheering. The people organized themselves into volunteer military companies. Arms and ammunition were being collected privately and publicly. Everything showed it was a unanimous move of the people, led by the higher and educated classes of society.[3]

Abraham Lincoln, a man whose political life was almost as unknown as his private life, had been announced as a can[d]idate for the Presidency of the United States and had been elected by a large sectional majority. He was not, however, to take his seat without increasing the troubles already showing their heads in the heavens. Newspapers declared an almost equal amount of feeling to be displayed in the Cotton States, and things looked as if it only required some one to take the lead in the matter. They did not have long to wait.

From Charleston I went to Wilmington North Carolina, where I was ordered to report to Mr. Bolles. This done, we soon spoke of public matters. His preconceived opinions had already been much shaken by the progress of current events, and he almost conceded the possibility of a separation. Still he deprecated such a result much. My vessel was soon fitted out and in due season I set sail for Little River, South Carolina. In the mean time, reports were received from other parts of the South. Persons felt doubtful of the action of the border states[:] Maryland, Virginia, North Carolina, Kentucky, Tennessee, Missouri, Arkansas. . . .[4]

While at Little River news came of the secession of South Carolina. The ball was set in motion by the most high spirited, yet the weakest of the Southern States. Commissioners were at once dispatched to the other States including Virginia and Maryland—to agree upon a line of action. Virginia still trusted that the whole matter might be arranged peaceably, yet made no endeavors for sometime to come to provide for and arm herself in case of a failure of the Peace Congress which had been called.[5]

The people were largely in favor of standing by South Carolina, inasmuch as the withdrawal of the Senators and Representatives from that State threw the Southern States in a decided minority. The executive of Maryland played hot and cold, vaciliating between a desire to join the South and a fear of the consequences, being right on the border. Thus it was clearly evident to me that no count could be made on that State.

The secession of South Carolina was hailed with acclamations of joy and firing of cannon throughout the Cotton States and soon the infant Confederacy was brought into existence. Georgia, Alabama, Mississippi, Louisiana, Texas and Florida followed one after another to join the first sister State. Elections were soon held, a government organized with Jefferson Davis as President, Aly [Alexander H.] Stephens as Vice President, and immediate preparations for war made.

Each state as it seceded from the Federal union seized upon the public property within its limits. South Carolina alone seemed still destined to fire the first shot as well as [to become] the first one to break up and dispel the halo which had surrounded the Federal union during the last eighty years. Batteries had been directed against the forts in Charleston harbor. The Federal executive tried to blind the Commissioners from South Carolina who were in Washington trying to arrange a peaceable separation. A distinct promise had been given by the Government that no attempt would be made by the authorities to change the condition of affairs. To give the lie to the honesty of purpose claimed by the U.S., Fort Moultrie was set on fire and evacuated during the night. A steamer the "Star of the West" laden with troops and provisions and accompanied with an adequate naval force attempted to pass to the relief of Fort Sumpter [Sumter], into which the garrison of Fort Moultrie had been thrown, and was fired upon and turned back by the batteries on shore. Subsequently another attempt was made to relieve Maj. Anderson who commanded.[6]

The attack of the "Star of the West" having failed, Genl. [Pierre G. T.] Beauregard who commanded at Charleston telegraphed to Montgomery, Ala., the seat of Government, for orders what to do. The fort had been gradually surrounded by batteries bearing immediately upon it and the approaches from seaward. He was directed to reduce the place. The attack commenced, and lasted thirty-six hours. Maj. [Robert] Anderson replied for a time. His garrison was small and numbering only some seventy or eighty men, and soon worn out by work and exertion in reducing the fires in the fort. They surrendered as prisoners of war. A large Federal fleet was lying outside Charleston Bar watching the progress of the bombardment.

I had as before stated taken my vessel down to Little River. I remained there only a few days, receiving orders to return and discharge the crew, and lay the vessel up. This done, I returned to Little River to watch the progress of events. I remained at Dr. Frinks until after Christmas; then returning to Wilmington found but a small prospect of getting funds to pay my way. Discussions went on [in] the mean time. Events were progressing and daily accuminating.[7]

I returned to New York by way of Washington, having an interview with Prof. [Alexander Dallas] Bache [the superintendent of the U.S. Coast Survey] regarding Southern matters, and found him rather more favorably disposed than I expected. I remained in New York, closely watched in the meantime, but striv[ed] to get the consent of parents etc. to return South. I deemed it as being in honor bound; I had preached secession and passed my word to return. Fort Sumpter fell while I was in the North. Maj. Anderson was received with glowing honors fit for a conqueror. Daily bulletins announced in the press his passage from one point to another; and it became dangerous to express publicly an opinion favorable to the South.

Buchanan still remained President. With a vaciliating policy, he was at once foolish and unwise. Perhaps he might have delayed the progress of events by decissive action at once in the premises, because the Southern people were illy prepared to assume the defensive.

Officers of the Army and Navy were daily resigning their commissions and going South. Names which were soon to come into every ones mouth were quietly passing from one camp to another. Gen. [Winfield] Scott, a Virginian, was showing signs of turning renegade. . . . He was then hatching his scheme of a vast project, most illy called by himself "The Anaconda." Serpentlike in its workings, it was he who first counselled the destruction and pilfering of the private despatches of the various telegraph offices throughout the United States. How the coils of the Anaconda were broken will be seen. The April riots had occurred in Baltimore. The passage of troops from Massachusetts through Baltimore had called forth the music of the mob; the troops fired upon the citizens without doing much damage except to the upper stories of the houses; some eighteen or twenty soldiers were killed during the affray. This doomed the city and decided the fate of Baltimore.

Lincoln had assumed the reins of power [on March 4, 1861, and] had called for 75,000 troops in the vain thought that such a display of force would be sufficient to break down the wicked rebellion. Arsenals and dockyards were busy preparing the means for the Anaconda. Vessels were purchased at an exorbitant price to commence a rigid blockade of the Southern coast and harbors.

Along the whole coast, Fort Pickens at Pensacola, and Key West were the only places still held by the United States, and the former place was only kept by them through the cupidity of Mr. [Stephen R.] Mallery [Mallory], once Senator from Florida. Genl. [David E.] Twiggs had surrendered his forces in Texas to the Confederates and offered himself to their cause. Loud were the outcries against him and his treachery. Troops were massed in and around Washington. Baltimore City was strongly occupied and the leading men of the City and county confined to prison; nearly all were first sent to [Fort] Lafayette and thence to Fort Warren in Boston harbor.

In the meantime the Southerners were not idle. Upon the failure of the Peace Congress[,] Virginia joined her Southern Sisters. North Carolina followed. Norfolk and Gosport Navy Yard were taken possession of after being fired [upon] by the orders of the Government at Washington. With the Navy Yard were also captured several vessels in a damaged condition, among which was the famous Merrimac, or Virginia as she was afterward christened. Washington was being strongly fortified to prevent capture, which at that time was hardly dreamed possible. Maryland was then completely in the hands of the Federals and, joined with the treachery of Governor [Thomas H.] Hicks, was delivered over bound hand and foot.

Remaining in New York until about July, I received orders to report to I. Hull Adams, Assistant U.S.C.S., for duty in Maine. Finding it impossible to get away from the North, I had written to Mr. Bolles in Wilmington, some friends in Charleston, and offered my services soon before the April riots in Baltimore to the President of the Southern Confederacy, the name of the new infant republic of the South. From subsequent circumstances I became convinced that my letters never reached their destination. Time passed on. I proceeded to Boston, reported to Mr. Adams, and went to Maine to prosecute the survey of the Sheepscot River.[8]

Towards the close of the season, orders came for all employees of the Government to take an oath of allegiance to the United States. Firmly resolved to join the fortunes of the South, I hesitated. By maneuvering around, I gained time sufficient to write home and learn their opinion of the case, resolved to act as became the circumstances. The advice received was not to take it [the oath]. Circumstances in the meantime arose which in a measure frustrated the intention of bringing matters to an issue. During the time previous I had been unable to draw my pay, and funds in hand were not sufficient to cover my expenses home in case I should leave at once, or anything should happen. Hence I was compelled to swear, yet making on the face of the oath the stipulation that it was not to be binding upon me after leaving the service of the United States. I never dreamt that it would be received and [therefore I had] resorted to this means of getting my pay and enabling me to furnish my way South.

Time was drawing near when within a few weeks the weather would compel the stopping of work. A few days before doing so, a messenger came from Bath to me, directing me to come over at once to see Mr. Adams. I went at once knowing what it was all about. Mr. Adams received me most kindly yet not without embarrassment. A delicate duty had been imposed upon him, to gain my adhesion to the Union cause. Coming from one of the oldest families in New England, proud of his name and ancestry, he combined true gentlemanly qualities such as are seldom found. I believe he saw as well as I did the drift things were going to take and had fixed upon leaving the country, ostensibly for the benefit of his health, yet more truly speaking to get out of a dirty and disagreeable mess.

He had been sent on from Boston for the special purpose of bringing back the oath of allegiances. The reason why my adhesion was so much desired by the Government was, that upon the secession of South Carolina, Mr. Bolles had resigned and had carried with him the manuscript charts and archives of our joint work at the South. I was the only person then at the North who was acquainted with the latest surveys, and in connection with the before mentioned Anaconda, any sacrifice I might have demanded would have been fully given. Thus I had them in a measure in my power, and was going to use it for my own safety. Mr. Adams laid the case very clearly before me, handing me at the same time a letter from Prof. Bache to the same effect, yet intimating in a language not to be mistaken, that in case of a refusal to take the oath, arrest would be resorted to.

During our conversation, Mr. Adams carelessly threw an open letter on the table. My eyes followed his movements, and caught the words "arrest him." The letter fell towards me, and I read it throughout. I[t] was an order from the Treasury Department instructing Mr. Adams in case of a refusal to take the oath to procure my immediate arrest and confinement. It was an act of courtesy and kindness on the part of Mr. Adams [that I] little expected. He informed me he could do nothing in the case beyond his advice, which was to take the oath. Accordingly next morning we both went to a Notary Public where the oath was taken; I nevertheless verbally made the same stipulation which had been made in writing previously, namely, that it was not to be binding upon me once I had left the service of the U.S.

I then wrote to Prof. Bache saying what I had done, commenting upon proceedings regarding me, and announced to him my intention of quitting the service and leaving the country. We spoke of matters very plainly, and though nothing was said to incriminate either party, still it was felt by him that ere long, if I resigned, I would be found among the Southern army. Accordingly he tried to induce me to give a distinct pledge that[,] before anything was attempted, he should be informed of it. To this I consented conditionally. We parted mutual friends yet with doubts and misgivings.

Soon after, the battle of Manassas had occurred and raised public excitement to its highest pitch. . . . The result of the action was rendered nugatory by its not being followed up. The state of the Federal army was such that ten thousand [Confederate] men might have entered Washington and held it and thus given to the people from and of Maryland the chance they were wishing and praying for of identifying themselves with the Southern cause. It was left undone; and hence time given to the North to put forth and bring about the scheme of their Anaconda.

Frequent skirmishes occurred which generally resulted in a victory to the Confederates [for example, the Battle of Ball's Bluff]. The Potomac was lined with batteries which prevented the passage of vessels to and from Washington, and appearances looked as if they were going to make Washington a very uncomfortable place to live in. Troops were on the field which had not been engaged, and it remains a mystery why the pursuit of the enemy was not ordered. It can be accounted for in no other way than he [Beauregard] was unaware of the crippled state of the enemy.

Soon after seeing Prof. Bache, I discharged my party and returned to New York[.] I was endeavoring to fix matters so as to be able to go South, but found myself completely blockaded and watched. Matters remained in this condition until Mr. Bache returned from his visits of inspection [in the] North, and I went to see him to ask permission to visit some friends in Maryland. He gave me a verbal order to report to Genl. [Ambrose E.] Burnside at Annapolis [to support his Roanoke Expedition] upon the expiration of my visit. This settled all controversies at once. Preparations were immediately made and I started for Maryland.

No. 28 Broad Street, New York
April 8, 1861[9]

To His Excellency
Jefferson Davis
President of the Confederate States of America

Sir,

I would most respectfully offer my services to the government and people of the Confederate States, of which you are the chief, as Topographical Engineer, or in any other capacity that you may deem fit. If any reference be necessary, permit me to mention Major W. [William] H. C. Whiting, of Engineers, Lieut. Commdg. Thomas B. Huger, of the Navy, and Gen. Wm. B. Taliaferro of Gloucester Co. Hs. Virginia.

Hoping that this may be favourably noticed by you, I am, with greatest respect,

Very Respectfully

Your Obdt Servant
Oscar Hinrichs
U. S. Coast Survey

Care of Carl E. L. Hinrichs
Consul for Saxe Altenburg & Coburg Gothe

Revere Ho. Boston, Mass.
September 24 1861[10]

I. Hull Adams, Esq.

Dear Sir,

In order to settle the matter of Mr. Hinrichs' oath & to obtain the public property in his charge, I advise you to proceed to the station of your party & make the necessary arrangements, & not to send by mail to him the papers etc. There is a tone of defiance about his letter to me which is very unpleasant & which indicates the moral fury to which he has been exposed has tainted him. So be on your guard.

Yours Respectfully
A. D. Bache

I enclose you a private note to hand to Mr. Hinrichs. [Below]

Boston, Mass.
September 24, 1861

Mr. Oscar Hinrichs

Dear Sir,

You will see on reflection that the case wh. you present is more simple than you suppose. The law to which you refer has been the law of the land for some seven months, & under it you have received pay & emoluments. When it became the law had you found objection to it you should have withdrawn from the public service. Neither you nor I can modify a law. Nor can I accept any modification [meaning Hinrichs's attempt to add his own caveat]. The case provided its own penalty & I have simply to administer it.

As a friend I would advise you for your own sake to make no difficulty in taking the oath prescribed. If after that you choose to leave public service you do so with an honorable discharge, under which you may obtain employment elsewhere. You can obtain no passport to leave the country without taking the oath & must in fact be in the hands of the government as a suspected person.

Whatever small griefs you may have about pay & the like should yield to the great principle of obedience to the laws, & this I hope you will see clearly.

As you have addressed me privately, so I reply in the same way and not as your official chief.

Yours truly
A. D. B.

2. Crossing to Virginia

November 20, 1861–January 3, 1862

Mr. Surrat [John H. Surratt Sr.] was a friend to the cause, and had
been made acquainted with our intentions. He received us most cordially,
giving us the use of his private parlor and prevented the numerous
strangers who came into the house from intruding upon us.

—*Oscar Hinrichs*

I left home on the 20th of November, 1861, and after seeing how matters stood in Baltimore[,] passed on to the home of my friend Mr. [Harvey] Stanley, an Episcopal minister, a native of North Carolina. I remained there until the 18th of December. We were in daily communication with Dixie, and soon heard fabulous stories of the prowess of this and that person. Mr. Stanley was rather violent in his expressions regarding persons and events as they occurred, which frequently gave rise to conversations of too much personal character. He was much esteemed by his congregation.

While in that neighborhood I made the acquaintance of Mr. Edmund Duval[l], a gentleman and planter living near Mr. Stanley's. Also that of Mr. John Contee, formerly a naval officer. At the house of the former, I was invited to meet some parties recently from Virginia, Edward MacNeu [Mason Edwin "Ned" McKnew] and George Lemmon. The former [was "one of the most daring and successful of 'blockade-runners'" and] made the arrangement with me to give me timely notice when he was about to leave, and agreed to let me go with him. Circumstances prevented him however, from fulfilling his engagement, and consequently I was left to shift for myself.[1]

Time was passing rapidly, my stay at Mr. Stanley's was already growing more protracted, and which Mr. Stanley was desirous of protracting still more. I was afraid of drawing upon him the suspicions of the Government,

the more so as persons whose political creed was rather loose informed me that he was so regarded as destroyed. All contributed to make me desirous of leaving as speedily as possible. Capt. Contee undertook to get information for me, Mr. Edmund Duval[l] to make the necessary arrangements with George Lemmon. I soon began to receive from George frequent messages, and at last he came himself to give the order to march, I meeting him some twelve miles distant at the house of another gentleman, Mr. Richard Wootten [Wootton].[2]

I left Mr. Stanley's house on the 18th of december, his son Charlie driving me down there [to Richard Wootton's house]. Upon arrival I was most cordially received by all members of the family, Frank, Lizzie, and their mother, I remained there until about the twenty-third or fourth. At Mr. Wootten's house I first met [Walter] Wat Bowie, also recently from Virginia. It was here that a great council of war was held regarding our future movements.[3]

We determined that Lemmon and Bowie should bring their men down to the river (they were on recruiting service and represented that they could easily bring some fifty or sixty men) and that there we should watch our chance and capture the first Federal cruiser that came along. It was ascertained that their crews were but small in number, heavily armed, yet withal small boats, being nothing more than the old river tugboats converted into armed vessels by putting some navy guns aboard and altering them for the accomodation of officers and men.

This plan met with my hearty approbation. The party was to be under the command of Lemmon and Bowie as they might choose until they arrived at the river. There the command by their own consent was to devolve upon me. The reasons for this were that they knew the country perfectly, of which I knew nothing, I knew more about a vessel than they did and consequently was more competent for that part of the business.

On the night of the twenty-third or fourth a covered wagon came up to Mr. Wootten's, called for me; my small baggage was speedily placed in the wagon, our arms buckled on, a parting glass taken, mutual good wishes expressed, and away we went full of hopes bright and sunny of the future.

Our first camping ground was an old deserted negro cabin on the plantation of Mr. John V. [B.] Brooke, formerly Speaker of the House of the Maryland Legislature, and subsequently Provost Marshall at Winchester: We arrived at the place about one o'clock at night. Bowie and myself remained by ourselves. George Lemmon went off on business with Harry Brogden who drove us down. Bowie and myself remained quiet the next day, he riding off in the evening and soon returning. It was here my Christmas was spent. In the meantime George returned with Watkins Richardson, Fred Stewart, and Alexander Hamilton, reporting at the same time that this was the total number of disposable men for our undertaking.[4]

Bowie was inclined to back out of the agreement, the others knew nothing of it and only George stood up to the mark and said he was still willing to hold out if there appeared any chances for success. Arms had been secured by both Lemmon and Bowie, in the shape of dragoon sabres, one or two officers side arms, and about twenty Colt's navy pistols with ammunition. On the night of the twenty-seventh we held a council of war. Mr. Brooke came up frequently to see us, after sending provisions, and sometimes something to drink.

The night of the twenty-eighth was spent in considerable trouble. George and Bowie had ridden off early in the morning to prepare for a move forwards, expecting to return in the afternoon or evening. A little after dark, Mr. Brooke came up and informed us that a large cavalry force was on the road to [Upper] Marlborough, and that George and Bowie unless informed of the fact would run some risk of being captured. He advised the keeping of a guard during the night to prevent anything of a surprise, and promised if anything turned up to let us know and [he would] lend a helping hand.

The party having been left in my charge during the meantime, I ordered the removal of the contraband baggage in our possession into the woods. Arms were brought into requisition and freshly loaded, and all preparations were made for a stout defence.

The house itself like nearly all of its class in this section of the country was built of hewn logs firmly pointed and strongly built. It stood on quite an eminence of ground and was proof against anything except artillery. It commanded the approaches from all sides so as to compel any force to come out into the open field which surrounded the place.

A sentry was placed with instructions to call the rest of us quietly if anything strange occurred. I took the first round myself, and moreover took occasion to examine the ground more closely than I had done before. All passed off quietly however, and without being disturbed by the false alarms of one or two who imagined that they saw many things which did not exist. This was natural. None had ever seen service in any shape or form, and their imaginations soon supplied cases of alarm and sometimes fright.[5]

Bowie and Lemmon returned during the afternoon of the twenty-ninth, and about eight o'clock we commenced moving forwards. Hamilton driving the wagon containing our traps and Stewart, Lemmon and myself riding. From Mr. Brooke's place we struck out towards "Surrat[t]sville," a small hamlet on the Washington and Port Tobacco turnpike. Mr. Surrat [John H. Surratt Sr.] was a friend to the cause, and had been made acquainted with our intentions. He received us most cordially, giving us the use of his private parlor and prevented the numerous strangers who came into the house from intruding upon us.[6]

We remained here until the night of the thirtieth, when we again moved after dark to the house of a person whose name for the time has escaped me. Here we remained during the night of the thirtieth and were joined by five other persons desirous of crossing to Virginia. Two were mechanics, brothers and with good faces, one a boy who was unable to render service, [and] a small negro belonging to the apparent leader of the gang. This leader struck me at once as not being quite right. I communicated my apprehension to Lemmon, who did not see fit to enter into any speculation regarding him. I nevertheless kept an eye on him.

We arrived at the [Potomac] river on the night of the thirty-first of December. It had been reported to us that we should find here two boats in a warehouse which with little work could be made to carry us and our baggage across. After bringing them out of the house, finding oars etc., and placing them in the water, no easy matter with the thermometer below freezing point: and working until nearly daybreak, we were compelled to retrace our steps.

Surrattsville, the home of John H. Surratt (From *Harper's Weekly*, 1867; used with permission of Surratt House)

Approaching daylight prevented our going back to our resting place of the night previous, and after considerable talking to no effect, made up our minds (George and myself) to go to a negro quarter which we had observed while passing towards the river, and about three quarters of a mile from it.[7]

The leader of the party who had joined us refused to go with us, saying it was too risky to remain so close to the river, that we all should be undoubtably captured, yet advised our going there. I felt very much like putting a ball through him. I believed him then and do still to be a spy of the Federal authorities; it was not the proper time nor place, however, for doing anything of the kind. He passed on his way and we on ours.

The negro inhabiting the house was waked up, required to open the door and in we went. We soon set her mind at ease regarding our intentions toward her, got her to cook something for us, and after eating and thawing from our night's adventure; while Bowie and the balance were sleeping, George and myself commenced studying out how we were to get out of the box we were then in. The wagon which had hauled our baggage down had returned.

Sickles' Brigade picketted to within three hundred yards of our quarters. Soldiers, teamsters, servants, and camp followers generally were continually prowling about, and the chances were considerably in favor of our receiving during the course of the day a polite invitation to dine as Hamilton expressed it, "with Mass Dan." None seemed to recognize our situation.[8]

George and myself put our heads together to study out what was best to be done. A certain Dr. Thomas lived somewhere within a dozen miles from where we were, and [a prior] report mentioned him as being a friend to the cause. To him then we must make known our situation and get assistance from him.

Between us then we got up the following plan. George, knowing more of the country, was to call upon him for assistance to have the boats repaired, and make arrangements with him regarding a move should necessity require it. The land upon which the negro quarter stood as also the warehouse containing the boats, belonged to a violent Union man: To him I was to go, representing myself as a Federal officer looking after the rebels. I was to tell him that I had five men with me disguised, was on the track of some persons about to cross to Virginia; had captured their baggage, and if he would keep quiet regarding [the] boat matter, [we] would be enabled to capture the whole party. To aid me in my deception of him, I got a large overcoat belonging to Bowie, a sword belonging to Lemmon, and when dressed up [I] did much resemble a Federal officer.

As soon as the details of the plan were settled, George started on his mission and I on mine. My road lay close to the river, and while walking along, saw rising above the top of the trees which fringed the river bank, the tall spars of a tolerable sized schooner [anchored in Mattawoman Creek;] this fact ascertained beyond a doubt, the next thing was to examine her more closely. Sword and overcoat were laid aside, and down to the river I went. She was a vessel of about 120–150 tons burden, with but a small crew.

This ascertained by hailing her, I went back to our temporary quarters, and waiting for George until he returned, I took a nap. He returned on the road by the river, and luckily found a couple of bateaus hidden away in the bushes. He had found Dr. [John W.] Thomas, and had made all the arrangements contemplated by us. I told him then about this vessel, when we concluded that she must be our conveyance across the Rubicon. Preparations were immediately made to carry this into effect.[9]

The bateaus were brought down to a point from which we could speedily reach the schooner before much damage could be done to us by her guns; the baggage was brought down close to the river and left in charge of Hamilton. Richardson, Bowie and Stewart remained with one boat; George and myself took the other, and coming down on her from opposite sides, we reached her simultaneously.

Once on deck I knew she was ours. The jump on deck called up master and crew. Bowie immediately negotiated for them to carry us [across the river] peaceably. This the skipper refused to do under any circumstances. Commencing to talk about his wife and children etc., when seeing that the conversation had lasted longer than there was any necessity for and moreover seeing the light of a steamer coming down the river, I went up close to him and fired my pistol on the deck. This cut the whole proceeding short. Our baggage was placed on board in a hurry. While this was going on, the skipper recovered his senses and, rather than lose his vessel, he consented to carry us over.

While we were in the act of weighing anchor, the steamer poked her nose into the creek in which we were lying; and as it would have been more than madness to have made any attempt upon her we kept quiet. We should have been smashed and blown to pieces before we could have finished getting under weigh and closing in upon her. She soon went off however, and speedily making sail, with a strong breeze and favorable current, we reached the Virginia shore of the Potomac. We landed a few miles above Occoquam [Occoquan Creek] at Hallowing Point on January 1st, 1862.

Wat Bowie [had] evidently become much disgusted with proceedings at Surrat[t]sville. Information gathered there showed considerable danger of capture existed if we took the route eventually taken and which was at first decided upon, and [Bowie] seriously counselled our going down the country to St. Mary's, and crossing into the neighborhood of Port Tobacco. Not knowing anything of the country, I was per force compelled to keep quiet, and the discussion was left intirely to George and Wat. It was only from their statements that I could gather the true state of the case, and when called upon, decided against Wat. From this time on he did not seem to care much about anything connected with the party; he commenced drinking and nearly brought us into trouble, by calling attention to us.[10]

All passed off, however, pleasantly and without any hard words and feelings. As above stated we arrived on Virginia soil on the night of January 1st, 1862.

After spending the night most uncomfortably near the river bank, we proceeded next day to the encampment of Col. Wade Hampton, now Brig. Gen. of cavalry. [Hinrichs converted his diary into a narrative during winter quarters at Moss Neck in February 1863; Hampton was a general at that point.] Gen. Hampton received us most kindly, setting the best he had before us, giving us late Southern news in return for Northern news, and between frequent drinking and talking we passed a most pleasant evening. Bowie who had gone ahead of us to camp, had further proceeded to Fredericksburg and Richmond to deliver despatches brought over from the United States. Gen. Hampton placed at our disposal an ambulance to carry our baggage and ourselves from thence to Manassas near which the main body of our forces were then encampt. We arrived at Manassas on the evening of the 3rd instant.[11]

Col. Hampton appeared to be a good officer. His men were in a good state of discipline and well cared for. In personal appearance, he is a large man, heavily built, a good face and open countenance. His manners were polite and

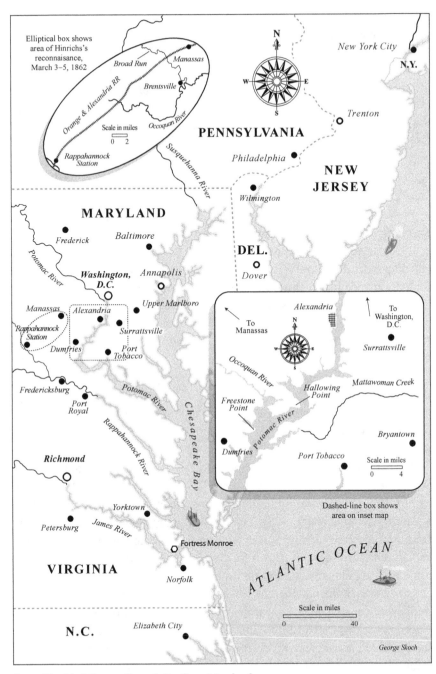

Oscar Hinrichs's Escape through Southern Maryland

affable, and likely to make an impression upon strangers[.] I was very much pleased with him. Since then he has risen to a General officer, and as such has done good service, and if properly supported will eventually make his mark.[12]

Nothing worthy of remark transpired during our stay at Manassas. We arrived late and camped that night at the camp of the 1st Maryland Regiment of Gen. [Arnold] Elzey's Brigade, in which George had several brothers and numerous acquaintances. During the evening I expressed a desire to hear the then favorite song of "Maryland, my Maryland," and to welcome us nearly the whole regiment turned out with its fine band and sang it for us. Later in the evening I made the acquaintance of Gen. Elzey; of him, more will be said hereafter.[13]

December 1861 Correspondence Regarding Oscar Hinrichs

Coast Survey Office
December 17 1861[14]

O. Hinrichs, Esq.
U. S. Coast Survey

Sir,

Please make arrangements immediately and proceed to St. Louis Missouri with the requisites for executing field topography, including suitable paper for plane table sheets, instruments etc. At St. Louis you will report at once to Col. R. [Richard] D. Cutts who is aid de camp to Genl Halleck, and may be found at Head Quarters. Take up such topography as he may suggest is desirable for the use of the military department and continue as on field duty heretofore to produce plane table work until the receipt of other orders from the Superintendent.

Your transportation to St. Louis, and subsistence as heretofore will be met by the fund of the Coast Survey, as also your pay at the rate of $30 per month. It is supposed that you will be furnished with transportation from the Army while employed in topographical duty.

Yours respectfully
A. D. Bache
Supdt

3. Appointment in the Engineer Corps

January 4, 1862–March 1, 1862

On the 27th [of January 1862], I returned to Elizabeth City
and found preparations going on for a speedy evacuation of
the town in the event of the capture of Roanoke Island.

—Oscar Hinrichs

We left Manassas early next morning for Richmond arriving there about six o'clock in the evening of the 4th [of January 1862], and stopped at the Exchange Hotel. The next morning I presented myself at the office of the Attorney General, Thomas Bragg, of North Carolina to whom Mr. Stanley had given me a letter of introduction meeting also at his office the Hon. W. N. H. [William N. H.] Smith, Member of the Provisional Congress from the Edenton District. I presented my case to them, regarding an appointment in the Army and on their joint advice, made a formal application for an appointment in the Engineer Corps of the service, backed by such testimonials as I had brought with me.[1]

I also wrote to Gen. [William H. C. "Chase"] Whiting, Mr. Bolles['s] brother-in-law, whom I had known previous to the war, and who, I was informed stood high in the appreciation of the Confederate authorities. This, however, mattered but little. My endeavor was to show the honesty of purpose in joining the cause at so late a day and substantially gave them a short history of my past career. I also wrote to Mr. Bolles. After waiting some days in Richmond, looking around me and studying my chances for success, I found that they were good, though it might take time to complete them.

I was prepared to start for Elizabeth City, as my funds, never at any time plentiful, were commencing seriously to ebb, when I was arrested by Brig. Gen. [John H.] Winder on the afternoon of the seventh. The circumstances were these. We were all sitting in our room in the Exchange Hotel talking about one thing and another, when a person entered desiring to see me, and upon [my] answering to the name politely informed me that Gen. Winder wished to see me in his office at once.

I went at once and after being introduced by this person to Gen. Winder, he asked me many questions regarding myself, and finally told me that I must consider myself under arrest with liberty to move about the city at will until he could adjust [address] my case with the Secretary of War, to whom I had referred him. It was in vain that I tried to find out from him who his informant was. Nothing was to be done now but to get my friends to work in the case.[2]

Accordingly I set [Attorney] Gen. Bragg and Mr. Smith to work; George Lemmon and Watt Bowie, and some friends whose acquaintances I had made in the city, among them J. Adler Weston. Upon calling at the office of Gen. Winder the next morning I found myself released, the explanation made to him at the War Department having satisfied him as to my suspected loyalty. As soon as I found myself released, I talked in very plain English to him and told him the day would yet come when he and any body else who had business with me should await my pleasure in the antechamber. The Provost Marshall, Col. Jones, a long, lean, lank, crabbed and yankyfied individual, appeared to be the person who laid the information before Winder, and while getting my papers to go to Elizabeth City, I had another talk with him. Who the person was that gave him the information upon which I was arrested I have never been able to find out.[3]

At any rate, I bade my friends temporarily good bye and started for Elizabeth City on the morning of the 8th arriving on the 10th. Letters which I had sent ahead announcing my arrival from Richmond, however, never came to hand, and it surprised them much to find me suddenly among them. My greeting was not over warm. The younger members of the family soon got over their first shyness as also did their Mother and Grandmother. Their Grandfather however, kept much to himself, and judging from appearances would rather have had me anywhere else except where I was.[4]

There was much talk during my stay here of the attack upon Roanoke Island by the expedition fitted out under Burnside at Annapolis. This gave me much trouble, inasmuch as they seemed afraid that I would not take part in it and they seemed to want my services. These I was perfectly willing to render them, provided it did not interfere with the program which I had already laid down of my intended movements [to join the Engineer Corps].

I did not come down to the South to play attendant upon anyone. My purpose was to fight, and nothing except the presence of my own parents was likely to prevent my gratifying my own personal inclinations. Day after day the storm became more threatening. On the 17th of January I started for Richmond to press my appointment. Remaining there until the 27th, without any material change in my prospects, except that they appeared to brighten up.

The day following my arrival in Richmond, I saw George Lemmon who gave me a very interesting account of a correspondence between himself and the editors of the "Examiner" Newspaper touching myself. It appears that a day or two after my first leaving Richmond for North Carolina an article appeared in that scurrilous sheet implying great censure on the Government for allowing me liberty to go where fancy or inclination might lead me, and more especially for permitting my visiting North Carolina at that present time. It was replied to by George in a very strong manner and which induced them to withdraw the previous publication and offer a species of apology for what had been previously said.[5]

Upon receiving the narration, I called at the office of the newspaper and desired to see the things published[.] This was abruptly refused. After some conversation which gradually grew more and more personal, I offered him in as many words the choice of being a scurrilous rascal and scoundrel or of a fight; the latter was avoided, and I have had no oc[c]asion to complain of the paper in a manner personal to me [since that episode]. Thus ended the matter.

On the 27th [of January] I returned to Elizabeth City and found preparations going on for a speedy evacuation of the town in the event of the capture of Roanoke Island. This event seemed to me a foregone conclusion.

By means of the usual want of energy nearly always displayed by the Southern Government at that time, the fort was not in a condition of defence. A few hastily and badly constructed earthworks, a few old pattern cannon, hardly any pieces of more modern manufacture, a half a dozen river steamboats turned into gunboats and placed under the command of a gallant old navy officer, were about the most important means of defence of the place. The channel of the Sound had been partially obstructed by means of sunken boats and badly placed. The garrison consisted of about 2,400 men.[6]

Towards the latter days of the month increased anxiety became manifest throughout. Many people had already left the place and many were preparing to follow. On the 3rd of February, Col. [Charles F.] Henningsen made his appearance with a battery of light field pieces. This was the same person who had figured so largely with [William] Walker in Nicaragua, and who from his experience, was certainly entitled to a larger and more influential command than that of an Artillery command under a crazy old politician, [Brig. Gen.] Henry A. Wise. He arrived, nevertheless on the fifth instant finding it impossible to get the necessary transportation to go to Roanoke, and finding it moreover, useless to go there, he reconnoitered the country bordering the river below the town.[7]

And I offered my services as a volunteer engineer officer[.] They were accepted through the instrumentality of Col. W. [William] E. [F.] Martin who had but shortly before returned from Fort Warren as a released prisoner of war. I was accordingly installed at Cobb's Point about four miles below the town and where an impromptu battery of four Navy thirty-two's [thirty-two-pound guns] had been established. This battery was badly placed[.][8]

The guns, on heavy carriages, could only be trained to bear on the river channel directly across, leaving the enemy the advantage of a long approach before a shot could be fired at them. The training braces had never been used, the ropes and blocks stiff from exposure to the weather, no men to handle the guns, and above all no powder to fight with.

I started the men sent down to me, thirty where there ought to have been three hundred, at strengthening and extending the works so as to receive a ten inch rifled piece placed at our disposal by Commodore [William F.] Lynch. My going down to Cobb's Point evidently threw everything into confusion, and much as I disliked to displeasure or disappoint my entertainers, it could not be avoided to remain consistent with my previous confessions.

On the 7th took place the engagement at Roanoke [Island], and most anxiously were tidings looked for by all. On the morning of the 8th, a fleet of some steamers came up the river and the excitement grew to be intense. By many they were supposed to be the advance guard of the yankee fleet. To an eye at all practiced by water, I quickly discerned the Confederate flag. This in a measure allayed the excitement, which was however, soon brought up to a boiling point again by the boom of a cannon.[9]

I was at Elizabeth City at the time and words cannot express the feelings that were set in motion on viewing the crowd collected around the wharves. No reply was made by the vessels, but soon a boat was seen going from one of them to the shore, and soon after the vessels cast anchor in front of the town. They brought the first reliable tidings from below, the enemy had been badly repulsed and our fleet returned to bring up some wounded men and to get another supply of ammunition, not having enough to fire a single gun.

One of our vessels was lost, the "Curlew" being sunk by a shot from the enemy. All the vessels fought most nobly, as also the only battery engaged on the Island. They predicted that if ammunition came in season, we might still hold the place, relying mainly on the naval officers to do so. Two [hours] past and no ammunition. By prowling around and working on the authorities of the place, I managed to get 200 pounds of powder, which I had made up at once into cartridges. The naval forces managed also to get a small quantity.

On the ninth news came of the fall of the island, the surrender of our troops to Gen. [John G.] Foster. Gen. Foster was an old Army Officer, and I had made

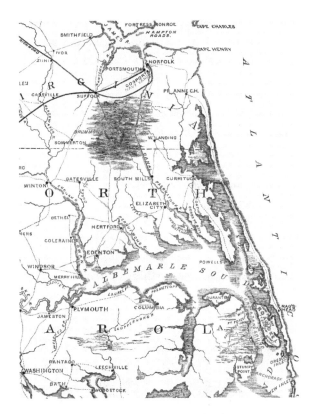

Elizabeth City and the Albemarle Sound (From *Harper's Pictorial History of the Great Rebellion*)

his acquaintance at Smithville, N.C. [today's Southport], two summers previous while on duty there. He seemed to be a quiet modest gentleman, and in the frequent discussions which took place regarding political matters, universally took the side of the South. He was now fighting against us. Lieut. J. P. Bankhead of the Navy who was frequently present, generally took the other side as he said for argument, but bore it out in practice better than Foster.[10]

As an Engineering Officer, Foster is no doubt an able man[.] I never considered him as a match for Whiting or even any person to command large numbers of men. How far my conviction then was borne out by subsequent events time has shown. He has characterized himself with an unenviable name for brutality and rascality, and as a leader has not shown any ability commensurate with the greatness of his command.

On the 10th [9th] I went down to Cobb's Point, [and] kept the working parties going all night. At daybreak on the 11th [10th] I received a note from Commodore Lynch, telling me to prepare for action, as the enemy were coming up the river. The authorities from the town had sent me down 7 men and one non-commissioned militia officer. They all made loud protestations of what they would do if the enemy came up. My experience of humanity had already been taught by bitter lessons [regarding] what faith to put in loud talking. And accordingly, while a message was being sent to Commodore Lynch to send men to fight the guns, my own men took out [off], and I am glad to say [I] have never seen them since.[11]

Commodore Lynch sent me the crew of the gunboat Beaufort, which was sent up the canal to Norfolk. The enemy approached slowly and cautiously, keeping well on the star board side of the river. When supposed to be within range of the utmost trailing of my guns, I spread fire. They slowly returned the same, and kept on the approach. Commodore Lynch came on land and took command by reason of his superior rank. The engagement soon became general. The Flag ship was soon disabled, and placed in a sinking condition, eighteen shots having pierced her hull and having lost some twenty men in killed and wounded. She surrendered.

The "Fanny" a vessel captured from the enemy near Chicomicomico [Chicamacomico] was run ashore and set on fire[;] not however, until she could no longer be held and had done much damage to the enemy. The Appomatax [Appomattox] ran as soon as her ammunition was expended. We stopped firing from the battery after every grain of powder was shot away and the majority of the vessels had passed by us out of range. Commodore Lynch then took down our flag, our guns were spiked, spiking the last one ourselves, and we took to the woods, and [moved] onward towards Norfolk by way of Suffolk. I now represented my case to Capt. [William H.] Parker and was by him introduced to Commodore Lynch.[12]

After many troubles and many adventures, we arrived in Norfolk on the 13th. On the morning of the fight I had with me one twenty dollar bill, clean clothes, but which were now somewhat begrimmed with gun-powder. (My money was now all expended.) I wrote to Governor Bragg at Richmond begging him to push my appointment through as soon as possible, and by doing various small jobs about the town in the way of carrying luggage from the railroad and coping, managed to pay my expenses.

On the 17th I fell in with Col. Martin, and left on the 18th with him for Elizabeth City, in the hopes of recovering my clothes. This I succeeded in doing to some extent though not all. I went to Mr. Frank Charles, at whose house my mother's parents were stopping, and gave them a full account of my maiden fight.

I returned to Norfolk on the 21st. Here Col. Martin lent me 20 dollars, which, with employment as before mentioned paid my way. Never shall I forget my last five days in Norfolk, for forty-eight hours no morsel of food crossed my lips, because I would not beg, I could not buy [food], and [would] rather die from hunger than do anything else. Whatever faults of my previous life had been, now I believe I redeemed many of them.[13]

Amid my troubles on the 26th, I received my appointment as First Lieutenant of Engineers, and [was] ordered to report to Gen. J. [Joseph] E. Johnston at Centreville near Manassas. How now to do [that with] no money, no friends, and possible be obliged to vacate the appointment for want of means to obey orders. I wrote a note to Mr. W. H. Thompson begging of him a loan for the purpose; it was refused in the most polite terms imaginable. I wandered the streets until after night, and on my way found the means of going on to Richmond. I left Norfolk on the 28th, and arrived in Richmond the next day, and on the second of March reported to Gen. Johnston. While in Richmond Gov. Bragg lent me $50., Mr. Ashe $20.

January 1862 Communication Regarding Oscar Hinrichs

Richmond, Va. January 4th 1862[14]

Hon. J. P. Benjamin
Secretary of War, C. S. A.

Sir

Having been engaged during the last six years in the Survey of the Coast of the U. S., and during that time been allmost allways in charge of the surveying party, I would most respectfully present myself as an applicant for a position in the Army of the Confederate States as Topographical Engineer. From the practical experience gained while on the U. S. Survey I know myself qualified to fill the position sought, in as much as I had been ordered to join and report myself to Gen. Burnside at Annapolis for further orders, and having, in the face of a refusal to take the U. S. Oath of Allegiance, been promoted to a Sub. Assistant U. S. C. S. Owing to reasons of a private and pecuniary nature, I could not leave the U. S. until this time, otherwise my services would have been at the disposal of the Confederate States long ere this. I would most earnestly and respectfully request your favorable notice to this my application, and remain

Very Respectfully

Your Obedient Servant
Oscar Hinrichs
Late Sub Assistant: U. S. Coast Survey

Confederate States of America
Department of Justice
Richmond Jany 4th 1862[15]

Hon. J. P. Benjamin
Sec of War

Sir,

The accompanying letter is from an old friend and schoolmate of mine. You will observe that it has no directions, signature or place from which it is dated. [This letter was smuggled across the Potomac River by Oscar Hinrichs.] The writer is the Revd Harvey Stanley, an Episcopal Minister, residing for many years in Maryland but a native of New Berne North Carolina. This letter was handed to me by Mr. Hinrichs, and although there are some things in it intended for my eye only, yet as I only know Mr. H. from what Mr. Stanley says, I have thought it best to send it to you with the application which he will make to you. I know J. C. Ehringhaus, his grandfather on the mother's side, very well. He is an old and very much respected citizen of Elizabeth City N. C.[16]

I will only add that in the interactions I have had with Mr. Hinrichs, I have been favorably impressed, and state I trust that he is fully entitled to all the consideration bestowed upon him by Mr. Stanley.

Very respectfully
Thomas Bragg

Nov 30 1861

My Dear Sir,

I regret that I cannot in person introduce to your kind consideration my young friend Mr. Oscar Hinrichs, who will probably meet with you.

By his mother's side he is connected to John C. Ehringhaus Esq. of Elizabeth City. His father, Carl E. L. Hinrichs Esq., has been Consul General for Altenburg, & Consul for Saxe Coburg to the United States, for the last twenty years.

Mr. Hinrichs' talents together with his experience in the Topographical Department of the U. States are well known to his superiors & colleagues. But as he is his own best epistle, I leave to him to explain further the purpose of his visit, & to bespeak his claim to your courtesy & attention . . . .

Stanley

Hon. J. P. Benjamin
Secretary of War

Mr Oscar Hinrichs who applies for an appointment in the corps of Topographical Engineers of the Confederate States is of German parentage. His maternal grandfather [step-grandfather], John C. Ehringhaus Esq. of Elizabeth City, N. Carolina[,] has resided in the state near a half century [and] perhaps is one of our best and most exemplary citizens. A son [Blucher], maternal uncle of the young man, now deceased, was a prominent and worthy member of our bar—has been a state Senator—and was an ardent and resolute advocate of Southern interests and rights.[18]

While I know by reputation only the immediate parents of the applicant, and had no personal acquaintance with himself until since his arrival in the city[,] my knowledge of his family relations leads me unhesitatingly to accord him a sincere loyalty to our cause and to believe his future conduct will merit the confidence of the public authorities.

Very respectfully
W. N. H. Smith

The *Richmond Examiner*, January 10, 1862, under the heading "Spies":[19]

We are informed that, on one day this week, a letter was conveyed to General Winder stating that O. Heinrich, of the United States Coast Survey, and attached to the *Burnside Expedition*, was in Richmond, and at the Exchange Hotel. The detectives found him, but did not arrest him, as it is said he had letters to some of the public authorities here. It was possible that he came here with the report that he had abandoned the United States service.

On Wednesday last Mr. Heinrich applied to the passport office for a passport. For the purpose of ascertaining what and how many points he wished to visit, a passport was granted to him to Petersburg, Norfolk, Portsmouth, Elizabeth City, Wilmington. On making his application he did not state—what was already known to the passport agent—that he was just from the North, but came in with a crowd of Southern men, and made his application as they did.

But a few minutes after the passport was written out, a note was sent by the passport agent, through the hands of a Georgia officer, to General Winder, stating what had transpired, and urging that Heinrich should at once be arrested, here or at Petersburg. . . .

The *Richmond Examiner*, January 11, 1862, under the heading "The Case of Mr. Hinrich":[20]

We received the following communication in relation to the case of Mr. Hinrich, mentioned in yesterday's Examiner, with relation to the statements of fact made therein of his having, upon his arrival here from the North, been furnished with a passport to visit military stations and important points on our coast.

"To the Editor of the Examiner:

In yesterday's morning issue of the Examiner, I noticed that, under the designation of "Spies," you allude to the arrival here, a few days ago, of Mr. O. Hinrich, and state that he was not arrested, though charges were laid against him to General Winder.

The facts of the case are: That Mr. Hinrich was arrested and discharged promptly on evidence which might be of credit even to the writer of the article.

I write, in simple justice to Mr. H., that you would publish a statement that he showed himself instantly, to the proper authorities, that his presence here was for the good and advancement of the Southern Confederacy. Very respectfully, [George Lemmon]"

Elizabeth City, NC Jany 11th 1862[21]
[received January 17, 1862]

Hon. Thos Bragg
Atty Genl
Richmond Va

Mr Oscar Hinrichs has called on me for a letter of recommendation for some position in the Confederate Army connected with the Engineer Department and I very cheerfully on his own account and that of his family write you what I know of him & give you my opinion of his fitness morally & intellectually.[22]

I have known Mr H from early boyhood though I have not seen much of him for some years. His father resides in New York, [having] married in this town the daughter of Mr John C. Ehringhaus the oldest most respected citizen of the town. . . .

Some four or five years ago Mr Ehringhaus procured for young Hinrichs an appointment in the Coast Survey of the U. S. in which Department he has been serving until his recent appearance in the Confederate States. When the troubles first broke out I think he was with a Surveying party in the neighborhood of Wilmington and I have understood from Dr. [Rufus K.] Speed, the member of the convention from this place, that through him he applied for service to Govr Ellis but his services were declined by the Govr and I understand from Mr Ehringhaus that he, like most of us not dreaming that the war would assume the proportions that it has, advised Mr H not to resign his current position without some certainty of a permanent position.[23]

From my knowledge of Mr H, his father, step mother & her family, I am convinced that he is honest in offering his services to the South, that his being here comes from an unwillingness to fight against us. In fact the day after I was landed at Governor Island, New York Harbor, a half brother of Mr H's, a lad of some thirteen or fourteen years, was permitted to see me, and in this little conversation I was allowed with him, he told me that his brother was anxious & determined to go South & that he was encouraged in it by his father & mother. . . .[24]

Yours with great respect
[Col.] Wm. F. Martin

Elizabeth City, NC January 14/62[25]
[received January 17, 1862]

Thomas Bragg Esq.
Attorney Genl

Col. Wm F Martin & Doctor R K Speed having in their letters to you, in regard to Mr O Hinrichs, in a measure made reference to me I consider it my duty to make the following statement to you in regard to O Hinrichs early desire & request of entering into Service of what now is the Confederacy.

Sometime in the early part of last April I received a letter from my daughter, married to the father of O Hinrichs, writing that O Hinrichs, then in the Service of the Coast Survey Department of the U. S., was anxious to come South and requested I would endeavor to obtain for him a situation with the Government of our State. Doctor R. K. Speed having been elected a member of the Convention to meet in Raleigh I asked him to call on Governor Ellis & endeavor to obtain from him some suitable appointment, which the Doctor at that time thought could be readily obtained.[26]

In the mean time I wrote my daughter the step I had taken in this matter advising her however regarding my opinion of the uncertainty of success not to allow her son in law [stepson] to resign the situation he then had under the federal government until I had better & more certain reason to expect success in my application.

Early in June then I received a letter from Doctor Speed then at Raleigh advising me of the Governor declining giving to O Hinrichs any situation in the State. I therefore informed my daughter of this result of my application, repeating the suggestion of his [Hinrichs's] holding on & retaining the situation he then held till a more favourable opportunity.

[I will allow] O Hinrichs to speak of his qualifications but this much I may say that he entered the Coast Survey in 1856 & that during all this time he has given entire satisfaction as to his conduct & abillities, not only to his superior officer & those in command & service with him but also to those with whom in any way he was connected.[27]

Having now resigned his situation from a sincere desire to serve in the Confederacy, it would be truely gratifying to me & his friends should the Confederate Government give him such employ[ment] as he may be qualified to discharge. . . .

Very respectfully yours
John C. Ehringhaus

Rec. Jan 14/62[28]

Prof. A. D. Bache
Superintendent U. S. Coast Survey
Washington, D. C.

Dear Sir

Circumstances beyond my control, and of which you have been previously informed, must now cause me to request of you my discharge from the public service of the United States and from the corps of which you are the distinguished chief. I herewith beg leave to present for your acceptance my resignation as an officer of the U. S. Coast Survey, to take effect immediately upon your receipt of this letter, and would beg of you to forward the honorable discharge promised me in your letter dated Boston September 24, 1861 to my Father Carl Hinrichs Consul Gen. of Saxe Altenburg & Coburg Gothe, No. 28 Broad St. New York. As I leave the limits and jurisdiction of the United States with a view to naturalization elsewhere the conditions and penalties & degree of the Oath of Alliance to the U. S. become null and void, in as much as I am no longer a citizen of the U. S.[29]

While thanking you most sincerely for the many kindnesses received at your hands both publicly and privately, and wishing you success in all your undertakings, I am with the greatest respect & consideration

Yours very respectfully
Your obedient servant
Oscar Hinrichs

Coast Survey Office Jan 17, 1862[30]

Oscar Hinrichs Esq.

Dear Sir

Your letter without date or place was received this A.M. Its vague & inappropriate character must prevent me from complying with your request to give in reply an honorable discharge. I do you the justice to suffice knowing that this is accidental, and that you will be prepared to give me assurance of continued loyalty & to state without reserve where you intend to go after leaving the loyal states.

Yours respectfully
A. D. Bache
Supdt

4. Retreat from Yorktown

March 2, 1862–May 6, 1862

I heard something whiz past my head and next moment fell backwards.
The gun had burst, throwing a piece weighing about half a ton just
touching my feet as I lay. But for my fall I should have been crushed.

—Oscar Hinrichs

My arrival at Manassas was by no means the most pleasant. After a walk of some seven miles through wind and snow and rain, I arrived at Gen. Johnston's quarters, and introduced myself by handing him my commission. While he was reading it I had a good opportunity to study his face. He appeared to be a person of great strength of will and endurance; his countenance bespoke much kindness of heart and firmness of character, and he made altogether a most favorable impression upon me. After pressing me to take a seat and dry myself, he asked numberless questions, and last, if I had any acquaintance with whom I might remain until wanted. I mentioned Gen. Whiting's name. His manner became changed at once, and turning to an aide directed him to get a horse for me. Then turning to a large map of Virginia, pointed out the route I was to pursue on the reconnaissance I was intended for.[1]

Brig. Gen. [Isaac R.] Trimble was directed to furnish me with as much cavalry as it might require, and before many more moments I was for the first time in the saddle as a Confederate Officer. Owing to my not being able to see Gen. Trimble in time on the same day, I was compelled to remain over until the next morning, when some cavalry was placed at my disposal, and I started on my journey.[2]

The night of the second of March I remained at the quarters of Gen. Trimble. He appeared to take some interest in me and listened to such parts of my story as I was willing to tell with much attention. He appeared to be a kind and affable old gentleman. His attentions to me were certainly of the most kind and considerate character. As a fighting man, I did not think much of him, but am happy to state that these first impressions have been materially changed since then. I have seen him stand cool and quiet among a shower of balls that might have excused anyone from desiring any more of them, and perhaps seeking other and more comfortable quarters. His disposition seems to be exceedingly charitable, during [doing] many things which are of great comfort to the recipient, though some fault perhaps may be found in the manner of thus doing. Plain and straight-forward in his doings, he seems desirous of correcting at once and in the shortest way all that is or appears to him wrong, and he thus commands himself highly.

On the Morning of the 3rd of March, bright, clear, and cold, I started on the reconnais[s]ance ordered by Gen. Johnston. Now that no harm can be done by giving his orders to me, let it appear. He seemed anxious to have some one to whom he might unburden his perhaps somewhat heavy heart, and with a view to that effect he spoke to me. Calling me to one side of the room, near where was hanging a large map of Virginia, his eye and hand quickly fixed itself upon the region about Manassas. Thence he laid out the route I was to pursue, via Brentsville to the Rappahannock, thence on the north side of the Orange and Alexandria Railroad back to Manassas. Reporting to him the condition of the roads and the chances of making use of the ground for defensive purposes.

I was to explore thoroughly the country thus indicated for about fifteen miles on each side of the Railroad. Recent heavy rains and thaws had swollen the streams to such an extent that it was exceedingly dangerous to ford them; the bridges where they existed, in many instances having washed away. Broad Run proved to be the first difficulty of the kind. The weather had moderated much during the day, so that the temperature of the air was pleasant enough; that of the water however, was exceedingly cold. With much risk the Run was crossed by swimming the horses. My first days ride was forty-seven miles without getting out of the saddle. The second days ride seventy-two, and the third day eighty-four miles, total 201 [203] miles in three days.

I returned to Manassas on the 5th day of March, and reported next day to Gen. Johnston. He seemed pleased and gratified at the results of my reconnaisance, and the despatch with which it was made. The evening of my arrival I reported back the cavalry to Gen. Trimble and remained at his quarters. He desired me to see Gen. [Richard S.] Ewell, then commanding this division. The first impression of this great Captain, was anything but prepossessing.[3]

The night was cold, chilly, and dark, with a slight sprinkling of rain. A ride of about two miles brought us to a long low house; dismounting and tying our horses to a portion of the fence we advanced toward the house. A low, but sig-

nificant growl intimated that we might not find the entrance as easily accomplished as we might at first have supposed. A servant appeared and called the dog off, and after we had knocked somewhat loudly at the door, a gruff voice bade us enter. Seated in a large arm chair, wrapped in a large dressing gown with a military cloak thrown over his shoulders, slippers on the feet, sat the redoubtable General Ewell.

Upon being introduced he gruffly inquired what I wanted. I made known my errand in the shortest manner possible. He told me to come again in the morning. I then mentioned to him having just returned from a reconnaisance, I should be obliged to report to Gen. Johnston in the morning, and did not but know that I was already doing wrong in coming to him at all, inasmuch as I had matters and things to report with which I did not know if Gen. Johnston wished him to be acquainted. His manner then changed very much and he asked me to be seated, which he had not done before. I politely declined. He offered me something to drink which though I felt much in want of something of the kind, I also declined.

After a few more words of no import, I took my departure returning to Gen. Trimble's quarters about ten o'clock. The balance of the evening was spent in pleasant converse at that place, and next morning early I got underway and reported to Gen. Johnston. After reporting to him all that I had found out, he desired me to make it out in writing and upon doing so, again met Gen. Ewell. He desired to know where he had seen me, I told him. He then had a conversation with Gen. Johnston, evidently regarding our conversation of the previous evening; the General had a hearty laugh. Gen. Ewell took his leave, offering his hand to me before doing so, and asked me to come and see him. Gen. Johnston told me I had done well after Gen. Ewell left.

On the strength of the information given him, I presume Gen. Johnson ordered the retreat from Manassas. Stores of all kinds were being shipped quietly away by rail, and on the morning of the 7th of March, the backward movement took place. On the afternoon of the seventh, I was ordered to get in readiness all the lumber I could, men were furnished, to proceed to Rappahannock Station and place the bridge across the river at that place in a condition to carry the trains and Artillery over it. I set out immediately, arriving there about 11 o'clock at night. After looking after the bridge, and deciding how to do the thing in the best and most expeditious manner, I sought some quarters, believing myself to be fixed there for some days. I was not disappointed.[4]

On the morning of the 9th the bridge was finished, and about ten minutes after the last nail was driven, the troops and trains commenced to arrive. On leaving Manassas, the troops and trains took different roads, all coming together at the above named station. So quietly had the movement been made, so careless was the enemy that he was unaware of our movement until all idea of pursuit was hopeless. Everything crossed the river in safety. Gen. Johnston expressed himself pleased with the work and directed me to proceed to Rapidam [Rapidan] Station and do likewise. The lumber from Manassas having given out, I was compelled to go to Culpepper [Culpeper] Court House, the county seat of Culpepper County, and remained there two days, gathering the timber necessary and waiting on the railroad for transportation for my men and timber.

I reached Rapidam [Station] on the 11th, and at once set to work on the bridge. I found very pleasant quarters at a connection of Gen. Taliaferro, of Gloucester, and remained at this house several days. However pleasant it might have been, there were, however, too many ladies to suit me. I accordingly shifted my quarters to a Mr. Antrim's. Here things were a little better. As the bridge was finished, the troops and trains arrived. I concluded we might possibly remain here for sometime. The positions occupied by the troops was good, provisions and forage in plenty[,] and as we did not have force enough to make a regular field fight with the enemy should he come up, I concluded we were to fight him here.

Gen. D. H. Hill still remained at Culpepper Court House. Gen. Johnston ordered me in connection with my friend [Henry J.] Rogers, who had been ordered to the party near Rappahannock Station, to bring up Gen. Hill from up there. Rogers started on one road, I took another, and on the day following, Gen. Hill was safely lodged near Rapidam. As this was the hero of the Big Bethel fight I felt very anxious to see him, but was disappointed by his being sick. Brig. Gen. [Richard] Griffith was in command of the Division, and a more affable gentleman never lived. I saw him frequently until the troops moved to near Richmond. He was killed during the battle of the Seven Pines [Savage Station] later in the year, May 7th, 1862. He died nobly, at the head of his gallant Brigade.[5]

From Mr. Antrim's I changed quarters again to a place where we might all be together (Rogers, Douglass, Randolph and myself) [at] Mr. Lawrence Taliaferro's house. Here we remained in a delightful condition. Female society sufficient to make it pleasant, an old and very agreeable gentleman and a fine old lady. I was sorry to part from them, and leave them to the tender mercies of the Yankies, who soon after flooded this part of the country. Having two sons in the service, when the enemy did come they soon deprived him of everything; he lost nearly all his negro property and from the sum total of his fortune has been able to save very little. The opportunity has never occurred when I might be able to revisit this part of the State, but from all that I have been able to hear, it is completely desolated.[6]

We remained here quietly until April 10th, when orders were transmitted to Rogers and myself, under Capt. Prestmann [Steven Wilson Presstman], Engineer P.A.C.S., who had joined us a few days previously, to report to Gen. Johnston at Yorktown, Va., he having left early in the month for Richmond. Prestmann started by rail at once for Richmond, Rogers and myself started on the 11th overland to Richmond, and from thence per steamer to Yorktown.[7]

Remaining in Richmond several days [we were] waiting for further orders from Maj. [Walter H.] Stevens, Chief Engineer. We received orders at last to proceed to Yorktown, examine the condition of the lines of defence erected by Maj. Gen. [John B.] Magruder, and report on them to Gen. Johnston on his arrival there. After much trouble in getting our horses on board one of the boats carrying artillery horses down, and further trouble in getting passage ourselves. We started about sundown on the 19th down the James River, arriving at King's Mills wharf on the 20th.[8]

While going down the river, the night was very cold and disagreeable, Rogers and myself worked our way into the cabin of the boat. This part of the vessel appeared to be occupied by quite a rowdy set of people, whom we afterwards found out to be [with] Brig. Gen. [George] Pickett of Longstreet's

Division. After some words of not exactly the most pleasant nature, we were informed that this part of the vessel was reserved for the Gen. and his staff, and that we would be obliged to move out. Unpleasant as it was nothing could be done to prevent it, and our night was spent most disagreeably.[9]

However, the worst of things must have an end, and next morning among the bright sunshine and fine weather, the disagreeable experiences of the previous night were soon lost sight of if not forgotten. I had made myself the promise however, to be even with Mr. Pickett on the first opportunity that might offer itself, and we did not have to wait long. Gen. Pickett was fond of his toddy and had on this occasion drunk a little too much; as a soldier he is a gallant fellow and will fight the Devil himself if directed to do so. He has from time to time done good service.

Riding over to Yorktown that same day, along the line and from thence to Williamsburg where we remained that night, my opinion of the defencibility of the line was soon formed. I found that works had been constructed on a large scale running entirely across the Peninsular, from river to river. They were placed in every conceivable position, where they ought to have been, and where they ought not. About two thirds of the line was commanded by the Yankee side, and the works themselves badly constructed and weak. Our report was given verbally to Gen. Johnston the next day. He was much exasperated, but said nothing. We rode out with him the next day, when I pointed out to him the various things with which I had fault to find. He then expressed himself satisfied.[10]

We, Rogers and myself, were then ordered to report to Gen. D. H. Hill, commanding Left Wing at Yorktown proper. Reporting there as speedily as practicable, we were soon set to work on the defences of the place. I think from what I saw at Gen Johnston's Headquarters that his mind was made up either to make a grand fight with the enemy or retire from the place. The former was a doubtful proceeding. We knew nothing of the works of the enemy, except that they were approaching the place by regular approaches, which our works could not stand.

To have commenced moving at once would have placed the army in a very bad predicament, worthless and disorganized as it was by the intrigues going on among the officers and men for positions at the coming election. Never was a greater mistake made by any people tha[n] to hold on to the principle of electioneering in military matters. Discipline becomes from necessity slack and indifferent. Officers are afraid to do what they know to be right, because it would endanger their chances for reellection. There were some few honorable exceptions to this general rule, and they were few and far between.[11]

Upon reporting to Gen. [Harvey] Hill, we were set at work strengthening the work and mounting guns which I felt would be left in the hands of the enemy. Our time at Yorktown, at our quarters[,] was pleasant enough if I may throw out the difficulties we had with Gen. Hill. [Lieutenant William E.] Harrison who had been acting as Chief Engineer of the place until our arrival had already had several disagreements with him, and soon after our arrival he put us all in the same category.[12]

Holding that the Engineer officer is the only and proper judge of where works are to be placed, and not the General except by his consent and concurrence to make the details necessary, it does not follow that we are blindly to obey the dictates in that respect of any person; we may obey an order of the kind under protest. This I did. A letter was written by Gen. Hill to Gen. Johnston complaining that "certain Engineers" would not obey his orders. Gen Johnston replied "if they do not obey your orders put them in irons." It is evident to us all that something else beside the above quotation must have been written by Gen. Hill.

Accordingly, as I was the only one who cared to risk the irons, I wrote to Gen. Johnston setting forth the true state of the case, whereupon Gen. Hill was informed that there was a vast distinction to be observed between persons detailed as Engineers and Commissioned Engineer Officer[s], and he must in the future be guided by their opinion or refer the matter in dispute to him. This Gen. Hill never forgave me. In my frequent intercourse with him, he has always borne the rebuke administered to him by Gen. Johnston in mind.

In appearance he [Harvey Hill] is anything else but pleasant and prepossessing. Uncouth and ungentlemanly in his manners, he has never yet failed to make himself highly unpopular by both officers and men. People from his own state refused to serve with him. The small notoriety gained by him at Big Bethel, seems to have turned a not oversteady head and made him proud, fastidious and unrelenting. As a soldier he is no commander for a separate command. A mind narrow and shallow, he possesses no genius for command, yet as a subordinate he has done good service. He fights hard, yet without judgement. His reputation is rather of a shadowy one than a real achievement. As a soldier he is nothing extraordinary, a gentleman he is not, and by his manners he is a disgrace to the rank he now holds. So much for him. At another occasion I had an opportunity of speaking to him on equal terms, and did not hesitate to do so.[13]

On the 24th of April I was standing in the Rifle battery near a gun about to be fired at a Yankee battery; I was protected in a manner by a series of sand bags and upon which I rested a spy glass to watch the about being projected shot. The gun exploded with a dull heavy sound, I heard something whiz past my head, and next moment fell backwards. The gun had burst, throwing a piece weighing about half a ton just touching my feet as I lay. But for my fall I should have been crushed. Two men were slightly injured. The gun carriage was completely demolished. It was a most narrow escape, yet not the first of the kind I had passed through.[14]

May 1st I received orders from Gen. Johnston through Maj. Stevens, to report to the Engineer Bureau in Richmond. Owing to the almost insurmountable impossibility of being able to get transportation on the steamboat from Yorktown to Richmond for my horse, Capt. Prestmann and myself started on the 3rd [of May] over land for Richmond. We arrived the night of the 3rd near Williamsburg.

The retreat from Yorktown having commenced on the night of the 2nd. On the morning of the 4th I heard firing in our rear, and as I knew the enemy to be on the lookout for us this time, and not having seen any fighting since I left Roanoke and Elizabeth City, I turned back, just in time to get on the ground during the hottest of the fighting. Contributing my small mite toward beating back the enemy, I followed up my journey that evening arriving in Richmond on the 6th. Never had I seen so gallant and pleasing a picture as this short but glorious fight. Gen. Johnston came out noble and smiling. Going everywhere where his presence seemed needed, for the enemy came with a whoop and a run. Yet our gallant boys repulsed them at all points, and then quietly resumed their backward movement. The cavalry acted handsomely and finely, charging the enemy's infantry and cavalry both, and making many prisoners.

Conspicuous among the whole crowd was my old friend Brig. Gen. A. P. Hill[,] formerly 1st. Lieut. of Artillery, U.S.A., and formerly Assistant in Charge of C.S. [Coast Survey] office in Washington. He fought hard and well, and earned for himself an enviable reputation for hard fighting and good generalship.[15]

As before stated I arrived in Richmond on the 6th. Rogers soon came up also, and we took up quarters at Mrs. Raines. Throughout all my acquaintance with Rogers, now running over some two or three months, I took a peculiar liking to him, and it seemed to be a mutual one. He never started to do anything but what I was informed of it and if deemed necessary, my advice asked. We rode and went out together so much that for a time strangers supposed we might be brothers. From our first intercourse there seemed to be some tacit understanding that we were to be thrown much together, and it seemed to give him much pleasure whenever we have subsequently met.

5. Jackson in the Valley

May 7, 1862–June 25, 1862

I mounted and was no sooner in the saddle than five Yankee cavalry turned
the corner on me. Taking advantage of their moment of surprise, my sabre was
drawn in a moment, my road lay through [the cavalrymen], and giving a
cut right and left, dashed through them with three at my heels.

—*Oscar Hinrichs*

I remained in Richmond until the 21st of May. I first made efforts to go out
to Gen. Beauregard, but finding so many going out there, I made application
to be ordered to Gen. T. [Thomas] J. Jackson in the Valley of Virginia, a man
whose fame as a soldier was already reaching far beyond the limits of the in-
fantile Southern Confederacy. I received my orders to report to him on the
21st and started on the 22nd. [Henry] Rogers who made application to go also
was disappointed, Maj. Stevens having appropriated him for the defences on
the James River near Drury's and Chapin's Bluffs, since made memorable by
the fight with the Yankee gunboats on the 14th [15th].

On the morning of the 13th, Rogers asked me to assist him in posting some
infantry on the river bank in anticipation of the coming attack of the enemy. I
went down with him on the morning of the attack [May 15]. Four vessels came
up and came close up to the obstructions and commenced the fight. Our batteries were admirably served and soon one of their ironclads got underway
and steamed out of range. Their loss must have been quite large, inasmuch
as our sharpshooters three times drove the gunners from their guns. Our own
loss was slight from the fact guns were on too high ground, and their shells
and shot went over instead of into us. It was a handsome fight for the time it
lasted. However, I started for Gen. Jackson on the 22nd.[1]

At Gordonsville I met with [George H.] Bier[,] an officer of the old Navy.
As he was bound for the same place as myself, we made common cause and

traveled on together. Nothing of importance occurred until we reached the neighborhood of Front Royal, a small town on the Shenandoah. Jackson by means of forced marches had fallen on the enemy at that place, and after an obstinate fight, killed and captured nearly the whole of the 1st Maryland U.S. Regiment. This fight took place on the 23rd.[2]

On the 24th [Jackson] fought and captured the garrison at Strausburg [Strasburg], and on the 25th fought and routed Banks at Winchester. The combined results of this movement were about 3,000 prisoners, many hundred stands of arms, wagons, horses, cannon [as well as] Quartermaster and Commissary and medical stores etc. It completely loosed the hold of the enemy on the lower valley and gave to these poor people another breathing spell.[3]

At Winchester I reported to this redoubtable captain [Stonewall Jackson], and for the first time saw him. Although flushed with a series of victories which should strike terror into the ranks of the enemy and make his name a terror and reproach to them, with a force so small that it might have been hidden by that of the enemy, he routed three times his own number; and then too with men nearly broken down by heavy marches and heavier fighting, against men who were fresh in all respects, finely equipped, and coming with all the preparations of war. It was truly astounding.

In person, quiet, modest, diffident and unassuming, [Jackson] bears upon him his honors lightly and meekly. Attributing nothing to himself but all for the glory of God [on] high. "By the blessing of Providence" is his customary and stereotype phraze, and only too much bespeaks the man entire. Religious without fanaticism, without cant and hypocracy, he commands himself to the good will of man. Brave to insensibility, insensible to rashness and obstinacy, he stands firm and cool among a shower of shot and shell which makes men stand aghast at the apparent tempting of God's mercy and kindness.[4]

[As I transcribe my note-book in February 1863, I'm reviewing my notes about Jackson.] I have been with [him] in many hard-fought battles, I saw him at Malvern Hill, at Cedar Run, at [Second] Manassas, at Sharpsburg, and among all none were more cool and collected than he. His sunburnt famous cap and coat, a lean lank horse, a not by any means graceful posture, imperturbable among the din and turmoil of battle, he seems with lifted hands and lifted eyes to call down victory upon his standard. His call has never seemed to be in vain.

Once only and only once have I seen him at all excited, and then only for a moment. His quickness of disposition once accomplished, and again the cool and quiet smile. His movements are quickly conceived and equally as quickly carried out. Attempting things which at first seemed rash and impossible, it seems that Providence so managed things for him that it all turns out right.

Stonewall Jackson, Winchester, Va., 1862 (From Henry Kyd Douglas, *I Rode with Stonewall* [Chapel Hill: University of North Carolina Press, 1940])

Upon introducing myself to him on the afternoon of his fight at that place [Winchester], I found him exceedingly affable and polite. Giving me his own seat, taking my cap and talking pleasantly about things in Richmond. I complimented him on the recent fine work he had done lately. Thanking me for the compliment he told me as I had come to him for work I should not be disappointed. On the 28th [of May] he directed me to report to Gen. Ewell at Charlestown, where our forces were then hedging in the enemy. Here I stopped at a most delightful place [with] kind, pleasant affable people.[5]

On the morning of the 28th Gens. Ewell and Jackson directed me to find out roads leading from [Charlestown] towards Hallstown [Halltown] to Shepherdstown and elsewhere. I started out, and during my absence, Gen. Jackson received news of the movement of Gen. [James] Shields which caused him to turn up the Valley in a hurry. This movement commenced on the 1st of June. I returned to Charlestown on the evening of the 1st.[6]

On the 2nd I went through Berryville, at which place I was led to believe I might find Gen. Ewell. I stopped until after dinner and after dining ordered my horse. Mounting very leisurely, some person called to me to be quick; I mounted and was no sooner in the saddle than five Yankee cavalry turned the corner on me. Taking advantage of their moment of surprise, my sabre was drawn in a moment, my road lay through [the cavalrymen], and giving a cut right and left, dashed through them with three at my heels. My horse having had a good feed and rest, was fully equal to the emergency. After a run of about four miles, they quietly dropped behind and let me proceed on my way rejoicing. I have been gratified since to learn that one of the two whom I had cut at died that night and the other one was severely wounded.[7]

I stopped that night at Winchester. Great was the excitement in that town.

Rumors of the close approach of the enemy, and great fears were entertained that we might be captured. On the 3rd I caught up with the army at Strausburg, and after assisting in posting our troops against a possible attack of the enemy, I strolled off reconnoitering the country. A heavy rain storm came up and I sought refuge for the night at a neighboring farm house. About 9 o'clock at night the army made a new move, leaving me behind again. On starting out the next morning, no signs of a confederate was to be seen. Pushing on I came out on the turnpike about three miles from Strausburg. Here again I came near being captured.[8]

On the 4th I again caught up with the army near New Market[,] a small town on the Valley turnpike. I here find an entry in my note-book to this effect, "Old Gen. Ewell [is] an old ass, the same as Gen. D. H. Hill; neither fit for their positions." I do not remember the exact circumstances under which the remark was made, yet how much the opinion then expressed has changed, what has been previously written may testify. A more gallant fighter and truer man never breathed. The Confederacy has lost a valuable officer in [Ewell's] misfortune of being wounded and rendered in a measure unfit for service. As the companion in arms of Jackson, and as the hero of the battle[s] of Cross Keys, Port Republic, and many other hard fought fields he has acquired a just and highly earned renown.[9]

On the 5th [of June] at 5 o'clock a.m., we passed through Harrisonburg. On this afternoon a gallant fight occurred near Harrisonburg between our rear guard and the advance guard of the enemy. I[t] was here that the gallant [Turner] Ashby, the terror of the Yankees, was killed. How much his loss was regretted, how much the cause lost will probably never be appreciated. Brave and daring to a fault, openhanded and high toned, we may long mourn him.[10]

As an officer [Ashby] was invaluable and as a scout and gatherer of important intelligence. As an cavalry officer he was not much account; I mean by this as a carrier out of discipline among his men[.] He sought to lead them more by his example than by authority, and the consequence was he could seldom gather more than two or three hundred men around him to carry out any project. The majority of his command was usually scattered from one end of the Valley to the other. With what few men he generally did have around him, he did wonders. It was a serious loss to us and a decided gain to the enemy.

We remained camped on the road between Harrisonburg and Port Republic until the 8th, when a portion of Shield's cavalry made a dash into the latter place, and came near capturing Gen. Jackson. His escape was almost miraculous. Dashing through the enemy[,] turning their cannon, and across the bridge over the Shenandoah was but the work of an instant. A few moments later and our troops came pouring into the town and drove the enemy out.[11]

At the same time [Maj. Gen. John C.] Fremont with 7 brigades of infantry and a proportionate force of cavalry and artillery made an attack on Gen. Ewell near Union Church and Cross Keys. At this juncture I met Gen. Jackson and the only time when he appeared to be at all disturbed. A short conference with Gen. Ewell and he returned with quite a different expression of countenance. The fight near the church was most hotly contested, and ended by the enemy leaving the field sometime before sundown. Gen. Trimble quite took my fancy by the manner in which he fought his brigade and deserves great credit for the stubborn manner in which he[,] with one small brigade[,] fought them. Gen. Elezey [Elzey] also fought well and was wounded slightly. Things looked very unpromising that night.[12]

Gen. Trimble was left to guard our rear and keep back the enemy should they attempt another attack from toward Harrisonburg. The balance of the troops were moved towards the river in anticipation of the advance of Gen. [James] Shields who was reported in strong force near Snifbrue [Swift Run] Gap in the Blue Ridge.

It is argued that the movement ordered by Gen. Jackson was made on the spur of the moment and not made the subject of deep and anxious thought. I am unable to say whether this is so or not. Be it as it may, this much is certainly true and lends somewhat of might to the argument above mentioned, that our trains certainly did not start on the road towards Staunton and were turned off by courier from the General over some very rough and almost impassable roads, to the inherent roughness of which was added recent heavy rains. I am inclined to think from what I saw myself, that the movement was premeditated, and that the sudden order to change the direction of march was given at such a late hour more to keep his own place a matter of secret and conjecture, and thereby cause diversion among the enemy.

Gen. Ashby who commanded our rear, certainly did receive orders to keep the enemy in as much check as possible on the morning in question. When we

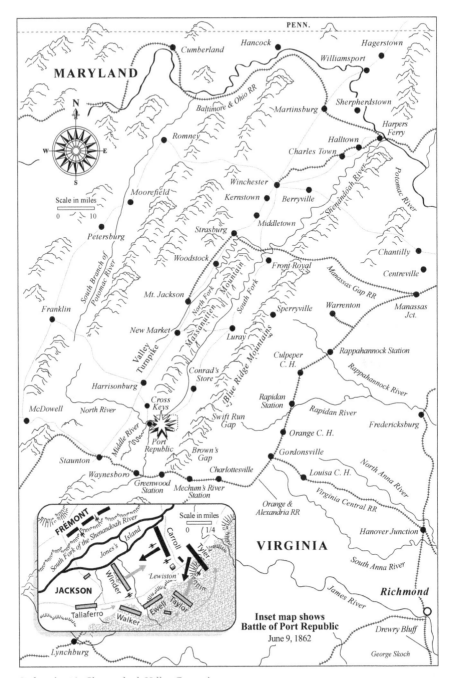

Jackson's 1862 Shenandoah Valley Campaign

Map labels (clockwise):

PENN.

Cumberland · Hancock · Hagerstown · Williamsport · Sherpherdstown · Martinsburg · Harpers Ferry · Halltown · Charles Town · Romney · Winchester · Berryville · Kernstown · Middletown · Moorefield · Strasburg · Petersburg · Woodstock · Front Royal · Chantilly · Centreville · Mt. Jackson · Sperryville · Warrenton · Manassas Jct. · Franklin · New Market · Luray · Culpeper C. H. · Rappahannock Station · Conrad's Store · Harrisonburg · Rapidan Station · Rapidan River · Fredericksburg · McDowell · North River · Cross Keys · Swift Run Gap · Orange C. H. · Port Republic · Brown's Gap · Gordonsville · Louisa C. H. · North Anna River · Staunton · Charlottesville · Waynesboro · Greenwood Station · Mechum's River Station · Orange & Alexandria RR · Virginia Central RR · Hanover Junction · VIRGINIA · South Anna River · James River · Richmond · Lynchburg · Drewry Bluff · George Skoch

MARYLAND · N · W E · S · Baltimore & Ohio RR · Scale in miles · 0 · 10 · South Branch of Potomac River · Shenandoah River · Potomac River · Manassas Gap RR · Massanutten Mountain · North Fork · South Fork · Valley Turnpike · Blue Ridge Mountains · Middle River · Rappahannock River

Inset:

FREMONT · South Fork of the Shenandoah River · Jones's Island · Carroll · Tyler · Scale in miles · 0 · 1/4 · Winder · 'Lewiston · JACKSON · Taliaferro · Walker · Ewell · Taylor

**Inset map shows
Battle of Port Republic**
June 9, 1862

add to this the fact of the badness of the roads, and that after leaving Harri-sonburg there was no position in which we might advantageously offer or accept battle should Fremont and Shields still determine to pursue us by dif-ferent routes, until we reached Staunton, it becomes highly probable that the General did select the juncture of the North Branch and South Branch of the Shenandoah as the battle ground on which to fight each one separately, and beat them in detail.

We have seen how Fremont was beaten at Cross Keys, and it now remains to be shown that Shields met with a like reverse at Port Republic on the day following. Gen. Trimble as before stated was left with his brigade to guard our rear from a renewed attack of Fremont's; and being obliged to fall back from superior numbers, reached the bridge across the river at Port Republic just in time to have a safe passage. The bridge was burnt and Fremont compelled to remain on his side and view the defeat and rout of his brother commander.[13]

The morning of June 9th opened fair and hazy with much dampness in the atmosphere, so much so that the powder smoke hung in the air in heavy clouds above the field of battle. The opening of the [Port Republic] fight was seriously to our disadvantage, the enemy driving us back over the corn and wheat fields something like a half a mile. As soon as more troops could be brought to bear, the face of affairs soon changed.[14]

On my way down to the field I met numbers of our men coming back, many without arms and all concurring in the expression that we were beaten. These men I gathered up, soon amounting to about 200, which I proposed to fight myself or turn over to some regiment. The former course being more conge-nial, I soon had them placed in a break in our line and was leading them for-ward in the general advance when I was sent off by General Jackson to con-vey an order to General Ewell[.] This spoilt all my fun. However, as there was nothing else to do, I could [not] but obey.

The place where I had left General Ewell, something like an hour before in our repulse had been occupied without my knowing it by the enemy and be-lieving General Ewell still to be there, as it was a commanding position and a central one, I inadvertantly rode right into [the Federal line]. I was called upon to surrender, which I did with the best grace imaginable, desiring, how-ever, to yield my arms only to a Staff officer of like grade. I was quietly carried to a house, was met in the yard by several Yankee officers who very politely asked me to dismount, and ordering my horse to be tied by an orderly, I found myself in the presence of General Shields himself. He soon left, however, turn-ing me over to several of his staff officers. I was most politely treated by all, and strange to say none of them ever asked me for my arms.[15]

Being invited to sit down, I chose a place by a window from whence I could see what was going on in the field. I saw the Louisiana Brigade make a gallant charge on a battery and capture it, and saw the columns of the enemy retreating behind a piece of woods. Having previously ridden over much of the ground of our present battle, I knew at once how to act.[16]

A Captain and two Lieutenants were sent with me and leading them through paths and roads hidden from our troops, I brought them suddenly right among our cavalry. Finding themselves surrounded in an instant by many who recognized me, I politely demanded their arms and returning from a trooper's canteen the civility they had done me, offering something to drink, I sent them to our rear under an escort of cavalry. They laughed at my maneuvre and said I was perfectly right in returning the compliment of being captured, and that I had done so in a manner handsome and creditable.

[The captured Yankee officers] with our other prisoners were forwarded on to Richmond, at which place they soon met with more of their friends. I visited them at the Libby Prison and caused a little more comfort to be allowed them. After sending them off I pushed on with the cavalry in pursuit of the flying enemy and assisted in capturing some twenty three more, among whom were several additional officers. On the occasion of my visit to them at Libby they recognized me, and upon the tale being told of my own capture and escape, made a great deal of merriment over it.

Fremont as before stated had occupied the opposite side of the river with his whole force; seven brigades of infantry and cavalry and artillery in proportion, a marching order of which force I had captured and given to General Ewell on the day previous. After the pursuit was ordered to stop, our army retraced their footsteps and entered Brown Gap in the Blue Ridge to rest our men from the exertions of the two days hard fighting. The fighting was very severe for what time it lasted, namely from about 7:30 in the morning until about one in the afternoon. Much credit is due the Yankee battery, Co. "E" 4th U.S. Artillery, for gallant fighting.[17]

We rested in Brown's Gap the 10th and 11th and took march again on the night of the 11th crossing the Shenandoah about two miles above Port Republic, and stopping near Mt. Meridian on the Staunton and Winchester Turnpike and about fifteen miles from Staunton. Here we rested from the 12th to the 15th inclusive, marching again on the 16th towards Waynesboro, a small town on the Virginia Central Railroad, thence to Nuchums [Mechums] River—a station on the same road about 20 miles from Charlottesville.[18]

Here I was detached from Gen. Ewell's Staff and placed on Ordnance duty as Assistant Inspector of Ordnance by Gen. Jackson; my immediate chief was Lieut. George H. Bier, C.S.N., an old acquaintance who had frequently desired to have me with him. In many respects this was much more pleasant to me, inasmuch as it gave me more to do and relieved me from the association of persons who I could not respect and much disliked. I was detached on the 19th of June. After inspecting the stores, all captured from Banks in the Valley, we went to Greenwood Station on the 25th to do likewise there.[19]

6. The Fights around Richmond

June 26, 1862–July 6, 1862

Night closed in on scattered and shattered regiments; fifty men of a regiment could hardly be found together; the field in front was strewn with the dead and dying, lying even under and among the enemy's guns and pieces.

—Oscar Hinrichs

On the 26th [of June, Major George Bier and I] received an order from General Jackson directing us to follow and join him at Ashland on the Richmond, Fredericksburg & Potomac R.R. We reached Gen. Jackson's headquarters about 11 o'clock on the night of the 29th. He slept in advance of the battle-field of Mechanicsville, where A.P. Hill gained so much credit for himself. It was here that Gen. Jackson's forces, after a forced march from Ashland fell upon the enemy's rear [on the 27th, which] was the opening of the day's fighting about Richmond. Not expecting any attack from that quarter, we came upon them unawares, and [they] did not know our whereabouts until the rifles and muskets dealt destruction among them.[1]

After passing a most unpleasant night, we were in the saddle [be]times on the morning of the 30th, and Bier and myself were ordered to take twenty cavalry and lead our column under Jackson himself on the pursuit of the enemy. We rode after them for some ten or twelve miles, and the sight was handsome. Guns, knapsacks, overcoats, canteen, etc. etc. strewed the road from the beginning to end. Squads of the enemy, numbering from three to thirty, were being captured at almost every step of our road and delayed us much. Sending them at first to the rear under guard was found at last to be impracticable as it took from us our cavalry, which after [all] was not much account anyhow. I determined to give them a fair trial anyhow should the opportunity offer itself. During the afternoon a small artillery fight took place, which resulted in our driving them from their position. July 1st opened as finely as yesterday.[2]

The General seemed much pleased with us for work [earlier in the day], and gave us some cavalry again. Bier being called off, [he] left me with them. The roads were found again filled with stragglers, arms and accoutrements. I followed them, capturing many prisoners for about 5 miles, when we came to a dead stop. The bridge leading across the branch or run of White Oak Swamp was on fire and [on] the other side the enemy were drawn up in line of battle about 75,000 strong.[3]

Yesterday [June 28th] occurred the hottest of the fights around Richmond, and where our men displayed themselves to immense advantage, I mean Cold Harbor [the Battle of Gaines's Mill]. Whiting, Trimble and [John B.] Hood deserve great credit for the manner in which they fought their troops and the good work done by them. Our loss was very heavy.[4]

Before coming down on the Yankee brigade [on June 30] we saw a troop or squadron of Yankee cavalry coming up the road towards us and among them a man who seemed to hold some considerable rank. They advanced upon us to within sixty or sixty-five yards. My own number had dwindled down to less than thirty, these I formed in a single front and ordered the charge. The enemy instead of meeting us as I confidently expected turned and ran in spite of all the efforts made by the officer above alluded to.

Now commenced a most exciting chase but the Yankee horse, being more fresh, kept ahead. Beside my cavalry thought it more prudent to keep out of arms length[, and our horse soldiers] gradually dropped off one by one hunting prisoners, until at last three men only remained with me. These three kept close to my heels all the time, and seemed as anxious to have a small skirmish, as myself. These three and myself were within twenty yards of said officer as he dashed into the run or branch near the burning bridge; and finding infantry fire coming among us and nothing but certain destruction to be gained, I withdrew.

Here I lost my horse, my poor old gallant grey. I had owned him since being in service near Rapidan Station. He had carried me safely and truly through many a long march and hard fought field, yet all things must have an end. The faithful animal that would follow me like a dog and only wished to be able to speak; his bones lie whitening and enriching the soil of the Chickahominy. A horse captured from the enemy during the morning soon mounted me again. About one of the last men to reach the burning bridge was a Yankee trooper, who had been strapped in the saddle to prevent his falling off, a practice largely resorted to by the enemy, to balance the defects of bad riding; [he] unstrapped himself and was subsequently captured. He informed me that the before mentioned officer was no other person than [George B.] McClellan himself. Comment is useless.[5]

Upon finding the enemy posted to receive the rebels [across White Oak Swamp], I sent a Courier to General Jackson with the information and a request to hurry forward the artillery and infantry with him. After sending him off I commenced reconnoitering the ground, selected positions for our artillery and waited the result. Our artillery [was] coming up the positions being approved by General Jackson; after about twenty minutes [of] heavy firing, the enemy abandoned the position, withdrawing their artillery and infantry. Owing [to] the nature of the ground [and] the immense superiority of the enemy, no attack by our infantry was made, and we rested on the ground.[6]

July 1st opened finely and gave promise of a handsome day's work. Early in the morning we were moving, the enemy having abandoned the position of yesterday and continued to fall back until late in the afternoon when we came upon them and compelled them to fight, though at great disadvantage to our-selves. General Robert E. Lee had command of the whole Confederate forces and to him must be laid the blame if any, of the escape of the enemy. Longstreet, Huger and Magruder it appears were directed to move in concert with Jackson and allow him a chance to gain their rear on one side while [Maj. Gen. Theophilus H.] Holmes kept them from the river and consequently the support of their gunboats. [Maj. Gen. James] Longstreet fought hard and well.

Huger did make an attack upon them with one brigade [on June 30 at Glendale] and drove them back some distance, but finding the enemy heavily reinforced, did not support the brigade sent forward and which consequently had to fall back on him. Magruder got drunk and failed to do anything. The results of Longstreet's fights were some eight hundred prisoners and fourteen handsome pieces of artillery, but without horses. Huger's and Magruder's [attacks] amounted to nothing, and hence the enemy finding themselves but slightly pressed on their front had time to concentrate on their two wings, thus rendering ineffectual the attempts of Jackson and Holmes.

It saved the Yankee army from complete destruction and capture and would have avoided to a very great extent the fighting of today [July 1]. I have said if any blame is to be attached, it belongs to Gen. Lee, for as soon as he found how feeble Magruder and Huger were doing their work, he ought to have suspended them at once, for the power to do so lay with him. However, the results of yesterdays fight on their part was to be retrieved today. The opportunity was speedy to offer itself to show their incompetency and his want of military genius in the field. As a thinker Lee has probably no equal, but he appears to be sadly deficient in a quality which enables Generals to make their mark, a coup d'ocile [d'oeil] as the French call it.[7]

Early this morning [July 1] I was sent out by General Jackson to find a connection between the Charles City and a county road on which he wished

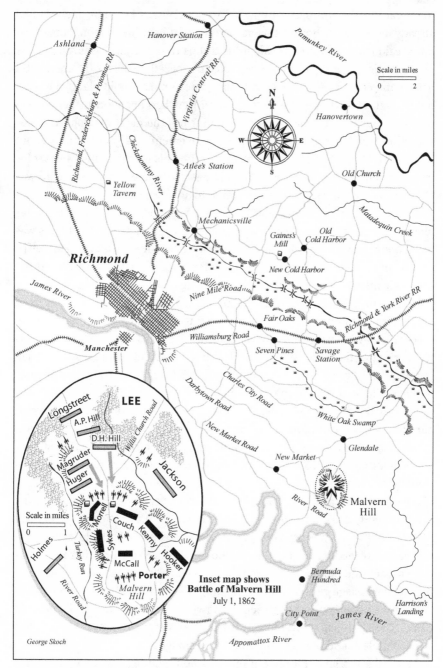

Scale in miles
0   2

Ashland

Hanover Station

Pamunkey River

Richmond, Fredericksburg & Potomac RR

Virginia Central RR

Chickahominy River

Hanovertown

Atlee's Station

Yellow Tavern

Old Church

Matadequin Creek

Mechanicsville

Gaines's Mill

Old Cold Harbor

New Cold Harbor

Richmond

James River

Nine Mile Road

Fair Oaks

Richmond & York River RR

Manchester

Williamsburg Road

Seven Pines

Savage Station

Charles City Road

Darbytown Road

White Oak Swamp

New Market Road

New Market

Glendale

River Road

Malvern Hill

**Inset map shows
Battle of Malvern Hill**
July 1, 1862

Bermuda Hundred

Harrison's Landing

City Point

James River

Appomattox River

George Skoch

LEE

Longstreet

A.P. Hill

Willis Church Road

D.H. Hill

Magruder

Huger

Jackson

Scale in miles
0   1

Holmes

Morell

Couch

Kearny

Sykes

Hooker

McCall

Porter

Turkey Run

River Road

Malvern Hill

The Seven Days Battles

to operate. I was compelled to pass through Huger's Division. Jackson had already moved three hours previous, and I could hear his cannon. Huger had not breakfasted. In riding through his troops to the front, I was stopped by his outer pickets, saying it was dangerous to proceed further as the enemy still held their picket post opposite to them. Nine Yankees could plainly be seen, but no sign of anything else, and knowing they had abandoned their strong position opposite Jackson at ten o'clock [during] the night previous, the presumption was fair that their retrograde movement was general throughout their front. Huger had in the meantime finished his morning meal and set his troops in motion; a courier from Gen. Longstreet passed saying the road was clear for miles; still Gen. Huger hesitated to advance.[8]

The slow process of ordering forward a regiment from the rear, its deploy[ment] as skirmishers consumed much valuable time and while this was being done the Yankee picket of nine men were captured by Bier and myself[,] thus demonstrating the futileness of the effort to drive them away by one thousand skirmishers. Three hours had a whole division been stopped, without a gun being fired by the enemy. It was an offence highly culpable and deserved a severe punishment. Magruder also failed to make good his blunder of the preceding day. Coming from the troops from Jacksons extreme left to the extreme right of the whole line—Gen. Holmes,—I found them massed in such numbers as to render their movements difficult and uncertain, and in consequence the real fight of the day did not take place until late in the day and then most[ly] on Jackson's side. The center did fight but the right was almost paralized by want of room. The enemy had in the mean time drawn themselves into a handsome position on Malvern Hill under the protection of their gunboats, the shells from which frequently fell among our men doing occasionally much damage.[9]

The fight at Cold Harbor [Gaines's Mill] was a very hard one, especially the infantry fight, and I am doubtful which to class as the hottest. The infantry fire at Cold Harbor was probably greater than at Malvern Hill. The cannonade was certainly terrific. During the afternoon [at Malvern Hill], after returning to Gen. Jackson, I found myself caught in advance of a brigade charging a battery of eleven siege guns. I certainly did not expect to get off with life much less with broken skin, yet although repulsed twice, I managed to get clear after a while. The fight lasted until late at night, the cannonading not ceasing until 9 o'clock. Flesh and blood could hold out no longer.[10]

We had lost a large number of men, without gaining any material advantage and if anything came out rather worsted. Night closed on a very disordered host. Gen. Ewell, gallant old man that he is, after the 1st Brigade under [Brig. Gen. Charles S.] Winder was repulsed after having driven the

The Battle of Malvern Hill (From *Harper's Pictorial History of the Great Rebellion*)

enemy from their guns, begged and entreated the men to try another charge, promising them to lead them himself, yet all to no avail. The men had fought until flesh and blood could hold together no longer, and though they were willing to defend themselves from an attack, they positively refused to make one. Night closed in on scattered and shattered regiments; fifty men of a regiment could hardly be found together; the field in front was strewn with the dead and dying, lying even under and among the enemy's guns and pieces.[11]

McClellan, supported on his flank and rear by the enemy's gunboats, had opportunity to devote his entire strength to his front, and thus ended the fight around Richmond with the exception of some small skirmishes in which the fortunes of war were varied on both sides. From within two and a half miles of Richmond we had now driven them nearly twenty-five miles under their gunboats. They lost from twenty to twenty-two thousand men, of which ten to twelve thousand were prisoners in Richmond including a Major General, four Brigadiers, and other officers in proportion.

Bier and myself, including the cavalry on our first day's trial and tramp, captured about five hundred prisoners from Major downwards; my own share amounted to ninety-seven alive, and eighteen killed for not giving up their arms. The second day I captured and sent to the rear seven hundred and forty-three, including three Majors, eight Captains etc. etc.

July 2nd opened quietly and raining heavily and continued all day. Our men were employed largely in burying the dead, and we could now commence to count the cost of these fights. Major [C. Roberdeau] Wheat of Wheat's Louisiana Battalion "Tigers" lies numbered with the dead. Pierced with eleven balls he lays within a few feet of a stack of Yankees; twenty-eight men without any commissioned officer were all that remained of the Battalion. He was a brave man and seemed to love fighting for its own sake. Col [Joseph V.] Scott [from the 3rd Virginia] also fell at the head of his regiment. Col. Moore [William G. Meares] of the 3rd N.C., from Wilmington was killed gallantly. Our loss was about half that of the enemy which is heavy enough.[12]

July 3rd. Nothing doing today except continuing to bury the dead and gather up arms and ammunition. Towards evening indications were felt that the enemy intended continuing their retreat down the River from Richmond and preparations are being made to follow them.

July 4th. Today I am announced to the Army as Assistant Chief of Ordnance, Valley District[,] and Inspector of Ordnance, V.D.

July 5th. After overhauling and replenishing the stock of ammunition, I started the train for the army.

July 6th. Our men today captured a strong box with $200,000 in specie intended as pay for the Yankee troops. The Government took possession of the same. During the afternoon I was directed to return to my old camping place near White Oak swamp. About 35,000 stands of arms have been collected from the battle field and sent to Richmond.

7. The Maryland Shore

July 7, 1862–December 31, 1862

It remains to be seen now how they will fight on the enemy's territory,
for I believe that we shall cross to the north side of that river, and
may be try to raise up a rebellion in Maryland.

—Oscar Hinrichs

We remained quiet from this [time] out, with occasional trips on duty to Richmond and Ashland until the 15th instant when reports having been received of Gen. [John] Pope's advance along the line of the Orange and Alexandria Railroad. Gen. Ewell was started off to head him off and prevent his getting possession of Gordonsville, the juncture of the former road with the Virginia Central. Jackson's Division followed soon after.[1]

[As Jackson's acting chief of ordnance,] I marched the train off towards Louisa Court House on the afternoon of [July] 15th, following myself on the 16th reaching Gordonsville on the 19th. On the 21st marched again about noon, and camped about 3½ miles from Liberty Mills, and stopped here until the 26th. While here laid the foundation for a source of ammunition supply of all kinds preparatory to the expected campaign after Pope. This Yankee general had issued a most extraordinary proclamation upon assuming command and I confidently believed that Jackson would soon teach him a lesson, and have his Head Quarters sooner and more constantly in the saddle than he had anticipated. During the interim marched over to Orange Court House, and again on the 27th to Green Spring Valley, near Mechanicsville.[2]

On the 29th I was ordered to Richmond after Ordnance Stores, returning on the 4th of August. On the 5th again went to Richmond and returned on the 8th. On my return found the General had decided to divide the train into two, reserving a part as a general reserve train for his command, now augment[ed] by the accession of Gen. A. P. Hill. On my arrival at Gordonsville, found the train had been moved forwards to Orange Court House, and while following it during the night with some wagons sent or left back for repairs or stores, missed the main body.[3]

On reaching the Rapidam river, I found that the balance of my wagons still remained at Orange Court House. Lee's train—Division train—had been fired into and stopped by some Yankee cavalry on the other side of the river who had managed to elude our pickets and thus got in our rear. I at once sent off for some infantry and under its protection passed the train over, then believing that the Yankees would return in greater force to capture the train, I post[ed] the 13th Georgia, [under] Col. [Marcellus] Douglass, near by and waited their coming up. This they soon did and were received in the most handsome style by the men; some thirty saddles being emptied and about fifty prisoners taken.[4]

This was the opening of the battle at Slaughter's Mountain or Cedar Run. Finding no more danger after the repulse of the cavalry, I returned to Orange Court House about sun rise, having been in the saddle all night, and from thence was ordered to Gordonsville with the train; this fight occurred on the 9th of August. We captured Acting Maj. Gen. [Henry] Prince, but lost our gallant Winder, commanding the "Old Stonewall Brigade." Our loss was about 1,000 [and] that of the enemy about 3,000; and thus opened the campaign ending with the battle of Sharpsburg.[5]

Gen. Jackson after the fight returned to near Gordonsville thereby causing the enemy to believe that from the smallness of our force we were retreating being unable to make our victory good. Pope readily fell into the trap thus laid for him, and instead of making good his retreat, remained near Culpepper Court House. Reinforcements continued to arrive from our army near Richmond, and soon Jackson moved with the first column, flanking Pope and compelling him to recross the Rappahannock. I remained at Gordonsville until the 20th of August when orders were received to move forward and join him.[6]

At Gordonsville I worked hard establishing a handsome depot of Ordnance Stores from which our part of the army could draw supplies. I came up with our troops at Jeffersontown, a small town on the Rappahannock. Every attempt to prevent our crossing, and succeed at this place assisted by heavy rains which caused the river to rise very rapidly, were made by the enemy. Early's Brigade and Field's [Lawton's] Brigade were thrown across the river, but had to be withdrawn on this account. Jackson, however, flanked the position, cooped en masse on the 27th, my train following in the extreme rear.[7]

Here let me say that it appears to me that if anything should go wrong on our front, our army be beaten, it would be almost impossible to secure our trains. The confusion on the road near Jeffers[on]town, augmented by bad roads and the most culpable negligence of the Quartermaster Department, was beyond bounds. Any description will beggar the reality. Gen. Lee is in supreme command, and instead of things being bettered, they are only made worse by that fool of a Chief Quartermaster, [James L.] Corley.[8]

Jackson however, cannot wait to unravel the Gordian knot of wagons and trains, and has pushed on and engaged the enemy's rear near Manassas. Gen. Lee remained at Salem. This person I believe to be exceedingly overrated by both troops and people, who will one day be slaughtered like sheep by him. I cannot believe that he is the great General in the field. His talent appears to lie more in planning than in executing his plans when conceived. This appears to be Jackson's great forte. But to proceed.

My train crossed on the evening of the 27th with a most beautiful confusion of trains. About one o'clock I reached Salem, rested my teams and waited further orders, which arrived about eight o'clock. Went on my way with a cavalry Col. as guide over a new road, with the enemy at times within easy cannon range. How the General managed to pick this road for an indispensable Ordnance train to pass over, I cannot imagine, unless it be that he was mislead by the cavalry reports, a not unlikely thing, when we come to consider the value of Confederate cavalry. Writing at this late day, many things are plain to me, which would appear at first almost inexplicable. When we bring in to account the intire worthlessness of our cavalry, which was bad then and is infinitely worse now, it explains much.[9]

Passing through Middleburg and Aldie where we rested again waiting further orders. At Aldie met with Gen Taliaferro going to the rear wounded in the first of the series of fights [at Brawner's Farm on August 28 against the Iron Brigade] near the old battle ground of Bull Run. He represented the whole as a most decided success, but much heavy fighting. At Aldie received orders to move forwards to Sudley Mills on Bull Run; this was a verbal order, and from subsequent proceedings, I asked the General whether any such orders had been sent me; which he denied.[10]

When near Sudley's Mills, I found that the place was in possession of the enemy. Contrary to the advice of those with me I determined to carry the order out not doubting but that when the General sent the order to me, the road was clear. I gathered together about two squadrons of cavalry [composed of] some 600 stragglers, which with my own guard made my force about 1,000 men; with about a third I pushed forward, felt the enemy and finding them in small force, engaged them, drove them from the place, passed my trains through, and captured some 150 prisoners, which I presented to General [Jackson] next morning. The enemy numbered about 2,500 men. My cavalry, taking charge myself, did excellent service. As soon as their line was broken by the infantry fire, I charged them with the cavalry and put them to flight, capturing the above prisoners. I reached my destination safely, having run a great risk, however, inasmuch as the train passed through the enemy's line into our own. This I call fighting the ordnance.[11]

The next morning fighting was resumed, and went on with varying success until near night, when McClellan [Pope] came up in person and assumed command. The day on the whole, and especially towards evening, had gone too much against him, and all he could do was to save as much of his command as possible.

The fighting of our men was splendid. Earlys Louisiana Brigade at one time lay behind a railroad embankment, and running out of ammunition, fought the enemy with stones. Thirteen Yankee regiments were more than half represented on the field in dead and wounded. They fought well however. If our men could only be as well disciplined as the Yankees are, they would indeed be invincible. However, they fight well, and deserve every success which can be awarded them. It remains to be seen now how they will fight on the enemy's territory, for I believe that we shall cross to the north side of that river, and may be try to raise up a rebellion in Maryland.[12]

Jackson instead of following the enemy on their retreat towards Centerville, and Fairfax Court House, pushed on by them, fighting again at Ox Hill, where Gen. Harney [Phil Kearny of the] U.S.A. was killed.[13]

[We] went on to Leesburg, crossing the Potomac at Edwards Ferry [White's Ford] on September 5th. I think without exception it was the grandest sight I ever saw, to see our dirty boys crossing the Potomac. Heretofore everything had gone smooth and well, save a great deal of confusion among the wagon trains at times, not a wheel broke, and it looked more like a huge wave rolling in towards the beach and breaking upon it. So our lines of troops [were] crossing the river. The day was beautifully bright, the air balmy and pleasant, and as each successive regiment touched the Maryland shore, shouts and music rent the air. Brigade after Brigade thus passed on; cannon upon cannon, wagon upon wagon, until nothing was left behind save our tracks.[14]

D. H. Hill and Longstreet crossed at other points. We all joined hands again near and at Frederick City. The Potomac was crossed without difficulty. The previous fighting however, was very severe and our loss proportionally very heavy. That of the enemy, however must, judging from the men laying on the field at Manassas and Bull Run, be at least ten to our one. Our brave old fighting cocks, Ewell and Trimble, were both wounded near Bristoe Station: and we miss them much. We could have more readily lost 20,000 men than these two, for they both are invaluable in a fight.

We remained near and at Frederick City until the tenth [of September]

The Confederates crossing the Potomac River
(From *Harper's Pictorial History of the Great Rebellion*)

resting and recruiting our men and horses. Although our previous fighting, especially of Jackson's Corps, was almost unparalleled; still I think a great blunder was made in allowing so much and valuable time to escape unimproved, inasmuch as it permitted the enemy to concentrate their shattered forces and recruit them with new levies from the border states.

The small garrison left by the enemy at Harper's [Harpers] Ferry, seems also to have been completely overlooked, and it necessitated the detaching of 30,000 men under Jackson to reduce that place and thus keep open our communication with our rear. After so much time was wasted and thrown away at Frederick City, the detaching of so large a force in the face of an advancing enemy whose only salvation lay in fighting us soon and driving us away was a fatal mistake, inasmuch as it weakened our anyhow small army of invasion to a little over 50,000 men. These men if perfectly fresh, would be equal to twice if not thrice that number of the enemy, demoralized by recent defeat and disaster, but they were not fresh, and I think it would have been better to have detached a large force of cavalry to watch this garrison until the enemy could be whipped, when Harper's Ferry would have fallen of itself.

Be that as it may, Jackson was detached with his own, Ewell's, Hill's (A. P.) and McLaws Divisions, nearly 30,000 strong, to capture that place. Jackson left Frederick City early on the morning of the 10th. Harper's Ferry surrendered to him on the 15th with the garrison of about 11,000 men, many stores and supplies, all of which were saved with comparatively small loss on our side.[15]

I was ordered to follow D. H. Hill's division, and after much confusion again, left Frederick City on the morning of the 10th and moved out towards Boonsboro. The balance of the army moved also. This move was necessitated by [the march] on which Jackson had to make on Harper's Ferry, so as to be within supporting distance of each other.

I do not believe that it was the intention of the army to return in to Virginia without making some demonstration beyond our mere presence, but D. H. Hill left his copy of instructions, detailing the whole plan of campaign, on his table at Frederick City, and it now became a matter of absolute necessity to return to Virginia with as little delay as possible. Accordingly the army moved on towards Hagerstown, camped there two days to allow Jackson to come up and protect our numerous trains in crossing the river, and to prevent our being whipped in detail.[16]

In passing through Boonsboro, and camping there for the night, was informed of the presence of the escaped Yankee cavalry from Harper's Ferry. Went out and reconnoitered them, and then sent to Gen. D. H. Hill for more men to resist the attack if made. He sent me a regiment of infantry and four pieces of artillery, but nothing came of it. From Hagerstown my train was moved to Funkstown, and from there to Williamsport, recrossing the Potomac at that point. Some 50 of Longstreet's ordnance wagons were captured by the Yankee cavalry, which had threatened me at Boonsboro. Stuart is said to have captured some of the wagons and the greater part of the men who did the damage. This, however, is very doubtful; it was a disgracefull piece of business anyhow.[17]

After I crossed the Potomac I went through Martinsburg, on to Harper's Ferry, and thence to Shepherdstown, again crossing the Potomac on the morning of the 17th about an hour before day. Upon reporting to the General [Jackson], who had rejoined Lee [in Sharpsburg] the evening previously, leaving A. P. Hill in command at Harper's Ferry.

D. H. Hill had been left on the Boonsboro road with his division in a most advantageous position to hold the enemy in check should they attempt to follow us up. They did follow us up in force, nearly crushing this little division on the top of South Mountain south of Boonsboro. Their loss was very heavy before they could compel him to retire and it made him slow and cautious.[18]

On the 17th [of September] orders were sent to A. P. Hill to join us with his division. The enemy under McClellan [came] in force against us, and as we had yet much property to save, a fight was compulsory on our part. Both

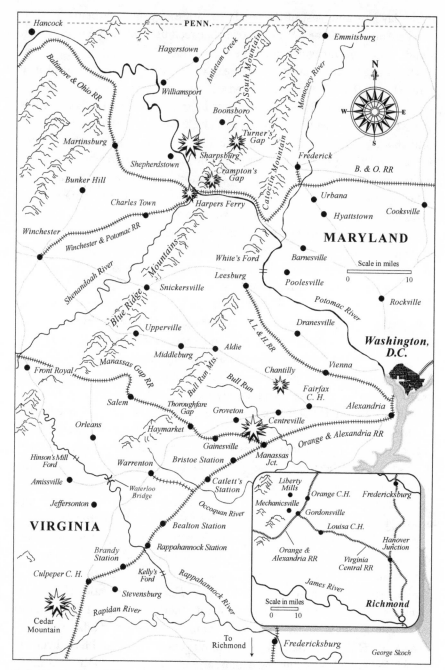

Cedar Run to Second Manassas, Antietam, and Shepherdstown

armies lay east and west of the small town of Sharpsburg, it being between us. The Antietam River [Creek] also lay between us, rendered famous by the pseudo charge of Burnside across the stone bridge.[19]

The engagement opened at daybreak of the 17th and lasted until near 9 o'clock p.m. The tide of battle raged with varying success on both sides, at one time we gaining a little, another time loosing, except on the extreme left, where we gained steadily. Centre and right, however, were loosing ground, until about 4 p.m. when A. P. Hill came [from Harpers Ferry with his 3,300 troops], and charging the enemy's lines with his whole division, restored to us the line of battle of the morning. It was most opportune that he came just as he did, for the enemy were making strenuous efforts to interpose themselves between us and the river, and would have succeeded but for A. P. Hill. Our men, however, were much worn out by constant and heavy marching and consequently the straggling from the field was immense. From my own observation I estimated it as fully 25,000 between the battle field and the river.[20]

From what I saw of the battle itself, if [at] about 6 o'clock, 10,000 fresh men could have been thrown in on the right it would have resulted in a most complete victory, for so far the slaughter of the enemy was immense. Our own loss was probably between 12[,000] and 15,000, that of the enemy at least one half more. But even the longest day must have an end, and it appeared to me that when exhaustion and night put a stop to the conflict the battle was as near a drawn one as could well be. I confidently expected that the enemy would make another attack, on us the next morning, inasmuch as he could receive further and fresh reinforcements, which we could not, unless we count the small army of stragglers; many of whom had crossed the river during the night and made their way to Winchester, and they would not be worth much[.] To those who did fight too much credit cannot be given.

Allowing a loss by battle and sickness of 25,000 men since our occupation of Maryland, we have a force of only 60,000 to begin the battle of Sharpsburg, which was further reduced by casualties and straggling to about 35,000. With [a] handful [of soldiers] we fight, hold in check, and nearly whip at least 150,000 of the enemy. It was then, as far as mere fighting was concerned, a glorious triumph of Southern prowess over Northern bravado. There were many occasions during the battle, which if taken advantage of and pursued with vigor, would very materially have changed the aspect of affairs even before [A. P.] Hill came up, and to him in all probability would have been assigned the duty of pursuing the enemy, and my impression is that not much of the vaunted Army of the Potomac would have remained. The fates willed otherwise, however, and night closed in on a vast battlefield and hospital.[21]

Morning found the enemy's pickets withdrawn some distance from our front, which intimated one or two things. His reinforcements had not come up, or he was even with them in no condition to renew the battle. The morning [of September] 18th found us much recuperated and somewhat strengthened.

Finding the enemy did not make the attack, I think it would have been a good thing to make the attempt ourselves, and if finding the enemy too strong for us, the engagement could have been broken off, [our commanders] feeling confident that the enemy would not molest us after having seen our disposition to continue the fight. The day however, was consumed in burying the dead and attending to the wounded. Towards 10 a.m. the enemy's pickets, reoccupied their ground of last night, but did not molest us.

At night preparations were made for recrossing the river. I received orders to move my train, and at the same time to report to General Jackson for instructions. On my return I lost my way, and ran into a Yankee picket post of some 20 men, from whom however, thanks to my sabre, good horse and the darkness I got away. Arriving at the river side, I found a most endless confusion. I got across after much trouble and difficulty, to find my train split up into about 20 different parsels and scattered I knew not where. This occupied my time on the 19th in gathering them together again.

The army had all crossed during the night, and this morning the enemy came down to the river side [near Shepherdstown] and shelled our wagons without doing any material damage. A brigade of Yankee infantry crossed over under the protection of their guns, but was pitched into by A. P. Hill and nearly killed out. Our whole army now moved backwards towards Bunker Hill, between Martinsburg and Winchester, rearming the men, reorganizing the army etc., preparatory to falling back to a good line of defence.[22]

From this [point] until November 10th the army was moving to and from, ranging from Martinsburg to Berryville and Millwood on the Shenandoah. Longstreet and [John R.] Cooke have gone with Lee to Fredericksburg and on that date received orders to reinforce him there to check the Yankee advance on Fredericksburg. Passing up the Valley as far as New Market, and crossing the Blue Ridge at that place, passed on through Madison Court House to Guinea Station near Fredericksburg, where we remained quiet until the 13th of December.

On the evening of the 12th the enemy crossed the river in force occupying the town and in the morning made an assault upon our lines on the heights in the rear of the town. They were most signally repulsed with a loss of about 20,000. Why Lee did not attack them the next morning is more than I can say, for never was a finer opportunity offered for the complete destruction of the Yankee host. McClellan had in the meantime been superseded by Burnside, who afterwards gave way to Hooker, who again, in his turn, will give away to some one else. At any rate, the Yankee host lay in front of us for 24 hours, the pickets frequently not 60 paces apart, quietly looking upon each other. On the night of the 14th to 15th during a very dark rainy and dismal night, the enemy left, without one picket becoming aware of it until broad daylight next morning. Thus ended the campaign for 1862.[23]

8. The Pennsylvania Line

January 1, 1863–June 28, 1863

General Jackson took us on a flank movement in the rear of Chancell[or]sville, where Hooker had crossed en masse. It was the opening of the spring campaign and most brilliant it was, though the victory cost us dear[ly].

—Oscar Hinrichs

The troops soon went into winter quarters on the line of the Rappahannock, fortifying their positions and preparing for another year of war, bloodshed and desolation. On the 20th of December I was relieved from Ordnance duty and ordered to report to Brig? Gen. Taliaferro, then commanding Jackson's old division. Taliaferro is a very pleasant, nice gentleman; [he] socially possesses, however, too little of the qualities which I think requisite for a general officer in a service where everything depends upon political power to secure advancement. Could he be retained in his place as Brigadier, he might do well enough, but [Taliaferro] was never fit to command a division. This however, was no fault of his; 'twas his misfortune. At any rate, as long as he had command of the division, I had a very pleasant time of it with pleasant and agreeable quarters.[1]

Gen. Trimble relieved Gen. Taliaferro from the command of the division on February 1st and assumed command. If any previous time at Headquarters had been pleasant, it was surely so now, as I was associated with the most gentlemanly staff I have ever met with in the service. The Adjutant General I was made acquainted with when I first came to Manassas. The other members of the Staff were as equally pleasant to deal with, and my opinion of Gen. Trimble has already been recorded.[2]

Unfortunately towards the close of April General Trimble was taken seriously sick, and the command of the division devolved upon Brig. Gen. R. [Raleigh] E. Colston, a most gallant and accomplished soldier and gentleman. Shortly after his assuming command, the enemy began to show signs of returning life and animation by effecting a crossing in small force at Port Royal. They did but little damage and much good, by taking the worthless horses of a still more worthless cavalry company, on picket at that place. They returned however, to their side of the river before our troops could reach them.[3]

We also returned to our quarters and remained there until the 29th of April, when, the enemy having crossed about 15,000 men at Fredericksburg, our winter quarters were broken up, and we were ordered at once to Fredericksburg. Here we confronted them until May the 22nd [2nd], when General Jackson took us on a flank movement in the rear of Chancell[or]sville, where Hooker had crossed en masse. It was the opening of the spring campaign and most brilliant it was, though the victory cost us dear[ly].[4]

Our first attack upon the enemy was a complete surprise, and we ran the immortal 11th Army Corps [commanded by Maj. Gen. O. O. Howard] some six miles when night closed in upon our jaded troops. Much confusion was brought about by the thickly grown-up country we had to pass through, so thick that we could not see 50 paces ahead or [on] each side. The enemy were run into their lines of fortifications, hastily, yet well constructed. During the night in attempting to pass some troops from their left to their right, they commenced a most terrific shelling, probably the heaviest I ever was under.[5]

The troops in many instances became panic stricken and in attempting to run created still greater confusion. By the individual exertions of Jackson, Colston and their respective staffs, it was soon stopped, but, for the time being the scene of artillery without drivers, horses running madly, men struggling to get out of the way of dashing artillery etc., is beyond description.

After quiet had been restored, General Jackson rode to the front, and Lane's North Carolina Brigade, mistaking him and Staff for Yankee cavalry, fired, wounding severely General Jackson, Gen. A. P. Hill and killing my friend Captain [James K.] Boswell of the Engineers. After being wounded, and while being carried to the rear, one of the litter bearers was shot, by which accident the General received a very severe fall. Extreme imprudence after reaching the hospital brought on pneumonia, from the effects of which [led to] amputation of one arm, he died on the 5th [10th]. He lived to know of the complete victory we had gained over the enemy on the 3rd of May, and died, as ever the humble, penitent and upright gentleman and soldier.[6]

The loss [of Jackson] was for several days hid from the army, but this could not succeed long. Thus ended the mortal career of the brightest and best jewell in the royal crown of the Confederacy. His mantle may have fallen upon

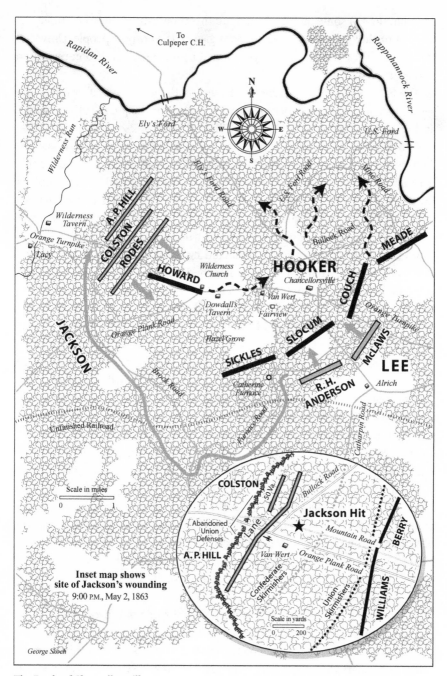

To
Culpeper C.H.

Rapidan River

Rappahannock River

Wilderness Run

Ely's Ford

U.S. Ford

N
W · E
S

Ely's Ford Road

U.S. Ford Road

Mine Road

A.P. HILL

Wilderness Tavern

COLSTON

RODES

Orange Turnpike

Lacy

Bullock Road

MEADE

HOWARD

Wilderness Church

HOOKER

Chancellorsville

COUCH

JACKSON

Orange Plank Road

Dowdall's Tavern

Van Wert

Fairview

Orange Turnpike

Hazel Grove

SLOCUM

McLAWS

LEE

SICKLES

Brock Road

Catherine Furnace

R.H. ANDERSON

Alrich

Catharpin Road

Furnace Road

Unfinished Railroad

Scale in miles
0   1

**Inset map shows
site of Jackson's wounding**
9:00 P.M., May 2, 1863

George Skoch

COLSTON

50 Va.

Bullock Road

Lane

Jackson Hit
★

Mountain Road

BERRY

Abandoned
Union
Defenses

A.P. HILL

Van Wert

Orange Plank Road

Confederate Skirmishers

Union Skirmishers

WILLIAMS

Scale in yards
0   200

The Battle of Chancellorsville

the shoulders of some one else, but up to this time [winter quarters, 1863–64] he has not shown himself to the anxious gaze of the army or people. Universal throughout the country was the gloom cast by his death. Hill soon recovered and went on duty again.

The fight of the 2nd was renewed by day on the 3rd when, after much and severe fighting, their entrenchments were carried at the point of the bayonet, and thus virtually ended the battle of Chancell[or]sville.

Gen Colston behaved very handsomely. His staff was redeuced by casualties from six members to three; poor Duncan [McKim] being killed. A more noble hearted, wholesouled gallant gentleman never breathed and he died nobly at the head of a brigade leading it into action. The enemy retired across the Rappahannock after receiving a most severe chastisement. Their loss was probably some 20[,000]–25,000 in killed and wounded and prisoners. Our loss amounted to about 12[,000]–15,000 including poor General [Elisha F.] Paxton [who was] killed. Two brigades were detached from the division and returned with the rest of the army to Hamilton's Crossing, the balance remaining at U.S. Ford for flag of truce purposes, and to bury our and the enemy's dead, as well as to clear the battle field of all things left by the enemy in their hasty retreat.[7]

We remained here until May the 20th when we took [up] our line of march for Hamilton Crossing, [and] reported to Maj. Gen. Edward Johnston [Johnson] of western Virginia notoriety, who had been assigned to the command of the Division vice Trimble removed. Gen. Trimble remained in Richmond and from thence after his recovery, rejoined the army during our subsequent sojourn in Pennsylvania. We remained at Hamilton Crossing until June 5th employed in reorganizing thoroughly the command preparatory to moving forwards upon the enemy. Our line of march was already forshadowed and nearly indicated by the disposition of the enemy, and as our army was small, comparatively to the undertaking in hand, it was to our interest to accomplish our foothold upon the enemy's territory with as little previous loss; and to keep the troops as fresh as possible for the coming battle which had to be fought on Pennsylvania soil, and which had to be in the neighborhood of the Valley of the Cumberland.[8]

As said, we left Hamilton Crossing on the morning of the 5th and took up our march in easy stages for Culpepper Court House, from which place the enemy had been run by the previous advance of General Hood of Longstreet's Corps and Stuart with his cavalry. Soon after leaving the vicinity of Fredericksburg, however, the enemy made a counter-move, which did not alter the condition or posture of affairs. Early's and Johnson's divisions were delayed a day, but finding Gen. A. P. Hill strong enough to hold the ground against the

enemy, we were pushed forward to Culpepper Court House. Here we rested a day.[9]

The enemy[,] finding themselves likely to be taken at serious disadvantage and also our threatening [Maj. Gen. Robert H.] Milroy's command at Winchester and Harper's Ferry, gathered a large cavalry force [at Brandy Station], threw them on our supposed front upon Stuart, and came very near making their point. The timely arrival of reinforcements of cavalry, artillery and infantry, soon restored the day and eventually [turned] it in our favor. Some 500 prisoners, among whom were many officers, [and] a battery of field pieces captured by the cavalry were among the trophies of the fight.[10]

This [battle being] over we continued our march on towards Winchester where we arrived on the 13th [of June], driving in the enemy's pickets and confining Milroy and the major part of his command in Fort Union and the adjacent outworks; his force numbered about 5[,000]–6,000 men of all arms. We lay in front of Winchester two days; allowing Early to gain the command and approach from the Valley Turnpike, while Rhodes [Maj. Gen. Robert E. Rodes] went away to cut off their retreat from Harper's Ferry and Martinsburg.[11]

It was confidently expected that Rhodes, after getting on the road leading to those places, would move forwards on to Winchester, join on his left with our division occupying the approaches from Front Royal and eastern Virginia; and join on his right with Early, who would move across the Prighton [Pughtown] road and cut the enemy off from escape into western Virginia. In this manner Milroy would have been completely enclosed and his capture made certain. Instead, however, of quickly destroying the depots of supply at Martinsburg and intermediate towns and moving on towards Winchester, he [Rodes] moves from Martinsburg on to Harper's Ferry and goes about the country generally picking up supplies and provisions. This was no doubt supplying a very useful place, but was not doing the things required.[12]

In consequence of the non-appearance of Rhodes, three brigades of Johnson's division were sent across from Front Royal road to take position on the Martinsburg road, to intercept the retreat of Milroy, now made certain by Early's having stormed and captured [West Fort] on the evening previous. General Johnson took two brigades and the artillery himself, while I was detailed to bring Brig. Gen. [James A.] Walker up, who was posted near and in the town of Winchester.[13]

The enemy left their works about 3 p.m. on the 15th, leaving their wagons and artillery behind them. They were encountered by Johnson about four miles from Winchester near Jordan Springs about daybreak and brought to a stand. Hearing the firing I hurried up Walker's Brigade just in time to prevent a flank movement apparently, but in reality an attempt to escape. The engagement lasted about an hour and resulted in the capture of about 3500–4,000 prisoners, some 1500 horses, 8 stands of colors etc. Milroy with about 1,000 cavalry made good his escape. The enemy fought well for a short time.[14]

On the 16th [of June] we marched on to Sheppardstown and after delaying two more days, crossed the Potomac into Maryland at Sheppardstown on the 17th. Thus commenced the great move so anxiously looked forward to by so many, and from which so many good results were predicted. The scene of crossing the Potomac was widely and vastly different from that of last year. The weather was cloudy and rainey as if already then mourning the loss of our great Captain [Jackson]. The masses of troops moved quietly but surely on their way; the silence was only broken by the voices of command, the rumbling of artillery and wagons and the usual clatter of arms. Only now and then when some more than usual lively individual passed along, would a faint cheer rise from the ranks, soon however, to die out. In my mind, misgivings soon began to rise. Not that the men would not do their duty faithfully as usual, but that the officers were not competent to understand the true interest of the cause and the true manner of advancing that cause when in the enemy's territory; that the real issue would be lost sight of in the midst of plenty and the new scenes in which they were now called upon to act. How far I was correct let the result show.

We marched to the neighborhood of Sharpsburgh, the scene of our last summers grand fight and camp. With this the men were much dissatisfied. Partially camped on the battle field, evidences of the carnage and destruction were everywhere visible. Pieces of exploded shells, round shot, broken swords, and muskets, ever and anon mixed up with human skulls and bones of both man and beast, broken artillery wheels, in fact everything which could bear witness of a terrible conflict were strewn around. Sitting around their camp fires at night there were no sounds of revelry and joy, but the veterans who had taken part in the battle of last year related their own deeds and of those who slept around them in the ground to the gaping multitude of younger men, many of whom now for the first time assisted in the great drama in which we were all acting our part.

On the 19th we moved on through Hagerstown and were most heartily received by the secessionists of the place; ladies waving their hankerchiefs, kissing their hands; the men cheering, what few were left of them. This little episode put our men in somewhat better spirits, and never had our army appeared to better advantage. Our entry into Hagerstown last year showed no doubt a fine looking body of men, but dirty, filthy and worn down by incessant marching and fighting from the Blue Ridge to Frederick City. Today they were in good spirits, well clad and shod, clean with muskets and accoutrements in place and clean.

The tread of the men was lively and quick, and none elicited more admiration than the Old Stonewall Brigade and the First Maryland Battalion. This latter body of men was formed with new additions from the remains of the old 1st Maryland Regiment [along with the 2nd Maryland Infantry and Baltimore Horse Artillery]. Having the advantage of an excellent drill master and officer, formerly Captain, now Lieut. Col. [James R.] Herbert, they presented without exception the most military appearance of any body of troops which passed through. We camped that night about one half mile from the Pennsylvania line, on the Green Castle Turnpike.[15]

We now commenced seeing the evidences of the utter helplessness of the Pennsylvanians, who though they did not received us with open arms, with firing of cannon and rejoicings, nevertheless showed very plainly that many would do so if they dared, and in my opinion it needed but one successful issue of a general engagement to open the door of the whole state of us. Many at first were inclined to fear, perhaps the majority of the people with whom I conversed. Their country was rich, filled with all manner of supplies needed by the army. The Quartermasters were occupied daily in gathering supplies and sending them to the rear, likewise with the medical and commissary departments. I estimate the whole number of horses and cattle sent to Virginia and appropriated to our use while in the state at 4,000 and 20,000 respectively. Coffee, sugar, tea and other things of the kind were gathered up and either disposed of on the spot or sent to the rear, most of which reached its destination safely. Our army moved in three columns (I speak now of Ewell's Corps only) into the enemy's country, marching and resting as occasion required until we reached Carlisle, Pennsylvania, and passing through Green Castle, Chamber[s]burg and other smaller and minor towns and villages.[16]

Gen. Meade who had superseded Gen. Hooker, finding that Lee had the start of him, gradually abandoned his position in front of Fredericksburg, thus releasing Hill's Corps and permitting it to join Longstreet a little beyond Chambersburg. Early made a circuit, taking York and other towns on his route, all being engaged in gathering supplies. The strictest discipline was maintained throughout, and but for the losses of horses and cattle, no one could have told by the appearance of the country, that a hostile force was in the state.

Meade fell back on Washington and covered Baltimore, thinking perhaps at first that it was [in] reality nothing more than a raid by [Albert Gallatin] Jenkins with his cavalry and of [General John D.] Imboden who crossed at Cumberland doing much damage to the public works along the river and gradually made his way down to Williamsport[,] and covered the rear and kept open our communication from excursionists from Harpers Ferry, which place still held a small garrison. Hill and Longstreet however, out maneouvered him and had joined the rest of the army before Mr. Meade was fully aware of it. He then commenced drawing his forces together, sending them off in small squads of two or three divisions at a time who fell across our course at Gettysburg.

9. General Lee at Gettysburg

June 29, 1863–August 31, 1863

The possession of [Culp's] hill by us would have virtually ended the battle, for it would have compelled Meade to seek another line of defence, and compelled the removal of the remainder of his army.

—Oscar Hinrichs

We were recalled from Carllisle, and in sight of Harrisburg to join Gen. Lee at Gettysburg. It had been confidently [assumed] that a brush would occur near or at Carlisle with the New York troops sent down in poste haste for the defence of Pennsylvania, but who had retreated on our approach, burning the bridges on the Susquehannah [River] behind them, thinking thereby to stop the advance of an army that yet had to cross a bridge in pursuit of an enemy. The chances are that even Philadelphia would have surrendered without making any serious resistance, and perhaps by that move would have inclined the Northern States to enter into some preliminary proceedings, having a peace for its objective. We turned off short to the right however, and suddenly confronted Meade near Gettysburg.[1]

Johnsons division came in time to hear the cannon of our victorious forces booming after a retreating enemy, and on the night of the 1st of July the Confederate lines included the town of Gettysburg with about 6,000 prisoners, captured by Early, Rhodes and Hill. It was the opening of the grand battle at that place. The enemy after their first repulse on the afternoon and evening of the 1st instant, fell back to a very strong position south of the town which they furthermore strengthened by the erection of logworks and earthworks.

The fight was recommenced the following day [day two], but our success had so far ended. We gained nothing beyond the knowledge of the position of the enemy that in all probability, at best, we had disabled as many men as we had lost, which were not few, and that otherwise we had lost no material advantage.

The fight reopened at daybreak on the third and [after Pickett's Charge] closed with the same success. It was then deemed advisable to withdraw our forces to the range of the hills from which the enemy had been driven on our first advance on the afternoon of the 1st. This was accomplished at two o'clock on the fourth [of July]. Here we remained in position during the day, vainly hoping that the enemy, elated with their success, would follow us and attack, in which case, the Army of the Potomac would have ceased to exist.

During the night of the fourth we commenced our retreat on towards Fairfield, camping near there on the 5th, Hagerstown on the 7th and rested several days, offering battle to Meade on the south side, which he refused to accept, and recrossed the Potomac on the night of the 14th [13th]. Thus ended the invasion of the United States from which so much was promised and expected, but which in reality demonstrated two very remarkable things. First, that the real issue of the war will not be fought by the sword, but by the pen; second, that the Federals are incapable of making an aggressive movement successfully, at least until some man, as yet unknown, shall take charge of it.

The failure of the campaign of 1863 may be accounted for on two different principles, each one of which may or may not be correct; for as far as I am concerned, it can only be guess work, and after all not by any means reliable.

First, it may never have intended to have been more than a grand raid, to gather material and supplies, to last during the coming winter and to show ourselves periodically on the borders of the North. Our march last year was by no means as far into the interior, nor did it do as much damage. We must have destroyed between $10[,000,000]–20,000,000. of property, fed our army four weeks certainly beside feeding their own, reduced our expenses at least five times that sum, taught the enemy a severe lesson and recrossed the Potomac saving everything.

Second: It might have been for military reasons, outside of those existing in Virginia, to make the invasion which we did not have force enough to make in the enemy's country and at such a distance from our base. A shadow of truth is lent to each one by different circumstances.

My own opinion is that the movement was intended to be a permanent one if it could be effected, but was terminated at Gettysburg. It was terminated there because I do not think the right means were employed for ensuring success and making it good, which was at the opening clearly and surely within our grasp. Never were a people so completely paralized and left at the mercy of an advancing army fresh from a recent victory.

Seldom has a victorious army advanced into a enemy's country which was

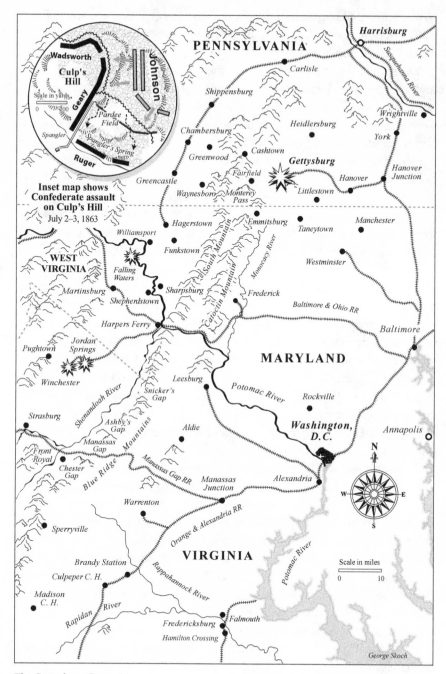

The Gettysburg Campaign

so well appointed in its minor details and working qualities, and which felt as confident of success as the one under the leadership of General Lee [that] advanced into Pennsylvania.

The start was good. The division of the army into three invading columns under Longstreet, Ewell and Hill, three as gallant men as ever straddled a horse, necessitated an equal division of the forces of the enemy, if Lee's forces were kept apart, but always within reach and support of each other. The cavalry force under Stuart comprised another invading column falling on the flank and rear of the enemy, which even in his own country make him cautious how to advance. Passing through a country which had seldom if ever been visited by an army either friendly or not, inhabited by a people quiet and industrious, but of small education comparatively, all tended to increase our force rather than detract from it, and a great blow might have been struck [if] the enemy in reality found out our real strength, and attempted anything serious.[2]

My own conversations with people along the road proved to me beyond a doubt that our force was very much overestimated, ten and twelve thousand being frequently reported at thirty and forty thousand. It was not until the whole army was drawn together near Gettysburg that Meade really knew what he had to deal with. It is currently reported that Gen. Lee did not wish or desire to [precipitate] a general attack from our side on the afternoon of July 1st, but [A. P.] Hill finding himself upon the ground and sorely pressed by the enemy, to extricate him, Rhodes and Early had to engage one [Yankee unit] after the other, which made it a general engagement, driving the enemy with much loss from their position.[3]

Johnson's division appeared upon the scene about 3 o'clock in the day [July 1] after the main fighting was over, and was assigned a position on a small ridge about 1½–2 miles from Gettysburg, at that time more to prevent the enemy from executing a flank movement than anything else. Much very valuable time was lost bringing Johnson into position, and not until nearly 9 o'clock was the movement completed and the division in position. The artillery did not arrive until about 10 o'clock A.M., on the 2nd. In the meantime the scouts reported no enemy on the hill which commanded our position (Johnson) as well as the main point held by the enemy. Later in the night the hill was occupied by a small force of the enemy.[4]

By daybreak [on July 2, Culp's Hill] was heavily occupied and the construction of logworks commenced. Our division of artillery was not assigned a position until about noon, did not arrive on the ground until 3 o'clock, when fire was opened, and the division did not engage the enemy until nearly dark. Early attacking at the same time with Johnson, both found themselves heavily opposed by the enemy's artillery and infantry, but steadily gained ground. Early effecting a lodgement on the cemetery Hill, and Johnson in the first line of entrenchments on the Hill [Culp's] opposed to him.[5]

A reconnaissance [during the late afternoon of July 1] disclosed the enemy in but very slight force on our left flank, nothing but cavalry with a little infantry and artillery who seemed placed for no other purpose than to impede our advance on their wing and flank, as the force was insufficient for anything else. The reconnaissance developed another thing, that by extending our division line more to the left and occupying another wooded ridge [Culp's Hill], which woods conceal our movements, a command of the Baltimore pike could be gained, thus cutting off all supplies from that direction and of rendering much greater assistance to our attacking columns.

I believe if this plan had been followed, the hill which Johnson contested would have been gained and thereby a command of the other ground [Cemetery Hill] held by the enemy secured. The possession of this hill [Culp's Hill] by us would have virtually ended the battle, for it would have compelled Meade to seek another line of defence, and compelled the removal of the remainder of his army, which being beaten from an admirable position would have fallen an easy prey to our cavalry.[6]

This delay in attacking, if such was to be the thing, characterized all the movements of the whole army [from July 1–3]. Early not being supported was compelled to retire from his lodgement, thereby loosing many men, and much "esprit." The attacks of Longstreet and Hill also were made separate and alone, which allowed the enemy to concentrate masses of troops against them from such parts of the field as were not pressed to repel us. The causes then for the loss of this battle lie, first in not getting possession when it was practicable of the ground commanding the Baltimore pike and the hill contested by Johnson. Second, the want of unity of action on the part of the attacking columns; third, the not supporting of those columns which had effected lodgements in the enemy's lines in a manner adequate to the occasion.[7]

The retreat was orderly and steady. Meade only following as we gave him possession of the ground and never pushing Lee. For three days we offered him battle at Hagerstown, which he refused to accept, and after crossing into Virginia, not daring to make an advance until allowed to do so. From what I have seen nearly the same reasons may be ascribed to the total failure of the campaign of invasion. I do not think there was any real occasion in Lee's making an attack in the first place, or when made, continuing the same under adverse circumstances as those under which he fought.

A great want of foresight appeared in the management of the supply of artillery ammunition especially. It is never just or desirable to count upon the supply you might gain from the enemy, for how much have ever the enemy captured from us during any general engagement? None to speak of. Artillery ammunition is [at] all times difficult to transport in sufficient quantities as long as that branch of the service seems to think that their only use is in making as much noise as possible.

Firing [artillery] without an objective is always to be condemned, and how much more so when the supply is attended with much difficulty and when in an enemy's country, with much danger of capture and destruction. Justice demands however, that admission, that the practice at Gettysburg was admirable, few shots being thrown away. The supply however, was not equal to the demand of 250 pieces, and though there may have been enough for another day's fighting, a backward movement was made compulsory upon Lee. Of infantry ammunition there was the greatest abundance, besides some little captured from the enemy on our first days fighting.[8]

On the whole Meade fought well, and [was] deserving of a much better cause. He was however a stranger to the troops and they to him. It may have been a particular instance, but to compell a success demands an intimate acquaintance with the material of the army, to know what it can do and what not. He is young in command and needs much experience to cope with such heads as Lee, Longstreet, Ewell and Hill, who may make blunders occasionally.

Meade ought never to have allowed Lee to leave Pennsylvania without making at least an effort to stop and compel a fight. An intimate knowledge of the country was at his disposal; persons thoroughly acquainted with the mountains and passes through which Lee had to go to get back might easily have been employed to carry a force sufficient to harrass Lee much [or] if not, capture most of his command. The capture of a large wagon train while crossing the mountains showed conclusively that Lee did not have the passes guarded, or if so, the guards were worthless.[9]

From Hagerstown we suddenly moved at night to Williamsport and Falling Waters. Longstreet and A. P. Hill's Corps of the army were employed in building boats for a temporary bridge on which to cross our trains and artillery, the river being entirely too high for fording owing to the recent heavy rains. Ewell['s] Corps reached the river about 11 o'clock p.m. Rhodes division leading and Early's bringing up the rear of our column. Contrary to all expectation, Ewell's Corps forded the river a mile above Williamsport. The water was very high, the current swift [and] the night very dark. Johnson's division did not finish crossing until near daybreak. Early succeeded in crossing without molestation from the enemy beyond an occasional shot from their long range pieces.[10]

About noon on the 14th [of July] the enemy's cavalry appeared near Falling Waters, a small place of two or three houses, and opened very nicely on [Brig. Gen. James J.] Pettigrews brigade which was still on the Maryland shore and guarding our rear on the columns of Longstreet and Hill. It turned out quite a surprise though after a little the enemy were handsomely repulsed, though not without wounding mortally General Pettigrew. He subsequently died near Bunker Hill. From now, when all our forces were across the river we moved slowly backwards, camping about in spots, and generally employed in reorganizing and destroying the means of communication likely to be used by the enemy. Thus the railroad near Martinsburg was torn up and the ties and stills burnt.[11]

On the 22nd we took up our line of march again from Martinsburg to Winchester, and continued the march on the 23rd to near Front Royal. This movement was made necessary by Meade having crossed in force near Leesburg and moving rapidly towards the lower Gaps in the Blue Ridge in the hope of cutting off Ewell's Corps, and crushing it by superior numbers. On our arrival in Front Royal we found the enemy in possession of Chesters Gap, from which point they had driven our cavalry, and appeared ready to pounce upon us. Fortunately the night soon approached, thus breaking off any chances for a fight today. Johnson [was] bringing up the rear of Ewell's column, Early having been directed another route, via New Market, was placed in line of battle ready to receive the enemy should they move upon us. Chesters Gap being closed against us, the Shenandoah behind us, and nearly all our trains near the troops, it was made compulsory upon us to choose another road and cross the Ridge under the protection afforded by Hill and Longstreet, who had already crossed higher up. Accordingly Johnson's division moved at early dawn, closely followed by the enemy's cavalry on the Luray road on the morning of the 24th. The enemy finding that nothing could be made out of us, left us to pursue our journey unmolested and we reached Luray and the mountains on the 25th. [Johnson] rested the troops on the 26th (Sunday) [due to] the troops being much exhausted and wearied with long marches and the intense summers heat.[12]

On the 27th [of July] we resumed our march for Sperryville at 4 o'clock a.m. and camped again about five miles beyond Sperryville on [the] road to Madison Court House. From here the Pioneer Corps of Rhodes and our division were sent ahead to prepare the roads so that our trains of wagons and artillery could pass along. General Jackson had a happy faculty of choosing "out of the way" roads, and I presume General Ewell, commanding Jackson's Corps, felt it incumbent upon him to try to do likewise, but as was most likely to be the case, [the move became] a most lamentable failure. I certainly never saw such roads in all my life, up hill and down dale, through mud and rock until the head swims. Here was certainly an opportunity of showing what good Pioneer officers could do in the way of making a bad road passable. The gentleman sent up from Richmond, as a general thing proved themselves totally incompetent, and when let alone, if anything made the roads worse than before. Indeed take them all in all, a more worthless act of appointments certainly never was made.

July 28th broke upon us with wind and rain and another slow days march, camping about 5 miles from Hughes River, a small and inconsiderable stream during the summer, but as reported, a young torrent in the winter. Marched again on the 29th camping about 3½ miles from Madison Court House. Here we were led to expect a few days rest from our fatigues which, though the marching itself was slow, was nevertheless great from the fact of being obliged to assist the artillery and wagons trains, which appeared to be without end, over the muddy and slippery hill of Madison.

Here a rumor, without much appearance of truth, came to us to the effect that Meade had made a forced march of several days, crossed the Rappahannock and gained possession of the heights at Fredericksburg. Improbable as it seemed to be, there was nevertheless much cause for anxiety, for the move to him was a perfectly feasable one, and one which would have put us to much trouble to counteract. Pushing on towards Richmond, that place would have fallen into his [Meade's] hands like a ripe apple; and a way of retreat still left opened to him to Fortress Monroe, if hard pushed and unable to hold himself. Cavalry alone guard the crossing of the Rappahannock, and from what has been said previously, it could be easily estimated whether they would have afforded much delay, if any, to the advancing columns of General Meade. Indeed I am generally surprised at the tameness and slothlike intellect of the Yankee Generals since McClellan's removal; except where it is a plain case of a damned fool. They ought to have been shot for not having got possession of that place long since. Several chances were open to them, which were never attempted and which certainly offered reasonable chances for success, more so than the attempted assault on Mary's [Marye's] Heights at Fredericksburg, December 13th 1862. However the whole thing turned out to be a rumor and there the matter ended.

In our expectation to remain in camp and rest we were, as might have been supposed, disappointed, we remaining only until the evening of the 31st, when we moved very unexpectedly at 6 p.m. through Madison Court House and camped a few miles beyond. On the march heard of the death of Lieut. [Thomas C.] Kinney who had been sent to the rear from Martinsburg to Staunton with Steinraker [Henry von Steinecker].[13]

August 1st finds us on the road again on the way to Gordonsville and Liberty Mills, and continue the same on the 2nd camping about three miles from Orange Court House on the Plank road. Here we remained for some time making a tolerable permanent camp, recruiting and amusing ourselves with working at our own leisure and convenience. Gayety and festivity among those who can afford the necessary luxuries are the order of the day. Officers are bringing up their wives, and those who have none are enjoying the questionable pleasure of public women. Thus wags the world.

The enemy leave us quietly in camp, merely picketing the line of the Rapidam and that of the Rappahannock to Fredericksburg. In the meantime Longstreet and [part of his] corps were detached from this army and sent to General [Braxton] Bragg in Tennessee, to which point Meade had also been sending men for a meal to Rosecranz [Major General William S. Rosecrans], consisting of some four or five corps.

10. The Battle of Payne's Farm

September 1, 1863–December 31, 1863

The fight was styled the Battle of Paynes Farm. This ended
the operations of the army for the year 1863.

—*Oscar Hinrichs*

Editor's note: this chapter concludes the final "winter-quarters transcrip-tion" of Oscar Hinrichs's diary. Starting on September 15, 1863, he began to chronicle his experience in commercially available, cloth-bound journals, which remained intact for the duration of the war. In this chapter and in chapter 11, Oscar's verbatim journal entries follow his wartime narrative. Only journal entries are provided thereafter.

Narrative

September opens and still finds us in our old camp until the 15th, when rumors of the advance of the enemy come from the direction of Rapidan Sta-tion. I was exceedingly unwell at the time the troops moved, which they did on that day. General Johnson had gone off on a furlough of several days, and the division was in command of Brig. Gen. Geo. H. Steuart. They marched to Orange Court House, fuddled and fooled about in the rain and mud for sev-eral days and quietly returned to some new camp near Orange Court House. Here I joined them on the 17th.

On the 18th [our Division] received orders from Headquarters to move in the direction of Rac[c]oon and Mortons Fords on the Rapidan, and camped about 5 P.M. near Mortons and left of General Rhodes. The whole army is strung out along the Rapidan from Rapidan Station to Mortons, the cavalry guarding the lower fords. Everything was set to work fortifying.

On the 19th I took charge of the front of our division, and could now form a better idea of the qualities of Brig. Gen. Geo. H. Steuart. It is very wrong to give a man status and reputation without knowing something about him and hence Gen. Steuart generally had a very poor one. From the fuss he now made it became evident that he was not the man for this division and it was a perfect God-send that the enemy made no attack.

On the 20th [of September] I was ordered by General Lee to make a reconnaissance of Germania [Germanna] Ford and vicinity, with a view to fortify, and moved down and commenced operations on the 22nd. The cavalry was soon relieved by a brigade of infantry under the command of Col. [Thomas M.] Garrett [of the 5th North Carolina], a nice clever gentleman, and brave man, but no officer in the specific acceptation of the term. He brought with him one battery.[1]

Col. Garrett was exceedingly desirous of having work done his way until [John M.] Jones came, who, being the ranking officer, decided to let me alone. It was indeed a very hard matter to suit him and the fastidious taste of the gentlemen of the artillery whom he brought down with him. After Jones arrival my task was much easier. Gen. Jones, I believe to be a gallant, good officer but rather too fond of the bottle.

On the 4th of October the Pioneers from our division, whom I had down with me, were ordered to return to the command. On the 5th received orders from Division Headquarters to be ready to move in the direction of Somerville Ford, but did not actually move until 2 P.M. on the 9th when we camped about a mile from [Mt.] Pisgah Church. We now started on a march which in my opinion should have been made several days sooner, having for its objective the expulsion of Meade, certainly from Culpepper County and possibly from Virginia.

Meade had further reduced his army by sending two more corps to Rosecranz, and we ought to have moved and concentrated at least two days sooner. At any rate the movement has begun, and I should not be much surprised if it did not turn out [to be] a complete fizzle. No Jackson here now to move at dawn on the enemy and flank him before night.

On the afternoon of the 10th I joined General Johnson on the road between Orange Court House and Madison Court House, just as the troops were going into camp for the night. General Jones with his command came up late during the night. Contrary to expectation we did not move until late on the morning on the 11th owing to Gen. Rhodes with his division taking more time than anticipated to get out [of] our way. The march was conducted with great caution and slowness. Caution was absolutely necessary to enable us to get around the enemy unobserved, yet certainly could have been conducted with much more despatch.[2]

Being obliged, by order to follow Gen. Rhodes, we were late at getting underway each morning, and soon found out that the enemy were made aware of our movements and that we were travelling on parallel roads in the same direction. Our line of march lay through fields and roads, theirs along the immediate line of [the] railroad. Our army kept diverging more and more from the rail road, crossing the Rappahannock at Warrenton Springs [at] which point we reached on the night of the 12th camping in and around the Springs.

During the afternoon of the 11th we came up with the cavalry of Fitz Lee, who had a handsome skirmish with the enemy under Buford, who fought well. Lee captured some 250 prisoners with a very small loss on our side. On the morning of the 13th we again pushed ahead at a late hour of the morning and reached Warrenton, a neat little town about 15 miles from the Orange and Alexandria railroad. Here the climax of dispatch was reached without a doubt. The enemy were and had been passing along the main railroad in three columns, their flanks guarded from sudden attack and surprise by cavalry. The bulk of their stores had been sent by rail from Culpepper Court House on towards Manassas and Centreville, and nothing but private baggage and such things as were absolutely needed by their troops were carried along in immense wagon trains.[3]

We reached Warrenton about 11 or 12 o'clock in the day, halted to allow Early to come up; cooked three days rations and went into camp where we lay. The enemy meanwhile camping and passing almost within hearing of our pickets. Indeed one corps camped within one and a half miles of our division, but moved long before day so that when our advance moved on the road to Cattlett [Catlett] Station it met with some little resistance from the enemy's rear guard. Some sharp firing ensued, our whole corps was speedily drawn up in line of battle, but after some little cannonading, the enemy had gotten his trains sufficiently ahead, and then moved from our front. A few prisoners were captured by Rhodes and Early, our division being held in reserve.[4]

Soon after the enemy moved, we moved again also, but changed our direction from Cattlett [Station] to Bristoe Station. Hill with his corps was to have been on the ground and to have intercepted them with his corps at Bristoe but, for some unaccountable reason, mistook the proper road and fell on their flank some three miles from Bristoe. A lively skirmish ensued between [Henry] Heth and [Dick] Anderson's divisions and the enemy, in which Hill was decidedly worsted, loosing a number of men killed, wound[ed] and missing, and six pieces of artillery which were captured by a skirmishing line of the enemy. It was without exception the most disgracefull fight of the war. The fault lay in bad judgement of the ground and of the force of the enemy; coupled with a too great extension of his line. Moreover the bad fighting of

Heth and Anderson occasioned the loss of the artillery. Ewell['s] corps came up just too late to retrieve the disaster.[5]

Meade's whole army had passed saving everything, and with great eclat made good their retreat on Centreville. Nothing more now could be gained from them, the season was too far advanced for any great operations, small ones did not pay and while the cavalry kept the enemy penned up in Centreville, the infantry devoted its energies in tearing up and destroying the [twenty miles of the Orange & Alexandria] railroad. The cause of Hill's not coming up in time and place is probably due to the fact that he had a much longer line of march than Ewell['s] Corps and encumbered as he necessarily was by his wagon trains, [which] caused the delay.[6]

The face of the country had been entirely changed, and many places which I had known, could not be found, having been totally destroyed by the enemy. Roads were everywhere, no vestige of fences left. Hence unless supplied with good and active guides, it was an easy matter to mistake the road. Guides from the country could not be had, as no people were living on the latter days line of march; having been either removed by the enemy or had done so of their own accord. There was however no excuse for the loss of the artillery, and [if we were] anywhere except here [in northern Virginia] a court of inquiry would have been called to investigate the shortcomings of both Major Generals. Such however, is not the practice here.

Gradually we took up our line of march for the Rappahannock, destroying the railroad as we progressed, and crossing that stream on the morning of the 19th; we camped in and around Brandy Station, and Stevensburg until the 9th of November. In the meantime I was temporarily detached and ordered to make a survey of our line of entrenchments on the Rapidan from near Germania Ford to Liberty Mills, a distance of some thirty miles. This duty I completed with the assistance of Priv. Von Steinecker by the 2nd of November.[7]

I had some time previously applied for leave of absence for several days for the purpose of going to Richmond, and left the army on the 6th, returning on the 11th. In the meantime while absent on the survey before mentioned, and while in Richmond, we had been in the habit of sending a brigade of infantry with wagons across the river to gather up and carry off the rails from the road, and transporting them to the south bank of the river.

The enemy came up in force [at Rappahannock Station on November 7 and] attacked a portion of Early's division; and after a handsome resistance by Gen. Harry Hays, who commanded the troops[, many] were obliged to surrender. About half of Hays Brigade and a large part of Hokes Brigade were thus lost [although Harry T. Hays escaped and Robert F. Hoke was away in western North Carolina]. They occupied some earthworks, assisted with four pieces of artillery. The disaster might have been prevented by manning the works on the south side with artillery, thus taking the enemy in flank. The position occupied by us was a kind of salient in the general line, and only defensible in connection with the balance of the line. They did not surrender however, until every round of ammunition had been expended and the enemy had entered the work at the point of the bayonet. Their slaughter is said to have been immense. Gen. Rhodes was also attacked near Killeys [Kelly's] Ford and suffered some loss.[8]

On my return from Richmond, I found all the troops on the south side of the Rapidan and in position near our old quarters near Mortons Ford. On the 15th came the sound of heavy connading [cannonading], and seemed to admonish us that the campaign was not quite over yet. On the 16th came orders to move to Mortons Ford from near Mount Pisgah Church where we were temporarily in camp. Marched down same day and at once commenced fortifying a new line, the enemy having shown a disposition to cross the river. We remained thus employed until the 26th when news came that they had crossed en masse at Germania and other fords, and the army was at [once] started to meet them.[9]

The enemy were met with on the 27th and an engagement [ensued] between our division and a large body of the enemy, said to be composed of about two and a half corps. The contest was spirited and resulted in our driving the enemy from the field. Ammunition running scarce, the army was withdrawn, although only our division had been actually engaged and drawn up again on the south side of Mine Run, a tributary stream to the Rapidan. Here we again set to fortifying, trusting that the enemy would attack us. In this we were disappointed.

As much has been said of the battle of Payne's Farm, it is due that I should record my own observations, and may place a different credit to the account of certain officers who gained a great deal of public favor by it. As before stated the enemy had crossed in force at Germania and other fords, moving in a direction nearly at right angles to the river until reaching the main road leading from Orange Court House to Fredericksburg. They then advanced up the stream.

Two or three corps had been thrown across between Germania and Mortons fords and had advanced up to Mine Run, their flank and rear being in direct communication and resting on the river. A. P. Hill was posted fronting the enemy across the main road above referred to (Plank road), Early joining Hill, Rodes joining Early. Johnson was to have been the extreme left of the line; but was formed nearly at right angles to the general line and facing the river. The country is thinly settled, and heavily wooded; [its] undergrowth [is] very much on the style of the Chancell[or]sville woods.[10]

Mine Run: recrossing at Germania Ford
(From *Harper's Pictorial History of the Great Rebellion*)

We marched out from our intrenchments about 7 o'clock A.M. on the morning of the 26th, crossed Mine Run at Bartlett's Mill and proceeded down the river towards Germania Ford. Leaving the Mill about two miles, the advance of the column, composed of one company of the 25th Virginia, afterwards increased to a regiment under the immediate direction of Gen. J. M. Jones, was fired on by some cavalry. It was known that a large body of cavalry, infantry and some artillery were camped opposite Finleys Mill on Mine Run and about one mile below Bartlett's Mill; the cavalry was still near Finley's at the time of our marching from our entrenchments, yet no precaution was taken to prevent a surprise. Brig. Gen. G. H. Steuart, who had held the extreme right of our division in the entrenchments, was to have led the column, but missing the road came up in rear of everything, Ordnance and ambulances.[11]

As soon as the advance was fired on the column halted, two companies sent out as skirmishers and flankers, and we again moved forwards. The two companies might scrape and search about two hundred yards of ground. An officer of Gen. Rhodes Staff came up and mentioned to Gen. Johnson that Gen. Rhodes was very anxious for him to come up, as he had serious fears for his left flank. I certainly thought that with such an intimation of danger a more thorough search would have been instituted. Yet such was not the case. Of course as far as the flankers extended no enemy was to be found. It appears however, that they were watching the movements of the column from the beginning.

The head of the column was halted about a quarter of a mile from Gen.

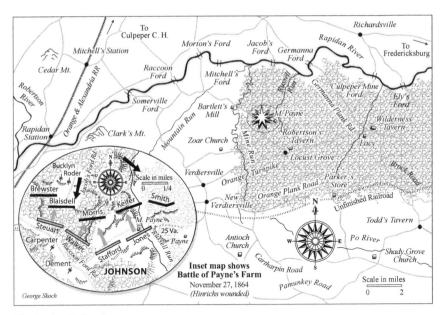

The Battle of Mine Run

Rhode's line of battle, and while a consultation was being held between Early, temporarily commanding the corps, [and] Rhodes and Johnson as to the proper position of the latter, a courier came up at full gallop from the rear of our column, saying that Gen. Steuart was fighting the enemy.

The column was counter marched a short distance, and placed in line of battle parallel with the road on which we had advanced, save Steuart's Brigade which was formed at right angles and facing in the direction [of the Rapidan] from which we had come. His fight amounted to nothing more than a handsome repulse of cavalry, who thinking the whole column had passed, had pounced upon the division ordnance and ambulance train. Everything however, for a moment was utter confusion, but all was saved. After moving by each flank successively for sometime, throwing out skirmishers and advancing them, we soon came upon the enemy, when a desultory fighting commenced, leading to no result, and without uncovering the main body of the enemy. The fair presumption is, that it was the same body who had camped near Finley's Mill.[12]

About three o'clock Gen. Early sent orders by one of his Aids, for our division to advance, engage the enemy, and drive them away. Steuart was half wheeled to the right and then the whole division advanced. The left encountered a heavy and destructive fire, and its advance was retarded much. The other brigades advanced steadily, gradually swinging around as it were towards the left. The enemy were successively driven from one position to another, until night set in and stopped the fight. I had been painfully though but slightly wounded about fifteen minutes after the fight opened and remained as long as the pain permitted.[13]

After night, the whole army was withdrawn across Mine Run and lay in line of battle from Zoar Church [south] to Antish [Antioch] Church. The men were immediately set to work entrenching. The enemy slowly came up after us on the next day, but made no attack. He suddenly during the night of the 1st of December returned and recrossed the Rapidan. No other troops were engaged during the [first] day, beyond mere skirmishing, besides our division; the fight was styled the Battle of Paynes Farm. This ended the operations of the army for the year 1863.[14]

Journal

Sept. 15th Rumours of an advance of the enemy came last night, from the direction of Rapidan Station. Troops this morning ordered to march to Orange Co. Ho. Div[n] under the command of Geo. H. Steuart. Dont like him a bit. Fuddled and fiddled about for two days; when troops went into the camp near Orange. Ordered to move *Sept. 18th* in the direction of Raccoon and Morton's Ford on Rapidan again under Steuart. Went into a temporary camp about 5 P.M. Troops engaged in fortifying Div[n] front all night.

Sept. 19th [T]ook charge of our front today and worked on same until *Sept. 20th*, when I was detached from the command by Gen. Lee and ordered to Germania Ford, to fortify there; moved down to Germania on the 22nd and commenced operations. Col. [Thomas M.] Garrett, comdg. Iversons Brigade, came down with 4 regiments of infantry on the 23rd.

Brig. Gen. J. M. Jones came down with 2nd Brigade on the 25th with four additional regiments. Worked by details from the infantry. Col. Garrett like most N. C. officers not worth much; too fond of gassing. Find much trouble in satisfying both parties—Arty. and H.Q.; don't care a dam[n] however for either and shall do as I please anyhow.

Johnson's Pioneers ordered to the Div[n] on the 4th October.

Enemy very quiet; dont seem to understand why we should be so busy fortifying along the river, and it dont make much difference whether they understand it or not. Rumour says that Meade has sent two additional corps to Rosecrans; if so presume Mr Lee will move on Meade. Would be a good thing anyhow I think; only want to make the Yankies fight with their front towards Washington, in which case Mr. Meade will be tolerably much used up. Moved my washing to Gen. Jones' [headquarters] on Sunday morning and remained very quietly in camp all day. Nothing stirring whatever.

———————

Oct. 5 Received orders to be ready to move at a moment's warning in the direction of Somerville Ford, [at] which point a heavy force of the enemy was said to be approaching. Don't think Mr. Meade will be such a damned fool as to try to force Early's line. It is much too strong for him; and he would get a thundering thrashing. Got anyhow a considerable piece of work done today. Spent evening very pleasantly; Gen. Jones was very communicative and pleasant. Steinecker came during evening and brought something to drink which made me feel much better. Weather getting very cold now at night, and days raw and thick. Hope we may soon get into winter quarters.

———————

Oct. 6 Everything appears quiet again this A.M. Sent Steinecker to McNeils Hill to sketch topography. Nothing of any moment occurs today.

———————

Oct. 9th At 2 P.M. received orders to march and join Div^n at Mt. Pisgah Church near Rapidan River. Marched at time appointed, but owing to the pleasant confusion existing among troops and wagons did not report. Camped within a mile of Mt. Pisgah Ch.

———————

Oct. 10th Marched again this A.M. and reported in the afternoon to Gen. Johnson. Camped within 6 miles of Madison Co. Ho. The whole movement appears to look like one of Jackson's dodges, but they cannot come [to] it; there is too much refinement of a nicety. Nothing will come of it. Camped this night again with the Pioneers. Another sprig of the Engr. Dept. is said to have come up from Richmond. Saw Mr. Lawrence Taliaferro at Orange Co. Ho.; looks very well, though communicates much that is unpleasant. Mentioned to Capt. Thompson again about entrenching tools left at Germania Ford. *Oct. 10th.* Marched this P.M. to within about 8–10 miles of Robinson [Robertson] River. Camped amid much confusion; slept however remarkably well considering all things—which the others did not. Hence they growl much about everything they would like to do but cannot. Gen's Lee and Ewell close by.

———————

Oct. 11th Marched again this A.M. and camped at night near Stonehouse Mt. Slight firing during day[,] supposed to be cavalry skirmishing. Meade seems to have smelt a rat and is clearing out. No authentic news today.

———————

Oct. 12th Marched this morning as usual. Heavy blunders again at Div^n Hd. Qrs. Find no orders countermanding time of marching issued to us here; we were kept up from two A.M. Second, Johnson failed to see where Rodes left wing was and consequently had the whole Div^n tailing after him while hunting a road to get away from Stonehouse Mt. Seems to be fatal to him in the shape of mistakes. Marched today through Rixeyville to Jeffersonton, crossing Rappahannock at the Fauquier White Sulphur Springs at about dark. Rodes being in advance of the column, crossing first. Early will cross tomorrow. Can see but little of this place tonight, it being barely starlight. Have heard much of this place but [have] never seen it. Can judge more about it tomorrow perhaps; it seems to have been quite an extensive arrangement. Weather growing very cold tonight.

Oct. 13th Marched again this A.M. for Warrenton. Passed over the field of the cavalry fight of yesterday; saw few signs of an engagement beyond some dead horses and a few dead yankees. Warrenton Springs must have been quite a pleasant place in former times, all gone to the devil now. Reached Warrenton about 1 o'clock P.M. and found it much deserted, very few women being in the place. Seems to have been a neat pleasant little place.

Rested here until the morning of the *14th* when we marched first in the direction of Cattletts Station on Orange and Alexandria RR. We came up with the enemy about 4 miles from town, Rodes pitching into them while Early flanked them and came in rear. As soon as the enemy found it out they limbered up and moved off. Our direction was now changed from the former to Bristoe Station, coming up with the enemy about 2 miles from Bristoe. Here Hill pitched into them. Cook[e']s N. C. Brigade acted very badly, running from a skirmishing line of the enemy and allowing 5 pieces of Rice's and McIntosh's Batteries to be captured by the enemy. Enemy got rather the better of us today and will probably escape altogether from us. Cook[e']s men acted disgracefully. More and more impressed with the faithlessness of the North Carolinians, and cannot understand it.[15]

Oct. 15th All quiet again this A.M. The enemy gone and Early in pursuit. Remained quietly in camp until about 4 P.M. when the Pioneers and myself received orders to go to work destroying the Orange and Alexandria RR.

Oct. 16th Continued the process commenced yesterday. Heavy rains during day. Will make the roads through this infernal region none the better; a regular "blackjack" county. Camped near Cattlett Station, near Cedar run. [Jed] Hotchkiss came and stayed with me during night.[16]

Oct. 17ᵗʰ Bright and clear this morning. Think we shall go back to the Rappahannock or Rapidan and move into Winter quarters soon. Dont think operations will be continued much longer if at all. Meade decidedly gained his point during this retreat, which he conducted very handsomely. Will probably go up the spout however anyhow. Rumour says he has left Centreville. Cavalry chased him across Bull Run anyhow. Cavalry gained laurels during this part of the campaign, which the infantry lost; they cannot brag much now since Cook[e']s N. C. Brigade acted in such a cowardly manner. Seems that Gen's Heth and Anderson are both in the dirt also. Heth is no account anyhow. Hill very unfortunate in his Brigadiers and Major Generals, Heth being a part of his [corps]. We continue the destruction of the road today.

Oct. 18ᵗʰ Continued destruction of the RR. Nothing of importance occurring. Our Divⁿ went to Bristoe Station and destroyed track there.

Oct. 19ᵗʰ Marched this A.M. towards the Rappahannock. Fauquier County seems to have been thoroughly sacked by the enemy. Many dwellings burnt along line of RR and county generally deserted. The few people remaining are mostly of the Yankee stamp. I do not trust them much. Crossed Rappahannock this day at noon. Again much confusion among troops and wagons. It is well that the enemy are not in a condition to pursue us else they might play the devil this morning with us. Camp about 1½ miles from river among a lot of dead horses. Did not gain anything by this trip except loose much of our prestige.

Oct. 20 Remained apparently quiet in camp today, allowing the men to wash and clean themselves up. Rumour says Bragg has been superseded by Longstreet and that Rosecranz had been captured with 22000 men. Don't believe it anyhow.

Oct. 21ˢᵗ Moved camp this A.M. to within a mile of Stevensburg between Brandy [Station and the Rapidan River]. Received an order from Col. Smith to make a survey of the fortifications on Rapidan. Pioneers ordered to river again.

Oct. 22ⁿᵈ Moved our camp this P.M. Camp picked out by [David S.] Hessey, a damned fool. Place unpleasant. Hotchkiss returned.[17]

Oct. 23ʳᵈ Rain in camp again. Nothing new.

Oct. 24ʰ Went to Gen. Lee and got information of projected survey. Am told I am to be ordered to Richmond. Made application for 3 days leave on 21st and got it today.

Oct. 25ʰ Start this A.M. with Steinaecker for Germania, taking my two horses along. Stopped at Mr. Pullman, left horses at $40 per month each.

Oct. 26ʰ Not well today, remain in vicinity visiting people.

Oct. 27ʰ Start work this afternoon near Willis.

Continue progress up river finishing on morning of *the 31ˢᵗ* [of October]. Got my leave on day of starting from camp. Return to camp on Nov. 2. Find Pioneers returned. Got a new hut and have a chimney built.

[*Nov. 6ʰ–12ʰ*] Start for Richmond on Nov. 6ᵗʰ. Return to camp via Orange Co. Ho. on *the 11ʰ*, remaining at Orange a day for want of transportation. Our army had a fight at [Rappahannock Station] RR bridge in which most of Hays and Hokes Brigades of Early's Divⁿ were killed, wounded and captured; lost 4 pieces of arty. Cannot understand the object in thus loosing men and material without some equivalent. Am much afraid that Meade is too much for Lee. He has shown decided genius thus far. Do not think Lee will command much longer. Enemy evinces a desire to push us as much as possible while this firm weather lasts. Nothing new of a gratifying nature from the West. [Major Gen. George H.] Thomas giving Bragg the devil. Captured from 5[00]–700 wagons from him and otherwise outgeneraled him and neutralized [him in the] fight at Chickamauga. On return from Richmond find whole army across Rapidan, and prospect of a still further falling back.

[*Nov. 15ʰ*] All quiet up to the *15ʰ* [of November]. Cannonading this A.M. and look for orders to move. This is Sunday morning. Heavy rains last night, heaviest of the season. Orders to be sent to Richmond approved today or rather yesterday, and look for them from Lee's Hd Qrs. Hope things will be more pleasant there than here. At least no Ed Johnsons to deal with. Plenty of fools down there though also. While in Richmond went down to Chaffins Bluff and saw Bradford; a great surprise to him. Receive frequent and kind letters from Till now. Chris wants to enter service again. Don't know how to advise him for the best. Am much afraid that I will let other things get the better of him and me. Am much worried on that score. Sends me a slip concerning Addie. Why will an old wound be continually torn open. Let her marry and be happy if she can. Tis more than I can be anyhow. Am a damned fool myself to worry about it. No news from home and very anxious about them there.[18]

Nov. 16th Fair and cold this A.M. Ordered yesterday to move and break up camp and move to meet the enemy who are reported to have made attempts to move. Countermanded however and we remain in camp till today. Moved down to the rear of Mortons Ford and commenced fortifying a new line. Remained in camp till *the 26th* when the enemy cross at Germania and Elys Fords. Marched this *27th* to meet them. Prospects for a general fight good.

Dec. 4th We meet the enemy as anticipated, our Div^n being the only one heavily engaged [at the Battle of Payne's Farm]. Was severely struck on the right arm by a musket ball, and had my overcoat torn on left arm. Went to the hospital on same night and went to wagons on day following—*Nov. 28th*. Remained with them until this date. Went to our old camp and put the tent to our old chimney. Bad news from the West in the meantime. Bragg badly whipped from Lookout Mountain. Lost about 50 pieces of arty. and 6[00]–700 prisoners.

Dec. 5 Remain here shortly. Move towards Orange Co. Ho. on *the 6th* with Pioneer Corps, they being sent to fix up the roads leading to Mortons Ford from Orange Co. Ho. Camp nearly 2½ miles from the Co. Ho. Am not on duty yet, my arm still paining me much; had a narrow escape of it; am not much sorry that I am not thrown [in] with the General. Remain quietly in camp until this *12th* day of [December]. Have been quite ill with diarrhea. Steinecker went to Tinsleys. Hear today that he had been arrested for threatening the life of a negro—by Gen. Johnson, and put into the 1st Brigade Guard house. Horse &c turned over to Maj. Mercer. Am not much sorry; he had commenced to get too large for his breeches—and withal I believe much of a rascal and scamp; think he will deceive Tinsleys daughter. Think ought to warn old man Tinsley—still it is none of my business. Nobody looks out for me and let them do likewise.

Bragg has been relieved of his command by request of himself and turned over [his army] to Lt. Gen. Hardee. Will now see what he can do with the Army of Tennessee. Bragg may not be so much to blame after all. Much blame is to be attached to D. H. Hill, [Thomas] Hindman, [John] Breckinridge and [Leonidas] Polk. Very good letter in [Richmond] Dispatch from "Sallart" about officers and how managed by Bragg which places things in an altogether different light. Anyhow Hardee will have a chance of showing what he can do to retrieve the disasters in that section of the country.

Dec. 31st Encamp near [Mt.] Pisgah Church and commence building quarters for the winter. Weather bad and cold. Steinecker was released from Guard [house] and sent to me, he promising to do better from this [time] out. Perhaps he may. Received a letter Christmas night from friend [Charles P.] Bolles, writing from Richmond. Tells me Whiting will apply for me if I apply to him (W) I did so at once, also writing to Hon. W. N. H. Smith and Col. [Alfred L.] Rives on the subject.[19]

11. Winter Quarters

January 1, 1864–February 29, 1864

Last evening a little before sundown [we] received orders to get in
readiness to move as the enemy were moving up the river. . . .
Rumour says it is the Yankee Cavalry on a raid.

—Oscar Hinrichs

Narrative

From this [time] out, although compelled to move about much more than
desirable, being occupied in repairing roads and putting them in condition
for the winter and coming spring, nothing of any moment occurred to disturb
the truce which nature had ordained should be. Thus ended the third year of
the war, and had brought us apparently no nearer a peace than when started.
To the superficial observer, such would be the conclusion arrived at without
a doubt. Yet to me it seems that we are approaching the end, and with the
coming spring and summer campaign, may confidently look forward to an
early establishment of peace. Many reasons induce me to believe such.

As for the results of the years [of] hard work, blood shed and labor, it does
not apparently amount to much. The Army of Northern Virginia has held its
own, despite the depletion of Longstreet corps and the casualties incident to a
campaign. The enemy it is true holds about the same stretch of country as last
year, but it was given up for motives of prim prudence. Throwing ourselves so
much nearer [to] our base of supplies, our front [is] protected by a well fortified river [the Rapidan], which could be held if necessary at any given point,
and leaving to the occupation of the enemy a section of the country thoroughly
devoid of anything else, subsistence for man or beast, and thereby compelling
him to furnish his supplies from a greater distance, besides from motives of
humanity to furnish supplies for the people.

The severe lessons taught during the year, the continually increasing demand for troops in the North, the unwillingness of those in service to serve longer, all tended to make the Union Generals in the Army of the Potomac very cautious how they risked their commands in a general engagement. Though much distressed, they found the Confederates always ready and willing to meet them, which proved to the soldier most conclusively that the "Backbone of the rebellion" was not much injured yet. Operations in the west and southwest did not seem to prosper so much.

The fall of Vicksburg relieved a large force of the enemy which he might turn successfully on either Mobile or Charleston or against Johnston or Bragg in Tennessee, besides weakening our forces by the amount captured at Vicksburg. Mobile, though not immediately threatened, deserved the close attention of the authorities. Charleston [was] besieged with more vigor than ever; Savannah and Wilmington, both threatened, all called for great prudence on the part of the Confederate authorities and Generals.

The battle of Chickamauga, though essentially gained by us, proved rather embarrassing than otherwise to Bragg, and compelled him subsequently to fall back from Mission Ridge, and open the door to mother Alabama and Georgia. Thus in the west we have lost ground which cannot be readily recovered, unless Meade be severely handled during the next year, or Grant or Rosecranz [are] totally whipped and routed from Tennessee and Kentucky. The military prospects of the Confederacy are therefore not much better than after the fall of New Orleans, Donalson [Fort Donelson] and Roanoke Island.

Politically however a great gain has been made. The people of the North are becoming tired of the continual drain for men and treasure, and gradual but certain depreciation of their circulating medium, paper. During the coming year it will fall as heavily on the market as ever did Confederate scrip, and what with the prospects of a vigorous campaign on the part of the South, it will end the war by the retirement of Lincoln at the end of his appointed term.[1]

There is however also much to be done by us, irrespective of what may be the action of the people of the United States or our army. Our Congress must aid our army in a manner more effectual than frittering away valuable time in fixing the term of office of the Executive Departments. The army must be increased by the enrollment of all such men as have placed substitutes in the army, and those who for the last three years have been making princely fortunes out of the distress of the country, and who have so far shirked military duty under the protection of foreign papers, or claiming to be Marylanders and others. This will either increase our army to a respectable standard, or relieve the country of the presence where it can do no good, but much harm.

The currency of the country must be brought to a more healthy condition, by the reduction of the amount now afloat. Restrictions will have to be placed upon foreign commerce, by excluding from our shores such things as are not absolutely necessary for the purposes of war, and manufactures of warlike material. All these things I deem [to be] of necessity, and should have been the prime duty of Congress in attending to it as soon as that body met. Then with ranks filled up to a fair standard, a healthy currency, and a prevention of the efflux of gold, or the commercial equivalent, we may safely go on in our work of renovation.

That these ideas have suggested themselves to many there can be no doubt, and time alone will show whether they will be acted upon. The stake for which both parties contend is a magnificent one, and well worth the herculean efforts made on each to wrest from and retain.

A quick and vigorous prosecution of the war, on the style and manner of the lamented Chief [Stonewall] Jackson, whose loss the Confederacy has not yet fully comprehended, and whose individual worth the world will hardly ever know, are prime requisites, and must be adhered to. Having a firm reliance on Him in the hollow of whose hand rests the shadow of the world, and a confidence in ourselves, we may speedily proclaim abroad to the world our well fought independence and assume our position among the great family of nations.

The reform commenced and inaugurated by the Southern States will, however, not end here. To prevent a like occurrence of strife the form and system of Government must be and will be changed also. Experience will have demonstrated to the dullest mind, unless he be fool or bigot, that the time and rule of republicanism has, to use a Yankee phrase, played out. As good institutions as [representative republics] may [be] in times of peace and prosperity, [they are] inadequate in times of calamity and peril.

The compulsion to keep a large standing army, the total overthrow of the former boundaries of society[,] will need the strong arm and hand of government to guide and check, for only in a well founded system of government and check upon the frailties of men, can perfect liberty be found. Thus upon the ruins of demolished republics will rise the fabric of a powerful state under the monarchal sway. It will not be brought about at once. Time will be required to accustom the people gradually to the new state of things. But it will nevertheless surely come. Already symptoms begin to show themselves, and ere long it will be wondered how it was resisted so long. Tis the only way of saving the country for it contains within itself the germs of either its own greatness or debasement, as the case may be. Nous verrons.[2]

Journal

Jan. 31st All remain quiet during the month. Averill [Brig. Gen. William W. Averell] has made a raid into western Virginia towards Danville. Six different commands sent to intercept him and all come back with a flea in their ear. Did suppose Early would do something; he will have some good excuse to offer no doubt. Am in our winter quarters now and am hard at work drawing. Steinecker so far has behaved himself according to promise.[3]

Feb. 6th Intimation of the enemy attempting to cross at Mortons Ford. Rumour says that they have done so; probably nothing more than a feeler to find out whether it be true that troops have been sent from this army towards Richmond, which point appears to be again threatened from the Peninsula. Am quite unwell with another touch of diarrhea. Seems to have become not an uncommon complaint with me. Heavy firing down the river on or about our Div^n front during day. Our troops (Div^n) has been ordered down.

Feb. 7th Went this A.M. to Mercers and breakfasted with him without a previous invitation. While there saw Wrights Brigade going to our reinforcement. Enemy about 20[000]–30000 crossed and yesterdays firing was on them. Gen. Walker had a smart skirmish, but held the ground assigned him. Craig came up and reported that the enemy had recrossed the river; they remain in line of battle on Culpepper side. Our loss very small, 4 killed, 17 wounded — 25 prisoners. Yankees left 17 dead on the field and 41 prisoners. Very good thus far.[4]

On the 4th of the month returned from a three days survey of our fortifications at Mine Run, as also those of the enemy. Steinaecker went with me. Sent him on the 6th to Orange to Col. Smith to draw our money, $260.; he returned saying he had lost it. Gave him a pass to go to Spotsylvania to get money. During night went off taking Cockrills horse with him. Cockrill sent Monroe in pursuit, catching him at Spotsylvania Co. Ho. with horse. On coming near Verdiersville, Steinecker broke guard and ran off. Subsequently recaptured near our picket line on [the] River by cavalry. Sent to Div^n Head Quarters and from thence ordered to Corps Guard House under charges. Hope this will be his last escapade. Can hardly believe he wanted to steal the horse and desert to the enemy. There is no telling however what is the truth. Charges are stealing and desertion.[5]

Feb. 14th Saw Steinecker today; will be tried tomorrow. Am summoned as a witness for him but cannot see how I can do him any good. Am sorry for him.

Yankees are said to have lost about 1200 men in the skirmish a few days since. One hundred and nine Yankee officers escaped from [Libby Prison in] Richmond recently. Col. Straight [Abel D. Streight] leading off. Hope they may catch him again; 34 recaptured so far. [Brigadier Gen. James G.] Martin had a fight near Newbern, whipping the Yanks; also Pickett captured two gunboats recently. New Year opens well. Trust it may be indicative of our success during the year and end the war. Everything quiet again.[6]

Feb. 15th Attended Steineckers trial today, but without being examined. Think he may get clear; am sorry for the poor devil. Rumour speaks of changes in the Yankee Army of the Potomac. [Generals David] Hunter and Thomas spoken of as successors to Meade. Nothing much new going on anywhere. Weather very disagreeable; snowing with a prospect of a heavy fall. About 50 Yankee officers have been recaptured thus far. Seems that the Yankee advance from Fortress Monroe was only to cover the escape of the said officers—the Yankees returning soon thereafter and going back to Williamsburg and Yorktown. Some few may yet be caught; doubt it much though.[7]

Feb. 17th Attended Steineckers court martial this morning; was examined extensively myself as to his loyalty &c and his capture of horses &c. Am afraid my answers regarding the disposition made of said horses may be misinterpreted. I was asked whether I knew what disposition was made of all of them—to which I answered no. To one horse I might have given an answer, but that did not come within the scope of the question. I am riding said horse myself. Think he will be cleared; at least hope so. Am sincerely sorry for the poor devil, in a strange land and among strangers—do not think much sympathy will be shown him anyhow. Everything quite satisfactory.

(Noon) Weather very cold—probably coldest of the season. Freezing all day, even in the sunshine. Hope this will be my last introduction to a Confederate or any other court martial. Rumours of a severe fight among the enemy themselves [and] not contradicted. Hope it may be as stated—only ten thousand times worse. The rumour in question says the fight occurred about certain troops refusing to reenlist again, preferring to go home to remaining in the field. Think it highly probable that even many who have reenlisted think likewise and may take their chances of capture during the Spring campaign, which I think promises to be vigourous, and looking right after their Haversacks. Dont think the Yankees will fight much.

Saw a good piece of poetry regarding Conscripts. Transcribed it below [see appendix 2]. Respectfully dedicated to those who have unfortunately put in substitutes; respectfully, piously, tearfully and sympathetically dedicated to all concerned, with the hope that it may assist them muchly by the Author—Old Soldier. Hope there may be many, so many that numbers cannot tell them. We may then confidently look forward to something like the beginning of the end.

Feb. 21 Nothing new thus far. [Major] Harry [W.] Gilmer caught a heavy train on the Baltimore & Ohio RR and got lots of money. [Former U.S. senator] Jessie D. Bright from Indiana was on board and was also relieved of his valuables. Averill said to be on also, but none knowing him he got clear. Sorry for it. One man got 29,800 dollars—25000 in Greenbacks—balance in gold and silver. Harry was doing a good business sure enough.[8]

Went to 3rd N.C. yesterday and saw Col. Thruston and the balance of the Wilmington boys. Had a visit today from Ellis; like him much and wish he were with us again. I am very desirous of going to N.C., if it can in any way be brought about. Have not much faith that anything will come of it. Will finish map of Mine Run line tomorrow for Gen. Lee. Hope it may do me some good. Congress passed an act increasing Engineer Corps to 120. Will it bring me any promotion? Dont much think it will—and believe to deserve it too. Time will tell.

Saw the address from Congress to the people—a poor document and hardly worthy of such a body; it is not what it professes to be on account of their stewardship to their constituents, but rather as bill of wrongs suffered by the people of the C.S. from those of the U.S. and an acknowledgement of weakness in trying to attempt so much; and an exhortation to the people to assist the government and its constituted agents in the discharge of their duties. It will not have the desired effect—certain—sure.

Davis' address to the Army very good. Have kept a copy. More I see of Davis the more I like him, and believe no other man in the C.S. could have done any better. Has his faults, but he means well and does it according to his knowledge; a good man.

Feb. 22 Nothing new today; had a visit from [Major] Edwin [L.] Moore of Charlestown. Finished map of Mine Run. Altogether a handsome piece of work. Like Moore much, seems to be a clever lad.[9]

Feb. 23 Delivered map today to Col. Smith. Let Gen. Johnson see it. Was much complimented on the execution; hope that it will bring in something more tangible than a mere compliment. Saw Steinecker today, he seems to be in first rate spirits, and thinks he will get cleared of the charge against him; don't know what to think of him. Stopped also at Mercers. Hear of Pierce being on a big spree in Richmond. Am much surprised at it. Wonder what he is thinking of. Paid a visit this evening to Dr. [R. T.] Coleman and wife. Very pleasant people in their own house, a very nice lady.[10]

Feb. 25 Took breakfast with Dr. Coleman and some company this morning. During afternoon Tom Taliaferro came over and spent the evening with me. Queer people all these Taliaferro's are. Like Tom however about as well as may be a little better than most of them. Warner is a fool. Wonder how he and Gen. Colston get along now at Savannah; presume Colston is worried half to death by him, for reason of having no sense.[11]

Am at work on map of Orange County. Will finish it in a day or two—and then go to work on Pennsylvania maps. Am tolerable confident of going there. Hope I may be able to make something out of it this time. Have been thinking much of the Stanley's yesterday and today; dreaming of the good time a coming; only wish it were here now instead of coming.

Wonder if any change will take place in my position with old Fencerail [Ed Johnson] during the coming campaign as it seems I am doomed not to get away from him. Sincerely hope so. Wonder if Coleman could not procure a change for the better? Perhaps so. Nothing new much. Feel anxious regarding Mobile, otherwise everything quiet.

Feb. 27 Went to the party at Dr. Terrells last night—a grand humbug; hardly any ladies came hence a great bore. Had a letter from Bradford. Wants me to go to N.C. with him. Wonder how I can manage it. Would like to go very much, but do not see how it can be brought about considering the happy state of the Treasury Department.[12]

Feb. 28 Sunday; am resting. My horse was stolen from me on Friday—and do not suppose I shall ever get him again. He was cheap, considering he cost me no trouble to get him or no money to purchase him with, having been furnished by the Yankees to Steinecker and by him to me. Had a letter from Bradford, wants me to go to E. City with him on a thirty days furlough. Would like it much, but do not know how to manage it.

Am trying to rest today from my labours of the previous week. By turns begin to feel solemn and religious nowadays and trust it may be a lasting feeling. Have now been reading morning and evening prayers from the Common Episcopal Prayer book for nearly a month—and will endeavor to keep it up. Have stopped my habit of swearing a good deal. The devil will get into me sometimes however and off I go like a gun cocked and primed. A bad habit and desire to stop it; no good can come from it and much harm.

Enemy are said to be preparing for an advance. Rumours of fights among the enemy mentioned some time since seems to be confirmed—growing out of troops refusing to reenlist. Gen. Taliaferro gone to Florida to take command. He will get his Major General commission after a while. Beauregard it is said thinks much of him. He will have an opportunity of showing what he can do with an independent command and with the inducement of promotion before him. Would much like to be in his place. A man lacking much which makes a good officer yet getting high up in rank by means of a wrong system of promotion and Congressional and family influence. Thus wags the world.

Weather beautifully pleasant and warm, roads good, and should not wonder if we did not soon prepare to move. Conscripts are said to be coming in large numbers, though I have seen none of them as yet. Hope our Army may swell to some respectable proportions. [Joe] Johnston in supreme command in Tennessee.

Feb. 29 Recovered my lost horse this morning at the camp of the Louisiana Brigade. A great set of thieves and rogues, though not so much worse than any other Brigades. Last evening a little before sundown [we] received orders to get in readiness to move as the enemy were moving up the river. Do not expect it to amount to much, though heavy cannonading took place close under the mountains towards Stanardsville.

Rumour says it is the Yankee Cavalry on a raid. Rosser is said to be in their rear picking up their stragglers. Presume it is nothing more. Weather threatening now or other inclement weather. Think it would be the best move for us [that] the enemy could make, as it may enable us if properly disposed to cut them off and annihilate them almost entirely. Early could come in on their flank, Hill to extend his line so as to be in supporting distance of Rosser and protect the Virginia Central Rail Road and leave Rosser with what force he has and what could be spared here as circumstances might require, which would best push them as much as possible. Think it amounts to an intention of Meade to be fully informed of any design on our part to flank him, as was the case in the Bristoe affair, by compelling us to expel the Cavalry first and thus give him time to secure his supplies and communications.[13]

Good news from the west. Telegraph informs us tonight of a heavy fight beyond Dalton Ga. in which the enemy were severely worsted and falling back upon Chat[t]anooga. Good for "Old Joe" [Johnston]. He will turn back yet and win the game. Feel very confident of the result. Enemy retreating to Jacksonville Fla. pursued by Gen. [Joseph] Finegan. Yankees intend giving up Charleston S.C. and will try their fortunes elsewhere, probably Mobile. Will get severely handled there in all probability. I have no doubts of the ultimate results of the coming campaign if our leaders will only do right which they are no doubt trying to do.[14]

Am sorely pressed for money now—and do not see where to get it from to liquidate my liabilities. A sad state of affairs for me sure. If I thought anything could be raised in N.C. would try to borrow the money to go down, but suppose everything is short up there also. A good Father in Heaven will help me out of my difficulties if I have faith in him—and I do try to have. Finished map of Orange today and started again on map of York Pa. commenced last summer. Will have use for it sure.

12. Nothing but Death

March 1, 1864–May 21, 1864

Eighteen days has the fighting been going on now, and nothing material gained by either side save the constant repulse of the enemy in their assaults on our lines.

—Oscar Hinrichs

March 1ˢᵗ The yankee raid mentioned in yesterdays note promises to be of greater dimensions and more important in its results than anticipated. The enemy are said to have started in two columns, one up the Rapidam and Robinson [Robertson] having the Central R.R. for its object—the other crossing the Rapidam at U.S. [Ely's] Ford, and cutting through the country and attacking the R.R. again lower down towards Richmond.

The reports today are two—first that Charlottesville had been captured and the University burnt—[R. Preston] Chew loosing two pieces [of] artillery. 2ⁿᵈ That [Thomas L.] Rosser had fought handsomely and with assistance of such forces as could be raised had repulsed them. Chew again loosing two pieces. On the other column it is said they had penetrated to Beaverdam Station burning depot and bridges. A. P. Hills entire corps save two Brigades is said to be gone after them—but which ones not stated—probably the lower ones.[1]

Received orders again last night to be ready to move at a moments warning. That Meade has not fallen on his head is certain, and the present opportunity is frought with much, which may make him [stronger] if he can bring his men to the sticking point. Should not be surprised to see all former blunders again committed by the Confederate commands in opening the line of the Rapidam and weakening the line so much as to be untenable for us. The cavalry camped about the country should be amply sufficient to check at least one of the columns of the raiding enemy—and still leave the line intact.

Meade will certainly advance his infantry and other forces as soon as he finds out that A. P. Hill has gone—and then the line cannot be held. There only remain 10 Brigades if it be true that Hill has gone. He himself is not in command being absent sick and has no Major General with whom I would trust so large a command. They are hardly fit to command Divisions.

Rumours say also that our Division shall be withdrawn and sent after the [Kilpatrick and Dalgren] Cavalry; in which case goodbye Mr Rapidam—and it will not be recovered without severe fighting, which will probably then be in the neighborhood of Richmond. So we have a fair prospect of another series of seven days about that infernal town. I do not cherish the prospect at all though I have no doubt of the results. The weather seems willing to aid us as much as it can while we remain in camp—it [has been] raining now steady for nearly twenty four hours and sleeting tonight. It will be terrible on both man and beast should we be compelled to move. A handsome fight will be made if they attempt to crowd us, and if met with they will get what they evidently come for—a sound drubbing.[2]

The roads will be in a terrible condition tomorrow. Many of the men are without shoes though efforts are being made to supply them. It is very hard on the poor devils, and I pity them, yet admire them much. Tomorrow may show another state of things. Hope the Yankee Cavalry will be rubbed out— which will damage the enemy much as they have no doubt mounted every man possible. Presume demonstrations will be made from the south side on Richmond simultaneously. Averill ought also to make another start to make the thing complete. Should not much wonder if it is not already done though not heard of as yet. Bully for K.—poor Duncan McKim. Continued work on York Co map.

March 2 Day commences with many rumours of the feats and doings of the enemy. Everything remaining quiet until late in the afternoon when we congratulated ourselves on the whole row blowing over without our being compelled to leave camp. The fates willed it otherwise however, for about 1 hour before Sundown [we] received orders to move at once towards the Wilderness. We camped at Rowes House on Mine Run, with Jones, Steuart and Staffords Brigades and a battery of [Lt. Col. William] Nelson's artillery. This movement is intended to intercept Kilpatricks Cavalry on their return. Believe it will be a complete waterhaul.[3]

March 3 Sandy Pendleton joined us last night and marched with us this morning. We left Rowes about 4 oclock A.M. Arrangements are perfect to catch my gentleman should he come, which I doubt very much. J. E. B. Steuart [Stuart] joined us today a short [time] during the day, but nothing came of it. Mr. Kilpatrick did not honour us with his much desired company. We camped near Wilderness Run at Wilderness Tavern, with the expectation of returning to camp tomorrow.[4]

March 4 During night programme was changed and we returned to Chancellorsville and patiently awaited the enemy. No signs of them. During afternoon the enemy attempted to cross at Elys Ford but on the appearance of [Brig. Gen. Williams C.] Wickhams Cavalry Brigade they returned. Tonight I think we shall go back to camp tomorrow, at least such are indications now. Kilpatrick so far has done little damage and has accomplished nothing so far. Am very tired tonight, hence shall say all about him that I know thus far tomorrow.[5]

March 5 Start this morning for camp, and when about 3 miles on the road, were stopped on account of the rumours of the crossing of the infantry &[c] at Germania and Elys Fords, which turned out to be a hoax—as anticipated. Reached camp about dark and thus ends the much vaunted Yankee raid.

Sunday March 6th In camp today, nothing further new; and to all appearances quiet though I do not think it will last very long. Kilpatrick divided his raiding party into two columns—one commanded by himself, about 2500–3000 strong—another commanded by Col. U. Dahlgreen [Dahlgren], about 500–1000 strong. They captured our cavalry picket at Elys [Ford] and pushed on at a trot to Spotsylvania C. H. getting there about 2 oclock A.M.—thence across to Fredericks hall tearing up the railroad and capturing several members of the Artillery courtmartial in session there—among them Capt. [William F.] Dement.[6]

Kilpatrick was met at the works on the Brock [Brook] Turnpike by Henleys Battalion, composed of Clerks of the Department[,] and with the assistance of the Tredegar Iron Works Battalion repulsed him. He then crossed to near Mechanicsville and camped. Wade Hampton with 300–400 men followed him from Hamilton Crossing—attacked and surprised his camp at night— capturing some 90 prisoners and divided his column, a part crossing the Pamunkey and escaping towards Fortress Monroe—under his own command— the other part retreating in much disorder towards Louisa Co. Ho.[7]

Dahlgreen upon hearing of Kilpatricks discomfiture returned—was met in King William County by a small squad of Fitz Lee's Cavalry [and his men were] killed, captured and dispersed. Dahlgreen himself reported killed. Fitz Lee captured about 200–300 of Dahlgreens command. J. E. B. Steuart left us on the 3rd and went with Rossers brigade and is said to have killed, captured and dispersed the column starting towards Louisa Co. Ho., capturing 1200. This is merely a rumour yet may be correct as the enemy was much jaded.[8]

We met none of them and as indicated was a complete waterhaul. Everything was nicely fixed to give them a welcome reception and they could not get to the river from Fredericksburg to Liberty Mills without meeting somebody. The enemy will have lost probably about 1/3–1/2 of the men they started with and nearly all their horses and will have to be newly mounted again before taking the field. Thus ends this raid.

The raid on Charlottesville turned out to be nothing after all. Hills Corps was under Anderson's command, and marched with all their camp equipage and trains. Consequently when they came on Sedgewicks Corps and started to make fight, he had to look out for the wagons. The cavalry returned between the river and Andersons rear, and the wagons had to be secured again, when Sedgewick escaped unhurt as also did the cavalry. Though Anderson was some account but he ought to be courtmartialed for such a piece of foolishness as the one just stated. Am sorry for him. The damage done to the Rail Road was repaired in three days.

The purpose of the enemy was to liberate their prisoners at Belle Isle, capture Jeff. Davis and Cabinet—kill them—and burn the "hateful" city. Such were their orders as found on the person of Dahlgreen. Truly a nice programme. The Lord however had his finger on them & they all came to nought. Bully for "we-enses."[9]

———————

May 4th Rumours of late had commenced to put the enemy in a state of motion. Nothing of any moment had actually occurred, save the appointment of Grant to a Lt. Generalship, and his assuming command of the Army of the Potomac. This morning orders were issued to hold ourselves in readiness to move as the enemy seemed intent upon crossing the river and measuring their strength with us. We marched during the afternoon and evening to Zoah [Zoar] Church, camping near Wilderness Run. The disposition of the troops of our corps were [made] while marching—Johnson leading, Rodes, Early. Rodes camped at Locust Grove, Early at Mine Run. A. P. Hills Corps marched down on the Plank Road and camped at Verdiersville and vicinity.[10]

———————

[*May 5th*] On the morning of *the 5th* Brig. Genl. J. M. Jones with his Brigade was sent forward in advance to reconnoitre and fool the enemy who had crossed in mass at Germania and Elys Fords. The enemy were found and about 10 A.M. the engagement commenced, all the troops of his corps being

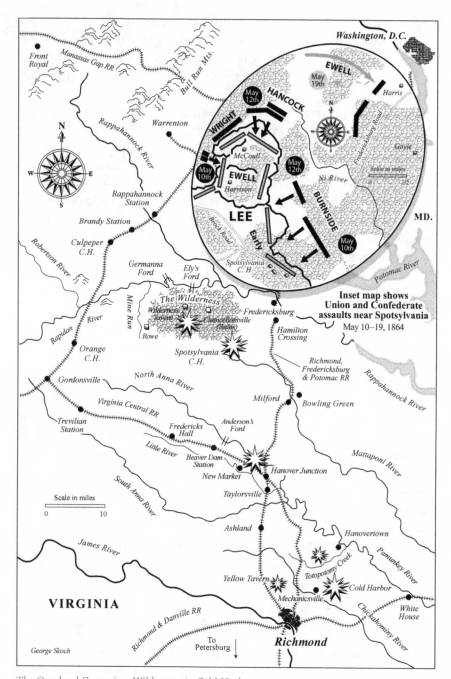

Front
Royal
Manassas Gap RR
Bull Run Mts.
Warrenton
Rappahannock River

Washington, D.C.
EWELL
May
19th
Harris
HANCOCK
May
12th
WRIGHT
McCoull
May
10th
EWELL
Harrison
May
12th
LEE
Ni River
Gayle
Fredericksburg Road
Scale in miles
0   1/2
BURNSIDE
Early
May
10th
Spotsylvania
C.H.
Brock Road

MD.

N
W   E
S

Rappahannock River

Rappahannock
Station

Brandy Station

Culpeper
C.H.

Robertson River

Germanna
Ford

Ely's
Ford

The Wilderness
Wilderness
Tavern
Chancellorsville
(Ruins)
Rowe

Mine Run

River

Rapidan

Orange
C.H.

Gordonsville

Virginia Central RR

Trevilian
Station

Fredericks
Hall

Little River

South Anna River

Scale in miles
0   10

James River

VIRGINIA

George Skoch

Fredericksburg

Hamilton
Crossing

Richmond,
Fredericksburg
& Potomac RR

Rappahannock River

Spotsylvania
C.H.

North Anna River

Milford

Bowling Green

Anderson's
Ford

Mattaponi River

Beaver Dam
Station

New Market

Hanover Junction

Taylorsville

Ashland

Yellow Tavern

Totopotomy Creek

Mechanicsville

Hanovertown

Pamunkey River

Cold Harbor

White
House

Chickahominy River

Richmond & Danville RR

To
Petersburg

Richmond

Inset map shows
**Union and Confederate
assaults near Spotsylvania**
May 10–19, 1864

Potomac River

The Overland Campaign, Wilderness to Cold Harbor

successively brought into action. Johnson on the left of the Old [Orange] Turnpike with Jones resting on it, and Walker left of the Div^n. Rodes was on the right of the pike, all occupying the western ridge of Wilderness Run. The enemy lay across the continuation of the Brock Road, Old Turnpike and [Germanna] Plank Road.[11]

After a hot engagement lasting until about 5 P.M. the enemy were repulsed at all points. In their assault on our right they broke Jones Brigade, but were reinforced by [Cullen A.] Battles Brigade of Rodes Div^n. Equilibrium was soon established, not however, without loss on our side. Genl. [Leroy A.] Stafford was mortally wounded and since died. Jones killed. From 5 until dark the enemy kept steathily moving to the left [right] with the intention of turning our left. Hays and [John] Pegram were brought up and placed on our left. A little after dark the enemy made a furious assault on Pegram but were signally repulsed. Pegram was severely wounded. All passed quietly during the balance of the night. Heavy attacks were made during the day on Hill and Rodes— Early being generally held in reserve to reinforce points critically assailed.[12]

[*May 6th*] The fight was reopened on the morning of *the 6th* by the enemy. [John B.] Gordon was brought down on our left, with two Batteries from [Col. Thomas H.] Carters Battalion who did elegant execution. The enemy were again foiled at all points without any more severe loss on our side. A little after dark Gordon and [Robert D.] Johnstons Brigades of Rodes Div^n, who had come up from Beaverdam during the day and been posted on our extreme left with the artillery, made a beautiful flank movement on the enemy, taking their trenches, and capturing Brig. Gens. [Alexander] Shaler and [Truman] Seymour with about 300 prisoners. Thus the enemy were driven from the Brock Road and Germania Ford. Their line of battle lay along the Culpeper plank road and following the Old Pike to Chancellorsville.[13]

[*May 7th*] The morning of the 7th opened without anything of any note save burying the dead—of whom about 1500 of the enemy were buried. At a moderate calculation their loss must have been about 20[000]–25000 men in the engagements thus far.[14]

[*May 8th*] On the morning of the 8th the enemy had disappeared from our front and moved to our right towards Spotsylvania Co. Ho. where they were met by our cavalry and held in check until Longstreet's troops could come up, when they were ejected from the place. The other troops soon came up and the army was again confronting the enemy. During the night the Div^{ns} of Johnson, Rodes and Early were placed in line of battle to the north of the Co. Ho.

During the day heavy fighting was going on in Hills Corps now commanded temporarily by Early; Gordon commanding Early's Div[n].[15]

[*May 10th*] On the evening of the *10th* an attack [led by Colonel Emory Upton] was made on [George P.] Doles line which gave way, admitting the enemy which cost considerable trouble to eject them again. Gordon came on in handsome style and repulsed them handsomely. Nothing of any very great importance occurred during the days of *8th*, *9th* and morning of the *10th* save some skirmishing with the enemy with occasional assaults of the enemy on the corps front in which they were uniformly repulsed with much damage.[16]

[*May 11th*] During the day of the 11th it was comparatively quiet. During the day Doles was removed and his place taken by Hays with Gordons Brigade in reserve. Johnsons line was weakened by stretching. During the night of the 11th [and at dawn on the 12th] the enemy massed a heavy infantry column estimated at from 20[000]–40000 in Johnsons front and about daybreak attacked the weakest point of the line occupied by Jones Brig. The artillery which had been there had been removed by Gen. [Armistead L.] Long and not replaced, one regiment, 21st V[a] [was] on picket, one absent to relieve the same and one regiment skirmishing in Steuart's front—which altogether weakened the point assailed that but feeble resistance was made and the enemy gained possession of the works [at the "Bloody Angle."] A battalion of arty. which came up was captured. During the melée Gens. Johnson and Steuart were captured with the greater part of their command. About 12[00]–1500 have been gathered together again. After the breaking of the Div[n] now temporarily commanded by Col. [Jesse M.] Williams of Staffords Brig., about 5[00]–600 were gathered again and led against the enemy, but broke soon losing Col. Williams and [Col. William A.] Witcher. What was now left of the Div[n] was gathered together [and] placed under the command of Col. [John H. S.] Funk [of the 5th Virginia], and at night came down to work on the trenches.[17]

The enemy had been able to maintain possession of a portion of the line, and it was deemed advisable to give their portion of it up to save further bloodshed and to get rid of a bad portion of the old line. Accordingly it was straightened, passing in rear of where Gen. Ewell had had his quarters during the previous fights. About 2[00]–300 yards of ground were thus given up.

[*May 13th*] Nothing of much consequence occurred on the 13th save heavy skirmishing along the whole front, during which the enemy showed a disposition to move further to the right and towards the R. F. & P. R.R. which also covered the Telegraph road.[18]

[*May 14th*] On the [morning of the] 14th having gone to the rear myself, orders came consolidating temporarily the Div[n] of Johnson with Early and Rodes — the latter taking the 2 No. Ca. [Carolina] regts., the balance being assigned to Early's Div[n] commanded by Gordon. [Maj. Edwin L.] Moore and [Lt. Skipwith] Wilmer were assigned to Gen. Ewell; [Capt. Henry Kyd] Douglas, [Maj. Robert W.] Hunter, and [Capt. Virginius] Dabney to Gen. Gordon [who was] now a Major General. No assignment of myself had been made as yet though I suppose I shall go to Gordon.[19]

Losses thus far are supposed to be heavy for the enemy. Of the enemy they will probably foot up:

Union: 10000 killed, 50000 wounded, 5000 prisoners — 65000[20]
Confederate: 2000 killed, 10000 wounded, 3000 prisoners — 15000[21]

Confederate Generals [who are casualties] thus far:
Maj. Generals killed — J. E. B. Steuart[22]
Brig. Generals   "   — J. [John] M. Jones, [Leroy A.] Stafford, [Junius] Daniels [Daniel], [Micah] Jenkins, [Abner M.] Perrin[23]
Lieut. Generals killed — none
    "   "   wounded — J. [James] Longstreet
Maj. Generals   "   — none
Brig. Generals   "   — J. [James] A. Walker, H. [Henry] H. Walker, [Harry T.] Hays, [Henry L.] Benning, [Robert D.] Johnston, [Stephen D.] Ramseur, [Samuel] McGowan, [John] Pegram, [Edward A.] Perry[24]
Captured, Maj. Gen. Ed. Johnson [&] Brig. Gen. S. [George] H. Steuart.

The enemy are supposed to have lost heavily in General officers; amongst them [John] Sedgewick [Sedgwick], Taylor, [Alexander] Hays, Carr, [James S.] Wadsworth, Talbot, [John C.] Robertson [Robinson], [William H.] Morris, [George W.] Getty, [Henry] Baxter, [Alexander S.] Webb — [Truman] Seymour and [Alexander] Shaler captured.[25]

[*May 17th*] Constant firing and skirmishing has been going on every day since (this is written on the 17th) and moving of forces to our right. Considering the forces engaged, this is the greatest attack the enemy ever have made on Richmond and the fighting has been the most persistent both in thought and action. The enemy have fought better and harder than they ever have done before and considered that attempts are made from the Peninsula under [William F.] Baldy Smith [and Benjamin Butler], things long hung in a trembling balance. There can I presume be no doubt of their final repulse at all points both here and there. Success has crowned our arms elsewhere. [Frederick] Steele has surrendered to [Sterling] Price—9000 men. [Nathaniel P.] Banks has been whipped again. [Franz] Siegel [Sigel] has been met in the Valley by [John C.] Breckenridge and whipped.[26]

May 18 The enemy this morning made two more assaults on our lines but were soon and handsomely repulsed with but slight loss on our side. Captain [George] Williamson of Gen. Steuarts Staff was severely and painfully wounded. The position of troops has thus far changed [so] that Longstreets Corps is again on the right and Hill in the centre. Rumour gives Early the permanent command of Hills Corps for which I am very sorry on Hills account, as I believe him to be a good officer and gallant soldier. Papers have reached us from Richmond giving an account of partial success thus far in repulsing the enemy from Richmond. Brig. Gen. [Chas. A.] Heckman with nearly the whole of his brigade was captured by the forces under Beauregard who has assumed command under Bragg. The enemy were driven off some two miles and still retreating. About 1,000 prisoners are captured and lodged and rumour says some 25 pieces of artillery. This will about square us with the enemy on the score of artillery.[27]

Old Joe appears to have had a brush but with what result I do not know, save that he says he has twice repulsed them. Everything appears to be working well. Think Grant has been already or soon will be heavily reinforced by troops from Washington and Baltimore. Siegel certainly already has done so to the extent of some 4000 men—chiefly infantry. McNeils [Captain John H. McNeill's] partizan Rangers have destroyed the buildings at Piedmont and many stores of much value to the enemy. We are not out of the woods yet, however, and things may change much in the course of a few days, should Grant be reinforced as I expect he will be. We may however soon expect to look for reinforcements from Richmond and No. Carolina. Rumour says Hardee's Corps is on its way here, though this is quite doubtful. I do wish that this horrid war would close soon, as I am getting heartily tired of it.[28]

May 19th Late this afternoon Ewells Corps—on information received at Gen. Lee's Hd. Qrs.—started on a flank movement on the enemy's right, with a view of finding him unprepared and with the hopes of capturing a wagon train. It seems however the enemy were fully informed of our intentions [in] a sufficient time to make the necessary disposition to meet him. Our skirmishers drove in their pickets and advanced into and among the wagon camp, when[,] it appearing that the enemy had thrown a heavy force to meet us, our command withdrew with slight loss. Col. Funk of the 5th Vᵃ Stonewall Brigade was slightly wounded. Some few officers and men were killed and wounded. It is presumed that the loss of the enemy was equally as heavy as ours plus some mules which were alleged to have been killed.[29]

The long and short of the matter however is that [the Battle of Harris Farm] was a failure and a fizzle. It was thought to make a Jacksonian movement but proved a lamentable want of brains to accomplish what to him appeared an easy task. How much we regret the loss of that man now. Eighteen days has the fighting been going on now, and nothing material gained by either side save the constant repulse of the enemy in their assaults on our lines. They have succeeded in crushing one Division completely. The attempts of Butler and Smith on Richmond have completely failed and the enemy returned to the cover of their gunboats.

May 21ˢᵗ Nothing new much this morning in the position of affairs here or at Richmond as near as I can learn. Banks has certainly been much depleted, it being claimed by many that he has been able to save but 5000 men out of 60000 with which he started [during his Red River Campaign]. Gunboats and transports have been captured with many prisoners. Some say he had surrendered to Dick Taylor. Whether so or not is doubtful either way. Joe Johnston has been fighting, repulsing the enemy with a loss of 12[000]–15000. Our loss estimated at 2500. Northern papers admit a loss of 70000 and 31 general officers during the fighting thus far with us. Gordon is certainly the Chevalier Bayard "sans pour et sans reproche" of this fight and of the army.

I am beginning to feel much depressed in spirits and energy. I wish the war ended so that I can take my leave—final and forever from a country where I can receive no remuneration for services. I will promise never to fight for a republic again, and will not live in one if I can in any way avoid it. Nothing more true than

> Despised by the land that bore us
> Betrayed by the land we served
> There is nothing but death before us
> And a failing of heart and nerve
> Yet stand to your glasses steady
> The world is a world of lies
> Here's a health to the dead already
> And hurrah for the next that dies.

I would willingly, gladly fight on could I see any fair prospect for advancement either in military or civil capacity. Our prospects for the future seem dark and blank. Could it only end now, I might be content to do allmost anything to make a comfortable living. Time may show what will become of us when the end comes—which I think is not far off.

Went to see Steinecker and Hotchkiss this morning and see about my orders from Genl. [Martin L.] Smith. Upon returning to camp I soon found everything in confusion in consequence of the enemy having retired towards Milford and Bowling Green and thus by their left flank towards and nearer Richmond. Having long expected this sort of a movement on the part of the enemy, this movement on their part did not surprise me. I certainly did not expect to see Lee so far behind him as nearly 20 hours. At any rate Lee this morning found their entrenchments vacated and the enemy gone. Orders were issued to follow them.

13. Attacks on Our Lines

May 22, 1864–June 14, 1864

*Grant certainly does fight us harder than any other
one they have sent down against us.*

—*Oscar Hinrichs*

[*May 22nd-23rd*] We moved through New Market, crossing the North Anna
River at Anderson's Ford, and thence down the [Virginia] Central Rail Road
to Hanover Junction camping there two nights. From there we moved (the
trains) about 12 o'clock M. on the night of the 23–24th, marching by Taylorsville accross the Little River, and camping a short distance from thence. *The
22nd* was employed by our troops in perfecting their lines in front of Hanover
Junction and getting ready generally to meet the enemy. Their cavalry had
forced a passage accross the North Anna above our left flank, thus giving the
enemy an opportunity and occasion of crossing their infantry which they were
not slow to improve. Hancocks Corps was crossed and prisoners report the
crossing of the major part of their Army.[1]

[*May 24th-May 25th*] Our lines on the 24th lay about a few hundred yards in
front of the Junction, stretching from Little River to the North Anna, and
thence down stream. This is merely my opinion from what I can learn to be the
case. Skirmishing was kept up with the enemy and a few prisoners captured
on both sides. I cannot think that Lee would have permitted Grant to cross
without opposition, unless he felt confident in whipping him in a general engagement and felt able of forcing him to one.

Reinforcements have come to us in the shape of Picketts and [John C.]
Breckinridge's Divisions and some small bodies of troops amounting to some
10.000 [10,000] men. I am writing this on the morning of *the 25th*. On the
night of the 24th Martin's Brigade, numbering some additional 4000 men, is

said to have come up, but I do not know positively. Some 3000 Southern cavalry are also said to have come up last night, but to whose command they belong I cannot find out. The situation is in my opinion a rather negative one.[2]

The enemy now holding the major part of the Central Rail Road, places the getting of supplies for them all within Rail Road reach by means of the V[a] Central, Orange & Alexandria, and Fredericksburg [Rail]roads with hardly anything to trouble them. By moving again to the left they can approach Richmond by the North side, and forcing Lee within his entrenchments about Richmond brings about the same result which he accomplished at Vicksburg and inaugurates a regular seige.[3]

Whether Lee will permit this is another question, and is not probable. By moving to the right and following the left bank of the Pamunkey they [Grant's troops] certainly approach nearer to the goal of their ambition and which is the prize of the fight, in actual distance of miles, but militarily speaking are no nearer than while on the banks of the Rapidam. If successful in crossing the Pamunkey [it] still leaves them another stream to cross, the Chickahominy, a much worse locality than any other as was shown by the experience of McClellan. Besides it places Grant in the unfortunate predicament of having been obliged to abandon the route selected by him, above all others, and giving credit to Little Mac for good judgement in selecting the Peninsula route from the first. Thus far it ruins him and his prospects, adds to McClellan's prospects, and besides ensures the defeat of his plans by being eventually compelled to abandon it also.

His [Grant's] chance of getting into Richmond is much better by moving directly on to the Confederate lines if he thinks himself strong enough to force the Confederates out—which I doubt—or moving to his right trusting to his numerous cavalry to keep open his communication with his base of supplies. This while placing [him] nearer Richmond offers I think much greater success if promptly and vigorously carried out, but at the same time annihilates his army if defeated unless he can so cripple Lee as to be unable to take advantage of it. By joining with Butler on the South side he gives himself an outlet while he is endangering our line of railroad with our depots of supplies to the South. . . .

I have received no orders and it appears irksome and uncomfortable to me. Doing nothing, staying in camp all may be construed unfavorably to me personally, and though I cannot say that I fancy fighting much, if at all. Still I might be of some good service to our new Major General Gordon.[4]

May 27th It now turns out that the arrival of Martins Brigade was chronicled rather prematurely. Still quite an accession to our servicable cavalry was made by arrivals yesterday and today by [Matthew C.] Butler's SC Cavalry Brigade numbering about 4000. The regiment I saw was quite a fine body of men. Everything yesterday looked quiet at the Junction. I went down upon the suggestion of Moore and half way reported to Gen. Gordon. He appears to be a nice clever gentleman with whom I hope my relations may be of a more pleasant character than with Old Ned [Gen. Johnson,] whom the Yankees may keep. Douglas has been ordered to Gen. Early as Chief of Staff. Much doubt is expressed in the confidence felt in the remnants of our old Div^n in the coming engagements.[5]

It is presumed that Lee will attack Grant soon. It would have been much better to have done so at a much earlier day as it would save the loss of many lives—in carrying the entrenchments of the enemy, as will be attempted should Lee make the attack. This appears to be what Grant is desirous of. Rumour says, with what appearance of truth I know not, that the enemy are trying to move further to the right and thence down the Pamunkey. This they might have done at an early day without the loss of a man or a[n] unnecessary fight, and place themselves much nearer Richmond. . . .

Saw a very good description of the [Wilderness] battle of the 5th & 6th from the correspondent of the London Herald writer [Butt Hewson] at Spotsylvania Co. Ho. under date of the 18th. It gives the Confederates much credit and especially mentions the handsome fighting of Gens. Gordon and Pegram. . . . We may [yet] be victorious over our enemies. Our loss is thought to be severe—and I am much afraid for poor Gordon will go up. Yet why should I predicate what is to be as regards persons.[6]

June 2nd We have been camped here within sight of Richmond for nearly a week, and still the enemy is no nearer and yet . . . skirmishing takes place every day but without any tangible results. . . . I wonder why no attack is made on the enemy, surely it cannot be for the want of men. On the night before last had to go to Genl. Gordon for information to work upon—and worked all night upon a map for him.

Yesterday morning on returning to my quarters at Ballards met with [Brig. Gen. James] Martin's Brigade [from Hoke's Division] near the entrenchments and for a few moments spoke with him. Want to see him a little more lengthily as I would like to hear of. . . . Div^n has come up and is now in line of battle. Poor [Edward S. "Ned"] Willis of the 12th Geo. [Georgia] was mortally wounded and since died from wounds received on the 31st of May.[7]

June 4th On the night of June 2nd [during the Battle of Cold Harbor,] an attempt was made on our part to dispossess the enemy of a portion of their lines

John B. Gordon (From Gordon, *Reminiscences of the Civil War* [New York: Charles Scribner's Sons, 1903])

which movement was entrusted by [John B.] Gordon's Division, the Stonewall [Brigade] under Gen [William] Terry leading. It succeeded admirably in capturing three lines of entrenchments [and] about 500 prisoners. Firing was kept up nearly all night by the enemy hoping to regain their works but without success. Gen. Doles of Rodes Div[n] was killed while forming his men. Gordon advanced his men through a piece of swamp deemed by the enemy to be impassable.[8]

During the 3rd the enemy made heavy assaults upon several portions of our lines but were severely repulsed at all points save in front of Breckinridge where they gained a temporary advantage, but were dislodged by Finnegan and the Maryland Line with heavy slaughter to them. Gens. [James H.] Lane, [Joseph] Finnegan [Finegan], [Alfred M.] Scales, [William W.] Kirkland, [Evander M.] Law and [Cullen A.] Battle wounded, Lane painfully.[9]

We have driven them at all points along the whole line. Gaines Mill and Cold Harbor are again rendered historic by our achievements. Heavy firing continued until late in the night but with what results is not known. We have been pushing them gradually towards the Pamunkey, our line forming as near as I can learn a crescent. Grant seems afraid of risking a general engagement in spite of his being reinforced by over probably 25000 men. Our loss therefore of the 2nd and 3rd is very slight, say about 600. Competent authority places theirs say 14[000]–15000 yesterday alone in their various assaults upon us.[10]

Grant certainly does fight us harder than any other one they have sent down against us yet, but has not at any one point made a point. He is now where McClelland started from during [18]62 and has lost nearly 100,000 men from all causes. Troops of all classes that could be raked, scraped and gotten together, have been brought down against us and thus far without avail. In the West Johnston seems to have worsted them considerably.[11]

Banks has lost everything, 1200 wagons, 22000 stand of arms, 15000 prisoners and has either surrendered or destroyed nearly the whole fleet of gunboats that accompanied his and Steeles Arkansas expeditions. Thus far everything here looks bright and cheering for us. God grant it may so continue, and victory final and complete settle down upon our flags and crown our efforts. As yet I am unable to do duty in the front — my horse being in a very bad condition. I would much rather be there than here.[12]

I received a letter from poor Charley Stanley dated Ft. Delaware Pennsylvania, which gives me indirect news from home. Date of letter April 24....[13]

June 5th Last evening the enemy made another of their customary attacks upon Fields lines, and were handsomely repulsed with much slaughter. [Robert D.] Lilly of the 25th Va was made Brig Gen and temporarily placed in command of Pegram's Brigade. [William] Terry is also made Brig Gen commanding the Va remnants of an old Division. Early has been made Lt. Gen. Ewell will probably be retired and Early will supply his place. R. [Richard] H. Anderson of Longstreets Corps is also said to have been promoted to a Lt. Gen. Large titles and small men. Brave and courageous, but no Generals. Thus wags the world. Where money and political influence is centered in some individuals anything can be had here from the highest to the lowest appointment xxxxxxx I presume it may be accepted as highly probable.[14]

Grant has found it thus far impossible to break through our lines, and he will in all probability try to divide our forces by transferring a portion of his troops to the other side of the James. As Richmond is the "sine qua non" of the combined efforts of the Yankee nation, I think it probable that we may linger about here during the balance of the summer, unless something should turn up which should change the complete aspect of affairs through out the land.

June 7th Yesterday came and went without anything new from our lines in front save a repeated rumour of the falling back of Grant towards the White House and a probable crossing to the south side of the James. Our troops advanced some distance without meeting with the enemy, and returned late at night to their old lines. Confirmed rumours came in late last night announcing the defeat of our troops [by Maj. Gen. David Hunter at the Battle of Piedmont on June 5] under Wm E. ["Grumble"] Jones, his killing and retreat of our forces near Waynesboro. Staunton is probably in the hands of the enemy for the time being, but is one of those positions which cannot be held.[15]

This morning Breckinridge leaves with his command for the Valley, and we may soon expect to hear of his having driven Hunter out & away again. All our stores, sick, artillery and wagons are said to have been saved. The force under Hunter is estimated at about 10[000]–12000 men, most Ohio volunteer militia—at least it is so reported. Saw [Major William W.] Thornton a little while yesterday—he tells me that Lewis, teacher at Mrs Frink, is up here with Hoke. I would much like to see the boy.[16]

[William H. C.] Whiting is apparently in disgrace for short comings during the fights with [Benjamin] Butler on the Southside. It is charged he was drunk, but I do not believe it. I have yet to see him so, and have known him now about as long as most of those who speak about him. He has however, evidently made a mistake but as yet I cannot get the gist of it. Mason and Cooper left this morning with Breckinridge's command for the Valley. Personally I am not sorry that they have gone. Both became rather disagreeable companions & C especially. Mitchele and Brown are couriers for Terry and Gordon respectively.[17]

Some slight firing near Gaines Mill this morning, but does not seem to have amounted to much. Should not wonder if we did not move soon on the southside. Grant will find it anyhow a hard road to travel. The Baltimore Convention sits today. Wonder who will be its nominees for President and Vice President of the U.S. Think they might spare themselves the trouble. Richmond however, is not yet in their hands as was fondly hoped in time for the action of the precious conclave of rascals.

June 8th Yesterday passed another day of quiet and rest. No news of any character were received from the front yesterday. Cockrill returned yesterday and looks about the same as ever. He seemed much tickled at something, but could not make out what until late during the night when Browns returned telling me it was rumoured that Steinecker had gone to the enemy. This morning he told Lyons that Steinecker had been guilty of some more stealing, and to avoid punishment had left for parts unknown. This much I dont believe. I know him to be a grand rascal, yet do not suppose him as bad as all that. Cockrill himself is much guided in his expression of unkindness by his antipathies and prejudices, and no doubt the only foundation for my remarks concerning Steinecker can very readily be traced to the intense desire manifested on a former occasion to injure and ruin him if possible and to the phantoms which generally hunt a diseased brain. The weather is very cool and chilly for this time of the year, an overcoat or other heavy covering being extremely pleasant at night; unusually cold and disagreeable. I feel very badly again today as if I were to have a spell of "hard times."[18]

June 9th Late last evening received a note from [Capt. Virginius] Dabny that the General wanted another map. Started down a little before dark, and when getting near the old camping ground heard that the troops had moved to the right, no one being able to tell me where or how far they had gone. I returned to camp fearful lest our wagons might also move. Heard from Major General Tanner [?] that the enemy had taken possession of Petersburg—an event for some time looked for. I wonder what the upshot of this business will be.[19]

Lee seems to be afraid of Grant who seems only fooling and playing with him. The Petersburg affair turns out to be a cavalry affair in which they were finally repulsed by a portion of Wise's Brigade, retiring in the direction of the Weldon railroad. The destruction of this road will prove of very material inconvenience to us at this time, as all our supplies are drawn over this road. Would not be surprised if some fine morning the Confeds are not whipped out clean on the Southside and the enemy entering with our men in Richmond. This will probably satisfy Grant, he then having accomplished what all others had failed in.

This morning I went down to the front again with Webb and found our Div^n camped near Gaines House near Gainesville [Gaines's Mill]. Everything seemed quiet; yet I do not understand the picture of affairs. There appears to be much indiscission as to what is to be done. One thing is certain: we have gained no very material advantage of the enemy which is here in front of Richmond while they have been able to keep our forces busy and occupied, thus permitting the sending off of raiding parties, who though they may not do much damage in the end, but what may be easily repaired, still occasion much inconvenience and frequently nearly miss doing a great harm by the purest chance and accident. This is shown by their sudden and unexpected attempt on Petersburg, the raiding parties of Kilpatrick, Dahlgreen, and Sheridan from the Army of the Potomac, and of Averill in Western Virginia.[20]

Dame Rumor says that Hampton has come up with [Maj. Gen. Philip H.] Sheridan somewhere in Louisa County, fought and defeated him capturing some 500 prisoners. Whether this be true or not is altogether another question. It is certainly desirable that something of the sort should happen. Pope has joined Hunter in the Valley with some 4,000 men. Averill has started on another expediti[o]n as also Cook [Brig. Gen. George Crook]. Averill and C[r]ook struck the C. R. R. [Virginia Central Railroad] somewhere near Covington, tore up the track &c &c and committing depredations. All quiet here.[21]

June 11th Orders came on today thick and fast regarding many points which would indicate a move of some sort. The intelligence from the Valley is of such a nature that it is highly probable that some portion of the army here may move in that direction. The enemy have occupied Staunton, burnt several buildings in the place and are crowding our forces near Rockfish Gap and are striking off towards Lexington & Lynchburg.[22]

In my opinion things generally look pretty dark. Lee does not seem disposed to crowd Grant away from his position, and Grant is gradually forcing him to detach men to support other points and with them force him into the fortifications of Richmond, where it becomes merely a question of time whether the enemy get possession or not. With a severing of the means of supplies—all coming from the South—it can almost be calculated when it goes into the hands of the enemy. Our army is hopeful, bouyant and strong, in point of numbers and might [succeed] in an open field which still play[s] fearfully with Grants pretensions [apprehensions].

I am much afraid Lee is not the man for the times now, and has fritt[er]ed the opportunity away. I suppose Bragg will also come in for his share of abuse should such a disaster occur. With a fall of Richmond the enemy can then continue the war for several years longer. Lee with a damaged reputation will be laid on the shelf and the "rebellion" virtually ended. Richmond's loss will compel the evacuation of Virginia and North Carolina, there being no line that I know of capable of the Santee or Pe[e]dee [Rivers] in South Carolina.

The disaffection existing in North Carolina would of itself make our tenour [tenure] even in N.C. of a questionable character, even if everything else would work right with us. Besides being crowded with a heavy army in front, both flanks open to an attack from the mountain passes on the west and Sea Coast on the east, while our forces with each retrograde movement would be constantly diminishing, not alone from battle but from active desertion. These people are fighting not so much for their much vaunted patriotism and love of country as from a desire to retain their property. Wherever their property is there their hearts will be also, and good morning Virginia & North Carolina.

All this is merely a possible contingency, which God grant may never occur. What my own course of action will be must be determined by circumstances which I cannot control. I hope I may never be called upon to debate the said [situation] with myself. I am afraid that I should not have nerval courage sufficient to enter into it fairly and without prejudice. My Father and Mother would occupy too large a share of the calculation. Self interest next. As I have nothing to hope from the C.S. and still less from the U.S., I might with perhaps perfect propriety do what I pleased. Evil tongues however, would have their say to my damage.

June 14th We moved as indicated by orders on the morning of the 12th. Rogers was in charge of the trains, and consequently everything was bungled. I hear & see much confusion, much to [my] disgust, but never saw trains willfully carried over roads which almost as soon as tried had to be abandoned. Rogers is a good, clever fellow, but can't keep hotel. We camped about 15 miles from Richmond. Nothing occurring to my knowledge. On the morning of the 13th we moved bright and early under better management than yesterday. Harman was placed in charge and brought us into camp by times. Have been able to learn of no news, nor seen a Richmond paper. Things to all appearances were working smoothly and nicely. This morning we moved by good times and camp at night about 8 miles from Gordonsville in the Green Spring country.[23]

I saw a Richmond paper yesterday, which confirms the rumor of Grant moving his forces from our front at Cold Harbor. He moved during the night of the 12th to and near Malvern Hill, and occupies McClellan's old lines of '62. We have moved our forces and front him still. Success has again crowned us at the hands of Forrest, he having captured 250 wagons, 2000 prisoners, 20 pieces of artillery [during the Battle of Brice's Cross Roads] and plunder[ed] generally, scattering the Yankees all around.

Hampton has come up with Sheridan [at the Battle of Trevilian Station and] killed and captured about 2000, and drove him across the North Anna on Sunday P.M. and follows in pursuit. Averill and Crooke—not Cooke—advanced on Lexington, but turned off and are moving on Salem or on the Salt Works. The party that tapped the C.R.R. [Virginia Central Railroad] has turned out to be a small raiding party and have left the vicinity.[24]

Advices [advisers] had been received in England up to the 16th of May and the comments, though of a non-committal specie, were favourable. They estimate Grant's losses as being very heavy—about 2000 per mile—and give the Confederates credit. Thus far then everything works smoothly, more so than anticipated. Grant is still in a condition to afford much uneasyness, though I believe the crisis has past. Our own movements seem to be made on the Upper Valley as a blind, my opinion being that we are bound as an advance corps upon Maryland. My bet with Cleon Moore may yet turn out to be correct that we should be on the other side of the Potomac before the 1st of July. Things look very much like it, and I think it is the beginning of the end. Have thought much of home lately and do hope and pray hopes may not be disappointed. The whole movement of our Corps affords much ground for speculation, which may or may not prove true. God grant it may.[25]

14. In Front of Washington

June 16, 1864–July 15, 1864

Reach the front of Washington this noon. Men very much exhausted by heat. . . .
Am afraid we shall miss our opportunity of getting in. Reinforcements are
said to be arriving rapidly from in front of Richmond.

—Oscar Hinrichs

June 16th March again this morning and camp at Charlottesville. Presume
we will go to Lynchburg, as trains have been sent down from there to here to
carry troops. Madame Rumour says that Early telegraphed to [Superinten-
dent] Vandergriff [of the Orange & Alexandria RR] for information as to how
much transportation per rail he could furnish. Vandergriff answered by asking
to know how many troops he had and he would furnish the cars. "Tell him to
send all he has got, it is none of his dam'd business how many men I have" was
Early's answer. Had an elegant bath near the University.[1]

June 17th March this morning towards Lynchburg over a road which promises
to be very rough; and camp near Cavesville [Covesville] about 18 miles from
Charlottesville. Nothing of importance transpired during the day.[2]

June 18th March again this morning and camp 2 miles from Lexington—the
county seat of Nelson—towards Lynchburg. Marched about 20 miles over a
very rough road. Heard today that Grant had crossed to the South side of the
James, and that heavy fighting had taken place. Grant crossed on the night of
the 13th and day of the 14th. He pitched into Beauregard and worsted him considerably, driving him some distance. On the following day however, having
been reinforced by Lee, Grant was in turn driven, loosing many prisoners,
and general loss heavy. Grant had thrown himself in full force on Beauregard,
crossed to Petersburg Rail Road and temporarily held the town. All the ground

Oscar Hinrichs's journal drawing: *Outside Lynchburg, Va.*
(Richard Brady Williams Private Collection)

lost was recovered and much more. Forrest is rumored to have increased his number of prisoners to 13.000 [13,000] which is very doubtful; probably about 3000. Hunter has thrown himself towards Lynchburg and some fighting has occurred; result not known. He is supposed to have concentrated all the detached commands in this section—in all about 25000 men.[3]

June 19th Sunday This makes the seventh day of our travel and we are about 30 miles from our first destination. We camp within a mile or two of James River and Lynchburg. Nothing new of any moment that I have been able to learn.

June 19th Passed through Amherst Co. Ho. yesterday, which is a neat little town. It is the county seat of Amherst County.[4]

June 20th Passed through Amherst Co. Ho. yesterday and camp within a mile or two from Lynchburg near the river.

June 20 Pass through Lynchburg this morning bright and early, and before anybody was stirring. Met Tom Taliaferro in the street looking most anxious for the breakfast time of day to come. Marched to a mile or two beyond Liberty, one of the neatest little places I have met with yet in Virginia. Our days march was about 28 miles. The road from Lynchburg out is lined with dead horses and chicken feathers. Indeed the destruction of property by the enemy along our march today has been very great. They appear to have passed along in great haste and in three columns of march. The people are suffering for food and I do not see how they manage to get along; as not alone [only] are all the provisions taken away, but the mills are destroyed.[5]

The more I can hear and see, the more fully convinced [I am] that this move as far as fighting and capture go, will turn out a grand, the grandest fizzle. We have marched, I don't know how many miles, broken down both men and horses and teams, and will probably within a day or so give up the process of following them. Their purpose seems to be to do as much damage as possible and avoid a fight, in which [case] they completely succeed. We catch up with them once in a while and make preparations for a fight, when away they go and do not stop short of another 30 miles. We shall in all probability never repair all the damage inflicted on the Virginia and Tennessee RR[d] as it is so open to raids. This may secure the people from a repetition of such visits as this one was from the enemy.

June 21st March again this morning at a more reasonable hour than heretofore—and camp near Congress Springs on the railroad. Maj Ballard joined us again tonight but brought no news. On our march we passed through Bufords Gap on towards Salem. The Gap is a very pretty one but the road miserable. Surprised that the enemy should have given it up without something more of a struggle. The same sights of destruction as heretofore only it appears that they were more in a hurry about it.[6]

June 22 March again this morning. Rumour says that the enemy have left completely, abandoned their artillery, mounted their men and gone entirely and that hence the pursuit will here end. The whole tale of abandonment appears very doubtful, though there is no telling what may not be done by an enterprising man. Maj. Ballard has just returned from the front and reports that the enemy have entirely left. Our captures amount to 10 pieces of artillery, a few wagons and 175 prisoners.

What our movements will be now it is doubtful to conjecture. From our position here we may go down to Richmond and strike at Grant, Hunter having gone in the direction of Lewisburg—or we might go by way of Lexington Station down the Valley to the Potomac, cross and perhaps by threatening Washington relieve Richmond and Lee to a very considerable extent. The latter movement would be the most effective I believe and secure us the position. Hunter having gone to Lewisburg in the Kanawha Valley may join Sherman in the West and thus be made effective again, though I believe it will be sometime ere he will have his command fit for service again.[7]

Rumours came from Richmond that considerable fighting has taken place there and at Petersburg. One rumour says that Grant has been severely handled, we having captured from him some 30,000 prisoners. Another account says that we were fighting in the streets of Petersburg. Loss on each side very heavy. At any rate fighting has taken place but with what result it is very doubtful. I hope the first rumour given will be made correct, if not so already. Prospects are I think much brighter for us than when we left Richmond.[8]

Sunday June 26th We took this back track on June 22nd passing through Lexington on the 25th. I did not omit to pay my last respects to the last remnant of that old hero Genl. Jackson. The enemy have burnt nearly all the buildings of the Vª M. I. [Military Institute,] including the dwellings of the Professors. Jacksons grave was not much disturbed. The flagstaff was much cut and the foot board obliterated. I presume for to sell by some enterprising Yankee.[9]

We march this morning again towards Staunton for which point rumour says a heavy yankee force [is] driving to connect with Hunter. Hunter is now said to be moving parallel with us down toward Staunton on a mountain road. Grant has made a furious attack on our lines near Petersburg and was most handsomely repulsed. They have it reported in northern papers that Petersburg has been captured by the Union forces in consequence of which gold fell to 195 3/8. I believe. About 700 men were captured by us.

Morgan appears to be alive again to the fact that there are still some yankees to demolish and consequently is occasionally letting into them. Another handsome repulse is claimed by us in front of General Johnston. About the fighting in the streets of Petersburg it turns out to be all bosh. Visited the Natural bridge on yesterday; was very much pleased with it. Hope however, I may not be called upon to visit it again. I do not much fancy this country; it has a little too much hills in it for comfortable riding unless it be in peace times and [I have] plenty of time.[10]

June 27th On the night of the 26th we camped about four miles from Lexington on the Staunton road and marched again next day camping about a mile from Gainesville [Greenville]. On the 27th we camped at Staunton, and marched again during the forenoon of the 28th for Mount Crawford on the Valley Pike. Nothing new from Richmond save that [Brig. Gen. William] Mahone had executed another flank [attack] on Grant in which some successes were gained by us. The raiders on the Danville road are progressing on their work of destruction, but yesterday were reported to have been severely punished. While in Staunton saw Mr. Tarus again who gave a very interesting account of the Yankee occupation of the place.[11]

We are moving down the Valley with Pennsylvania very near us, our probable destiny [destination]. Be that as it may, all seem to be of the opinion that is thither we are wending our foot steps. I trust it may be so. Few if any Yankee

Oscar Hinrichs's journal drawing: *Natural Bridge, Va.* (Richard Brady Williams Private Collection)

forces seem to be in the Valley save some 5000 men and a few cavalry at and about Martinsburg. They will probably not offer much resistance to our advance and for a short time we may count on having things our own way.

Another reduction of baggage took place day before yesterday P.M. in which I was despoiled of my desk and had to leave it with Major [Henderson M.] Bell at Staunton [who served as assistant quartermaster]. Some few effects were saved but do not know low long it may last to keep them. Saw Hotchkiss about making some arrangement to change my boarding house and may possibly be ordered to the command of Genl. Breckinridge. Gordons Div^n and Breckinridge form one corps with B. as corps commander. Ramseur [Maj. Gen. Stephen Dodson Ramseur] and Rodes under Rodes [constitute] another corps, and the whole under Early; quite a good combination if Breckinridges men are worth anything.[12]

June 30th March again this morning camping last night near Lacy's Spring or Big Spring about midway between Harrisonburg and New Market. Nothing of any moment has happened to my knowledge. I believe more firmly than ever that we are bound for Pennsylvania as it is reported by those who ought to know that no arrangement for getting supplies for our troops have been made, beyond those gotten at Staunton and vicinity while there and now following us.

Rumor says that Warren's Yankee Corps has been detached from Grant to meet us and check us. Be this as it may, I hardly believe he will be of much avail to accomplish his purpose, as it will take something more than one corps to effect such an object. Once [we] whip the force sent against us roundly, and peace negotiations will at once be opened, and lead I believe to satisfactory results. I am very much in favor of working the knife to the hilt this time and believe Early has the spirit to do it, if not controlled by higher authority. His action regarding the supplies of clothing, shoes and provisions at York last year bespoke the right thing. Were he to do it now that he is uncontrolled to a much greater extent and left to be the sole judge of what is expedient, I hope he may.[13]

July 2nd On the night of June 30th camped near Mt. Jackson and marched on the 1st to Strasburg. Saw Hotchkiss at Woodstock who told me he had had a talk with Gordon and had consented to my leaving him and going to General [Dodson] Ramseur. Have said nothing to anybody about it as it may give rise to the asking of impertinent questions which I do not care about hearing. This morning we marched from Strasburg to within a few miles of Winchester, camping near Kernstown at an old Church. Received my orders to go to Ramseurs this morning shortly after leaving camp and reported at once. I am not sorry that I am going to leave this old Div[n] and don't think anyone will be sorry I am gone.[14]

Rumour says that A. P. Hill [Dick Anderson] is now camped at Madison Co Ho on his way to join us on our trip. If so it will spoil calculation somewhat. Mr. Lee will be wanting to come next and then it will be a pretty little kettle of fish. Rumour also says that Grant has received another drubbing, the most severe of the series loosing 40000 men in killed wounded and prisoners. Can not believe it to be as serious as that, but should not wonder if there had been a fight in which he had been worsted. Rumour again says that Burnsides and Warrens Corps have been detached and ordered to meet us while Hunter is said to be coming down the Baltimore & Ohio Rail Road. If these rumours be

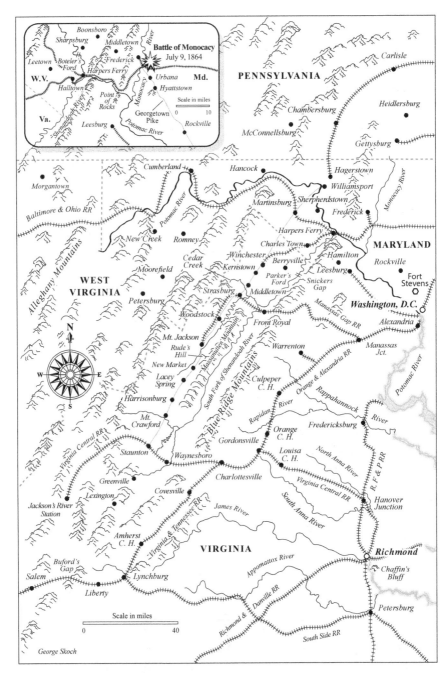

The First Half of Early's 1864 Valley Campaign

correct they may be able to give us some trouble, but I do not think there can be much confidence placed in them.[15]

The enemy up to today were not looking for us. [John S.] Mosby and Gilmer [Harry W. Gilmor] pitched into them and captured quite a number of them at Berryville on the Shenandoah. I believe that we have war and peace in our own hands if we only play our cards right. Grant whipped from Richmond, Hunter and his party whipped from Maryland, we can at least for some time to come do as we please. I do not think that another army can or will be raised shortly—and the militia will not offer much resistance to us. However we shall see. I am much afraid that a botch will be made of the whole business and that we may be glad if we can get away with a whole skin. General Jackson is not here now and things will not be managed as he managed them. Early is a good man but may now be rather over crapped. "Nous Verrons." Find young [Lt. Randolph] Ridgely who was aid to Genl J. M. Jones here but do not know as yet in what capacity. Douglass [Henry Kyd Douglas] is Chief of Staff. Will say more probably anon. Have not heard from E. City now in a long time, wonder what can be to pay there.[16]

July 5ᵗʰ We marched on the 3ʳᵈ from the neighborhood of Winchester and camped near Smithfield at Leetown. Our cavalry under [Brig. Gen.] Bradley Johnson had been fighting the enemy all day with varying success, it resting somewhat with us at nightfall. Shortly after getting into camp a report came that our cavalry was falling back before the enemy and our Division was got out under arms to meet the advance of the enemy. It turned out to be a hoax however.[17]

On the morning of the 4ᵗʰ we started for Charlestown, but were turned off when about 1 1/2 miles from the place towards Harpers Ferry. The sharpshooters of Johnston's Brig. met the yankee pickets at Hall Town and ran them into the Bolivar Heights. The heights were soon after carried with but slight resistance from the enemy. Our further advance was checked for the time being at the town of Bolivar, which from this time out was persistently shelled by the enemy from their fortifications on the Maryland side of the Potomac, and very much injured. Several women and children were wounded by their shot. About dark our skirmishers were pushed forward and entered Harpers Ferry without further opposition from the enemy. Most of the stores had been previously removed; among the most important of the captures was a bridge train almost complete, and a large quantity of forage in the shape of oats and corn, which at this time came in quite opportunely. The railroad bridges were partially burned. Everything was prepared for firing but was fortunately saved. Several houses in both Bolivar and Harpers Ferry were burned.[18]

5th day we remain quiet resting the men and sparing shoes, which are much wanted. Our cavalry and the Divisions of Gordon and Breckinridge crossed the river at Shepardstown yesterday, and will I presume gain some point in the rear of Harpers Ferry by which the retreat of the enemy may be cut off. At least such I suppose is the programme, if not I can not see much sense in the movement. I presume we shall move towards Shepardstown tomorrow and also cross the river, as we can do nothing more here. The Yankee force here in our front consists of probably about 4500 men, they being reported to have been reinforced by some 3000 last night. Think it probable that the enemy will evacuate the position tonight as they cannot expect to gain anything much by remaining where they now are. Our casualties thus far very slight, and that of the enemy about the same. I presume losses anyhow not much on either side. Made no private capture as yet but soon hope to be able to do so. Drew my pay for three months today up to June 30th and paid Jim $60 (40 as hire, 12 mess, 8 private).

July 7th Sunday Camped at Sharpsburg. We left the vicinity of Harpers Ferry today and marched to Botelers Ford on the Potomac. Nothing of much importance occurred during the time save the movements of troops on this side. Mosby cut the Baltimore and Ohio RR^d at Point of Rocks and has thus far prevented the enemy from sending any reinforcements to Harpers Ferry. The garrison at that place seems to take matters and things very quietly. Brig. Gen. [William G.] Lewis was left in command at Harpers Ferry with his Brig. but orders have been given him to return to the Div^n. Gordon's Division has been in position near Harpers Ferry on the Maryland side. I presume that we shall move early in the morning on towards Boonsboro Gap in the Blue Ridge.[19]

July 7th Remain contrary to expectation quietly in camp resting the men and animals. Nothing of any importance occurred save that it appears that nearly all hands got drunk at Corps Hd. Qrs. and got into a row with each other. Green had a fisticuff fight — Harman and Hotchkiss — &^{c} &^{c}.[20]

July 8th Marched early this morning towards Fred[e]rick City and camp about 4 miles from Fred[e]rick. Our Division in the lead. Cavalry fight a little on the mountain near Fred[e]rick. Pass through Boonsboro. Camp near Middletown. Up all night making a map for the General.[21]

July 9th March this A.M. on towards Fred[e]rick. Slight skirmishing with the enemy on approaching Fred[e]rick. Got into town with the skirmishers. Pass through town and take the Washington & Georgetown pike towards Monocacy Junction. Fight the enemy under [Erastus] Tyler and [Brig. Gen. Lew] Wallace. Gordons [Division] makes a handsome flank movement. Enemy driven away in utter route [rout]. Capture but few prisoners. Among them is reported E. B. Tyler Brig. Gen.[22]

July 10th March this morning from Monocacy Junction on the Georgetown road. Our Div[n] brings up the rear of the army. Fight with the enemy near Urbanna [Urbana]. Camp between Rockville and Hyattstown. See no signs of the enemy in our front.[23]

July 11th Reach the front of Washington this noon. Men very much exhausted by heat. Cannot get anything much out of them today. Am afraid we shall miss our opportunity of getting in. Reinforcements are said to be arriving rapidly from in front of Richmond. Skirmish with the enemy this afternoon.[24]

July 12th Lay quietly in front of Washington. Skirmish with the enemy all day. Preparations are made to leave here in a hurry.[25]

July 13th Marched last night as indicated, on the Leesburg road. March all night and rest within 10 or 11 miles of the river near a church. Bradley Johnson is reported to have captured Maj. Gen. [William B.] Franklin on a train between Baltimore and Washington; burnt Gov. Augustus Bradfords residence near Baltimore. We camped at F. P. Blair's place. House gutted of everything of value.[26]

July 14th Continue our march, and cross the Potomac today about 12 M at the same place where Jackson crossed in [18]62. Camp at Col. [Armistead T. M.] Rust's place about 4 miles from Leesburg. Nothing of importance occurred during the day save an reported advance of the enemy.[27]

July 15th I find that these dates are all more or less wrong. This day we rest at Col. Rust's place about 1–2 miles from Big Spring. Mournful recollections of Genl Jacksons first campaign to Maryland.

15. On the Valley Pike

July 16, 1864–August 18, 1864

The enemy in retreating set fire to several barns and burnt much wheat.
They told the people that the only way to keep us out of the lower
Valley, was to render it impossible for us to subsist.

—*Oscar Hinrichs*

July 16th March this morning at 11 ½ A.M. via Leesburg and Hamilton to Snickersville Gap. Yankee cavalry pitch into the train about 3 ½–4 miles from Snickersville and capture, burn, and run off some 50–60 wagons of the cavalry belonging to the cavalry of this command. Cavalry force along with the train act shamefully on the occasion, and run off leaving the wagons to take care of themselves. Our Division being rear guard pitch into the enemy with 2 regiments of infantry and drive them off. Rodes also sent a Brigade and did likewise. The 21st N.C., Kirkland's old regiment, capture a piece of artillery and one caisson. Brought piece off. Saw Col. Mosby. Was agreeably disappointed in his appearance [but] appears to be a quick, clever, gentleman. [Major Gen. Robert] Ransom, now commanding the cavalry of the Valley District, does not seem to be gathering many laurels on this rampage. Don't think him worth much. Face expresses indolence and want of decision.[1]

July 17th Rear guard again today. Camp last night at Snickers Gap after a march of about 20 miles. Yanks considerably worsted yesterday. Captured some 30 including one or two commissioned officers, killing and wounding several. Hope things will go on a little more quietly today.

July 20th We went only a short distance on the 17th camping near Berryville on the Charlestown pike. On the 18th we shifted camp among many rumours of approaching foe. Towards night the enemy crossed a very considerable force

General Jubal Anderson Early (From Early, *Lieutenant General Jubal Anderson Early, C.S.A.: Autobiographical Sketch and Narrative of the War Between the States* [Philadelphia: J. B. Lippincott Co., 1912])

in front of Rodes Div[n], which lay in line of battle [at Cool Spring Plantation] near Parker's Ferry on the Shenandoah. A considerable engagement took place lasting until some time in the night; the enemy were finally driven back across the river with much slaughter, some supposing their loss to be near 1500 in killed, wounded and prisoners. Rodes lost about 270. About 2000 Yankees attempted to cross in front of Gordon but were driven back by a heavy skirmish line. About 5 P.M. our Div[n] received orders to move to Berryville and take position to the eastward of the town. This done, I was sent on a goose hunt after Gen. Early. Returned to camp about 12 oclock at night.[2]

On the 19th our Div[n] remained quiet until about 4 P.M. when orders came to move at once to our first position on the Charlestown pike, and moved again to Berryville at night. Rumours a thousand and one came pouring in of Yankees advancing on Winchester by way of Bunker Hill, and hence we are turned off at Berryville to Winchester, making a forced march so as to reach that place by daylight. We arrive and upon examination find the enemy almost nowhere. They do not seem to be quite sure of how to play their game, and I expect some of these fine days quite a number of them will find themselves in our Hotel de Libby.

We are now lying in form of battle north of Winchester on the Martinsburg road, and about two miles from Winchester. I presume we shall move again this P.M. on the Staunton pike, probably to New[town] and Middletown. [John D.] Imboden had a fight with the enemy at Ashby's Gap and Berry's Ferry [Ford], punishing the Yanks severely. Thus far they have not made much out of us, and dont think they will.

July 23rd On the afternoon of the 20th the enemy advanced on Genl. [John C.] Vaughan [at Stephenson's Depot] and compelling him to retire. Our Divn was brought into requisition, but was soon panicstruck and ran like good fellows. Our loss was comparatively slight considering the chances. Much blame rests on both Genl. Vaughan for deceiving us regarding the strength of the enemy, and on Gen. [Robert D.] Lilley for not obeying at once an order given him by me to form his Brigade on the left of Gen. [William G.] Lewis. Lewis was wounded. Poor little [Lt. Randolph] Ridgely and Calloway was wounded severely, the former left in the hands of the enemy. I am much afraid he will not survive it. At night we left Winchester, camping at our old camp near Kernstown.[3]

On the 21st we marched and formed line near Newtown on the Valley pike. We soon moved from thence and marched slowly on to near the bridge near Strasburg and camped for the night. On the 22nd we marched to within a mile of Strasburg and leaving the Valley pike formed line on the "Back road." The whole command is in line here. Gordon on the extreme right, Rodes on the left. Head Quarters are fixed near Mrs. Millers on the Valley Pike south of Strasburg.[4]

July 26th We remained in line during the day of the 23rd and moved early on the 24th towards Winchester. On nearing Kernstown we found the enemy in position. Lines were immediately formed and the enemy driven from his position towards Winchester. The enemy's command consisted of [George] Crooks infantry, Averill's cavalry and some 12 pieces of artillery: in all some 15-20.000 [15,000-20,000] men. They made but slight resistance and fled. Bradley Johnson and [William L.] Mudwall Jackson followed them at once, forcing them to burn 93 wagons, 19 caissons, and capturing some 5[00]-600 prisoners. Col. [James A.] Mulligan of Lexington notoriety was severely wounded and left in our hands; he will probably die. Gen. Lill[e]y lost his right arm at the shoulder, besides wounded in the thigh. Ridgely is doing very well.[5]

On the 25th we remained in camp until about 5 P.M. when we marched towards Martinsburg, camping at Bunker Hill near Genl. Jackson's old Hd. Qrs. On the 26[th] we march to Martinsburg and camp near the Hedgesville road, and near our camp of last fall when we came down to destroy the B. & Ohio Rail Road. The command of Crooks has always boasted that they had never been whipped—which commencement I presume will now for a time cease.

July 29th On the 27th we remained in camp amusing ourselves last evening until about 12 oclock in tearing up the B. & O. R.R. On the 28th we are again in camp, but towards afternoon get orders to continue the destruction of the road. Saw [Col. Stephen D.] Thruston [from the 3rd North Carolina] in Martinsburg—he being Provost Marshall. About night receive orders to move by day in the morning towards Williamsport, I presume. Do not think much will come of it and dont think the whole command will march.[6]

On the 29th we march as indicated and am now writing this under a big oak in a small field about a mile from the Potomac. Sure enough only Rodes and our Div[n] comprise the command, with its complement of cavalry and arty. Should not be surprised if we did not get into a snap before a great while as this promiscuous cavorting of Brother Jubal A. is pretty sure to bring down the Yanks in pretty good numbers. They got awfully scared though, from the effects of the Winchester affair and are said to have arrived safely at Carlisle and Harrisburg.

[Lieutenant Gen. John B.] Hood has superseded Old Joe [Johnston] in command in Georgia, has had a fight, and claims a victory. The northern papers of the 25th say that Sherman has been badly handled and was then in a rather critical condition. Unfortunately for us, nearly all news of fighting in the west comes so pleasantly at first and winds up so disastrously for us, that I for one am rather disposed to discredit the victory though he may possibly have gained some slight advantages. Be this as it may, Hood is a good man and will do well if not interfered with. Another story will probably be told by the friends of Old Joe who are with him and are conversant with the situation. Thus wags the war with its ups and downs. I believe him to be the best man they could possibly have out there, save perhaps poor old Jackson were he alive now.[7]

July 30th On the 29th we marched to in front of Williamsport, crossed the cavalry and Doles Brigade of infantry. Set men at destroying the canal. The whole expedition amounts to nothing more than a grand plundering expedition, in which Mr. Rodes displayed his great proclivity for appropriating everything to the exclusion of everyone else. During the afternoon everybody gave themselves up to drinking whiskey, and in consequence everyone, from General officers down, got exceeding[ly] merry. We marched at dawn on the 30th back to Martinsburg without any further molestation, and continued the march to Bunker Hill on the 31st getting into camp between 10 and 11 oclock in the morning.

Have been reading a small work edited by Col. Frank Shaler [Schaller,] 22nd Mississippi Regt., called "Spirit of Military Institutions" [by Auguste Frederic Marmont]. . .[8]

July 31st March from near Martinsburg at early dawn towards Bunker Hill, getting into camp between 10–11 oclock. From this until the *3rd August* nothing of any moment occurred with this command. Rumour asserts that the enemy have taken two corps from Richmond—the 6th and 8th—and deflected the 19th, one corps assigned to the defences of Washington and two to the defence of Harpers Ferry and the passes of the South Mountain. No troops of the enemy are said to be on the south side of the Potomac.[9]

From Richmond news comes of the blowing up of a mine [known as "The Crater"] under Pegram's Battery, an entry of the enemy into the defences of Petersburg, but also of their speedy expulsion with considerable loss to both us and them. Be this as it may, it has developed that the enemy have been and are willing to mine and will put our glorious Engineer Department to their trumps regarding such operations. Would much like to see them engaged in the beauty of not knowing what to do with a Yankee mine. Am sure that they know nothing of such operations.[10]

Mahone is also said to have flanked a portion of Grant's command, killed and wounded about 500, and captured about 800 privates, 73 com[d] officers and one Brig. Gen. [I don't] know how much truth there is in it. Hope it may be so, and that the enemy have been severely punished. Dame Rumour also speaks of an armistice of 60 days having been agreed upon, in which case I think peace may be looked for upon our own terms.

August 4th March this morning at 4 A.M. in the direction of Martinsburg and camp at about 12 M. at Haynesville, 15 miles from our point of starting. I see that in looking over yesterdays writing that I forgot to mention the burning of Chambersburg, Pa. by our forces under [John] McCausland, for noncompliance of a military requisition of 100.000 [100,000] in gold or 500.000 [500,000] in greenbacks. About 350 houses were burned in the heart of the city and some 3000 people put out of doors. In all probability they thought it was an idle threat on our part and that their money might be saved. Am sorry to say that this course of proceeding is the most harsh and renders the carrying on of the war much more inhuman and unpleasant. Believe it however, to be the right policy, and am therefore glad to see that we have one man among us who has the nerve and heart to retaliate for the atrocious vandalism of the enemy in our own country.[11]

Richmond papers say that about 20.000 [20,000] men have left Grant's army for Washington. If this be so, Richmond is probably safe from any future assaults of a great character this summer. The investment may continue until fall but somewhat in the character of Charleston and not amount to much. Lee's army—at least the bulk of it—will then probably be transferred to this section of the country and another invasion of Pa. attempted. The Rocking-ham Prophet may then have a chance of seeing his prophecy verified. I believe we are merely the forerunners of the main bulk of the Confederate forces. A few days will show what is out and it will either result in a big fight or a foot race. Which shall it be?

August 5th Marched this morning from Haynesville, cross the Potomac at Wil-liamsport and after seizing some more whiskey march on towards Downsville, and camp at St. James College. The President [the Reverend Dr. John B. Ker-foot] and another gentleman connected with the institution met us, and after some little palaver invited us in to quite a substantial dinner. Soon after din-ner I went to Hagerstown to make some few purchases for the General. Again met a young lady friend of last summer, who recognizing me, was most kind and attentive. Indeed a few more visits and I dont know what might become of the heart of the Subscriber, if he had any. I spent a most pleasant afternoon and evening and came away with a solemn promise resting on me to return next day[;] am withal rather blue. Got to camp about 11 oclock.[12]

August 6th March today about 10 oclock, after arresting said two gentlemen of the institution as hostages for Dr. [Andrew H. H.] Boyd and another clericus, but release them again on parole to see after Dr. Boyd and procure his release. We march back again to Williamsport, cross and camp near the Big Spring and Hammonds Mill on the Back road to Martinsburg. My little Hagerstown friend is running through my head to an alarming extent, and I cannot quite understand it. I acknowledge myself much demoralized by said visit and little piece of calico. She did look mighty sweet and her little hand was so soft and kind, and rested very affectionately in mine. Bad things these Mr. H.[13]

August 7th March this morning and camp at our former camp at Bunker Hill. Nothing of moment occurred. Hear of General [Alfred] Iverson having cap-tured Maj. Genl. [George] Stoneman, 1000 prisoners and 9 pieces of arty. A very good thing for the good health of Mr. Stoneman if true. It appears that Stoneman with a body of the enemys cavalry made a raid on Macon, was pitched into, defeated and captured by Iverson, who seems to have come out with flying colours on this occasion.[14]

Hagerstown has ruined me I am much afraid. Dreamt last night of my little friend, and she said many kind and pleasant things to me. Would much rather have gone into Hagerstown than march to Williamsport. Will keep her in mind and good remembrance however, until another time and another meeting. How comes it that our female friends on the other side of the river [Maryland] seem so much more friendly and sincere, and a kind look and smile go so much more further than when coming from those on this side? Is it the contrast between the two classes of people which strikes us so forcibly, or the bright, hopeful and joyful faces of our friends look so much more to our hearts than those of the Union people.

God help the poor people of Maryland. Those of the South will never perhaps fully understand the trials and tortures of our friends north of the Potomac, until long, long after the war. Watched, spyed [upon] and followed even to the innermost recesses of their homes, they are compelled always to look out for some serpent that has crept in perhaps unawares. Much could be said here to show how matters and things stand there which it would be improper to write—for fear of others reading what is here written.[15]

All I may be permitted to say here is God bless our good loyal and true friends in Maryland, and to pray to take them under his good and gracious protection and safe guard. Should I live, I would desire to embody in a popular work, and which at the same time would be an accession to the military library of an officer, the opinions &c as gathered from this war . . .

August 13th March the 9th to Winchester and expect to meet some of Averill's cavalry pursuing Bradley Johnson. Camp our three Brigades on the roads covering Pughton, Romney and Cedar Creek. Nothing further of moment. On the *10th* about 4 P.M. received orders to move at once to reinforce Rodes who was reported to be pressed by the enemy near Stevensons Depot. March down in a hurry to find it much of a hoax, proceed to camp near the place of our unfortunate fight, and move from thence again to Winchester and on the pikes leading from Winchester to Millwood and Front Royal.

On the *11th* skirmish with the enemy's cavalry on the Millwood road and march to near Newtown and camp for the night. All the troops in the command in line of battle.

March on the *12th* to Strasburg and first are placed in reserve, but subsequently are placed in line of battle fronting towards Winchester. Late in the afternoon am sent off with Johnston's Brigade on the Wardensville road, but move from thence at dark towards Strasburg and camp for the night on Fishers Hill.

On the *13ᵗʰ* form our lines at daylight and proceed to entrench. The movements of the enemy decidedly indicated that he had been strongly reinforced and assumed the offensive by attempting to flank us. The country not allowing us to hold it successfully, we were compelled to fall back to this place, with a strong probability of a still further backward movement.

[Lieutenant Gen. Richard] Anderson (Dick) with a Division of infantry and some cavalry was at Culpeper Co. Ho. on the 8ᵗʰ and was sent to watch the movements of some enemys said to be moving from Washington along the Orange and Alexandria Rail Road. Since then nothing but rumours have come to us—nothing certain.[16]

In the meantime comes authentic accounts of McCausland's raiding party. It appears that after burning Chambersburg Pa. the command retired towards McConnellsburg thence to Cumberland, Hancock, crossing the Potomac at Old Town. At all of these places fights occurred, of more or less magnitude. So far so well. After crossing the Potomac, the command moved to Romney and while encamped near there, was surprised. About 250–275 men and 500 horses were captured by the enemy, besides all the artillery wagons of the command. Since then the commands have all reached our lines. Saw Col. Wᵐ L. Jackson [commanding the 19th Virginia Cavalry]—surnamed Mudwall—today and had quite a chat with him about old times. Asked most affectionately after Bier. Nothing more at time of writing which is on our lines.[17]

August 15ᵗʰ Yesterday morning the enemy left our front and retired to the north side of Cedar Creek and encamped. Our Divⁿ skirmishers with Hokes Brigade—and Smith's Brigade from Wharton's Division and sharpshooters from Grimes Brigade, Rodes Division—were advanced and skirmished slightly with the enemy. All returned to our entrenchments at night. Report says that Fitz Lee had a fight at or near Front Royal with Sheridan's cavalry in which the enemy got smashed and may account for their retiring from our front. Again from the west comes a rumour of a fight at Atlanta—Hood and Kirby Smith wounded, Marmaduke killed, enemy beaten. Nothing more from Mobile save the blowing up of one fort and the shameful and cowardly surrender of another—a third was evacuated, thus leaving the entrance to Mobile almost open.[18]

On the *15ᵗʰ* remain quietly in camp until about 2 P.M. when Pegram's Brigade and our sharpshooters were ordered to report to Genl. Gordon, who with one Brigade from his Divⁿ moved on the enemy, pushed them through Strasburg and past Hupps Hill on the north side of the town. Webb was unfortunately badly, if not mortally, wounded and left in town. Thus goes another good man. Our troops withdrew about sundown and went into camp. All quiet again. Anderson is reported to be at or near Front Royal with two Div^n of infantry and one of cavalry.

August 16th Remain contrary to expectations quietly in camp, the enemy still in our front. No customary reconnaissance made today, from which I judge that Gen. Early must have some positive information regarding them.

August 17th Enemy reported to have left the vicinity of Cedar Creek last night. The whole army is put in motion down the Valley Pike towards Winchester. Gordon in the lead and Rodes bringing up the rear. The enemy in retreating set fire to several barns and burnt much wheat. They told the people that the only way to keep us out of the lower Valley was to render it impossible for us to subsist. They behaved in a most shameful manner to the citizens, hanging a member of the 54th N.C. as a spy at Middletown. Of course he was none such.[19]

Upon nearing Kernstown the command is halted and soon after moves down to Rudes Hill near Winchester. Find the enemy in position near the Winchester fortifications. [Gabriel C.] Wharton's Div^n advanced on them from the Romney side, Gordon from the Valley Pike and our skirmishers at right angles to both. The enemy were dislodged after a spirited resistance by some cavalry and a portion (two brigades) of the 6th Corps. Capture in all about 350 prisoners, loss to them in killed and wounded about 200 — our loss about 150. Camp for the night near Kernstown.

August 18th March this morning about 9 A.M. through considerable rain to near our fighting ground of the 20th of last month and camp about in the same position as formerly. Had quite a talk with Bradley Johnston. Enemy reported to be in line awaiting us from Berryville to Smithfield. The much talked of reinforcements under Anderson and Fitz Lee are at last here. Hampton with another Division of cavalry reported authentically on the other side of the mountains, with Fields (Hoods old) Division of infantry following.

It seems determined to transfer the theatre of the war from Richmond and suppose the attempt will succeed, though cannot give much promise as to the result of it. Anderson comes over merely as a "cooperating column" from which I argue that Beauregard will be left in command at Richmond and Gen. Lee will come up here.

A portion of Sheridan's Cavalry under Custar [Brigadier General George A.

Custer], pitched into Wickhams Cavalry Brigade and after whipping it out, pitched into two Regiments of infantry, [the latter] routing them and capturing some 5000 prisoners. Truly a good beginning for Anderson. The infantry was from Woffords Brigade. Enemy behaved better than usual in Winchester, which does not promise much for another occupation by them, which I presume they will have in a short time. All supplies for our Army have been exhausted in the lower Valley by both parties.[20]

16. A Game of Bluff

August 19, 1864–September 5, 1864

The Yankee army of the Potomac deserves a great deal of credit for its
behavior during the past summer.... If they were fighting in another cause
the effusion of blood might bring tears into ones eyes, but not so now.

—Oscar Hinrichs

August 19th March this morning at light to Bunker Hill and camp. Before
marching from our camp, the valiant cavalry came in and reported the enemy
advancing about an hour before day. Quite a stir was made about the camps,
but it turned out [to be] nothing. We arrived at Bunker Hill about 2 oclock and
after placing our pickets and eating a sort of dinner, went to sleep. Our Div^n
in the lead, Breckinridge bringing up the rear. What a game of bluff Jubal is
playing; it is astonishing how the Yankees allow themselves to be fooled and
trifled with in this manner.[1]

Aug. 20th Slept till quite late this morning, but soon after was stirred out by
Col. Lee's pickets firing rather too heavy for good luck. [Ramseur] got the Div^n
under weigh and moved down to nearly Smithfield without seeing much, and
thus returned to camp at Bunker Hill. It seems as if a raining spell has set in
now, it raining now for several days at intervals. Rumours come of another
big fight at Petersburg resulting as usual in the repulse of the Yankee attack.
Our loss said to be 5000 killed and wounded and 1000 prisoners. Yankee loss
much heavier than on any previous fight. Hancock it appears got his corps on
Transports, sailed down the river, and returned on the 17th and participated
in the attack. They were repulsed with immense slaughter after breaking our
centre three times during the course of the day.[2]

Grant is much of the Bull dog and has his tenacity of purpose in fighting us.
Hope from this last experiment, if true, that he is throwing away both time,

money and men to no purpose. I wish they would all of them quit this business and let us alone.

Some may consider fighting fun, but I am somewhat like that Georgian who on seeing a rabbit run between two lines of battle, gave vent to his pent up feelings by saying "Go it Molly Cottontail, if I had as little character at home as you have to save, I should be found keeping you company."[3]

Anderson is now with us and I am wondering what good he will do us now that he is here. His Corps is proverbially as slow as a snail, and dont think the Richmond and Petersburg trenches have improved his locomotive qualities much if any. Camped in an old deserted house with the windows out, fireplace open and no doors. Some person entering this morning asked whose hospital this was.

Aug. 21st [Aug. 20th] Remained quietly in camp during the balance of the day, it continuing to rain heavily at intervals. About dusk received orders to move at daylight or sunrise tomorrow morning.[4]

Aug. 22nd [Aug. 21st] Ordered the Div^n to march as indicated yesterday and move on the road towards Smithfield. Rodes leading and Breckinridge coming up in rear. In crossing the Opequon, Rodes had a little skirmish, loosing some 3 or 4 men killed and wounded. We soon took the Charlestown road, and continued to advance cautiously until we came [to Cameron Depot] within 3 miles of Charlestown, when we struck the enemy. Skirmishers were soon thrown out from both Rodes and our Div^n, who soon engaged the Yanks. Skirmishing was kept up until quite dark. Had quite late riding . . . while everything was quiet.[5]

Enemy seem to be willing to dispute our further advance and Early seems equally disposed to fight them. The enemy are supposed to number about 35 thousand men of all arms. Anderson and Fitz Lee engaged the enemy [at Summit Point] between us and Berryville and appear to have driven them. Enemy strongly entrenched. Our trains were left behind at Bunker Hill, and soon after our leaving took to the woods and mountains. They were ordered up at a late hour of the night. The enemy seem to be rather fearful and should not be much surprised if they left in the morning.[6]

Aug. 23rd [Aug. 22nd] At light this morning finding no response to our firing, ordered the skirmishers forward, and found that the enemy had abandoned two lines of entrenchments and retreated towards Harpers Ferry. Came up with their cavalry rearguard about a mile from Charlestown, and drove them without much difficulty through the town and on towards the Ferry—to a

Henry Kyd Douglas shortly after the close of the war (From Douglas, *I Rode with Stonewall* [Chapel Hill: University of North Carolina Press, 1940])

point about 1½ miles from town. Our Div[n] soon after came up and about 1 oclock went into camp on the Smithfield pike 1½ miles from town. Anderson came up during the day and Fields [Maj. Gen. Charles W. Field] is said to have reached us also. Towards the evening Douglass was sent out by Gen. Early with [Brig. Gen. Archibald C.] Godwin's Brigade on the road leading to _____ Ferry on the Shenandoah, to make a reconnaissance and find out how the enemy stand. Came near getting into a snap, lost some 4 or 5 men wounded and prisoners. Head Quarters established at a Mrs Briscoe's.[7]

_____

Aug. 24th [Aug. 23rd] Rode out early this morning, everything appearing quiet, in search of a swordbelt, but got none. On my return from Wickhams Cavalry Brigade stopped at Mr Kennedy's and saw the Ladies. Promised to come back, but dont know whether it can be done or not. Good and kind people. Return to camp and keep quiet.

Aug. 25th [Aug. 24th] We are turned out tolerably early this morning and march through Charlestown in search of the enemy who were reported advancing on us. Turns out however, that it is nothing more than a Demonstration of some cavalry upon our skirmishers. They caught a few and killed a few of the 58th Va. It raised quite a hubbub. We slept in rear of our troops near the Episcopal Church.[8]

Aug. 26th [Aug. 25th] Ordered to be ready to move at sunrise this morning. Rodes and our Divn to be relieved from the front by Gen [Joseph B.] Kershaw of Anderson's command. Kershaw came up about four hours behind time as was to be expected, and we move off towards Sheppardstown. On nearing Kearneysville run foul of two Divisions of Cavalry just starting out on a big raid. Gordon who was in front was pretty heavily engaged. Whartons skirmishers were charged by their cavalry and some of them also picked up and hurt. The cavalry gets the worst of it and soon leaves the troops, following them up however, as fast as possible. Later in the day and towards evening got among them again in which fight Col. [William] Monaghan of Hays La. Brig. was killed, Col. [Robert W.] Withers of 42 Va wounded. Col. W. L. Jackson was accidentally wounded by his pistol going off. Gordon was slightly wounded in the head. We got into camp about ten oclock near Mr Schleys place about 3 miles from Sheppardstown.[9]

Aug. 27th [Aug. 26th] March this morning about 12 oclock towards Smithfield and camp near there. Nothing of importance during the day. Quite heavy firing was heard during the morning towards Whitepost and late in the day towards Charlestown. Have heard nothing from it.

Aug. 30th Quietly in camp today at Bunker Hill with nothing of any importance occurring during the day, save that everybody is lazing around loose sleeping and keeping as quiet as possible. Yesterday [August 29] we were stirred out very unceremoniously by an advance of the enemy's cavalry [under command of Brig. Gen. Wesley Merritt] on the Smithfield road. Our Division [Ramseur's] was immediately advanced and commenced skirmishing with the enemy near the Opequon [at Smithfield Crossing], driving in their skirmishers towards and across the river. Gordon's Division subsequently joined us on the right and soon both Divn crossed the river driving the enemy gradually towards Charlestown. After pressing them about 2½ miles beyond the town the troops returned to camp. The enemy soon after occupied the lost ground up to the Opequon. This morning their cavalry fell back to beyond Smithfield, our cavalry occupying the ground. The cavalry also made a demonstration on the Martinsburg road in front of Rodes Division, but it amounted to nothing. Our loss yesterday in both Gordon's and our Div^n will amount to some 40–50 men killed and wounded; that of the enemy certainly to [be] equally as much if not more. But few prisoners were taken—we loosing none that I have learned.[10]

On the 28th [27th] we marched from Smithfield about noon and camp at the old deserted house at Bunker Hill. Another fight has taken place at Richmond (26th) [25th], in which A. P. Hill with three N.C. Brigades made an attack on Grant's extreme left, capturing 2[000]–3000 prisoners among whom Brig. Gen. Spears, 9 pieces of artillery and some colours; also driving them from a series of earthworks. Grant must evidently be playing out here soon.[11]

Yesterday the Democratic Convention met at Chicago, and various are the surmises made here as to who will be the successful nominee of the political scoundrels assembled there.[12]

Aug. 31st Rodes was this morning directed to proceed to Martinsburg and drive the enemy's cavalry away who were becoming troublesome to our pickets. Our Div^n was ordered to support him if found necessary. Not hearing anything from him however, presume that he succeeded without any assistance from us. He brought out with him two young ladies recently from Philadelphia, relations of General [John] Pegram.[13]

On the 1st September everything remained quiet, and all hands remained in camp at Bunker Hill. The weather is now growing quite cold and unpleasant at night, and I am beginning to feel the want of the underclothing stolen from me at Martinsburg. I wish the devil had those who are wearing them now.

Received a letter from Chris and Till which is the first since the fight at the Wilderness in May last. Brings some rather astonishing intelligence—namely the departure of Chris for New York. Am much displeased with him for acting thus against my wishes. Have no doubt but that he was in a very great measure led into it and sustained by his Grandparents. Wrote to Till at once, and am afraid the poor thing may feel hurt at what I said regarding the matter.[14]

Rumours come from Yankeedom of the nomination of [ex-president Franklin] Pierce and [former Whig nominee John] Bell, then the withdrawal of Pierce and the substitution of [former general in chief George] McClellan in place of Pierce. Then comes another rumor of McClung [Alexander C. McClurg] and [James] Guthrie with a six months armistice, reconstruction of the Union &^{c} &^{c} which if all these rumours comes anywhere near the truth, no one can pretend to say. This much however is I think pretty certain, that none of these people will be elected. Reconstruction under no manner of terms. This the north will concede to be impossible and the independence of the Confederacy will be an established fact. It makes but little difference to me which is nominated and elected, be it Lincoln, Little Mac, Pierce and who not, as long as they will unite on terms of peace. What becomes in the future of the north I care not one whit. Let us alone here—to make cotton and rice, and no cares here.[15]

No news further from Richmond. Everything appears quiet again there, preparing possibly for another slaughter. The Yankee army of the Potomac deserves a great deal of credit for its behavior during the past summer. Beaten, cuffed and slaughtered like sheep, they nevertheless have come up each time to the notch when called upon. If they were fighting in another cause the effusion of blood might bring tears into ones eyes, but not so now. Built up of the rakings and scrapings of Christendom, it is much better that they are killed and left to fatten the worn out lands of Virginia. Had a valuation of horses yesterday which seems to be the enactment of another farce—for no one will ever be paid for their loss of them should such ever happen. Damn such foolishness. What next?

Sept. 2nd March this A.M. on a fools errand towards Summit Point—a depot on the Winchester and Harpers Ferry Rail Road, but after getting within a couple of miles of the place, turned back and camped on the Jordan Springs road, about a mile from the Winchester and Martinsburg pike. Gordon leading the column and our Division bringing up the rear. Rodes was left behind on the pike to guard the trains. It was very well that such was the case, for Averill with about 4000 cavalry pitched into our cavalry on the Smithfield road, who gradually fell back fighting to Bunker Hill, and finding our infantry gone, ran like thunder. Bradley Johnson who was guarding the Back road lost all his wagons by the operation, together with the wagons of Braxtons Battalion of artillery and divers other wagons. The main body of the enemy's cavalry started towards Whitepost and Newtown, but Early put small confidence in the report.[16]

On the 3rd our Divⁿ is started down the road to Charlestown to meet a reported advance of some cavalry, which turned out to be [Col. Henry A.] Cole's Mᵈ Battalion some 200 strong. We drove them across the Opequon without much difficulty and return to our camp of last night. The enemy's cavalry are now reported to be on a raid, and great activity is observed among our cavalry to stop them. Fitz Lee and Lomax put after them with a great chance in their favor. Just a little before dark the enemy's infantry pitched into Anderson near Berryville, and got soundly thrashed for their trouble. Anderson makes a handsome fight of it. Gordon is started down to support him after night. It was the intention of moving down to Bunker Hill again by the whole command, but the movements detailed above altered things very much and changed the programme. We shall move down to Berryville in the morning—and if the enemy are so very anxious for a fight, they can doubtless be accommodated.[17]

On the 4th we march as anticipated last night and contrary to expectation still find them in the neighborhood of the fight of last night. Our Divn is put on the left of Anderson—Wharton, Rodes on the right. Gordon is left at Winchester to march things from thence. We skirmish with the enemy all day. Wharton and Rodes towards 2 P.M. start out on a flank movement, but do not do anything. They both return to their original positions at dark. Had quite a ride reconnoitering. We camp in rear of our lines. Weather rainy and unpleasant. Prisoners say that the fall of Atlanta was officially announced to them, [Lt. Gen. William J.] Hardee killed and various other little pleasantries of a like nature. McClellan and [George] Pendleton of Ohio are the nominees of the Chicago convention.[18]

Sept. 5th Today was quite a lively one, and one which may be set down on which an anomaly in the history of modern warfare was successfully accomplished. It had been decided late yesterday afternoon that it would be best for us to retire, inasmuch as nothing could be accomplished beyond bringing the troops into a difficulty from which they might not easily be extracted. Accordingly orders were issued to be ready to move at an early hour, and Anderson commanded to withdraw his troops and skirmishers about 7 A.M. Our Divn was moved across the Winchester and Berryville Pike, our skirmishers following us to our new position. This gave rise to quite a lively picket firing—the enemy having reinforced their lines during the night and morning, and showing an evident disposition to molest us, if anything was attempted. However, the change was successfully accomplished—heavy firing continually being kept up on our right and in Whartons front.[19]

About 12 oclock Whartons and our Division filed off into the road leading to Winchester—Rodes leading the column—we bringing up the rear. No cavalry being on hand the entire rear was composed of nothing but a strong skirmish line. In this manner our march progressed without interruption, the enemy only following us a short distance, probably only to see what we were doing. Fitz Lee having been directed late yesterday to return to this command, camped last night a little to the northward of Winchester. Our progress was interrupted however, when nearing an old camping ground of a few days since, by the appearance of a large body of the enemys cavalry, said to be Averill with two Divisions of cav. who had pitched into Lomax cavalry composed of Johnsons, Vaughans and Jacksons Brigades and was soundly thrashing them when Rodes came up, whereupon they hurriedly retired. Firing was kept up at till a late hour during the night.[20]

It is highly probable that [with] Fitz Lee having headed off the raiding party near Newtown, the enemy concluded, inasmuch as we were down near Berryville, they would just walk around the left flank of the army and go on with their "rat killing." How this was frustrated has been detailed. Late in the afternoon it commenced raining, and rained like the devil nearly all night. Our quarters were in an old house near Stevensons depot on the old Winchester and Harpers Ferry Rail Road. We made out quite comfortably considering the condition of things.

An unpleasant rumour comes to us of the fall of Atlanta through northern journals, which bear a considerable impression of truthfulness. Should this prove correct, it will place the Southern Confederacy in an unpleasant predicament and probably lead to the capture of Mobile. It is to be hoped however, that it is nothing but a grand lie, gotten up for the benefit of the Chicago Convention—and which if true, it is hoped will considerably change the peace prospects on all hands. "Never say die" is an old and very good adage, and a very good one and one which ought to be borne up manfully now. All hands here are much depressed by this rumoured intelligence, but a good drink of whiskey last night dispelled much of it, which depression was probably owing to an empty stomack and nothing to eat save a piece of a sour green apple, and mighty little at that.

We most cordially congratulated ourselves on getting away from Berryville as well as we did, and give old Jubalee the credit for a vast amount of impudence and presumption. Never perhaps was a withdrawal accomplished in broad daylight under such circumstances. It certainly never entered the heads of the enemy that we would attempt any such foolhardy movement, and really intend carrying it out. It was done nevertheless. Bully for old Sneak Jubalee.

17. Calamity and Defeat

September 6, 1864–September 17, 1864

I do hope this struggle will assume some definite shape during the next two months one way or the other. I am much tired of war and its scenes of slaughter and bloodshed. I wish it would stop.

—Oscar Hinrichs

Sept. 6th Rainy, disagreeable weather all day today and for a wonder have not heard of any rumours of a move or anything else. Remain amiably cooped up in our house like so many pigs in a stye, for our house appears to be nothing more or less upon a close inspection by daylight. Last evening it was however a perfect godsend to have it, otherwise the court would have had quite an uncomfortable nights rest. Got up this morning at a more seasonable reasonable hour than usual, eat my piece of bread and meat, and kind of thanked the Lord to be able to do so.

Wonder what so much rain is now falling for—no crops in the ground, and would much prefer good weather to bad; it makes everybody feel and act so dull. Am not in the best humour imaginable and would much rather be able to sit down to a game of whist with its accompaniment of hot whiskey toddy than anything else. Have read the papers over and over again, even to the advertisements; played our game of chess—the first of the season, and want to play another but cant get anyone to play with. So wags the world allways wanting what we cannot have or get.

Sept. 7th After various rumours of the enemy advancing in a thousand and one directions, our Div^n remained quietly in camp during the day. Our Head Quarters were shifted a few hundred yards into a piece of an orchard and there we remained quiet. The enemys cavalry made demonstration along our front (of the army) but it all amounted to nothing. Gordon who was camped near Winchester caused Terry's Brigade to move out on the Berryville road and drove a few skirmishers supported by a few companies of cavalry back from whence they came.

Another heavy advance was reported to Gen Anderson who moved his division out to repel their attack, and found that the skirmish line of a mile in length reported to him consisted of thirty men who had crossed the Opequon and their two lines of battle to be five squadrons of cavalry. At Brucetown the cavalry pickets were driven in but our lines where subsequently reestablished everywhere.

We have now authentic advices from Atlanta which go to show that Hood was compelled to evacuate the place on the first of the month with severe loss in Hardee's Corps. He was completely outgeneraled by Sherman. Although a great misfortune to us, it is not irreparable and can with proper management be made good again. It is only bad inasmuch as it will stimulate the war feeling at the north and thus lead to a prolongation of the struggle. It is a sad occurrence.[1]

I went over to Corps Hd. Qrs. and spent quite a pleasant evening, the first for many a long day. Birdhunting seems to be quite the rage among a certain class of men, and not satisfied with the thunder of guns during an engagement, seem to be most anxious to prolong the sound of bursting villainous saltpeter. Success to their undertaking. I only wish I could enter into the spirit of the thing and enjoy myself as much as they do. I feel most uncomfortably lonely and desolate. Bound up within myself, am much afraid that I shall run into excesses should the opportunity offer. How much would I not give for a visit home, even for a short time, to hear and see them all once more.

Fool that I was for entering the service I did, when in all probability I might have kept clear of it altogether by proper management. Still I have nothing to blame myself with—a plighted [solemnly pledged] promise so to do could not be disregarded and lightly cast aside and here I am. Whether anything is to be gained by it by now is altogether another question and one which time alone can decide. God help me—I am here alone.

Sept. 8th Rainy and disagreeable this morning. Went out with Capt. [Don P.] Halsey and the General shooting partridges. Not that I did any shooting myself but went to see them shoot. In the afternoon went with the General [Ramseur] and Russel to Winchester and visited little [Randolph] Ridgely. Was very glad to see him getting on so finely and nicely. Indeed the people of the Valley when true to us and our cause, are true indeed, and to their honour be it said few of them are not so. Met also with a most pleasant Lady in [the company of] his mother who has come up to see him. Was much pleased with her and young Miss Kate Conrad, the kind nurse of Ridgely.[2]

A very pleasant rumour comes from the West to the effect that Hood has had a fight with Sherman at Lovejoy Station, in which our army was victorious and Atlanta retaken. Regarding the fight it seems probable enough that it has occurred and from what I know of Hood personally, I believe that if anyone is able to make the Western Army fight, he can do it. That he is personally brave all who know him know, and if his Army is in any kind of condition, victory is pretty certain and sure. Atlanta however, is another question altogether and his part of it may not prove true. Should Sherman have been driven out of the place with a severe defeat, peace will be an allmost dead certainty. God grant we may not be mistaken in our calculations, and be able to maintain ourselves until after the November elections. Can Lincoln be defeated is a question asked everyday, but without any tangible answer being given. The most powerful argument that can be made use of against him will be the success attending our armies in the field. Lee, Hood and Early have the whole business in their own hands, and may the good Lord in his kindness grant they may succeed.[3]

Sept. 9th Fair, clear and pleasant today after the terrible weather of yesterday. Nothing new of importance occurred save the General [Ramseur] and Halsey again went out and got a few birds from which we shall have a grand Supper tonight. About dark orders came to move at sunrise tomorrow in the direction of Bunker Hill.

Sept. 10th We march this morning as indicated yesterday through a terrible rain to Bunker Hill. Our Cavalry preceeded the infantry column and soon came upon the enemy who were speedily driven from all their positions to Martinsburg and through the town. Rodes Division preceeded our Div[n] and followed them up to near Martinsburg. Vaughans Cavalry Brigade behaved very handsomely to the enemy, sending their best compliments in the most approved style. While Rodes was moving down the pike, our Division lay quiet on the roadside at Bunker Hill waiting for orders what to do, and remained there until near night when we went to our old camps. After supper went up to Corps Hd. Qrs. and spent a pleasant evening. About 11 oclock receive orders to be ready to move at sunrise tomorrow.[4]

Sept. 11th March this morning after many delays back to Stephensons Depot on the Winchester and Harpers Ferry Rail Road. Our Div[n] leading and Rodes

John Pegram (Courtesy of the Virginia Historical Society)

bringing up the rear. It rains during the day in occasional showers making roads and ground generally heavy. No further news of any importance.

Dr. [Andrew H. H.] Boyd of Winchester returned from a long captivity yesterday and gives quite an interesting account of his stay at the north. He regards the election of McClellan as allmost certain but says the prosecution of the war will be the probable upshot of the whole business. Grant demands another 100.000 [100,000] more men, with which he says he can now capture Richmond. An addition of such magnitude will undoubtedly give Lee much trouble to manage, but another accession to our forces may still preserve us from calamity and defeat.[5]

Overheard quite an interesting conversation of [John] Pegram and Ramseur regarding Lee and the catastrophy of Rappahannock Station last fall. Pegram says Lee blundered considerably, and that the attack was most beautifully planned and managed by Sedgewick. Have my own private opinion regarding that affair—and blame all concerned in it, save those who fought it. Early and Ewell have their share to carry also but not in the same proportion. It was a sorry affair, costing us over 2000 men whom we could not well spare.[6]

Have had the blues now for nearly a week and am thinking much of home. Chris gives me much uneasyness and wish I could hear from him or from Till whether he got through safe. Would much like to pay them all a visit this winter, but see but a small prospect for anything like Winter quarters for this command. Remaining in the Valley as we probably will do, we shall be trotting after the Yankee cavalry continually and keep us in a constant state of mobility with little rest. I do hope this struggle will assume some definite shape during the next two months one way or the other. I am much tired of war and its scenes of slaughter and bloodshed. I wish it would stop.[7]

Sept. 12th Remained quietly in camp during the day without any news of any sort occurring that I know of.

Sept. 13th About noon today orders came to send a Brigade out on a road leading towards Charlestown and observe whether the enemy were making any demonstrations on our position, which judging from the firing they seemed disposed to do. It appears that their cavalry came up and crossed the Opequon at the point of crossing of the Harpers Ferry and Winchester Rail Road and also on the Berryville Road, where they ran into the cavalry pickets of Bradley Johnson, bounced Andersons infantry picket and captured about five companies of Andersons South Carolinians.

Their advance on the Charlestown road did not amount to much, they not crossing the creek at this point. Their skirmish line ran from the Rail Road Crossing across the Opequon to a point opposite the ford on the Charlestown road and about half a mile off. It was supported by a battery of five pieces on or near the Charlestown road, and another battery near the Rail Road Crossing.

Carpenters Battery went into position on the left of the Charlestown road and soon drove both yankee batteries from their first position without much difficulty and less loss. The battery near the Charlestown road moved however into a second position from which they continued firing—Carpenter losing about eight men killed and wounded by the operation. One prisoner was captured by our skirmishers. I forgot to mention that Johnsons Brigade moved down first and that subsequently both the other Brigades of Godwin and Pegram moved down also. These were the only troops brought out that I am aware of.[8]

On returning to camp found a visitor to Dr. [Samuel B.] Morrison—a Dr. Tanner, Chief Surgeon of Hoke's Div[n]—who gave quite an interesting narrative of operations in front of Petersburg since our leaving and makes the situation much more pleasant for us than anticipated. The health of the Army steadily improving and its strength augmenting, with full bellies and good spirits. Anderson is said to be on the march towards Richmond again, and I should not much wonder if some of our troops did not move down that way also pretty soon. If it will give any chance for a quiet Winter quarters I should not much care if we did go down and could stand perhaps the amount of trouble and disagreeable [conditions] though if the same can be had here, I should much prefer remaining here. However what is to be will be and nothing I can do will either alter or prevent any occurrence.[9]

Orders were left last night to be ready to move at daylight tomorrow morning, but judging from the movements of the enemy, I shall be much surprised if we move at all, or at least until late in the day; and as the weather appears to be threatening rain again, believe that the enemy are as little inclined to get a ducking as we are. However things are very uncertain, and nothing more so than Old Juballee, or Sneak as he has now been christened by the enemy.

Saw Bradley Johnson today for a few moments and listened to quite an argument pro and con for and against McClellans chances of election and its probable results. What is to become of us should he be elected, is a question much more readily asked than answered. If an armistice be agreed upon as [it likely] will be, should his election be made sure, it will in all probability be fritt[er]ed away in useless squabbles and contentions among our politicians instead of arming and preparing for another struggle, which if it does take place will be more bloody and sanguinary than any heretofore.

And should that be the case, the Southern Confed may as well give up, for McClellan, being possessed of the most consummate tact and military knowledge, will not move in the matter until he be fully prepared to do so; and when he does, it will be so as to tax the utmost abilities of our Southern generals, and it may not be amiss to keep an eye to windward and look out for a passage elsewhere.

Sept. 14th Remain quietly in camp today, it raining allmost cats, dogs and pitchforks. Weather therefore abominable and with leaky tents can be very easly imagined how much we enjoyed ourselves during the day. Nothing of any moment occurred to vary the monotony of the day. Wrote a letter to Till today which I hope may dispel any unpleasant feelings occasioned by my last.

Sept. 15th March this morning at sunrise to Winchester in obedience to orders received during the night to supply Kershaws place who goes probably to Richmond. Weather cool but clear and we make the trip in a short time. Anderson it appears has been ready to move for some days back, but owing to the presence and movements of the enemy did not move until this morning. I presume he is much disgusted by the kind and affectionate manners and attentions paid him by our northern bretheren, and has been long desirous of quitting us. Be that as it may.[10]

On the 13th the enemy drove in Bradley Johnsons cavalry pickets on the Berryville road and pushing on captured some seventy or eighty men of the 8th South Carolinians. They behaved in the most cowardly manner—giving themselves up without any cause whatsoever. Anderson is a good officer if he can be stirred and moved in time to do anything, but that whole teaparty is so very slow that it is surprising they ever come in time to do anything. He has managed to loose [lose] in his last and bungling manner of picketing some five to six hundred men for which there is no necessity. Early says that he wishes that they had all been captured for what good they have done us, and I do not think him far from wrong.[11]

We arrived in Winchester in due time and proceeded to put out our pickets in place of Andersons, who had gone glimmering. Johnson's Brigade was put on the Berryville road—Godwin on the Millwood road and Pegram on a road intermediate between the two others. A little after noon I rode into town—saw [Lt. Richard K.] Dick Meade—Aid to Gen. Taliaferro—Howell Brown and a whole lot of others. Nothing further occurred during the day.[12]

Have had the blues now for over a week and do really feel miserable on general principles. Would much like to see Ridgely but have nothing decent to wear in the presence of ladies—and dont care much to see them as it would only tend to increase my malady of heart and head. How much would I not give to be at home and see them all again—and allmost envy Chris being with them.

Saw a piece of poetry by a Lady of New Orleans on Maj. Wheats death at Gaines Mill, June 27. 1862, marked "Bury me on the field, Boys" [see appendix 2].

Sept. 16th Remain quietly in camp today without so much as a common grapevine rumour of the distant "raging battlefields." The day has been bright, glorious and sunny after our recent rains. How much a bright sunshine contributes to our good feelings? And especially so under existing circumstances. However to drop everything like this for the present.

Sherman upon entering Atlanta ordered all male and female citizens to leave the place as they might desire either to go north or South, and for this purpose proposed a ten days truce to Hood which he has accepted. Setting aside the suffering which these families will undoubtedly undergo, it was in my opinion a very foolish acceptance on the part of Hood, unless the accounts given in our papers regarding the efficiency of his army have greatly lied. Surely the mere fact of making the proposal, in view of Shermans past conduct to our citizens, must have convinced Hood of the weakness of the enemy, and time required to recuperate his allmost exhausted men and material, and give him the no doubt much wished for opportunity of wresting Atlanta from him and forcing him to retire in much greater speed than when he came.

Our accounts represent Hood's Army as being in elegant spirits and eager for the fray. That Hood needed rest is no doubt true, but probably not to the same extent as Sherman. Considering the condition of things in Shermans rear, the actions of Wheeler with a large Confederate force of cavalry acting upon his lines of communication, it was to say the least impolitic. Of course if Hoods Army is not in the condition it is represented to be, then the whole programme is much altered, yet I doubt not we could much more readily take the field against him than he against us. Therefore it was in any way impolitic.

With another four years prosecution of this cruel war, I may yet come to the yellow sash, if not killed or maimed in the meantime. However I would readily forego any considerations of military glory could I once more get home safe and sound now, without any more chances of getting involuntary holes punched through the tender fabric of my skin.

We had a visit today from Genl. [Lunsford L.] Lomax, now commanding the entire cavalry force proper of the Valley District, and if the Lord intended him for a Solomon, he did not write a good handwrite as he usually does. His features are rather on the common style, showing however much persever- ance when an idea has once entered his brain. It is to be hoped that he will bring out the cavalry in a better light than it has been heretofore with us. Poor devils they are much abused however, from all quarters, and no doubt much without their fault. Composed of first rate material, if it could only be remodeled and remanaged from the beginning to end. This however during an active campaign as we have had is impossible and we can only trust and hope for the best.[13]

If the enemy only knew and had the courage to find out how matters and things were situated with us, they would at once move upon us with their whole force, and force us back to at least Fishers Hill near Strasburg. A raid having Grant for its ulterior object could easily be carried out and bring at least this portion of the army to much sorrow. Passing through Lynchburg and Danville, and from thence rejoining Grant, burning and destroying as they went would hurt us much, and could be accomplished with comparatively small loss to them; and possibly without much hindrance from us.

It is said however, that the prince of cavalry—[Brig. Gen. Thomas L.] Rosser—is coming up here with his Brigade, in which event the Yanks will soon come to some sorrow. It is to be regretted that illnatured wounds have kept him so long out of the saddle. Hampton is doing good service, and with his command charged the Yankee entrenchments at Reams Station side with our infantry, carrying everything before them. Ours here would run at the bare idea of such a monstrosity. It shows that it only needs the proper kind of men with them to bring them to the same degree of superiority, which they enjoyed at the beginning of the war under Stuart.[14]

Got from Douglas the following piece written at Johnson's Island by a prisoner last winter. It breathes the right spirit. [See Wharton's *War Songs and Poems of the Southern Confederacy* for "The Guerrillas: A Southern War Song, Composed in the Bastille" by S. Teacle Wallis; see appendix 2 for "Damn it! Let it rip."][15]

Sept. 17th Turned out at an early hour this morning by the arrival of Lt. Joe Johnston, Aid to Brig. Gen. [Robert D.] Johnston, with a report that the enemys cavalry were rapidly approaching, having driven in the pickets of Bradley Johnsons Cavalry on the Berryville road. The whole camps were soon in a state of commotion to meet the threatened advance which upon a more minute inquiry and inspection turned out to consist of a squadron on the Berryville road and about a dozen or a matter of that on the middle road between the Berryville and Millwood road where they also drove in the cavalry pickets of Jackson's Brigade.[16]

One man was captured by them from Bradley Johnson and one man lost his boots in his hurry to get away on the Middle road. No other casualties reported. The men on the infantry pickets of Gen. Johnston who gave them a couple of volleys and thus quietly retired. Our picket lines were reestablished at once. Col. _____ now commanding Jacksons Brigade was relieved of his picket duty by the 5th V^a regt. cavalry and did no more service during the day. The officer commanding the 5th V^a reports that the enemy 1200 strong crossed at Snickers [Gap] and Berrys Ferry yesterday to the east side of the Blue Ridge bent on a raid.

During the forenoon accounts came in of Rodes and Gordon being ordered to cook up three days rations and be ready to march at two P.M. today. Old Jubalee seems bent upon making another raid on Martinsburg. What a fine chance it will be now for Sheridan to pitch into our small teaparty, especially as Lomax goes with him. We might stand the brunt of 4000–5000, but Sheridan could send us hopping up the Valley if he chose. Tomorrow may therefore be a day of sorrow to someone. Hope it may not be us.[17]

Yankee accounts lie beyond bearing about matters and things here in the Valley, when saying that Averill repulsed Rodes's infantry, Johnsons, Vaughans and Jackson's Brigades of Cavalry in the successive charges on the 10th of this month on the Martinsburg Pike, and was completely victorious.

Another paper however, gives Sheridan fits for not pushing us out of the Valley altogether. It says Sheridan cannot get more than 20 miles from Harpers Ferry without running foul of Early and then going back to Harpers Ferry. He might therefore be termed very appropriately "Harper's Weekly" as these attempts are made about once a week on an average. I shall close the entries in this book today, and if alive commence a new one tomorrow.

Saw a capital description of old Early from a yankee paper, which winds up with an anecdote to the effect, that when near Spotsylvania a S.C. regiment began to falter and waver when ordered to charge the enemy. Early rode up and said to them "Well boys you have got us in this damned scrape and you must help us to get out of it. Charge" in his cracked chinese fiddle voice. They did charge and cleared the yanks out. Nothing from Richmond or Atlanta today of interest, everything quiet save Grants shelling Petersburg day before yesterday to his hearts content.

Lomax is of [the] opinion that old Early will go fooling along until some fine morning the whole concern will be respectfully gobbled up by Sheridans forces. They outnumber us now at about the rate of about 2 ½–3 to one—and might any day force us hard were he [Sheridan] not so very cautious in his movements. We have never been able to catch them out of their entrenchments. Should they once be so caught, Early might turn damn fool enough to wade in and would probably come out [with a] whipping. Our boys are anxious to meet their old friends in an old field with no ditches or fences. Sheridan judging from his inexplicable maneuvres seems to be bound by orders from a higher authority than his own inclinations, and this he thinks probably bad to follow. Wonder what Early can be after now? Surely the mere capture of Martinsburg amounts to nothing as no stores have been brought there, the Baltimore and Ohio Rail Road not being in running order yet or the Chesapeake and Ohio Canal in operation. It must affect the people and authorities seriously in Washington and elsewhere, as most if not all its supplies of coal &c come by that route to Washington and Baltimore, and from thence through the state on the Potomac.[18]

18. A Day Long to Be Remembered

September 18, 1864–September 30, 1864

At daybreak the enemy, as expected, attacked....
It was impossible for our single line to resist this enormous mass.
So we were slowly driven back. Early during the fight Rodes was shot.

—Oscar Hinrichs

Editor's note: From September 18, 1864, to April 19, 1865, Oscar Hinrichs wrote his diary in German. As the reader will see in the upcoming journal entries, Oscar may have wanted to make it more difficult for others to learn about possible clandestine activities. Examples of such activities include:

- Oscar concocted a plot to foment rebellion among Germans in New York City to destabilize the Union.
- After Oscar received a letter from his future brother-in-law, Charles Stanley, he burned it, thus raising the suspicion that it was written using a CSA cipher like the one found in John Wilkes Booth's room.

After the war, Oscar or someone in his family translated the German diary entries into English. An expert in nineteenth-century Old German documents, on behalf of the editor, reviewed a sample of the Hinrichs transcriptions and found them to be accurate renderings without any postwar corrections or commentary.

September 18th Last night I rode to Winchester with our General [Ramseur] in order to pay a formal visit to General [Williams C.] Wickham, and later we reached the quarters of General Fitz Lee. On the way back many things were talked over, especially the situation of the population here in the country during the war. One hears much about their endurances, but it is not quite as bad yet, and it could be much worse. Douglas rode out with his sweetheart in order to have a good start over old Early, who is also crazy about that woman. But he won't succeed in doing anything because old Early has already too great an advantage. I wish him the best of luck in his courting.[1]

I heard at Wickham's [headquarters] that Mosby had a sharp fight near Middletown in which he was seriously wounded. This has not yet been confirmed, and it is to be hoped that it is not so. We hardly could spare him right now. It seems that Anderson is camped near Newtown, and if so, things do not look so bad for us, in case the enemy should attack us here. He would be a fool if he did not do it, since he will hardly have a better opportunity to destroy us completely while Early has gone to Martinsburg. Old Wickham seems to be a good old soul and wanting to satisfy all our wishes. The object of our visit was to ask him to have his cavalry reserves ready to come to our help in case we should be attacked in our position. The evening of our return General [Robert] Johnston was with us. We played several games of whist and went to sleep around 10 o'clock.[2]

This morning old Wickham came to us with his pistol and bayonet to help us out. But it seems that the enemy prefers to follow Early. There is a rumor that the 19th Corps went over the Potomac, probably in order to reach Richmond via Washington. Except 2 or 3 squadrons nothing is supposed to be between here and Berryville. All the rest of the 6th and 8th Corps is said to have gone back to Charlestown.[3]

The weather is getting worse and worse, and I don't know what to do in order to procure myself some winterclothing. It does not look as if our quartermaster would let me have anything, and I don't have money enough to get it otherwise. My only hope is that [my half brother] Chris is going to bring me some from the North. I wish I would hear from him what things look like there and what are the chances for peace there.

May Heaven bring this war soon to an end. Last night [the Reverend Beverley T.] Lacy, an old army chaplain[,] visited with us. He was engaged as such by General Jackson—a man with fine talents, but a wretched fellow and a still more wretched soul. I do not get much enjoyment out of him. This afternoon he called on us again, most probably hoping for a nice dinner. But he came too late, and it was good so, because our table was not too richly served. I did not like his ways ever since the battle of Chancellorsville, and I am afraid there won't be any improvement.[4]

Thanks to the Lord, today went by quietly and our enemies have not attacked us so far. Let us hope that they postpone it until later. It seems as if a great storm were coming up for the Aequinox. May Heaven take care of the enemy's seamen and see to it that they be readily handed over to the devil. There was no news from Early today. I expect I will have to wait until our quarters will be close together again before I can receive authentical news about his actions.

This afternoon General Fitz Lee came to us together with General Wickham—short and bowlegged—he seems to have a real horseman's soul and always is a capable officer. Both Generals highly praised our poor [Heros] von Borck[e]'s services in this land of heathen. It is a pity that he was wounded in such a bad way, that is to say, shot in the neck. It would be better if he went back to Europe. We have a wonderful character in our Medical Department. His name is Stewate, a Scotchman with a great gift for humour and fun. I should like very much to depict [draw] him here. Maybe I can do it later.[5]

Our Division doctor Morrison is also a rather good fellow, but could be better. He seems to have good intentions, but is not always able to carry out his ideas. All the rest of our dear men seem to have been born on bear skins (lazy), and they do not seem to have changed. I hardly have seen such lazy people before, except, perhaps, in the staff of Old General Jackson during the summer and winter [of] '62–'63. Today everybody lies down and sleeps because it is Sunday—and in this country one can't do anything on Sunday—and there isn't anything to read. Time is getting awfully long to me. I do not want to ride my horse around in the country for no purpose, and I do not feel like marching,—or am too lazy to do so. Dam'n it all, this is a contagious disease.

September 19, 1864 This is a day [the Battle of Third Winchester] long to be remembered. At daybreak the enemy, as expected, attacked the front of General [Robert D.] Johnston with cavalry and artillery, but was driven back by the outposts. Around 10 o'clock he started to show his infantry and at 11 o'clock he formally attacked our and Gordon's line. All the news were sent to old Early and he concentrated his troops—the Divisions of Wharton, Rodes and Gordon—in order to resist the attack. The enemy's first column consisted of approximately 10,000 men and was by and by reinforced to about 20,000. It was impossible for our single line to resist this enormous mass. So we were slowly driven back. Early during the fight Rodes was shot. Gordon of our Div. shortly thereafter. The whole thing went on with changing luck until 4 o'clock, when the entire line of battle was withdrawn. I am too confused today to be able to give a comprehensive account. More at a better and quieter time.[6]

September 20, 1864 Last night we marched until behind Newtown and slept in camp. This morning we continued our march calmly until we reached our fortifications near Strasburg, where we are camped for tonight. Today the enemy did not pursue and did not show himself until around 2 p.m. opposite Strasburg.[7]

September 21, 1864 The battle of the day before last was won only through the beautiful attack and the courageous conduct of the enemy's cavalry. After our infantry had withdrawn behind our lines, which were later restored, it remained rather quiet today til 3 pm, at which time the enemy's cavalry attacked McCausland. His line was broken and his men ran through Winchester as if the devil were after them. Carriages and wounded men, everything was running away tupsy-turvy, and it was the infantry of Wharton's Division which kept the enemy from taking the city. This meant giving up a rather good front, which was immediately occupied by the enemy's infantry, making it impossible for us to hold the rest of it. Almost a whole brigade—Smith's—was taken prisoner by the enemy.[8]

On our side we were forced to leave behind almost all of our wounded and dead. We have about 400 prisoners, among which there are three colonels, three majors—all in all we have fought well, and as far as I could hear, our Division is said to have done the best; it certainly was the only Division which retreated in line and good order. Between 9 and 10 o'clock the enemy's cavalry followed and the 9th New Jersey was almost completely destroyed. Col. [Anderson] Ellis [of the 54th North Carolina], the brother of the Governor of the same name, was wounded by our men in the darkness.[9]

The rest of yesterday's march was executed in best order, and many of the men, who fell back, came forward later. Our losses may reach 2000, but not more, I think. It is said that Grant was the commander in chief. But he is said to have been shot. Grant could have made things much worse for us, and it must have been only by chance, that it did not happen. As far as I could hear, we did not loose material of any kind. Everything was saved. The enemy's losses of men are said to have been extremely heavy, and this may be the reason that things were not worse for us. Thank God, it was not worse.[10]

This morning, at daybreak, the enemy's sharpshooters started to fire at our tirailleurs [sharpshooters], and it seems that we may have another little bout today. Will it be possible for us to hold these positions against 4 army corps? That is a great question. Yesterday General Ramseur was dismissed by this Division and transferred to Rodes' Division. The command of this Division was given to Gen. Pegram. We all are very sorry to loose R [Ramseur], but such is war. As soon as one has been able to gain somebody's favors, a ball comes flying and changes all plans. Last night I went to [Lt. Col. Alexander S. "Sandie"] Pendleton and asked for the position as Chief Engineer of the Corps, since I am the oldest officer here.[11]

[John C.] Breckenridge has also been discharged of his command and transferred to Dublin. This changes a lot in our whole program of the cam-

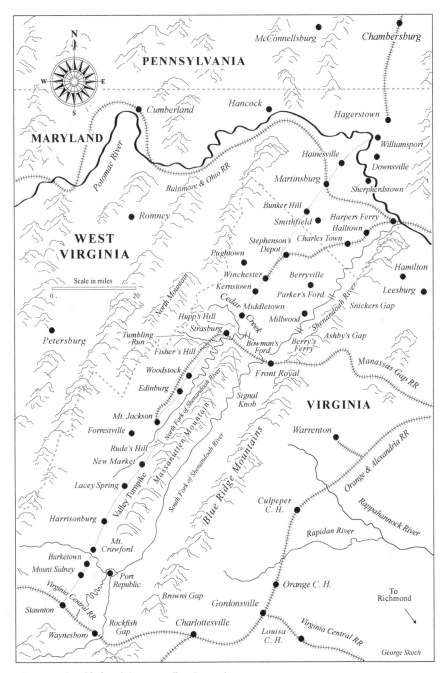

The Second Half of Early's 1864 Valley Campaign

paign. Whether it will be for the best or not, I could not tell; but let us hope for the best. Probably Gordon will take over the command which was taken from Breckenridge, and then, maybe, I'll be able to get the mentioned position for the whole Army. It's to be hoped for.[12]

September 22, 1864 Everything was quiet today up to 2 P.M. at which time the enemy started to send his troops over to our lines. Our cavalry held the fortifications to our left, and it was there that the enemy attacked. On the rest of the line he just kept us busy. The cavalry could not resist the attack and thus opened a door for the enemy [during the Battle of Fisher's Hill]. This was beautifully taken advantage of and a great many, I should say 10,000 men continued the attack on the flank. Two brigades of Ramseur's Division turned around completely, the manoeuvre being followed by all the commanders, one after the other.[13]

I have never seen such a thing before, and by the time I surveyed the show everything was in wild retreat, without order and partly without arms. Many efforts were made to restore order, but in vain. Artillery and infantry, everybody sought safety in running away. The Generals Early, Ramseur, Gordon, Pegram and their staffs did all possible efforts to stop this, but only around 10 p.m. they were able to get some order into the men. The march was immediately continued until 5 or 6 miles from Mt. Jackson where we camped at 1 o'clock in the morning. Today we lost 13 cannons, maybe 500 prisoners, one wagon etc. Among our dead and wounded we had to leave behind [Sandie] Pendleton—deadly wounded. He was shot late in the evening. Another day I shall say more about today's work.[14]

September 23, 1864 The enemy did not follow us last night, and this morning we continued our march orderly. A line was built on the other side of Mt. Jackson, and we expected an attack. Around 3 pm the enemy's cavalry attacked, but did not have any success. After dark we withdrew to this side of Mt. Jackson, cooked and slept undisturbed. Many of those whom we thought prisoners, showed up today, and most probably[,] many others will still come. I don't think that I underestimated our losses.[15]

September 27, 1864 In the morning of September 24 we retreated from Mt. Jackson towards New Market—after we had induced the enemy to reveal to us the strength of his forces. Our Division retreated in brigade formation, Gordon and Wharton in battleline. Ramseur marched in the same order as ourselves on our right. When reaching New Market the enemy showed up closely behind us with cavalry and artillery but stopped as soon as he saw that our lines were formed, and that we were ready to fight. Here Gordon made a big mistake. Early wanted to build up a new line this side of New Market, but Gordon went back and insisted that the whole army retreated in battle formation. This might have easily cost us dearly. We waited until the enemy brought forward his infantry and formed his battleline; we then continued our march.

After many more stops the day finally went by without bringing us serious damage, except for a rather heavy tirailleur battle which lasted till after dark about 12 miles from Harrisonburg, where we waited for nightfall. If the enemy should have chosed this spot for fighting us seriously, we most probably would have had many losses. After dark we continued the retreat. We left the highroad and took the country road to the left. May Heaven spare us roads of that kind! Never before we had marched on such a bad road. We marched till opposite Harrisonburg—about 5 miles, and camped for the night.

On the 25[*th*] we marched over Port Republic into Brown's Gap without seeing the enemy. Most probably he went to Harrisonburg with his infantry and stopped there. His cavalry went probably to Staunton. Our army with all of its trains is safe here and we can wait here for Kershaw's arrival. He is supposed to be only a short stretch in front of us. Most probably he will not get "jolly on his other boot" and we shall start the offensive as soon as arms and ammunition have been provided for men and rifles.[16]

On the 26[*th*] the enemy showed himself on the western bank of the river in great numbers and attacked us during the afternoon. But our sharpshooters defeated him, causing great losses. We are still camped in Brown's Gap, and it will be soon necessary—nolens volens—to attack the enemy in order to drive [him] out. This morning he burned four mills, and our rations of flour are getting low rapidly. Kershaw today personally announced his arrival. He also had a little fight with the enemy's cavalry in which he made a few prisoners. The position of the enemy's infantry is as mentioned above, near Harrisonburg.[17]

This morning, the 27[*th*,] the enemy made a feigned attack which we changed into a real one, chasing Averill with his Division of three brigades for some 5 miles, causing considerable losses. We might have almost caught his entire wagon train, if it had not been for General Wickham, who would not permit his brigade to attack. But he made a few prisoners. Tonight there is a rumor that the enemy entered Staunton and partly burned it down. Rosser with his brigade is supposed to reach Lynchburg tonight so we may expect him here in a few days. Then the whole cavalry question will be greatly changed and Mr. Averill will have to be a little careful about his ways of roaming around here, otherwise something may happen to him. This, however, is highly desirable.[18]

Tomorrow we shall, most probably, run into the enemy's infantry, and we hope to have better luck than in Fisher's Hill and Strasburg, so that we may repair the sad damage. Yesterday's and today's losses of our Division amount to approximately 10. We could not make out the enemy's losses, because he carries back his dead as soon as possible. If our chances are good we can at best show the enemy how to make a good retreat, and if Rosser arrives early, there won't be many who will see Winchester again, except as prisoners. Today we caught one of the enemy's surgeons, and did not know what to do with him. He was taken prisoner by our sharpshooters. He told us that Averill has been sent back because he had not driven us back from Mt. Jackson. It was very wise of him, not to do this, because it might have been disastrous for him. So, tomorrow there will be something new again. Taking everything in consideration, it was a wonderful week. I lived years within seven days. The enemy pursued us with approximately 15,000 men infantry, 6[000] or 7000 cavalry and 20 cannons, all together 25[,000]–30,000 men.

———————

September 28, 1864 Last night we received the order to be prepared for an early march this morning, but we did not start until 9 o'clock. We made a quick march towards Waynesboro, where General Wilson's cavalry Division was camped. Wickham and his Brigade were sent to Rockfish Gap to attack and cut off [the enemy] from there, while Wharton and our Division attacked from another side. As far as I know, Kershaw with the help of Gordon's Division was supposed to cut off the enemy from Staunton. Ramseur was supposed to protect the train. Wickham and our Division encountered the enemy and attacked him, driving him towards Kershaw, hoping that he would catch them. But things went wrong. Instead of continuing the way we wanted them to, they turned towards the train and so came in our back. Wharton did not attack from his side, and the end of the story is, that the enemy escaped us with sack and bag towards Staunton.[19]

This is very sad, since one Division had already marched towards Lynchburg to help defeating the enemy as soon as he came nearer to Rosser. Very seldom infantry has such a good chance to skalp the enemy's cavalry. As far as I could make out tonight, not many prisoners were taken, maybe a dozen. Besides [that], the enemy was not seriously damaged. I had been sure of seeing many prisoners, but, as it often happens, I have been deceived. It is to be hoped, that in the future Early prepares his plans a little better, in order to have more success.

Last night we camped in an old quarter of the late Jackson, but we had very sad thoughts. Here we had been after the battles of Cross Keys and Port Republic in '62 when he vanquished and decapitated Fremont and Shield.

Twice we were driven into the hole of Brown's Gap. Let's hope that we may finish the year as happy as the other time. Old Doctor Kemper seemed to be extremely happy to have us with him and he gave us a royal dinner, which did us an awful lot of good.

Tonight we lie in the same house which To[r]bert had occupied. It seems that we have driven the enemy out in great haste, because they had put up their tents and almost cooked their supper, when we fired. It seems that yesterday we came very near to having a great battle. Sheridan has lined up his entire army in battle order near Cross Keys and expected us. We were lucky not to have advanced any further. We might have taken too big a bite and gotten choked in swallowing it. Anyway "enough a day is its own evil," so we may be thankful to our Lord in Heaven, that things did not turn out worse for us. Let us hope that in the future Early will not try to chase the cavalry with his infantry.

Today we marched an awful lot, at least 25 miles. Unexpectedly we ran into those good people, whom, to make understand that we really are Rebels, we had, at first, some difficulty. Where shall we go tomorrow? May be to Staunton.

The events of the last 3 weeks seem to be a dream to me. This morning I received a letter from Till, but there were no news in it and no information regarding Chris' trip to the North. I wrote a short note to my father and gave it to the surgeon who was taken prisoner yesterday. He promised to mail it without fail, but I have little hope in this respect, because most of these fellows are rogues and rascals, and do nothing else but loaf around in the country and steal everything they can lay hands on. May the devil get them all!

September 29, 1864 Contrary to our expectations we stayed here in Waynesboro today and rested on our newly acquired laurels. In the morning I rode Erich to the quarter of Old Early and he sent me to examine the tunnel and the railroad to Rockfish Gap and then to take measurements for the reconstruction of the railroad bridge. This kept me busy almost all day long. I could not find out anything about the enemy today. It seems that around nightfall they lit large fires in the direction of Staunton, but till now we do not know what this means. Towards nightfall we received order to be prepared for marching at sunrise. Most probably they won't let "the sun rise" until 10 o'clock—which would be so much the better for us.[20]

It would have been much better if we had approached the enemy during the evening in order to attack him early in the morning. It is absolutely necessary to chase him out of this region and the earlier the better. It is also necessary that the enemy be beaten, but both these things will hardly happen at sunrise.

The old ways of General Jackson seem to be forgotten, and today we do just what pleases us. And therefore it is only a question of time for the enemy to chase us out of this region, and he will surely do it. Even the common people see this and speak and act accordingly.

Sunrise means a lot or nothing, and unfortunately it's usually nothing. The enemy's cavalry is riding rings around us and burns down our mills and barns, our wheat and hay, so that, even if we should wish to stay here, we won't be able to, because of lack of food for man and beast. We are in a very sad position. There are also rumors from Richmond which are not exactly bad, but could be much better. It is said that the enemy reached the town for a while on the northern side, and that a battle took place near the Chimborazo Hospital. I could not yet find out with what success. Yesterday's newspapers say, that everything is quiet, but that does not mean anything. Most probably it's General Gregg's or Kautz's cavalry which made an attack from the side. I suppose it's getting time for me to be looking around in order to quit this service and go elsewhere. It seems that we are quickly approaching the crisis since everybody says that troops are being sent to Grant and Sheridan. Heaven knows where they all come from, may be from the West.[21]

Forrest seems to have performed a master shot (bowling) when he occupied Athens in Alabama taking some 1500 men and officers, 500 wagons etc. and two railroad trains with supplies for Sherman's army. Of course, these are only small matters and won't help much to improve the situation. It seems to me that we are not able to make the best of everything whether it's for or against us. Sad to say so, but I cannot look at things differently.[22]

Tonight I had a long talk with Old Early regarding railroads and bridges—and had some very good ideas about this and that. Andersen [Richard H. Anderson] went to Richmond when Kershaw reported to us again, and he will take command of the two other Divisions of the 1st Corps. If at Richmond everything will end favorably for us, we may perhaps be able to face the enemy without fear. Decisive events are approaching rapidly there. May Heaven give us victory.

_____

September 30, 1864 Although the order was issued last night to be ready for march at sunrise, we remained, as expected, quietly in camp. Aside from my work on the railroad bridge there is nothing new. There is a rumor, that a battle is taking place around Richmond, but it is not authentic. Still, it may be so, at least I feel that way. My bridge does not make much progress, because beams for pillars are lacking. I should like to finish it as quickly as possible, because I believe it will be to my credit later on when I shall make my intended application for a patent in the regular army. But I'll wait a while with it. The enemy seems to endeavor to burn down all mills and barns along the high-road. I pity the poor people; as far as I can see they will have an awful time getting bread. The enemy has burned at least 1,000 tons of flour, 10,000 bushels of wheat destined for our corps and has abducted all horses and cattle. There will be, no doubt, orders tonight to march tomorrow.[23]

19. Put Them into the Infantry

October 1, 1864–October 14, 1864

It seems that the enemy assembled a lot of cavalry and ran over Lomax. . . .
Thanks to Rosser's personal efforts order was reestablished in the other brigades.
—Oscar Hinrichs

October 1, 1864. Although it is raining awfully hard, and therefore, it's terribly uncomfortable above the heads and under the feet, we start marching
today. We marched through New Hope and Mount Sidney towards Mount
Crawford, but stopped at one mile from Burktown, some 13 or 14 miles from
Staunton. We got on the highroad at Willow Pump, 8 miles from Staunton.
Our marching order was: Gordon, Wharton, Kershaw and our Division. Ramseur took another road. It looks, as if the enemy wanted to withdraw into the
lower part of the valley. The question is, whether we shall allow him to do so.
Most probably we shall.

Fort Harrison near Chaffins Bluff was taken by the enemy yesterday. This
will probably make us give up Chaffins Bluff and some other fortifications near
James River. However, near Chimborazo Hospital the enemy was defeated
and some 400 prisoners were taken. Taking everything into consideration,
things look rather dark around Richmond, and I would not be greatly astonished if the enemy should finally succeed in taking the town. A little bit here
and there and then somewhere else takes everything down to a small scale.
We cannot possibly send help to Lee from here, because, if we should do so
the road to Lynchburg and Danville would be open. And the enemy would
certainly take advantage of this opportunity, and then everything would go
to the dogs.[1]

With Richmond the enemy is going to take the whole state of Virginia, and
we shall be forced to build up new lines along the Roanoke River, or, maybe
even farther South. And then also the better part of North Carolina is going

to be lost, which will bring the war to such a small area, that one may easily see peace approaching. There is a large piece of territory westward from the Mississippi—a kingdom in the true sense of the word—which we might defend, and from where we might, later on, succeed in freeing the eastern part. I seem to be very fickle. Today I am speaking as if I were going to spill my last drop of blood for this question, and yesterday I was ready to leave for good. But such is human kind—never stable, changing all the time.

Our headquarters are in a tiny house, in a tinier room where there are 8 or 10 women, whose lords are soldiers. They told us a sad story about the actions of the enemy while he stayed in this region. They gave us also an excellent supper, and since our wagons did not arrive until 11 PM, it was not hard for them to induce us to accept their invitation. Up to now there are no orders concerning tomorrow morning. I would not be astonished, if another day would be wasted instead of being taken advantage of. Of course, the weather is abominable, and it is certainly much more comfortable to sit by the fire, smoke a pipe and do some thinking. Yesterday the Special Order Nr. 76—dated September 30, 1864—was published, with which I was nominated Actg. Chief Engineer A.V.D. Although this does not mean any advantage right now, it is a step in the right direction, and I hope, that later on I'll be able to make something out of it. So good so far.[2]

October 2 1864. Today the sun came up clear and bright, but we stayed in the camp and we are taking things easy. The enemy withdrew to the other side of the river and seems to keep rather quiet. During the afternoon the enemy's cavalry performed some demonstrations on the high road to Bridgewater, but we cut them short rapidly. One Brigade of the infantry went to a mill in order to save some wheat, which was safely brought back. Later on Pegram's Brigade was sent there too to protect the wagons.

I had a very pleasant time riding to our outposts with the General [Pegram], returning only at nightfall. I overheard a very interesting conversation regarding our Generals, especially Magruder, Lee and Johnston. Our General seems to like Magruder very much, and said, that after Jackson he is the only one to show some strategy in his works—and this on the peninsula in winter 61–62 and in spring 62. It must be so, because he succeeded in holding back McClellan and 135,000 men with his 9000 men for nearly 2 months until a part of the Army could come down from Manassas. He does not seem to know much about [Joe] Johnston, which astonishes me.

Forrest has again fetched the devil out of the hell by taking again 800 prisoners and a considerable amount of material. Rosser arrived tonight in General Headquarters. His Brigade is supposed to be here tomorrow. Tonight I visited [Capt. Don P.] Halsey. He is very sore about the slow advancement in the general staff and intends to ask for his retirement. I like him as far as I know him, and I wish he could get his advancement, which he certainly deserves. He and I lack public favor, and so we have to take things as they come, not as we should like them to come. Around 9 PM orders were given to be ready for marching at sunrise—and we may be sure to have a gay day tomorrow—but I have a hunch that nothing will come of it and that we may stay in bed undisturbed.[3]

October 3, 1864. As we expected and despite our things being ready packed, we stayed here. This morning I rode over to General Headquarters and heard that Lee had taken some 2000 prisoners. Day before yesterday [he took] 1500 on the south side and 500 on the north side of the river. These are most probably the outcome of the attack of Fort Harrison which went wrong and was only partially successful. If the real truth should be told, I am sure, this "partially" will amount to nothing at all, because I cannot see how such an attack can be "partially" successful. Rosser took over the command of the cavalry here this morning. His Brigade will arrive in Staunton tonight. It is said, that Fort Harrison is only an advanced fortification of Chaffin Bluff and was erected mainly to hinder and annoy the enemy in Dutch Gap; they say it is not at all part of the Richmond line. Anyway, it is easily possible that the enemy's engineers may transform it into a strong fortress and cause us considerable difficulties. It is said that Gen. Lee does not care about this loss. But of course, many things are said, although they are not true.[4]

It has been raining today, almost all the time, and I am glad to stay here. With me everything seems to go wrong. I am afraid that I will loose my attendant today, and I won't be able to replace him. I don't have time to curry-comb my horses and so on, and I don't see another way out. This morning I received a letter from Hall in Richmond telling me that he had some letters for me from my parents and from Maryland. I answered him right away, instructing him about the address. I am looking forward very much to receiving these letters and I wish I had them already, or, rather, I were where they are, that certainly would suit me quite well.

O, I wish the devil would get all those people who are so nastily getting in my way, as the owner of my attendant; dam'n it, I do not know what to do— and I won't be able to get along the way I suggested above. I need clothing badly, but I don't have time to be bothered with such things and on the other hand I certainly don't want to loose or ruin what I have. God knows what is going to happen—winter is approaching rapidly and I am only very scantily provided for—I especially need underclothing.

Late tonight a revoke of the special order given on the first of this month was published, and I do not have the slightest idea, why. Most probably one of my very good friends was so good as to want to save me some work—and he certainly deserves my highest gratitude for his friendly act! Today one tries hard to get somewhere, and tomorrow some scoundrel comes along and ruins everything.[5]

Tonight I paid 69 Dollars for cloth and buttons, and now I do not know what to do with it, since I have no time to run after a taylor for taking my measures and sowing my clothes. Such is life, and this here, certainly is a sad place to be in. It took almost my last cent to pay for it, and then some one or another will come along and ask for something and I don't know where to dig the money up. Only God knows what is going to happen to me.

October 4, 1864. Although last night we had no orders regarding today, we are still hanging around here and not marching yet. There does not seem to be anything new from our front. The enemy leaves us alone, does not disturb us the least bit, continues only to burn down everything and does not seem to think about tomorrow. He seems to get down to real war now, destroying everything which might be of help either to us or to the inhabitants of this region. Tonight we can see a big and bright light from some of his burning activity.[6]

I heard that some small battles were fought on the 1st near Richmond and were won by our troops. Fort Harrison was taken by surprise by the enemy's colored troops. At the same time troops of the same kind attacked Fort Gilmer and were almost completely destroyed. They are supposed to lye 10 to 12 on top of another and besides lost some 1500 prisoners. The newspapers of September 30 tell that near Sulphur Springs on the Tennessee line Forrest took some 800 prisoners loosing 35 men himself. His affair near Athens cost him 25 men. He was advanced to Lieutenant General and is now commander in chief of the whole cavalry down there. It is said that the President wrote to him, telling him that he expected him, Forrest, to chase Sherman completely out of Georgia, and that, if he should succeed in doing so, the highest honors the States can bestove upon somebody would be his.

Here in Virginia the enemy is reconstructing the bridge over the Rappahannock River. What does that mean? Will a new and fresh column attack us from there or does Sheridan want a new basis? Most probably this is his intention, because he does not disturb us at all, although we can notice a great activity in his camp. He won't be able to stay here very much longer without encountering transportation difficulties, and, therefore, it looks as if he wanted to go elsewhere. I was just interrupted by Douglas' return who brought orders to be ready at daybreak to attack and follow the enemy. So we'll have to be careful.[7]

Brigade General [William G.] Lewis has been called for by telegraph. It is highly desirable for him to come back here, because his brigade needs his or some other officer's good example very much. The commander they have now is a good fellow, but too afraid to really attack. His command is going to the devil a little more each day. I spent almost all day in Johnston's brigade and asked about my friends in Wilmington—heard many a good and many a bad news about this or that person, especially about the ladies.[8]

October 5, 1864. Today we are again staying here and don't hear anything from the enemy. There are no news about our front and none from Richmond either. It almost looks like an armistice. I was busy all day long writing letters. I wrote long letters to Till—Mad. [Madame] Medway—and—Frink. I hope to receive some answers some time. Am looking forward very much to receiving my letters from Richmond. Yesterday I had to pay 36 Dollars to the agent of Dolphs—Mr. Burson. Today Douglas paid 22.93 for me. I wish I could pay off all my debts, they are worrying me a lot.

Douglas had been to General Headquarters where he heard rumors about some more fighting near Richmond, in which we were defeated. Fort McRae on the right hand side of the Weldon railroad was taken by the enemy together with a great part of the rest of the line. But all was taken back, except the fort. Fort Harrison was attacked again, but with no success. There is a rumor that 8500 of our prisoners escaped from Camp Chase and are on their way south.[9]

October 6, 1864. This morning I rode over to Staunton in order to have my cloth cut and have a coat made from it. I left our camp at 10 and arrived in S. at 1 o'clock. After having attended to my business and while riding back leisurely I heard that the whole Army had started and was marching towards Harrison-burg. After riding for some 40 miles I arrived at our Headquarters around 10 o'clock. During the morning the enemy had hastily retreated. Many families in Harrisonburg took the oath and some of them left with the enemy. They burned down their houses and were gone. One of these people had packed everything and was waiting for a wagon, which the enemy had promised to send. He was so sure about it, that he burned down his house . . . but there came no wagon to fetch his things. All these families—some 50—belong to the socalled "dunkards" [Dunkers]. In their ways and manners they resemble the Quakers to some extent. We shall continue our march at daybreak and camp most probably near New Market. Nothing new or particularly interesting about the enemy.[10]

October 7, 1864. We started marching this morning around 8 o'clock. Nothing happened during the march. We camped as mentioned last night. Newspapers which were received by the commanders said that Hood changed his position, is back of Sherman, and is now in Marietta. [Maj. Gen. Sterling] Price is said to be at 25 miles from St. Louis Mo., marching towards the town. There is news from Breckenridge by wire that Echols with the militia and the reserves met the enemy (some 5000 men) under [Brig. Gen. Stephen] Burbridge near Saltville, and beat him so hard, that he had to leave his dead and wounded on the ground. No further news from Richmond. If it's true what is said about Hood's position, he most probably will force Sherman into an open battle, the result of which is easily to be forseen.[11]

There must be something wrong with the enemy. This morning Rosser stopped a currier [courier] with dispatches from Grant for Sheridan, containing orders, immediately to withdraw out of this valley. I cannot yet see what this means. The enemy left New Market this morning around 7 o'clock and is now on the other side of Mt. Jackson. All the barns and almost all mills have been burned down. This morning I saw a lot of smoke from some burning house. We have a very nice camp on the bank of the river, on the left hand side of New Market, about 1 mile from town. I am very tired from yesterday's long ride and the 18 miles I rode today certainly did not do me good. Besides I was too tired to sleep well. Tomorrow, we shall probably continue our march without obstacles until we shall reach Winchester. I guess that there we shall face each other. Nothing else for today.[12]

October 8, 1864. We stay in camp today. The weather is miserable. It rains, snows, hails, blows all together, and is cold enough to stand a coat and a fire very well. Rosser with one brigade met the enemy's cavalry near Forrestville and chased them for [a] good 5 miles. Along with quite a number of sheep and other animals he made 40 prisoners and some new field-forges. Lomax is said to have met the back guard of the 200th infantry near Woodstock, where they were busy putting fire to the place. 12 houses burned down completely, other houses could be saved in time. Later on the enemy was pursued until near Fisher's Hill, where his whole infantry was drawn up in battle order. Lomax was driven back to this side of Woodstock, where, according to rumors, Rosser tumbled on him from the back. This, however, has not yet been proved as to whether it is true or not. Anyway, finally the enemy has been chased. Besides it's good, that a new leader has taken command.[13]

It is said, that Beauregard was transferred to the southwest Department, and that Hood has taken up a position on the Macon railroad, while the Jackson Railroad has also been occupied. People say, that now Sherman's army is actually in such a danger as our's was believed to be in after Atlanta had been taken. General [Prince Camille de] Polignac with 5[000]–6000 men is said to have reached Hood. Price is within 14 miles from St. Louis. Therefore it is quite possible that the courier, who was made prisoner a few days ago, really had true dispatches, and that Sheridan is either approaching Sherman or nearing the Missouri. I had no news from Richmond. The different commands are making great effort to assign the single soldiers to the right division—this is a very important task right now, because it will be of greatest importance to have all fighting men ready to go to the front.[14]

October 9, 1864. Although it is Sunday today, we were awakened early this morning by gunfire near Mt. Jackson or maybe a little farther away. We did not hear anything definite about it, however, until 4 PM, when Lomax's men reported in New Market in great haste. It seems that the enemy assembled a lot of cavalry and ran over Lomax [at Tom's Brook]. This Division is not worth the powder necessary to shoot them down. They do not want to fight and run away from the enemy as soon as they can. The best thing to do with these people, would be to get them down from their horses and to put them into the infantry. May the devil get all these fellows. Around 5 PM orders arrived to get our Division moving towards the enemy and to fight him, if he should reach us. Anyhow, I hope they will leave us alone for today, since I do not at all feel peppy and ready for fighting. I did not yet receive my letters from Richmond. I am anxiously waiting for them, but maybe I will never get them. It's just my luck![15]

October 10, 1864. Last night we returned to our camp, because the enemy retreated after having chased these wretches of Lomax's to Meems Farm this side of Mt. Jackson with some 100 men. The whole thing was much more important than I first thought. It seems that their signal-troops found out what was in front of them and that the enemy therefore concentrated all of his cavalry on Rosser, who, at that time was marching near Edinburg on the road along North Mountain. With Rosser were his own brigade besides the one of Wickham and the former Lomax brigade. The enemy made a good attack, succeeded in getting Wickham's and Lomax's brigades into disorder, conquered their gun and was kept from advancing farther only by some fine attacks of Rosser's brigade. Thanks to Rosser's personal efforts order was reestablished in the other brigades and finally the whole affair was finished and the enemy retreated towards Forrestville.[16]

During all this time Lomax with Johnson's and Jackson's brigades thought to be pushing the enemy back, which was not so. The enemy was only slowly retreating, waiting for a decision from the decisive fight with Rosser, before he accepted the attack. Fortunately or unfortunately, I do not know, the enemy started the offensive too early, and before the cavalry, which had finished with Rosser, could get over, Lomax was already being driven back in such a hurry, that he had to leave his artillery behind and arrived in New Market around 3 PM. With a little less haste, Lomax and his whole brigade might have been taken prisoner. Lomax himself was taken prisoner twice, but got away again. Our losses amount to 9 pieces of artillery with horses, some 200 prisoners, around 10 wagons etc. A fine thing.[17]

Imboden and his brigade are on the other side of the Massanutten Mountains. He says, that a Division of the enemy's cavalry is in front of him. McCausland is on the other side of the Blue Ridge Mountains. Some of the enemy's cavalry is said to have advanced up to Rapidam Station and to have burned the bridge there. Mosby is said to have cut off two trains with their guards in Loudo[u]n or Fauquier, but has not the means of bringing them here. The enemy's wagon-guard is said to have taken up a very good position. Nothing new from Richmond. The weather is still cold and disagreeable.

Hardee is said to have been transferred to Headquarters at Charleston—probably because he is dissatisfied with Hood and Beauregard—and because his friend Joe Johnston was transferred. Magruder was dismissed from the Command in Texas and was transferred elsewhere. I could not find out where. Forrest is said to have made a start again, taking some 300 prisoners and 4 guns. Besides he destroyed the railroad from Franklin to Decatur (Alabama and Tennessee Railroad).[18]

I just saw the newspapers of the 8th of this month. It seems that the enemy on the 7th, or rather the 6th[,] sent two brigades of infantry, one brigade [of] cavalry and a lot of artillery within sight of the fortification line of Richmond. Near [Fort] Harrison he had a camp with more than 40,000 men. They had two lines with fortifications on the Richmond side and towards the town. These were attacked by our troops under Andersen [Richard H. Anderson] on the 7th and driven back by them and especially by [Brig. Gen. John] Gregg from Texas almost to Fort Harrison. We had small losses, while those of the enemy were rather heavy. Our troops took some 400 prisoners and conquered 10 pieces of artillery in their two lines. Now the enemy received reinforcements from his lines back of Fort Harrison and made an attack, which was beautifully rejected. The enemy had heavy losses. The lines and guns conquered remained in our hands. Gregg was killed in front of his column. Because of the darkness which was growing rapidly and since our troops were tired, our attack was not further continued.[19]

Nothing new, besides this. Near Saltville, under Burbridge the enemy made two attacks, but was driven back with a bleeding nose, leaving some 700 dead and wounded men behind. Joe Hooker was assigned to the command of Ohio and Illinois, while [Maj. Gen. Samuel P.] Heintzelman was ordered to report in Wheeling. This may mean a mixing up of the military powers with the rights of people.[20]

A lady, who recently came here from the west[,] tells a nice story about conditions there. She says that there are posters everywhere, on the roads and in the cities with slogans: Down with Lincoln—Peace with Union—Peace, but without Union etc. She also said, that the poor are much worse off there, because the rich do not want to help them along at all, that greatest economy is requested from everybody, that taxes are terribly high, and that all luxuries, such as coffee, sugar, etc. have been banned, even in restaurants. Of course, this may be highly exaggerated, but there must be some truth in it, because I often heard, how badly off they are there. Had no news yet about my letters. Today I made the request, through General [Robert] Johnston to be allowed to buy cloth from N.C. under the same understanding as for officers of the state; I had to report as a temporary resident of the state. I do not know how this is going to fit in with my further plans. Anyway, time will show it. I am more and more thinking of entering the regular service.[21]

October 11, 1864. Today we are still in our camp without disturbances. Did not hear yet of my letters. It's getting time for them to arrive. Received orders to cook rations for two days and to be ready for marching tomorrow morning. Many think that Sheridan has sent many of his troops to Richmond or has the intention of doing so. If this is so many of us will go to Richmond too. I do not know whether this is correct or why so many people think that way. Anyway, I am sure, there is something wrong. Maybe Lee is pressed for soldiers in Richmond and we may be of greater help there than here. On the other hand it will be difficult to take everything away here and to leave this valley open to the enemy up to Salem.[22]

The weather is getting more like winter and the roads are quickly getting too bad for quick marching. I do not think that we are going to have a quiet winter, but that Lee is planning a winter campaign. If this should be so and nothing of great importance come from it, I am afraid we won't be able to continue the war in the Spring with great energy. Our draught animals will be worn out by bad roads—and then we'll sit there just like the ox before the mountain (helpless). Let us hope that we (our Division) will be left here and that everything will come to a good ending.

Tonight further news arrived from Richmond about some more fighting on the 8th. Lee is said to have taken some 20 guns and 2500 prisoners. It is not said, where this happened. The news was brought by a surgeon, who just arrived from Richmond. Mosby has been able to free some 200 of our prisoners. Really, this man has given us great service and should be advanced to a high position. It took him hard work to get this position, but I am sure, he will some time be quite famous. I do wish him good luck. According to the saying of spies the enemy is supposed to be in three different places: 1) repairing the railroad from Manassas to Strasburg, 2) retreating through Middletown, and 3) camped near Winchester. And with such uncertain information the campaign is being planned here. Let us hope, that things will get better soon.[23]

October 12, 1864. This morning we started marching along the highroad towards Strasburg. Ramseur's, Gordon's, Wharton's, Kershaw's and our Division [Pegram's] with a battalion of artillery between each Division. We are camped at 4 miles from Woodstock. We received orders to march tomorrow morning at 6, in the following order: Gordon, Kershaw, Wharton, our Division, Ramseur, and the artillery as [of] today. When we started marching today, the enemy's cavalry was at about 4 miles on the other side of Woodstock, retreating. His infantry was farther away, and also retreating.

A new gun arrived from Staunton for our cavalry and was handed over the day before yesterday. Let us hope, that they will use it better than up to now. The worst of it is, that Ashby's old battery, at that time was taken under Chew. I can very well remember, how Chew would come to Ashby and say: I did not fire a shot in 24 hours, come on, let's have some fun. And off he went with 20 men cavalry, sometimes for 20 miles, round and round, and always came home safely. Things have changed since. At that time the enemy did not dare pursue us, except if they were in great number, and one shot out of a gun was enough to bring them to a standstill. Today we hardly can bring our cavalry near enough for some shooting.

October 13, 1864. This morning we marched a little later than said last night, in the order mentioned, but without meeting any resistance. At Fisher's Hill the last three Divisions were stopped and Gordon and Kershaw marched towards Hupps Hill on the other side of Strasburg. Here a camp of the enemy was taken by surprise, and almost a whole brigade dissipated. During this time we peacefully stopped at Fisher's Hill. After a few hours rest we were sent to Hupps Hill too. Our Division took up its old position on Caper Spring Grade (where formally we camped with Ramseur). We stayed there until dark and then camped nearer to our old tirailleur-line and our fortifications. Our Headquarters were with us, near a mill (Pfeifer). While we stopped on Caper Grade

I rode to the highroad with the General to see what things looked like there. It seems that the enemy did not know what was ahead of him, and therefore sent 2 brigades over Cedar Creek to lay hands on 4 of our guns. Old Early got sore and ordered, that Connors [Brig. Gen. James Connor] and a brigade of Gordon's Division should attack the enemy quickly. The enemy was beautifully defeated and 40 or 50 prisoners were taken, among which was the commander of one brigade. Nothing else happened.[24]

October 14, 1864. This morning I rode out early to see what the enemy is really doing. But everything seemed to be quiet. But shortly thereafter the enemy's cavalry came out and drove our cavalry (videttes) back. Then they sent over two squadrons to this side of Strasburg. There was some fighting and then the 2 squadrons retreated. Our sharpshooters advanced later on till half way to Hupps Hill and succeeded in driving away some 200 cavalry men. Our and Gordon's Division were advanced somewhat to check any possible advances of the enemy. We stayed here until nightfall, nothing happened. Our Headquarters are in the same location as yesterday.[25]

Tonight I overheard a conversation concerning several Generals, among which [Joe] Johnston, Rhodes, G. [Gustavus] W. Smith, Jackson and other were mentioned. They also spoke of some of the enemy's Generals. And even our *old* leaders were taken into it, and some of them criticized rather sharply, especially regarding the loss of a gun in this place on September 22. I should like to write down the whole conversation, but I am too tired tonight. But I shall try to do so tomorrow. I had no news about my letters, and am almost sure, that they must be lost.

The following was said about [Joe] Johnston: At the beginning of the war he quit his services with the U.S. and volunteered in Richmond, offering his services to the Governor. His offer was accepted and he was nominated Brigade-General. There was always envy between him and Lee about their advancement, and when finally Lee was nominated Commander in Chief, Johnston got sore and asked for his dismissal, which was accepted, after a commission of three of the first citizens of the State had visited him, telling him, how indispensable his services were for the State. But he was sore, insisted on his dismissal, and offered his services to the Confederate Government as soon as his dismissal was granted. He was accepted and ordered to Harpers Ferry where Jackson was in command.

As far as I could hear, all his [Johnston's] plans came from Richmond and the Council—and his injury during the battle of Seven Pines is considered a lucky happening for the State. The existing enmity between him and the Government seems to have been caused by his vanity and the fact, that he did not do anything. My personal opinion is, that the Government always tried to mix up with his plans, frustrating them. He is a very brave man and has the strongest brain in the union. As a General he has busied himself more with retreats than with anything else.

As a General, Rodes was one of the best Division Commanders of the whole army. As a commander of the whole army he seems to lack some of the talents absolutely necessary to make up a good and lucky commander in chief. He is said to have always been very careful about fighting and never to have to been taken by surprise. Yes, and during the fight he was efficient, careful and strong, besides quick in his movements and therefore hard to defeat.[26]

G. W. Smith is said to have been the best besides Lee and Jackson. When Gen. Pegram surrendered to McClellan at Rich Mountain he had a conversation with him regarding Smith, in which he is said to have asked, whether Smith was going to join the Southerners. He was told that Smith had been stricken by paralysis and that, therefore, he would not be able to participate any longer in the war. If one takes into consideration, how highly McClellan respected Smith, and that he asked for his opinion about everything, one realizes, how much the enemy must have been afraid of him on our side. Jasper Whiting—the brother of the General of the same name and my friend—did not tell that the Government was afraid to give him the command after Johnston had been wounded, although they thought him to be, may be, the best General.

Much is expected of Beauregard. He is supposed to be one of the best educated men, but he does not seem to be able to handle troops in great quantity. On the other hand his plans are good, so he really needs only a severe commander for his troops. Now he certainly has an excellent opportunity to show, what he can do. Bragg is an old woman, who has good plans occasionally, but cannot carry them out. His greatest strength consists in insisting on discipline. Everybody knows Jackson. Anyway it may be interesting to know, that after the battle of Chancellorsville the Government intended to nominate him to the full title of General, and to send him to the West. Certainly this would have been the best thing to do.

Whiting is said to be one of the best theoretical and practical Generals we have. But his manners and habits are against him and retard his advancement. This has always been also my personal opinion, without taking his manners in consideration. He always was a good friend to me, and I wish to see him in a better position. Early made some mistakes lately, but this is only human. Despite poor knowledge about the enemy's movements, he certainly made the best campaign this year, has succeeded in doing something and will render further good services. One thing is apparent: no general used much strategy, and he used it more than anyone else.[27]

20. We Lost Nearly Everything

October 15, 1864–November 30, 1864

Everything seems to go to the dogs. We really were beaten by our own men, who, instead of being on the front, were busy plundering. Things happened, as I feared.

—*Oscar Hinrichs*

October 15, 1864 This morning I rode to the front with the General [Pegram], since it was reported that the enemy was not to be seen. Many were already happy, expecting to be in Winchester soon. But everybody was disappointed. Soon the enemy showed up at Hupps Hill and advanced to the old railroad, where they built a rather weak sharpshooter-line. Some 300 steps behind this they put up a strong line. Shortly after we went there, almost a whole Division of infantry appeared on Hupps Hill. They stayed there for a short while, then they all left, sharpshooters and all. Gordon's Division was advanced. His sharpshooters advanced till Hupps Hill, stayed there for a while and came back again. Around 2 P.M. I rode out again together with the General in order to make a survey of the country at our Front and toward the left. We neither saw nor heard the enemy. We returned to our Headquarters and had a perfectly terrible dinner around 5 P.M.[1]

There are rumors that the day before yesterday the 6th Corps with 1500 cavalry men went to the Luray Valley, just at the time, when our first attack was made. But today everybody is said to have come back and to have gotten into position in order to give us a good reception, in case we should dare to come. Up to now our Old Man does not seem to be eager to do anything.

I could not get any news from Richmond or from the battlefields in the West, although I personally believe, that something serious and important is in the making. Yesterday I heard that Sherman has been cut off from his army in Atlanta and that he has wired to his faithful servant Burbridge to come to his rescue with all the men he has at his disposal. The future will show, whether this has been done. Hood is said to have reached a position in the last few days on the so-called State Road, taking some 4000 prisoners. I do not know yet, what this State Road is.[2]

October 16, 1864 Today is Sunday again, and everybody seems to keep quiet. This morning, after a long time, I had my first game of chess again. What amused me most were the faces they made, because it was Sunday! Towards 2 PM our old General [John Pegram] came back and we rode out together. We almost reached Cedar Creek, trying to find out, whether it would be possible to take our army through the woods toward Middletown and to attack the enemy there. We returned to our Headquarters only very late and found orders to be ready for marching in the early hours tomorrow.[3]

It seems, that our Old Man has something up his sleeve, because almost all the Divisions have received identical orders. I am afraid, nothing will come of it; our movements are too slow. For one thing, quickness is not one of our virtues, and, besides, we do not seem to be able to bring anything to an end. I had a long conversation regarding Europe and the science of war. I was very astonished to learn Brigade General [Robert] Johnston's views, which seemed rather strange to me, and which Gen. Pegram will probably call nonsense. This young man has still a lot to learn. It may be, that tomorrow we will have a big fight, but nothing may come of it. Had no news regarding my letters. A fortnight passed, since I wrote about them, so I gather, they were lost.

October 17, 1864 Today everything was quiet until midday. Then I rode out with the General in order to visit — at a distance — the camp and the "vedettes" (outposts) of the enemy. It has been decided to attack the enemy. We came to our camp around 10 PM after having had a wonderful ride. Tomorrow we are supposed to make one more excursion and then attack the enemy. We might make a nice job of it, if we only could keep our troops from plundering. I am rather pessimistic in this regard, but hope that I might be wrong.[4]

October 18, 1864 Today I spent most of the day in Gordon's Headquarter[s] waiting for General Pegram. He had promised to come by for me on his way back from the Old Early. We intended to go to the signalling station on the Massanutten Mountains. But he did not show up, and I stayed where I was. Towards night orders arrived to start marching right away, which was done. Our order was: Gordon — Ramseur — Pegram. All three Divisions were under Gordon's orders. Kershaw was meant to attack the following morning, after us, and Wharton should have followed, as soon as the road was clear.

We march along Tumbling Run behind Strasburg, over the [North Fork of the] Shenandoah, along the mountain range until [crossing Bowman's Ford] we reach the road from Middletown to Front Royal, where we shall attack the enemy. I still have the feeling, as if things would not come out as they should.[5]

October 19, 1864 We marched, as I pointed out yesterday, but in a miserable fashion. The night was extremely cold, and we marched very slowly, so we arrived at the point, where we were supposed to attack the enemy only about one full hour after daybreak. One cavalry brigade—Lomax's old brigade under Col. [William H. F.] Payne—joined us in the morning and took the outposts of the enemy by surprise.

Kershaw attacked at least ¾ hour before us. Quickly and neatly the enemy was driven out of his camp, suffering heavy losses. At 11 AM the battle was won. We had taken some 1500 prisoners, 18 guns, 50 wagons and at least just as many ambulances. But on the other hand our losses were also heavy. The enemy's 8th and 19th Corps resisted only very little, but the 6th fought extremely well and did everything a good troop can possibly do. Our lines were advanced and formed beyond Middletown. Wharton and our Division [were] to the [enemy's] left, [followed by] Ramseur, Gordon and Kershaw.[6]

At first the enemy tried only to make plans in order to save his trains, but when he saw, that we did not pursue him, but gave him time to recover, he attacked us, but was beautifully defeated. About an hour later the enemy [led by Sheridan] made a very heavy attack on the left wing and broke through Gordon's and Ramseur's Divisions. Kershaw gave in shortly thereafter, and seeing this, our and Wharton's Division did the same. All, except our Division, ran back as quickly as they could. Johnston's and Pegram's Brigades were handled well and acted like men.[7]

Our retreat was done quite well until we reached the Shenandoah Bridge [near Spangler's mill]. Here the enemy was reinforced by some 200 cavalrymen which attacked 50 or 60 men under General Pegram and two of his officers. The enemy was defeated, but he then tried to surround us, and now the whole thing broke down. We lost nearly everything: 34 guns, many prisoners, at least a 100 ambulances and wagons, if not more. The whole army was pretty well scattered. General Ramseur, who had been seriously wounded, was captured by the enemy and taken back. Late at night we arrived at Fisher's Hill, where I tried to gather my Division, but I had only some 60 men. Everything seems to go to the dogs. We really were beaten by our own men, who, instead of being on the front, were busy plundering. Things happened, as I feared.[8]

October 20, 1864 This morning we marched since 2 1/2 A.M. We finally reached New Market and went in our old camp. The enemy did not follow us. Everything looks quite sad. There are about 600 men in our Division here. I forgot to state, that on the 18th I received my letters from Richmond. One was from my mother [Amalia Ehringhaus Hinrichs] and two from [Mary] Mamie Stanley. There was no news in them, except that one tells me indirectly, that Chris arrived safely.[9]

October 21, 1864 Everything quiet today. This afternoon we had an inspection of our Division and there were some 800 men with 500 rifles. Otherwise there is nothing new. Today I wrote two letters to my parents, but did not send them. Then I wrote a letter to Till and started one for Mamie. I hope to finish them tomorrow. It is almost too cold to write out in the open, so I have to postpone it. There is no news from Richmond. It seems that there everything is quiet now.

October 22, 1864. Today we stay quietly in camp. I continue my writing letters, although it is frightfully cold. I could not get any news from anywhere. Now the newspapers already start to blame our Old Man for the excursion near Cedar Creek. In the end Gordon may get all the praises for the first attack, although it's the commander of our Division who deserves it.[10]

October 23, 1864 Again we stay in camp. Today I finished my letters and mailed them. As usually the newspapers are lying about the things which happened here and accuse our Old man and several officers of having been drunk. I wish I had had something to drink myself at that time. Great efforts are being made to improve the command, especially in regard to discipline. There are no news either from Richmond nor from Hood. I am afraid, that the concentration of the fleet in Beaufort N.C. and S.C. may mean an attack on Wilmington. I should like to ask to be sent there.[11]

October 24, 1864 Nothing new today. I heard today that Lomax and his men were at 6 miles from Winchester during our battle. It is said that the 8th and 19th Corps were taken completely by surprise. Only the 6th Corps resisted our attack. The Governors of the different States came together and decided to offer the negroes in the States to the government. An excellent thing to do, if it could only be carried out. This way it will be possible to put under arms some 30.000 [30,000] men, who now are serving as pioneers or drivers. I wish to see this thing come true.[12]

October 25, 1864 Today Lt. Col. [Charles S.] Venable of General Lee's Staff visited with us. He gave us a very interesting and comforting description of our position around Richmond. He said that now there are many men coming to our army and that the number of our men is increasing. Fort Harrison is said to have been taken by surprise through the friendship of the Old Ewell. Only a few reconvalescents ["returned convalescents"] and some artillery were in that thing. Ewell and the greatest part of his command were at Signal's Hill which was dodged by the enemy. He (Ewell) thought, Signal's Hill was the most important post. In the attack on Fort Gilmer, there were only about 50 men from Bennings Brigade besides the artillery in the thing and elegantly defeated that attack. The attack was carried out by negro troops. The field officers etc. stayed back at least half a mile in a little wood and sent forward the attacking column under the orders of the company-officers. The negroes marched right into the ditches of Fort Gilmer, and as soon as they fell into them the artillerists threw lighted bombs among them. Only a few were taken prisoners. I heard a fine thing said to have happened during our last battle. The 4th N.C. Regiment came upon some 200 enemies in a defile and did not wait to ask them to surrender but fired right into them, until all but some 40 men were shot.[13]

October 26, 1864 Today we had again a visit by Colonel [Walter H.] Jenifer—who used to be the chief of the Maryland troops. But he seems to be from Mobile and gave us rather good news from there. He told us, that after the attack by the fleet the enemy might have taken the town right away. Now it is too late. In the meantime batteries have been built up everywhere, so that a combined attack by fleet and army would be necessary to take the city. The newspapers are fiercely attacking our Old Man and say that Applejack is the reason of our defeat. I wish that all these damned newspapermen would be put into the service.[14]

October 27, 1864 Everything quiet today. We stayed here longer than I had expected. Lomax reports that the enemy disappeared from his front, and that some 500 cavalrymen showed up in Little Washington, the seat of Rappahannock County. Work on the Manassas Gap Railroad has been stopped, while it has been taken up on the Orange-Alexandria Railroad. The enemy is said to be very restless in his camp. It rained awfully hard last night. Yesterday I fell with my horse and sprained my ankle. We should start marching soon.

October 28, 1864 Nothing new today from our own fronts. Two small Brigades [of] Cavalry arrive today—Gillmer's [Harry Gilmor's] and Causby's [Brig. Gen. George B. Cosby], with some 7[oo]–800 men. The newspapers report some more fights around Richmond and Petersburg. It seems that the enemy attacked our left wing, but was repulsed with heavy losses. 500 prisoners were taken. At the same time our right wing was also attacked, but this, as far as I heard, did not amount to much. The enemy seems to want to extend his line to the right, which would take him right into a very swampy region. Gen. [James] Dearing, the commander of a Cavalry Brigade, was killed during the fight. Our losses are said to have been very light. Nothing new from the western Front. A few days ago, maybe on the 24th, the enemy attacked Lomax and his camp. Eight guns started firing at him, and since there came no response, the enemy asked, where Lomax's artillery was? Three attacks were defeated.[15]

Tonight I visited Early's Headquarters. I heard that he is very depressed about the newspaper articles. There seems to spring up an animosity between Early and Gordon, and it won't need much to blow this up into a roaring flame. It would be an excellent thing for the service, if some of the gentlemen would loose their positions through their talking. Now they are causing considerable damage, which may not be repairable. Today all the commanders of the Divisions of this army had a conference with our Old Man. I could not find out the reason for it, most probably some devilish trick. We shall soon find out about it.[16]

October 29, 1864 Today is Sunday again. And there is nothing new. We had a visit from the Cousin of our General—of the same name. He seems to be a jolly fellow. I heard that some changes—ad interim—will be made in the staff. A brother of the mistress of our General is supposed to come here as A.D.C. for the time being. He also is, as far as I could see and hear, a nice boy. As I said before, there is no news.

October 30, 1864 Our guest is still with us. Everything seems to be quiet. I had a chimney built to my tent and have some more comfort now. Sunday is today instead of being yesterday.

October 31, 1864 Our guest is still here and cheers us up quite a bit. No news from either here, Richmond or the West. But I heard that Mosby caught some Yankees near Bunker Hill, among which was a brigade of General Duffié. I just heard a little song, which the cavalry General "J. E. B. Stewart" wrote on his horse "Maryland." It sounds just as he used to be [see Appendix 2].

November 1, 1864 Today we still stay quietly in our camp near New Market without anything interesting to happen. As usually the northern newspapers are telling lies about our battle and make a great noise about the few prisoners, which—at their counting—have already increased to 1600. Besides they do not give us any credit for some 1500 who in the meantime safely arrived in Richmond. Duffié—a general on the enemy's side who was taken prisoner by Mosby—is a Frenchman and was commander in the Kanawha Valley. It seems that he was going to visit Sheridan and was on his way back to Winchester. His Cavalry-escort failed to follow the general's Ambulance closely and so gave Mosby an opportunity to catch the general and his staff before the cavalry could close up. Such is life.[17]

I read a little book by Captain L. E. Nolan (15th Hussars, English Army) regarding cavalry service. It seems to be a good little book and the rules contained in it would be of great advantage for us, if they would only be followed. I should like to change my status and join the Cavalry, because then I would have the possibility of advancement. Where I am now I stay were I am and do not get ahead. I have served now for almost 3 years without being advanced at all, and I am getting tired of it.

November 2, 1864 It seems to me as if we were going to stay here forever. We still are on the same spot. Quarters for winter are being fixed, and I shall be glad to see them ready. There is nothing new around here. Everything seems to be quiet, and even the crater of Richmond has given up spitting fire. It is said that Grant lost some 5000 men in the last affair, so he won't be in a hurry to expose himself to another defeat. Our armies are increasing. I should be surprized to see him stay much longer on the Northerner's side. I feel, that handling the thing right, we could make something out of an attack and probably defeat Grant almost completely. According to my opinion we should at least try it.[18]

There is something going on in Missouri, but up to now I could not learn how things really are there. It is said that a battle has been fought, and both sides claim the victory for themselves. But I should not be surprised to hear, that we were beaten. Price is a good old soul, but, as things are in this country, he cannot keep an inn. There is no discipline in his men, and they come and go as they please. Therefore one day he has an army and tomorrow nobody. Let us hope that Smith and Magruder get some order into things and—at least— keep the enemy busy. Right now they are in Arkansas.[19]

November 3, 1864 Tonight our new and temporary A.D.C. arrived. Nothing new either from Hood or from Richmond. The newspapers report that Grant wired about his last affair at Richmond as being a recognizance [reconnaissance]. A nice way of doing things, especially since such things do not cost anything, just some 5,000,000 Dollar[s] and 5000 lives. This is a small affair, and does not harm the world. I personally think that something at least has been gained, that is to say, that many of those scoundrels had to take their dismissals. Forrest made a tenspot: he captured some boats on the Tennessee River and besides some 60 wagons with shoes, which are good and come in handy for us.[20]

November 4, 1864 Nothing new today. Tonight I received a letter from Till. She wrote, that somebody, whom I would like to see, was going to bring me the letter, but she does not mention a name. I cannot figure out, whom she means.

November 5, 1864 Today it is agreeably cold. Nothing new. Last night I visited the General Headquarters and found out that something is in the air, maybe a march towards Winchester. It is said, that the enemy changed his position and retreated back of Fishers Hill. This is quite possible, because nobody could stand it in that position during this kind of weather. Most probably they changed in order to be nearer to the depots and in order to get into a decent camp. We do not march yet.

November 6, 1864 Today was a fine and important day for me. My father [Carl E. L. Hinrichs] arrived here. This is the person, Till was speaking of. My head and my heart are both too full for writing at length. It is enough that my father is here. I was just busy writing Till and scolding her a little, but I postponed it. Today I received my advancement to Captain [to rank from October 19.][21]

November 7, 1864 My father is with me. I hardly can believe it's reality. I would give everything to have both my parents here with me. There is no news regarding the military part. Everything seems to be quiet. Anyway I can't help feeling that something is going to happen before the week is over.

November 8, 1864 My father is still with me. Today we visited the different Headquarters together and I introduced him to Old Early. I should like to go to Richmond with him, but I am afraid, I won't be able to do so.

November 9, 1864 My father is still with me but wants to leave tomorrow. I asked to be allowed to accompany him till Richmond, but got a refusal. During the afternoon orders reached us to be ready for marching towards Winchester tomorrow. Nothing new otherwise.

November 10, 1864 After his short visit my father left today for Richmond. I am quite worried about him and I wish he were already in New York. We started marching and camped on the other side of Woodstock. We received orders to continue our march tomorrow morning. Today Kershaw was in front and our Division followed. Tomorrow we shall march ahead. It is sheer nonsense that my request for leave has been refused because nothing will become of this march.

November 11, 1864 We started marching this morning passing through Strasburg and Middletown, heading for Newtown, where the cavalry of Col. [William H. F.] Payne had a little fight. 20 prisoners were taken. We are camping at two miles from Newtown. The enemy does not seem to care much about us.[22]

November 12, 1864 Today we stayed before Newton. It is said that the enemy is advancing. Our troops have been put into line. But only a cavalry battle came of it. It is said that Rosser nicely cleaned up the enemy, and the same is said of Payne. When it became dark we retreated towards Fisher's Hill and camped in our old camp there. It is reported that McCausland lost 2 guns on the left of our line. It is strange that lately we cannot encounter the enemy without letting him have some guns. These last two have been surrendered now.[23]

November 13, 1864 Today we march back and camp near Edinburg. It is terribly cold. The enemy does not seem to want to follow us. Today we marched in the rear.

November 14, 1864 Today we marched to New Market and looked for a new camp. But since we could not find any suitable place, we went back to our old camp. It is still very cold. Today I received a letter from Charlie Stanley who is asking me for money. I do not know [how] I'll get it for him. I must already sell some gold in order to pay for my coat. I wish I could send some money to the poor boy, but I really do not know how to manage it.[24]

November 15, 1864 Today I wrote letters to Till, Rodgers and to Col. [Alfred L.] Rives and [Chief of Ordnance Josiah] Gorgas, the latter regarding the French affair. I did not hear anything new either from our or the enemy's front. Nothing new from Richmond either. Grant seems to wait for the return of his troops which went to the National elections before he thinks of starting something new. It seems that Lincoln has been reelected, so now we cannot count on more than 4 years. McClellan seems to have gotten only a few votes. He now will have to retire, there is nothing for him to do.[25]

Forrest succeeded again in scaring the enemy good and well by capturing and burning 3 gunboats, some 20 steamers and several small ships on the Tennessee River. Besides he burned down a lot of material stored on the Northern side of the river. The whole thing happened near a small village, "Johnsonville."[26]

The newspapers report the sad loss of our small battleship Florida in the Bay of Bahia by the U.S. Battleship Wachusetts under Capt. [Napoleon] Collins. It seems as if the Captain, C. [Charles] Manigault Morris—who formerly belonged to the U.S. Marine Division and later was lighthouse inspector—had gone to shore with about 70 men and several officers, and that there were only 56 people on board the ship. Let us hope that this affair may arouse some noise and excitement between the U.S. Marine and the other Seapowers, otherwise no port will be safe for us. Neither Southampton nor Cherbourg. As the story is told in the newspapers it shows that the whole crew of the Wachusetts including their fine Captain were extremely cowardly. At the same time arrives the unconfirmed report of the loss of the Tallahassee near Cape Hatteras on the North Carolina Coast. If this report is confirmed it would be only too bad for us, because right now we cannot spare any ships.[27]

I forgot to note before that Plymouth N.C. has been reoccupied by the enemy and that our iron Battleship Albemarle was exploded by the enemy [led by Lt. William B. Cushing], causing considerable losses to him. In Plymouth we lost nothing but the city. An extensive attack both by sea and by land is expected for this winter on the town of Wilmington. Let us hope that this town stays open for us for some time longer. Today has been designated by the Government as Church Holyday as a Fast—and Prayer day. Therefore everything is quiet in camp.[28]

November 16, 1864 Today seems to stay quiet and on both sides thoughts seem to be given rather to winter quarters than to fighting. Kershaw's Division, a few days ago, marched towards Waynesborough, most probably in order to join the troops in Georgia and to be ready to oppose the enemy there, who is led by Sherman. This General seems to have forgotten all the war rules known up to the present. He left Atlanta in a hurry and is now racing through the State towards Mobile, Savannah or Charleston; at least so say the rumors. Hood must have gone up in the air: not the slightest news about him.

November 17, 1864 This morning we started marching in order to reach a new camp near Lacy's Springs, some 8 miles this side of Harrisonburg. I called on Captain Smith in Headquarters and then rode towards our new camp. I had a pass for Staunton signed, where I intend to get my new coat. Nothing new happened otherwise.

November 18, 1864 Today I rode to Staunton and arrived there as wet as a bathed cat. It rained awfully hard all day long. I could not get my coat.

November 19, 1864 I shall stay in Staunton today in order to finish my business. I sold 15 Dollars worth of gold to my friend Tams, where I am spending the night.

November 20, 1864 I shall stay on in Staunton. Am feeling very badly, after the drinking and smoking last night. The weather is awful.

November 21, 1864 Today I rode back despite wind and rain and arrived at 5 PM. Nothing new. I received a letter from Mrs. Frink. I found everything topsy turvy and the chimney of my tent is missing. I do not at all like the way things are handled here, especially by our Division doctor. He should like to play the part of the fine gentleman, but does not know how to do it.

November 22, 1864 This morning we received the news that the enemy wants to pay back our last visit and that he camped in Woodstock. It seems though, that it is just a scouting excursion. Anyway Gordon, Wharton and Grimes started out and went to Rude's Hill. I started an answer to my letter, but it is too cold for writing. I am having a new fireplace built.[29]

November 23, 1864 My fireplace smokes terribly, so I had it torn down today. I had to let my letter go for the time being. Nothing came from the enemy's plans and the scoundrels went back into their hole.

November 24, 1864 The day is not over yet, and things might still happen. Up to now everything is quiet. I have finished my letters and have also written my diary. My new fireplace is something wonderful and behaves fine. I did not hear anything about Sherman except that he is marching towards Macon. I hope that the end of the march may displease him. It's night again and we are still here on the same spot. Nothing new happened.

November 25, 1864 Another day went by and nothing happened. There was no particular danger for us, as far as I can make out. Everybody seems to keep quiet. How long this will last, though, only Heaven knows.

November 26, 1864 It almost seems to me as if we were permanently camped here. We stay on one spot and wait for better times. There is no news from Georgia, except that Sherman's expedition is by and by taking form and spreading. It seems—since nothing is certain yet—that Sherman is headed for the coast and that he is approaching Charleston, Savannah or Mobile. The newspapers say, that soon he will come "to shame" but they forget to tell the public, in what way and manner this is supposed to happen. As far as my knowledge goes, I do not know of any mass of troops which could be sent against him. Hood is too far away—in Tennessee—and will therefore not be able to help either one of these cities. Besides, even if he should try it, he would have Thomas in his neck and be busy with him. It seems, as if something would happen to take us out of this position and enable us to oppose the enemy. Everything is quiet around Richmond. Bad weather and worse roads made an end of the war there, at least for the time being. All the interest concentrates upon Georgia. Tonight I received a very nice letter from W. N. H.

Smith—M. C. I wrote to him about some cloth from the State of N.C. and this is his answer to it.[30]

November 27, 1864 I cannot report anything new today. Yesterday I forgot to note that I rode to Harrisonburg in order to get my coat. I believe, today is Sunday. I did not hear anything yet about my letters to Rives and Gorgas and am wondering about it. This morning I called on the 20th N.C. Regiment and played a few games of chess. Today I had a little fight with our surgeon. It seems necessary for this gentleman to have somebody give him his mind every once in a while. He is an uneducated, uncouth fellow and in the wrong place since quite a while. I have an idea of asking for permission to go to New York for a while and start a little revolution there. The end of the story would most probably be, to be hanged on a lantern post—but that is a matter of no concern. Anyway, I should like to try it.[31]

November 28, 1864 Tonight I had the intention of telling the General [Pegram] about my ideas, only he had company, so I had to give it up for the time being. My ideas about it are stronger than ever. It can and must succeed, if done right, and I believe, I could. At least it is worth while trying it, according to my opinion. I hear today, that the last small affair near Mt. Jackson was of greater importance than we thought at first. It is said that the enemy had and acknowledged a loss of some 400. Our losses are very small, only 8 dead and 75 wounded. The enemy attacked with some 10,000 cavalrymen but seems to take his defeat calmly. I wish, the devil gets them all together. I wish to hear from my father in order to know whether he safely reached E. [Elizabeth] City.

November 29, 1864 Tonight I had a long talk with the General concerning a trip to New York in order to start a riot there. He seemed to like the thing and promised me his help. I am afraid, nothing will come of it, because the Government won't want to be mixed up in such an affair. Anyway, there cannot be any harm for me, if I do try it; I may get an advancement through it, and that is all I am after. We have marvellous weather right now. Warm and agreeable. We don't need the fire. I wish, I could have a talk with our Mr. President about my ideas. I think I could get my advancement in a much more agreeable way.

November 30, 1864. I visited the 20th N.C. Regiment tonight in order to play some chess. The newspapers report that our prisoners tried to free themselves in Salisbury, but without success. Some 40 were shot. Nothing new otherwise.

21. Leave for Petersburg

December 1, 1864–December 31, 1864

Everything seems to be quiet, and the year is coming to a close quickly,
and all the hopes we held in spring seem to be destroyed.

—Oscar Hinrichs

December 1, 1864 Today we received a dispatch from General Rosser, in which he reports that he attacked the enemy in a fortified position [New Creek on the B&O Railroad] near Moorfield and that he took the place with 800 prisoners, 8 guns and a great amount of material. Besides, many carriages were destroyed. Many horses and other animals, including Yankees, are reported to be moving towards their rendezvous, they have been longing for so much. A fine thing for us, and excellent right now! I wish, such news would come from all sides. Today I had my horses estimated. The heavy one brings 1050 $, my stallion 1800 $. So it is in this world. If I should have the bad luck of loosing one, I could not replace it with that money.[1]

December 2, 1864 Today it rained all day long and made any kind of outdoor activity impossible. Anyway I went out to make a visit tonight, which did not bring in anything for me, except some wet clothes. I haven't yet heard about my letters to Richmond regarding the Louis Galley matter. It seems rather strange to me, but I do not think, that I could do anything about it. Nothing new today.

Sherman seems to have everything his own way. Pretty soon, I am afraid, he will report in Savannah or Charleston, rather the first place, and that town will easily be his. Whether there will be anything gained, is another question. Anyway, he would then be free to move towards Charlestown and attack this town again with the help of a strong marine, or—and this seems still more probable to me—he may help Grant in his plans about Richmond. It will be hardest for us, to resist him there, without sending troops over from here. But where shall the troops be taken from?

It looks as if somebody was trying to spoil my chances in New York and started burning down public houses, and so on. Up to now nobody seems to have been caught, and I hope they will get away with it. On the other hand I wish things like that would not happen just as yet.[2]

December 3, 1864 There is nothing new, as far as I could learn. The weather is cold, and has stopped the war here for the time being. The newspapers report about Sherman's march through Georgia, but without making anything clear, so it is impossible to make head or tail out of it.

December 4, 1864 Today is Sunday again. I rode over to Wharton's Head-quarter[s] in order to talk over with him my plans about New York. He seems to be interested and thinks, that something could be done. The more I think about it, the more convinced I am, that something could be done successfully. He was giving me all kind of encouragement, but did not seem to take every-thing and every detail into consideration. I received a letter from our little [Lt. Randolph] Ridgely. His address is Dr. McClanahan, Charlotte, N.C. I shall write to him tomorrow.

December 5, 1864 Today I wrote to Ridgely and Col. Rives and Smith about the Louis Galley affair. I asked the latter one to take care of the matter and to write to me about it. Today I played a long game of chess with Dr. Hills with changing luck. Anyway, I am playing better now than before.[3]

December 6, 1864 Around 9 A.M. we received the unexpected order to march right away and to follow Gordon's Division. In a short time everything was packed and on the street. We camped in our old camp near Burkstown. Our Headquarters were in the house of Old Burk. There was a lot of speculating on the way, whereto we were marching. But since the whole thing is kept ex-tremely secret, it was just useless speculating. My personal idea is, that we are being sent to Richmond and Petersburg. Sherman has sent some troops there. One Corps and part of another are said to be already on their way.

December 7, 1864 We continued our march today and camped in our old camp near Waynesboro. The General's quarters are with the railroad agent Douglas and mine with Gallaher. Gordon left tonight with his troops by railroad. We are expected to follow early tomorrow, but I don't believe we'll get away before night. Otherwise nothing new.

December 8, 1864 I went to Staunton today because of my desk, and came back only after dark. Yesterday I received a letter from Tams with a check for $128, the balance for my gold. When I came back, the General had already left with a part of the troops. Our entire Division, except some 500[,] leave tonight. Douglas follows tomorrow with the rest.

December 9, 1864 We arrived in Richmond this afternoon after a very disagreeable trip. We stayed in Richmond for only 30 minutes, then we got into another train ready to leave for Petersburg. I saw George Lemmon very drunk. Around 6 we arrived at Dunlop Station and started marching to our lines right away. It snowed, rained and froze on the march of about 10 miles. We camped, for the night, near the Boydton Plank road. I had a terrible night, because, after the troops had settled down in the huts in front of Finnegans Brigade I went to Gordon's quarters in order to look for the General, but I did not find him. I had to go on to Colonel [William J.] Pegram's quarters, found him there, but could not stay with him, because the place was overcrowded. I finally camped at midnight with Gen. [Robert] Johnston.[4]

December 10, 1864 Today it is very cold and it looks as if it were going to rain. The reason for our haste is, that Grant had sent the 5th and part of the 9th Corps to Weldon in order to destroy the railroad. This caused the movement of Hill's troops, which caused a lack of protection on our right wing and no possibility of opposing the enemy there. Gordon's and our division had to take the places of these troops for the time being. All this happened between the 6th and 8th. On the 8th Hampton had a little fighting at Bellefield. It was, however, of little significance. The enemy destroyed approximately 15 miles of the railroad and subsided. Few prisoners were taken.[5]

12.11.1864 Today I am riding with the general through our lines. As far as the bulwark works are concerned, they are not in as good a state as I expected. Otherwise we are staying quietly in our quarters. Hope that Johnston, [William G.] Lewis, and [John S.] Hoffman are in the huts near the works.

12.12.1864 We are still in these quarters; expect, however, the daily return of the troops, we also will leave then. Last night Douglas arrived with the last part of our division.

12.13.1864 Marching out this morning since the troops returned this morning. Will camp on the south side of Hatchers Run, and approximately 3 miles from Burgess Mill. Have orders to build houses, nothing else is new.

12.14.1864 Riding out today into our new lines. Beautiful landscape with many swamps, firs, and pinewood and sand. No news as far as I could learn around here. It seems Hood had a battle at Franklin in which he did not win anything of significance, except the loss of many men. [Major General] Pat Cleburne was killed. After the battle the firing subsided until close to Nashville. That is the situation today.[6]

12.15.1864 Riding out again today. No news from either side. The newspapers report that Fort McAllister on the mouth of the river Oge[e]chee has been taken by the enemy. This opens the door for Sherman to get to the ocean and unite with the fleet. Nothing else.[7]

12.16.1864 Am going to stay at home today and relax. Nothing new on our fronts; nothing as far as I could learn. The battle at Franklin, mentioned on the 14th, did not accomplish anything except the loss of 13 generals. This is a great loss, and will bring us great damage should new operations be undertaken. It seems Sherman reached the coast safely.[8]

12.17.1864 Riding to the fronts with the general today. However, without any new information. Will have dinner with General Johnston.

12.18.1864 Today is Sunday and I am going to stay home and read. Tonight I received a letter from [William N. H.] Smith, an order from Governor [Zebulon] Vance for a piece of cloth for a uniform. Played a little chess at night.

12.19.1864 Early this morning I received orders from General Gordon to meet him not far from Crows Dam. Arrived a little late for the appointed time, yet still early enough for him. Rode with him and Gen. [Clement A.] Evans and a few other officers along our lines to view the construction crews and to select places for a few other dams. Coming back I stopped at Johnston's, ate my lunch, then went to Lewis' and returned home about dusk.[9]

Yesterday morning the enemy fired a salute of 34 cannonades. What could have been the reason for this? Deserters say it was for a victory of [George H.] Thomas over Hood at Nashville. Todays newspapers bring Thomas' official report in which he says that he made an attack on the left center, took 16 cannons, 800–1000 prisoners, a few wagons, and drove Hood 8 miles back. It seems Hood sent his whole cavalry and one division infantry, and Thomas took advantage of this favourable moment. My opinion is that this is the truth and no lie as it has been so many times.[10]

The war in the West seems to be very much misunderstood, for the same mistakes are always being repeated. The favourable outlooks of the beginning of this year are being lost, and it would not surprise me if the beginning of the next campaign would not end with the capture of Petersburg or Richmond; everything seems to indicate this. Talked today with several officers and exchanged my opinion, a few have agreed with me. No further news from Sherman. Savannah also is to be surrendered soon.

12.20.1864 Stayed today in my quarters and awaited orders from Headquarters of the Corps with regard to yesterday's inspection; yet nothing resulted of it, and everything seems to be quiet. Had a visit today, a brother of one of our generals — a lieutenant colonel of the artillery — a very nice little fellow. Nothing new on our fronts. Hood seems to have taken a few defeats, for one can see from the enemy newspapers that supposedly some 40 pieces of cannons have been received in Nashville.

It seems as if the enemy wants to move the seat of war further down to the South, for an excursion seems to have been made from Newbern without any effect. A large fleet of some 75 to 100 ships supposedly is armed for an attack on Wilmington. The advance guard supposedly appeared. I would not be surprised if a sizeable landforce would go along to possibly make an attack from both sides; anyone's attack from one side cannot do anything.[11]

12.21.1864 Staying at home again today. Last night it rained like mad, and takes everything away this morning. The newspapers bring only northern news about affairs in Tennessee; news of the same source say that Butler is supposedly in the land force which is directed toward Wilmington. D. [David] D. [Dixon] Porter, U.S.N., is in command of the fleet. The fleet is divided into five divisions. Some 30 ships supposedly arrived at New Inlet. Paid a visit to General Johnston with Douglas and spent a pleasant evening.[12]

12.22.1864 Going to stay in my quarters today and make myself useful in general. The family of this house moved out today, and the General [John Pegram] took his leave for a visit in Richmond and [to see] his beloved [Hetty Cary]. Also a nice scenery. Writing to my father c/o J. D. Schultz. Am also writing to General Whiting in Wilmington. Hear that Hoke and B. [Bushrod] R. Johnson went to Wilmington with their divisions. Last evening our general told us it is possible that we, i.e. our corps, would go there—which pleased me very much. Would like to go there to take part in the spectacle this winter. Tonight Dr. Grymes came to us, and as always, made himself extraordinarily unpleasant. Hope his visit will only last until the morning, and he will then make himself invisible for some time. No news in our front. Everything seems to be quiet. Wrote to Fains to send me my desk and table via Dr. Manson in Richmond.[13]

12.23.1864 [Major John P. H.] New left yesterday for a 15 day leave; today Douglas goes to Petersburg. Russel is taking care of his affairs and none but I stays in Headquarters today. Daniels [Capt. Raleigh T. Daniel Jr.] spent some time with me, played a few games of chess. In the evening I played with Douglas. No news on our front as far as I could hear. The enemy's movement on the coast did not enforce any change yet. A strong storm seems to prevail there, and not much is being seen of the fleet.[14]

An expedition left from Roanoke up the Roanoke river towards Fort Branch [located just south of Hamilton, N.C.]. A meeting took place in which the enemy has been driven off first; later, however, he managed to land a few sharpshooters. One can assume, therefore, that this little place was taken by the enemy. The enemy took 700 prisoners at the assault of Fort McAllister [near Savannah]. The enemy lost 2 can[n]onboats below Fort Branch, and a little steamer, which was being used as a dispatch boat, was also blasted in the air through a submarine device. Further news about the West, obtained from northern newspapers, say that our old Ed Johnson's whole division with all his brigade commanders has been taken prisoner. His capture is not known. It seems there he also had bad luck. No news received from our side yet.[15]

It seems the enemy became too troublesome for V.D. [Valley Department]. A cavalry force of circa 4000 men seems to have gone through Chester Gap and is supposed to advance through Madison County towards Gordonsville. According to today's news they advanced up to 12 miles. Lomax is supposed to be there. A meeting supposedly took place, which resulted in our favor. Today Lee's division marched out, probably to be ordered there. The enemy is supposed to have split and advancing partly towards Charlottesville. That is the situation today. The enemy easily could make a fine thing out of this if he would not be short of spirit. The departure of the cavalry could mean a fine trick for us if the enemy would try it. So far, however, everything seems to be quiet, and the year is coming to a close quickly, and all the hopes we held in spring seem to be destroyed.

As far as one can judge the military and political situation does not look particularly favorable. It seems our congress is withholding the really necessary measures until the end of the session and does not do anything in their power to improve our situation. They could do many things, yet, many things remain undone to give themselves greater per diem. In my opinion nothing better could happen to the state than if Lee or someone else who has the confidence of the public would give the congress a violent end, and put a form of monarchy in their place. However, the country does not seem to be ready for this, but I fear that if it does not happen soon, it will be too late; for the enemy will have gained ground in the house. Hope for the homeland that my judgment is wrong, but I feel very peculiar.

It seems that Hood's army, as far as one can judge by now, has been almost completely wiped out. Since Beauregard has permitted this excursion to Tennessee, he is partly responsible; I still see no reason to change my formerly passed judgment of this man. He is of no use in the field. Anyway, to give Sherman permission to split his army was a nice idea, theoretical, he hoped to destroy Sherman before he reached the coast. Only he did not have enough men and means to resist him. Wheeler, of course, probably killed and captured a few thousand; alone, this is a one time episode in the military history of this world, where one side was capable of marching right through the middle of enemy territory, to infest great damage, and to reach his destination in safety. He hoped that Hood would draw Thomas behind him to reach the enemy territory to put him on the defensive, and in this way free Tennessee and Kentucky of the enemy. Yet Hood first marched about 1000 miles, runs headlong against the entrenchments of Franklin, then Nashville, and to fill the measure of madness, divides his army in view of the enemy; lets himself be surprised by the enemy, and loses in this way the only chance to make good a fool trick.

I had earlier thought that he [Hood] was a good commander and would not multiply the mistakes of his predecessors—I was very wrong. He is only capable of leading one division, and should be transferred to it immediately. Who will be next in lead there to build a new army, and straighten things out again? I know of none who would like to undertake it. It might still turn out well for us, for with those victories the enemy becomes more daring, and might try to tangle with England. Judging from the received news, no favorable mood towards England seems to prevail, and it easily could lead to a little friendly war. Let us hope so. Today Grymes and Hewatt left for their hospital and may the devil keep them there. I have become very wary of both of them long ago. Wrote today to Dr. [Lorenzo] Frink. So ends this day.

12.24.1864 Riding this morning to the quarters of General Johnston to talk with him about the fortification of his encampment. Will then in his company pay a visit to General [Rufus] Barringer. Find him to be a very nice man with good ideas, i.e. they correspond with my own. No news in our fronts. From V.D. it is said that Rosser and his brigade attacks and persues him. Lomax attacks two enemy divisions near Gordonsville, with heavy losses for the enemy and is following them. These are the first news, however, and further news in my opinion will alter the situation very much, i.e. all that glitters is not gold, and this could easily change to another October 19 [Cedar Creek]. Tonight I am going to play a little chess with Daniel and Douglas. The enemy in North Carolina suffered another defeat below Fort Branch. No news from Wilmington. The fleet, however, showed up again, yet did not undertake any operations yet.[16]

12.25.1864 Today is Sunday, and Christmas. A terrible day for me. My thoughts are all confused, and with today's weather it is almost enough to drive one mad. Am all alone in our quarters. Douglas is out on a visit and to attend a big dinner. General Johnston is away also, and it seems the whole party is busy enjoying themselves, I alone cannot do it. Am busy writing and keeping my diary up to date. Wrote a letter to Smith and thanked him for my cloth. Toward the evening I will go to see Colonel Hoffman and shall return rather late. Had a visit from [Capt. William G.] McNeely and [Lt. Waller] Holladay—the former brought me a few drops to drink. Would like to know how they are doing at home. God help me, how I would like to be with them today.[17]

12.26.1864 Today I was alone almost all day; during the morning Captain Daniel paid me a visit and we played a few games of chess. This is my only pleasure now. About 3 o'clock Douglas returned with General Johnston from their patrol and made quite a scandal. Feel today quite tired and faint from sitting up so late for I did not turn into my bed until about 3 o'clock in the morning. The weather is so miserably bad that one cannot venture out side without great effort. A few rumors are circulating concerning Wilmington and Savannah, yet, I omit saying anything further today until I get better news; there is also a rumor about an attack on our lines yesterday about daybreak, yet this is not certain. I did not hear any shots, and it is possible that the whole story is a canard. —So ends this day.

12.27.1864 Am going to stay at home today until about 2 o'clock, at which time I have been told that an old acquaintance, a brother of General Lewis[,] will come to see his brother. I went right away to see him, and was very glad to see him after such a long and perilous time. After my return I went with Captain Daniel to his quarters for dinner, had a very pleasant time, and returned home about 8 o'clock. Today I received a letter from Charlie Stanley in which he asked me for money to buy a horse. I don't see how I can help him, yet would like to do it very much.

Today's newspapers report that Hardee left Savannah, and that Sherman occupied the place immediately. This was a necessity as soon as Sherman reached the coast, and would Hardee have stayed there, it only would have been a question of time when he would have been obliged to surrender to Sherman. I cannot see where the enemy gained anything great with regard to military importance, for the past two years there has been no haven, since the enemy held the encampments at the mouth of the river, no railroad concentrates there; it is not a industrial town, and it must necessarily take the enemy some garrison upkeeping. By now Hardee can oppose Sherman in his advances toward Charleston, and if necessary deliver his troops for the defence of this city. Sherman will probably now turn toward the North, and try to engage himself at Richmond. Only the future can tell how far he will succeed.

The attack on Wilmington finally took place. Some 50 ships bombarded Fort Fisher at the Inlet, they only landed three brigades and attacked from the flank. Fort Fisher is situated on the end of an expanding neck of land and protects the entrance to Cape Fear from this side. The land attack was warded off, the sea attack did not cause any significant damage. This is in my opinion only a question of time, for this Fort can be taken. But everything has to be held as long as possible, for I have no doubt that Whiting will do everything in his power, did everything[,] to make his position as secure as possible. [Braxton] Bragg is the high commander, a bad thing. We don't have any news yet from Hood's army. He is supposed to have only about 12,000 men infantry and 8000 cavalry with him—many deserted.[18]

See a long article in today's newspapers urging to give General Lee the high command of all armies of the State. In other words to give him the same rank as other generals, like Grant, have now. I have often wondered, that the southern awareness if not necessity for titles created a name of this kind long ago. I do not believe anything can be more urgent as the present necessity for it, and I believe that Lee is the best man qualified for it. In my opinion—one I always have expressed—He would be of more use here than in the field. Who then will take the immediate command here is also an important question. —Some say [Joe] Johnston.

_____

12.28.1864 Will have an official visit today from Major [Conway R.] Howard of the 3rd Corps and members of the staff of General [A. P.] Hill, regarding the improvement of the roads between here and Petersburg. Rode with him today along the road and then went to see General Gordon, where I spent some time—ate dinner—and it was a very good one—and returned home about dusk. We have no news from the West, except for some presumptions of northern newspapers—who state that our losses are not as meaningful as it is proclaimed there.[19]

At Wilmington everything is quiet again. Under the protection of his can[n]ons and warships the enemy took his landed troops on board and drew away in the meantime. Our losses in the whole incident are supposed to be only some 50 men. Whereas the loss of the enemy is supposed to be much larger. So far so good—if the enemy gives up the attack of this side, he will not need to make another one for it will not gain him anything except heavy losses. His loss until now can only have been very small, and of no significance. No news about Sherman either. Everything at our fronts at Petersburg is very quiet for a few days. The outposts shoot each other down every now and then without any meaning.[20]

12.29.1864 Staying quietly in my quarters—waiting for my horse until about 2 o'clock in the afternoon. Rode then to General Gordon to look after yesterday's planned shoveling, etc., and to plan the work-details. Return home at 6 o'clock. There are no news anywhere. The enemy marched off [from] Wilmington, and for the time being the beleag[u]erment of this place is ended.

The leave of Savannah proceeded quietly, if one can trust the telegraphs. Some 150 heavy artillery, 25000 bales of cotton—19 locomotives and maybe 100 railroad cars are claimed as captured by the enemy. Three steamships also were taken, which probably had to be left behind due to the blockade of the river near the city. The armored can[n]onboats were blasted in the air, and the marine arsenal burned down. Sherman offers the President the city with the above mentioned material as a Christmas present. One of today's newspapers (Sentinel) came to the conclusion that Hood is not in such a bad situation as many believed, and says that victory would be required in our advanced position, and that his withdrawal would be looked upon as a lost battle. The whole story is being told very colorful and may influence these people.[21]

Russel returned today, only he did not bring me anything of what I requested, said it could not be purchased but I don't believe it. Should it really be so, then it would be a good thing if the Yankees would take the town, only to teach the people some intelligence and energy. Everyone is supposed to have been drunk during the holidays, and I believe it is not much better today. May the devil take them alltogether.

I am pretty tired and bored with the whole thing, and I would like to see an end one way or the other. In congress time is only being wasted with useless talk and chat. To meet their own expenses they give themselves a raise in their wages—now up to $40 per day—but don't let anyone else near the cashbox. We get the purse and they take the money—probably a convenient practice of an old proverb. Wrote today to Smith to send me the official reports on these armies (No. V[a])—but won't receive them.

12.30.1864 Early this morning the General returned from his leave and made a long face after his indulgence. Shortly after breakfast I rode with him to General Gordon and we spent a long time there. We departed about 2 o'clock, passing our Div. Hospital and train, he went to see General Lee and I [visited] General Hill to look over the working equipment for our Corps. I returned home about 8 o'clock in the evening after riding back for circa 40 miles. That is why I am pretty tired tonight—and since I have to get up at an early hour tomorrow I will not write too much tonight. No news in the world, as far as I can hear and see, except that it is planned to consolidate the regiments of our brigades. This will probably stir up a great commotion. But more about this at another time. As I said I am too tired today.

12.31.1864 Riding out this morning before breakfast with a detail to start the work on the roads. It was raining right in, and developed into a strong rain. Then about 11 o'clock back to the quarters, and I remained there for the day. No news in the world as far as I could hear; even the newspapers, who so to say are ordered to always be ready with fresh lies, have nothing today.

And this is the last day of an eventful year. Thank God I am still alive to see it. May fate answer the beseechment of my parents and friends and help me safe through the coming year as it did in the previous one. And where do we stand now at the end of the year with our country and our situation. In spring we had every prospect to be today with our friends, and to talk with them about the past. Today, all prospects considered, we are further away from the peace which we all hope so for.

Yet out of all ill that has come to us, some consolation is to be drawn, for in everything one can see the protecting hand of fate, which has kept us until now. Our country suffered under the heavy hands of our enemy, as rarely any country did. Yet we lost little real ground, and our armies performed wonders.

Grant, with an army that cannot be equaled by any other of this country and continent, tried in vain to attain the possession of Richmond. He wasted one army after the other, and draped his country in mourning. Even today— after a beleag[u]erment of seven months, he is holding out without taking a toll, which we would not have given him. Of course Sherman with a large army had a few great victories, which however, he let slip through his hands. On our side mistakes also have been made, which could have made us pay heavy penance, if the enemy would have seized them. Alone herein, as so many times, fate has kept us. In the West we rather took than lost and freed a great territory of the enemy.

At the present time our country is not too well provided with food. However, with returning warm weather and hard work it will again give us everything to hold body and soul together; enough, even if not in abundance. One has learned to go without luxuries, nature provides enough to feed and cloth men. Yet, people still have to learn much, and may heaven help that it has not to be at once; mourning also came to our country, in abundance, but we realize that we have to comply to fate and bear it willingly.

Let us hope that with the passing year our mistakes will also diminish, and new laurels will wind about our flag, to hasten to a victorious goal. May spring with its young leaves inspire men and animal to rejoice—peace—or if not, that fate may keep us. Again, thank God for his good givings and for his mighty and strong help. May we carry on to deserve his further help and keep. Received a letter today from Till—so ends this year.

Poem: 1865[22]

22. Capture of Fort Fisher

January 1, 1865–January 31, 1865

*Today's newspapers carried Porter's official dispatches about the fall of
Fort Fisher. According to his and our own news it has been a bloodbath.*

—Oscar Hinrichs

1.1.1865 Staying home today in my quarters and write a real long letter to Till.
Playing a few games of chess even though it is Sunday. No news as far as I could
hear today, except the day before yesterday [when Maj. Gen. Cadmus M.] Wilcox undertook a little patrol and captured a few hundred blue-bellied fellows
on their post. Mosby has been wounded some time ago, but recovered [and]
may he soon be in the saddle again. Nothing happened today as far as I know.

May heaven give that today's first new year's day may become a symbol of
coming victory. Peace with the founding of this new nation. May this year
pass with as little bloodshed, and may we in the next new year be able to sit
at our own fireside and reminisce [about] the war. May heaven give all of us,
our relatives, friends and acquaintances a long and peaceful life; move our
enemy's heart and bring him to real understanding. May our plans prosper
and proceed safely; may mischief and rubbish be the enemy's. May God in his
grace keep us all healthy and well in body and soul for a new year, and give us
understanding and strength to do good and love; help and keep us.

1.2.1865 Riding out early this morning to start the repair works between here
and Petersburg. The weather is cold and uncomfortable. Return at 4 o'clock to
my quarters—pay then a visit to the 20th [North Carolina] Regiment and to
the quarters of General Johnston. The visit has not been particularly pleasant.
No news as far as I could hear, [yet] it seems an attack at Wilmington is terminated for the time being, and it is said that the fleet returned to Fort Monroe.[1]

A later rumor comes from the West which claims that Hood marched along the Tennessee River, had a battle with Thomas and defeated him. This would be very desirable, only it is not so; Hood is in no position to take the offensive, and could only have advanced if Thomas was mad or drunk, none of which is a possibility. No further news about Sherman. As far as we know he stays still quietly at Savannah. Let us hope he will stay there for some time and behave himself. The North, according to the newspapers, is still very upset about the failure of the patrol to Wilmington. May this always happen to them.

1.3.1865 Proceed this morning with my work on the road, however, without much progress. Believe it will take a long time to complete it, as the weather will not permit it. Tonight it is snowing already as if it will never stop. Absolutely nothing new. The newspapers are silent. However, some interesting northern rumors circulate concerning the Wilmington story. It seems that Butler and Porter cannot agree on the failure of the attack on Fort Fisher. The navy dropped 115 bombs per minute in it. Six of the 100 pound cannons burst on board and caused quite some damage. They probably tried to shoot too far—and—there lie six Parrots burst. The enemy placed a powdership [the *Louisiana*] with 300 tons (à 2000 pounds) close to the bulwark and ignited it in the hope that the explosion would cause great damage; yet this also failed.[2]

Nothing else from there. We also have some news about the patrol to Fort Branch from people of this vicinity. Much is definitely untrue—even though these news come from our friends, they also do things like that occasionally. Six of their can[n]onboats supposedly were detonated and lost with circa 1000 men, navy and infantry. Two little boats which were used to locate submarine matters [underwater mines] were also lost. The whole story traveled up to circa 18 miles of Fort Branch. This little fort is located at the Roanoke river and protects Halifax.[3]

1.4.1865 Continue my work today, despite last night's snow. Have no particular news today, everything seems to have been quiet at the seat of war. Sherman seems to want to make some way in the direction of Charleston, for he rounded up our outposts on Savannah river, and occupied the north shore of the river. The yesterday mentioned powdership supposedly cost $250,000. Nothing else useful. Rumors say that Colonel [John E.] Mulford will soon issue a new contract which should satisfy us. This would be very desirable and would free some 40[,000]–50,000 of our prisoners, half of which we probably could use in the field. Some 10,000 of the second corps are supposed to be there. This would help us very much in our present condition.[4]

1.5.1865 Continue with my work today. Weather pleasant but cool. Nothing interesting to report from either side. Everything seems to be the same. Outside of a few bombings now and then, and daily sharpshooter firings from both sides[,] there is nothing. Our General, for the first time [in a while] is at home tonight, writing to us as usual. The newspapers carry nothing. In congress one plays with the idea to consolidate the regiments, etc.—but will make a cow's foot of it, i.e. a fool trick, and unworkable. Would like to see the whole story go to the devil.

1.6.1865 It started to rain and storm this morning, but the air was warm and pleasant. Followed my work-detail about 11 o'clock on horseback. If this warm weather continues I could begin the real repairwork of my road by tomorrow. Hope it will not rain anymore until I complete it. Returned to my quarters at 2 o'clock, but had to leave after a short time to see General Gordon, to talk him out of a stupid idea. Succeeded with it for the time being, but don't know for how long. Nothing new to report. Rumors say that Sherman occupied Hardeeville [South Carolina]. This is however not certain. So far he still seems to remain quiet. Hope it will stay that way and we have nothing further to do with him.

1.7.1865 Continue with my work on the road, only today I am beginning the real repairing. Had in the meantime an official visit from General Gordon, and went later to his quarters. Just before I left I got news that the enemy is in the process of advancing toward Vaughan road, and our division was called to arms at once to meet the enemy. But as expected it did not mean anything, as the enemy only tried to align his outposts, and to accomplish this, moved some cavalry and infantry. No shot was fired as far as I could learn. As soon as the enemy retreated our troops also returned to their camp.

Had a letter today from my girl friend Frink—which amused me very much; paid a visit to the 20th regiment in the evening and returned to my quarters at 11 o'clock. Otherwise nothing new of any significance. Butlers Canal at Dutch Gap is supposed to be completed, only the upper patrol blew up the soil and rocks, and instead of falling into the river it fell into the canal. This canal is 560 feet long and 40 feet wide—has a depth of 15 feet long. It has been made to shorten the river some 10 miles, and brings the can[n]ons some 12 miles closer to the city of Richmond. Besides some of our batteries are being left too far inland to be effective. We have, however, some batteries at the upper mouth of the canal which could make the use of it very dangerous. Besides it is still questionable whether the canal will serve the purpose it was installed

Hetty Cary, fiancée of John Pegram (Courtesy of the Virginia Historical Society)

to serve, for usually a stream is never changed from its natural bed to an artificial one successfully. It has been tried at the beleag[u]erment of Vicksburg and did not bring any results except a vast output of work and money, without making it useful, and in my opinion, it will be the same with this canal. We have to wait and see how right I am.[5]

1.8.1865 Today is Sunday and I amuse myself answering yesterday's letter, which took almost all day. Completed then my previous notes. Had a visitor today from Chichester—what does he want here? He brought the work detail assigned to me by Rodes Division—it is possible that he was sent to help me. But it does not make any difference to me. Nothing new to report, for today is no newspaper or mail delivery.

Douglas left today on a 15 day leave to attend a wedding. Our general [John Pegram] also left today for Petersburg to attend church, and probably to have a good dinner. He also will get married in a short while [to Hetty Cary]. Everyone seems to have gone mad, for everyone is getting married—it seems in the end I will have to acquire a little woman too. Otherwise nothing new of interest today. Expect difficulties with my road tomorrow, for everything is frozen again.[6]

1.9.1865 Continue with my work on the road today. Yesterday's visitor is still with me and took over part of my work today. It would help my work a great deal if someone would be assigned to me. We have chances for some bad weather—probably rain, and then the roads will be in a fine condition. No news. It seems to be quite certain that Sherman's troops are moving, however, to which side still seems to be in the dark. It is possible that he will turn towards the Augusta and North Carolina railroad behind Charleston, to cut off communication and supply between Richmond and the South and Southwest. It is questionable whether the people of the three states—North and South Carolina and Virginia—in their present mood will supply our troops with bread and corn. It is available, yet, are the proper means being used to obtain those articles. Today I borrowed [Baron de] Jomini's Art of War from General Gordon, and began a study of it. Otherwise nothing of interest to anyone and I am going to stop writing for today.

1.10.1865 Staying in my quarters today, because it is raining as if the skies would fall down. My guest is still here. Going to write all day today. The general came about 1 o'clock in the afternoon, completely soaked. No news. Around us everything seems to be quiet; some shooting activity across from us at the canal (Dutch Gap); yet it does not amount to anything. From the South one hears nothing. According to today's newspapers Sherman is quiet around Savannah with his infantry. Kilpatrick with his cavalry captured Hardeeville, and watches Hardee and his maneuvering. I would not be surprised if he would pull out at Savannah and transport his troops to Beaufort, S.C., which is only about 60 miles from Charleston. From there he then can take the railroad and cut off our provisions. Thomas then would come through East Tennessee into western North Carolina, and would work himself between Sherman and Tennessee into southwestern Virginia, would then go towards Danville and Lynchburg. It will be questionable what Lee will do then.

In my opinion nothing is to be expected from Hood and his army. His troops without rest will not be able to do anything to help us out here, and [they have] lost all faith in him. A new commander in chief must be sent to them. It is said today that Steadmans [Maj. Gen. James B. Steedman's] cavalry caught and burned his ponto[o]ntrain, also a nice matter. He just is not the right man in the right place. Who should take his place? In my opinion this story will soon come to an end, for if enemy troops are able to march large and wide through the country, and not only are able to but are also doing so, the matter is certain to come to an end. An outside intervention would be able to make something out of it, if foreign nations would be willing to do so. There is a possibility that either France or England will be offered a proposition. We then will remain colonies until a later time. Nous verrons toujours.

1.11.1865 Going to continue with my work today, and am going to do a good deal. My visitor returned to his quarters today, but I hope he will return tomorrow to give me some more assistance. Have nothing new to report today from either side, which would be useful or interesting. According to rumors Butler has been relieved from his command to be ordered back to his home. This would be a great damage to us, for he is of no value as a general, and brought us—except as far as the question of our prisoners of war and their exchange is concerned—nevertheless more good than bad, and would most likely continue to do so. Concerning the exchange of prisoners, he most likely would not have had anything further to do with our people, and could not harm us anymore therein. As a commanding general in the field, however, it is another thing, and it would be very desirable if he would lead each patrol to Wilmington. Major General Ord is supposed to take the relieved command in his place.[7]

Hood withdrew to Tupelo in Mississippi to organize his troops. Also a nice country. It is being said that Thomas is preparing for a new campaign and the proposed direction is supposed to be Montgomery and vicinity to separate Hood's communication with the East. It is also being said that Grant sent a great number of troops from his army here, either to enforce Sherman or to undertake operations against Wilmington on a larger scale. As long as Sherman does not meet with him it still can take some time, and there might be a chance to give him a good thrashing. God alone knows how it will end. I am definitely very tired of it, and would very much like to withdraw honorably. Nothing else.

1.12.1865 It is again a beautiful day, and I would like to take advantage of the nice weather to continue the repair on the road and other chores alone but I don't have the means; am doing a good part of it with what I have available. The worst part is almost completed. General Gordon is hindering me more and more, but it cannot be helped; his presence, however, is doing much good, for it keeps the men at their work. Nothing new from any region. Rumors are coming precisely, that the enemy left Winchester and vicinity completely, and that the Winchester and Potomac railroad is being torn up. How far this is true is still questionable. It seems to me rather unlikely that they would destroy their own work when there is no occasion for it. But I would like to see our friends there delivered of this plague. Nothing else.

1.13.1865 Riding out today before breakfast to attend to my work and return about 11 o'clock, have breakfast, and will then ride to Monk's [Neck] Bridge at Hatchers Run, to look for a place to build a new dam. I would like to give this job to someone else, but will be satisfied to be relieved of the repair work on the road; one or the other has to be done. Have no news to report today. Everything seems to be quiet. The enemy reports his losses in the campaign in Tennessee to be 7,000 and estimates ours to be 19,000. Losses from all sources are claimed. In my opinion this could be correct, only Hood lost probably half of his army. Nothing further from Charleston. Sherman still remains quiet. Those last storms played havoc with us, and destroyed almost all railroad bridges between here and Weldon and Greensboro. It is a question of provisions, and at the same time will indicate on a small scale how far Sherman's influence will reach in case our southern communications are destroyed and held captive. We already are rather short on rations for man and beast, and several pilferings of the commissary took place by armed soldiers. A fine thing.[8]

1.14.1865 Will continue with my work today, but since it is Saturday not much will be done, and I will return early to my quarters to schedule matters for Monday morning. I have been relieved of the work on the road for sometime, and will start with my new dam on Monday. Tonight I am alone with our general [Pegram] in our quarters. We spend the whole evening playing chess. Tonight he received a letter concerning the matter of Louis Galley; nothing can be done about it. I am going to reply to it tonight with an answer which Mr. Gorgas may put in his pipe and smoke. Today it has been reported quite certain that Francis P. Blair is in Richmond just hanging around lacking courage. One does not know yet what his presence here means, probably to gain political capital for Lincoln. It will hardly lead to anything else. His visit here will gain us absolutely nothing. May the devil catch him and his superiors.[9]

1.15.1865 It is Sunday again, and this morning I paid a visit to General Lewis, in the first place to see him, and then to make the acquaintance of his wife. Then returned to my quarters, played a little chess and then went to General Johnston and had dinner. I came back home about 8 o'clock. The general went to Petersburg today to attend church, he returned about 9 o'clock and brought his wedding invitations with him. Nothing else of significance to report.

1.16.1865 Started building the dam below Monk's [Neck] Bridge today, and am busy getting the necessary wood from the forest. The general went to Richmond today to prepare himself for the wedding. He is getting married on Thursday. The newspapers don't bring any news, except that it is possible that the enemy is again attacking Fort Fisher at Wilmington. It seems some 60 ships had it under fire, and troops landed at about the same spot. However, we know nothing else, for almost all telegraph lines have been destroyed during the last storm. The attack is being led by D. D. Porter, USN. Blair took his leave and returned to the North. A fully authorized commissioner, Singleton, Senator of Illinois, one of the so-called Peace Democrats, supposedly arrived here, and everything is in a great uproar about it. It will hardly lead to anything. However, I would not be surprised if within 3 months peace negotiations would be under way. But we will have to wait and see, for one can never know here in the country what course a thing like this will take.[10]

1.17.1865 This morning after breakfast I am rode over to our division's quartermaster to see how my wheelbarrows were progressing. Found that nothing has been done, and I am obliged to issue orders for wood and nails. Then accompanied him to Petersburg where I obtained 17 wheelbarrows and 100 pounds of nails. Spent the night with him in his quarters. Through the newspapers we received news today about Wilmington, which do not sound too pleasant, namely the enemy's capture of Fort Fisher. Almost the larger part of the garrison is said to be captured. We have no further news. I don't have to mention that this is an unexpected mishap for us, since it closes our only remaining port. Probably a nice kettle of fish. It seems to me it must have been a surprise assault for one attack has been diverted, and reinforcements had been sent to the fort. Whiting is said to have been in command, and also probably has been captured.[11]

1.18.1865 Returned this morning to my quarters, and followed my work detail on horseback. Found them, however, returning and went and spent one hour with General Johnston; then returned to headquarters. The newspapers bring no further news today about Wilmington and the affair at Fort Fisher. Everything seems to be quiet. Grant fired a salute at us yesterday, probably about said affair. Nothing else of significance happened. Tonight I will receive 45 shovels, 25 hoes, and one axe from Farley's cavalry.[12]

1.19.1865 Continue today as yesterday with my work on the dam, the waterlevel is still too high to proceed further. Last night, after I closed my diary for the day, I received 15 negros from Major [Henry S.] Farley. This I hope will be of great help, for I am very unsatisfied with the detail. The day before yesterday I received a letter from Charlie Stanley, which I answered last night, wrote also to his sister, and mail the letter to Stall in Richmond today. No news, neither from Wilmington nor further southward. It says some changes are going to be made in the cabinet; Breckinridge is supposed to become Minister of War, and Lee general of all armies; and Johnston to resume Hood's command. These, however, are only rumors, and nothing definite. It probably would be good if it were true.[13]

In congress they also seem to have some uproar. Some of the gentlemen became upset about an article in the Sentinel and one of them wanted to resign. It would be all right if they would throw the whole of them into jail, and perhaps something could be done for the welfare of the country. Have a visitor from Chichester tonight. He is going to spend the night with me. The enemy's 15th and 17th army corps under Sherman are said to be in the process of moving forward, but it is not certain yet in which direction. After the crossing of the Combahee river his objective will be more defined. No further news. [Major] New returned from his leave the day before yesterday.[14]

_____

1.20.1865 Following my work detail on foot today and in returning stopped over at General Johnston's; went out with him to select a defense line for his camp, and did not return to my quarters until dark. General Pegram returned this afternoon with his bride. I did not meet her yet. No news from any one side in the newspapers. Wilmington surrendered according to rumors, but since we are still in telegraphic communication with this place those rumors must definitely be wrong as yet, although I would not be surprised if it would happen in a short time. Farewell until then.[15]

_____

1.21.1865 It is raining like mad today, for this reason I am staying in my quarters. General Pegram's mother-in-law arrived today in the heaviest rain, and since she promised to take my mail back I am writing today to my parents. The general appeared today for a while, and returned later to his quarters. Today's newspapers carried Porter's official dispatches about the fall of Fort Fisher. According to his and our own news it has been a bloodbath. The enemy lists his losses at 750 men but it is believed that the figure is much larger. Whiting and Lamb are supposed to be pretty badly wounded, especially the latter. They fought until the end. The enemy landed almost in the same spot as the first time, with circa 15,000 men. The prisoners are said to be about 3,000.[16]

Bragg was not far away, but did not seem to understand the intentions of the enemy, or else he might have been able to ward off the last attack. In my opinion steps should be taken immediately to recapture the fort, even at the cost of 10,000 men. The southern newspapers praise Whiting's defense. No further special news. A staff officer from Gordon arrived in the afternoon, he said that General Lee expects an attack from this side, and advises more alertness for our outposts. This weather will probably delay all the enemy's ideas for some time, if they really intended to undertake such tricks.[17]

1.22.1865 Today is Sunday—but not a sunny day, it is cold and still raining. For me it has been the most boring day in a long time. This morning I was awakened with the pleasant news that seven of my negroes ran away during the night; did not get them back. During the afternoon I received a letter in which I am informed to send them all back to their masters. This makes me very happy and takes a heavy load off my shoulders. Am going to play a little chess this evening. We received no mail or newspapers today, that is why I have no news. I forgot to mention Saturday that Minister of War Sedden retired at his request. It is not certain who will take his place. Breckinridge has been suggested by several. It all depends now on the President. According to the same news Lee has been suggested by congress as Commander-in-Chief; also that General Johnston would take over the command of Hood's army, who was relieved of it some time ago. I believe that both those orders will bring good results, and will pacify the public opinion.

1.23.1865 It is still raining today and I am going to remain in my quarters. Spent a boring day. There are no news, except congress' decisions to create the rank of Commander-in-Chief, and the suggestion to the President to give General Johnston another command. Further news about Wilmington add nothing about Fort Fisher; but endorse, however, the good conduct of my friend Whiting and Lamb. First of which is said to be wounded in four different spots in the hip, and that the latter was wounded very badly. Both have been sent northward. The newspapers report that all Government matters are being removed from there, and as far as I can see, one can expect the surrender of the place. The capture of Fort fisher was a very sad occasion for us.[18]

1.24.1865 Today is a beautiful sunny day, and I rode to my detail at the dam rather early. On my way back I stopped to see General Johnston, stayed a little while and returned to my quarters, where I learned that [Major] New and [Major William W.] Thornton had gone to see the General to pay their respect to his wife. I went there later in the evening to do likewise, did not see his wife, but met one of my first acquaintances of the war, a Major [Claudius L.] Goodwin, Quartermaster on the staff of General Hampton. I had not seen him since

I crossed the Potomac on January 1, 1862 [and entered Hampton's camp at Occoquan Creek]. It was after all a pleasant visit for the evening.[19]

Today's newspapers bring the news about the somewhat unexpected return of old Blair from Washington. It says he has complete authority to undertake peace negotiations. His propositions are supposed to be:

1st Absolute pardon as far as individuals are concerned and in as far as they have done since the beginning of the war.

2nd Complete abolition of slavery in all states.

3rd Return into the Union as *it was*, under a constitution as *it is*.

Or in other words, we are supposed to surrender, and accept the protection of Almighty Father Abraham, which he could not accomplish with his big armies and fleets. Should this be accepted, I would believe that each soldier who died in this war has been murdered with premeditation, which would be recognized by any legal court. But this will hardly be possible. It has been said that the reason for Blair's quick return, which is probably more truth than fiction, is that with the approaching of March 4 the European powers will not recognize the United States as they were but as they are, which included a recognition of the Southern States. This would not surprise me, and could be very good for us.

The day before yesterday we heard here at night heavy and light artillery fire, and I hear today that the enemy broke through General [William R.] Cox['s] line at that time but has, however, been repelled. Last night it supposedly happened again, but I did not hear anything. Tomorrow's newspapers will enlighten us about this.

1.25.1865 Today it is "can[n]on-like" cold, and I remain in my quarters. Turner paid me a visit this morning and gave me my bank-bill. Toward evening Douglas returned from his leave. Blair is supposed to be ready to start his return trip. It is another question whether or not he accomplished anything, and one I am not able to answer as yet. Our three can[n]onboats [gunboats] left for a little journey yesterday to destroy the enemy's bridges and communications between the north- and southside of the James River. The enemy had installed some obstructions across the river to prevent our can[n]onboats from coming down. One of them, a little nondescript thing, was entangled and had to be blown up, to prevent its falling in the hands of the enemy. One [the *Fredericksburg*] crossed over safely, two others [the *Virginia II* and *Richmond*] ran aground, and nothing was accomplished. For according to newspapers everybody returned to his position. Nothing else of significance from any side.[20]

1.26.1865 Am following my detail on foot today. Return rather late and very tired to my quarters. I see where the whole staff has been invited for dinner with the General, but I am not going, I am not in an appropriate mood. I will stay behind and write a letter. The advance of the can[n]onboats did not succeed, they all returned, except the one which was blown up. Blair departed. Today's newspapers speak of a recognition of the United States, and about a pact with such to execute the Monroe doctrine concerning Mexico [and together eliminate Napoleon III's control of the government]. This would be good for us, if we are careful enough to guard ourselves against any malice from the enemy's side, for I believe it is merely a speculation to involve us with foreign powers, to weaken us, and then to carry out their own intentions against us. We would not like that at all. Yet, I would not have any objections against a peace treaty in this way, just to let the enemy in to help give him a good beating. This I would like best. Would not be shy either to give the French a slap in the face.[21]

1.27.1865 I am going to remain in my quarters today, it is terribly cold outside, and besides I don't feel well enough to ride about 14 miles. Witnessed an execution today in our division. Two deserters who have been sent to die by the court martial. No further news from anywhere. There are rumors that the enemy sent about 10,000 men, artillery and cavalry, up the Roanoke River probably to attack Weldon. The preceeding night, Mahone's division marched towards Weldon and camped not too far a distance from us, and they continued to advance yesterday morning. For the time being Gordon's division is taking Mahone's place in the breast-works. For the past few days currency took a considerable drop, from 90 down to 33 for 1. Many believe it is due to pending peace negotiations. Although my own idea is that it is just a speculation of our finance minister, since a few days ago he sold circa 300,000 Thaler in gold on the market.[22]

1.28.1865 Remain in my quarters again today, keep busy writing to my father, friend [Charles P.] Bolles, and completing my letter to Frink. For the evening I was invited to have dinner with the General and made the acquaintance of his wife. I believe he made a good choice, wish him well. There are no news. It seems to be quiet everywhere, although there are rumors that our troops left Wilmington. This is almost impossible, for the enemy's occupation of this place would almost completely cut our communications with Charleston and the South. The news come from the enemy's side and some believe it. There is no other lead.[23]

I forgot one thing, today's newspapers bring Hood's farewell address to his troops—short and military. He takes the full blame for the campaign in Tennessee, which was so illfated. General Dick Taylor, the President's brother-in-law, has been named in his place. The only thing that speaks for this man is that he always has been very lucky in his enterprises, although, in my opinion, he lacks military experience. His promotion has been extraordinary quick, although he rendered some good services, his dealings were with mediocre generals on the enemy's side. Banks and [E. R. S.] Canby simply are not first rate people, except Butler. A little favouritism has been used. We shall see if things will get better in the coming campaign this spring.

_1.29.1865_ Today is Sunday and I remain in my quarters; amuse myself by reading and a little writing. Have nothing new to report, because we have no newspapers today, and did not see anyone to tell us anything.

_1.30.1865_ Riding this morning following my work detail. The day is beautiful warm and pleasant. I stayed until almost 3 o'clock, met a Colonel Houston [Lt. Col. George Huston] of the 33 Vᵃ Regiment there and had a long conversation with him about dams in general. Riding back I passed General Johnston's quarters, had my dinner there, and met Colonel Lee, who just returned from recuperating leave. Later I paid a visit to the General with New and spent a pleasant evening.[24]

Big news arrived today, three distinguished gentlemen, Vice-President [Alexander H.] Stephens, Senator R. [Robert] M.T. Hunter, and Judge [John A.] Campbell, one time assistant to the Minister of War[,] have been authorized by the president to carry on the Blair affair in Washington. It seems that finally something will be done, and Stephen's commission seems to be a good guarantee that everything possible will be done. [Tennessee congressman Henry S.] Foote also left again, to make peace on his own. One should have shot this fellow right after his first arrest, we would have saved ourselves much trouble. Now it is too late. I hope they will accomplish something. That something is going on has been confirmed by Blair's third arrival; and further by a letter I received from [William N. H.] Smith, in which he tells me that authorized peace negotiators have been in Richmond, although one does not know yet what it means.[25]

It is my opinion that the European powers intend to recognize the northern President as such, namely for his own states which voted for him in the last election. This of course would mean a recognition of the South. I believe this is the reason for Blair's frequent trips between Washington and Richmond. May heaven give that this is so, and that their meetings may lead to good deeds.

Although I would like to have a higher rank, and this war disables me in many ways, I might even forfeit earning a living for some time and I would gladly give up everything to see the end of the war. The Navy Department in Tallahassee above Cape Fear received a dispatch from Europe via courier which is reportedly of great importance. He did not arrive in Richmond as yet. According to rumors he carries news about our recognition. We shall see.

Breckinridge has been named Minister of War, and will take over next week the duties and honors of his position. The enemy's troop [column] which has been marching toward Weldon returned without success. Mahone's division is camping tonight near Dinwiddie Co. Ho. and will return to its former position in the breast-works tomorrow. I believe there is nothing further today.

1.31.1865 Rode out this morning and returned rather early. Lewis' brigade has been prepared for a division parade by rehearsing today. Spent the evening with the General, and had all in all a rather pleasant time. The commissioners mentioned yesterday really crossed our lines and are on their way to the residence of his majesty Abraham. I believe that is all there is new.

23. General Pegram Was Killed

February 1, 1865–February 28, 1865

I found our General's body on my bed. As long as I have been in service nothing upset me as much as this death. He was a good Christian man. May I soon find someone like him. I feel very much for his poor wife, she does not know anything yet.

—Oscar Hinrichs

2.1.1865 Today Pegram's brigade, like Lewis' yesterday, is being rehearsed. Johnston's brigade is also attended to, and tomorrow the division parade is going to take place. Generals Lee and Gordon were there to observe. I am going to remain in my quarters and am going to dine with Colonel Hoffman.

2.2.1865 Riding early this morning to check on my detail. Will then attend the parade. General Lee was there, also Gordon, both seemed to be satisfied. Later General Lee rode with our General [John Pegram] to the different quarters for inspection. They had quite a few ladies there [including Pegram's new wife, Hetty] and made a good show. Had dinner with Hoffman and did not return until dusk to my quarters. Sherman is reportedly moving and advancing toward Branchville [South Carolina]. We will have to wait a little before we are in a position to take the necessary steps. Nothing else of significance from anyone side. Everything seems to be rather quiet as in other areas. The trains of the Baltimore and Ohio Railroad reportedly are in the process of bringing Thomas' troops, it is said either for Grant or Sherman, possibly for the latter. Last night I paid a visit to General Lewis and made the acquaintance of his wife.[1]

2.3.1865 Remain in my quarters today; the weather is bad and unpleasant. During the day I received a visit from Colonel [William R.] Peck of the Louisiana brigade. While he was here, we received news from our outposts that an enemy corps prepared for an advance, and that orders have been given in case something happens. I would not be surprised if they would not take this chance to make another try at Weldon; nothing else is new. The newspapers have nothing yet concerning the commissioners. I don't believe that this will have any results here, except to prove to those who want peace under any circumstances that it is impossible as far as the United States will not or can not recognize our freedom.[2]

General Lee reportedly wrote a letter to one of the congressmen in which he requests abolition of the slaves of which he wants to draft circa 200,000. I think this would be very good if it would be executed properly, since they are of no value to us now, and do us much harm. Some day they will have to be set free, since the days of slavery have reached their end here. In field service they still could be made very useful, and could help to strengthen our armies for next spring. Yet it would not work, people here still have not the right attitude. If nothing is going to be done we will be in no position to put up much resistance, and the final hour of the South will have come.[3]

2.4.1865 Riding with the General and [Major John P. H.] New rather early today to inspect our outpost lines, and to show him the area. During the afternoon we rode over Hatchers Run, at Cummins House, only there we were in the open view of the enemy outpost. Met George there, one of our spies, who exchanged a newspaper for us. He said that his enemy contacts did not know of any movement, but believed that something was in preparation. We returned rather late to our quarters, and later I paid a visit to the General and his family. Met his mother-in-law, Madame Cary from Baltimore. After thinking about the military situation today, I believe it is not impossible that the enemy will attack this side within a short time. It seem[s] that some of Thomas' troops arrived here, and Grant will have to make room to bring them up to their lines. It is easiest to extend this flank, and if he is lucky, it will do the greatest damage to us. I would not be surprised if something happens tomorrow. Our peace commission supposedly returned today without having accomplished anything. Nothing else of significance.

2.5.1865 Today is Sunday. Cold and unpleasant. I got up late. While I was smoking my pipe after breakfast a telegram arrived stating that the enemy had attacked our outposts at Vaugh[an] Road, and overcome them. Our division has been called to arms immediately and marched off. The enemy displayed a big demonstration with one cavalry division—Greggs—advanced toward Dinwiddie Co. Ho., and sent from there a reconnaissance of circa 150 men from Boydton Plank Road. They came up to about one quarter of a mile

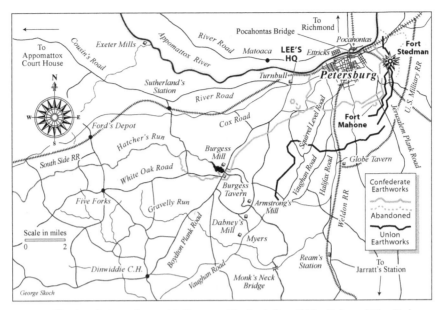

CSA Fortifications in Petersburg with Focus on Hatcher's Run, White Oak, and Five Forks

to our headquarters. We skirmished with the enemy nearly until towards evening, at which time we learned that his cavalry was about to retreat, [with] one corps [of] infantry which accompanied the cavalry, most likely settled across the Vaugh[an] Road.[4]

During the afternoon, Gordon with his division (Evans) and Heth['s] and Mahone's divisions, undertook a flank attack on the east and west side from Hatchers Run,—but did not accomplish anything, since our troops did not put up a resistance, I saw on our left a wonder of the war. While our infantry attacked, a battery of the enemy fired in their right flank; one of our batteries on [Brig. Gen. John R.] Cook[e']s line fired in the back and flank of this battery, while we and the enemy skirmished totally in the rear. Our tirailleure [sharpshooters] drove the enemy back to Hatchers Run in his breast-works. Nightfall came and the enemy held Vaugh[an] Road up to Gravelly Run and Armstrong's Mill. The General's wife was evacuated [but] she returned in the evening, first to our quarters and later to her own quarters. Everything seems to point to a hectic day tomorrow. May heaven give that all shall go well with us.[5]

2.6.1865 Our tirailleure advanced early this morning, up to Vaugh[an] Road, at the bridge over Gravelly Run. Much enemy activity everywhere, had how-

Confederate works at Hatcher's Run
(From *Harper's Pictorial History of the Great Rebellion*)

ever no contact with him until close to Hatchers Run, not far from Meyers [Myers's] house. Here we found a cavalry outpost and not far behind a rather strong line of cavalry. They also were repelled by our tirailleure and the enemy's cavalry retreated through their infantry line. We had about 500 men which later were enforced to circa 1,000. We skirmished until the afternoon.[6]

The General became rather anxious about Johnston's brigade, which was posted on our left and guarded their camp. He was just going to investigate when an attack took place on our left and upon us. The attack on us consisted of cavalry, but was repelled immediately with rather heavy losses. On the left, the attack was made by a corps [brigade] of infantry [from the Fifth Corps], and after some time, Johnston's brigade drove them back. The part of the division which was on Vaugh[an] Road was then withdrawn and moved to the left to reinforce this flank. Evans' division also came into it (but without doing or seeing anything) they turned around. During the attack of our division, General Pegram was killed [near Hatcher's Run]. A short time later Colonel Hoffman was wounded in the foot, and General Lewis took over the command. Mahone's division [led by Finegan] entered the activities later, and after a rather hard and hot battle, the enemy was repelled; however, not across the river.[7]

During the night our command was re-organized and a new line was taken up; and fortified. I remained with the troops until about midnight, and then rode to my quarters, where I found our General's body on my bed. As long as I have been in service nothing upset me as much as this death. He was a good Christian man. May I soon find someone like him. I feel very much for his poor wife, she does not know anything yet. He died at the head of his division, a good soldier and a brave gentleman. May God give him peace, and solace to his poor wife. Again I lost a good and true friend.[8]

2.7.1865 While I spent last night in my quarters, it began to rain and freeze. This morning everything is covered with ice. I am riding to the lines, put a new part down, and will then move our headquarters to a masons lodge. However, I will spend only a short while here. The enemy made some short demonstrations towards Finnegan's and Evan's lines, however, without accomplishing anything. I then rode along the lines, and my black horse took a fit and I had to shoot him. I am ashamed to have done this, and to have been driven to it by a beast. Alone it was enough to upset an angel in heaven. Toward evening our troops were withdrawn to be moved to the other side of Hatchers Run, but they are not going and remain again against all expectations in our quarters. It seems to me as if old Lee is somewhat disturbed to give up one of his reserve lines in such an easy way. More tomorrow.[9]

2.8.1865 During the night I receive orders to report to General Grymes [Bryan Grimes], but I am going to wait until morning. Ride later with General Cox to his lines not far from Burgess Mill, where we form a new line. I make an inspection of the area above the mill. From there I return later to my quarters. I have no news to report from our fronts. Our losses in the late affairs have been very small, scarcely 200, but we lost many officers.[10]

[John M.] Schofield's corps reportedly arrived here, supposedly to bring the enemy's advance to a halt. For how long we will remain in our outpost will depend upon the circumstances. The enemy led two corps [Warren's Fifth Corps and two divisions of Humphrey's Second Corps] and one division [of Wright's Sixth Corps] into the battle [with] altogether circa 30,000 men. Our division fought very well, better than usually, except for two regiments. I cannot adjust myself to the loss of our General, even though our present commander is a very good officer. After his return General Johnston will take over the command of the division.[11]

2.9.1865 Riding this morning with General Lewis to select a new camp for Johnston's brigade, and to become familiar with the area in general. The division's other two [brigades] are busy building the new lines. I hear that we captured circa 150 prisoners; we lost very few. Otherwise everything is rather quiet. Grymes and Cox are paying us a visit tonight, later I will accompany them to General Lewis' quarters. The weather is still very cold and unpleasant. I hope they will leave us alone for a while, before anything new begins. Nothing else new.

2.10.1865 I have no news from our fronts to report. During the morning I will remain in my quarters; in the afternoon I will ride out to see General Gordon concerning the new quarters for General Johnston's brigade; I then reported to General [Walter H.] Stevens, to select with him and Lieutenant Colonel [John A.] Williams a new front line above Boydton Road and along Hatchers Run. Having a pleasant time, and the General confer[r]ed upon me the duty to oversee the work—against all expectations. I then rode to the quarters of General Gordon to prepare for the necessary work for tomorrow.[12]

During the last few days they had two big mass meetings in Richmond. The speeches were made by several important persons. Every thing went well, the people decided that it would be best to take an initiative in this war. Even the negro question was mentioned and received a good reception. I hope something will be accomplished. Grant received circa 20,000 men reinforcement[s] from the West, and we could use a little more here, at least to keep an even balance.

Writing a letter tonight to Tams concerning my desk. Received an undecipherable letter from Charlie Stanley, which I am burning right away. I hear Madame Frink is fraternizing with the enemy at Smithville, giving and attending parties. Her daughter, nearly 16, married a 18 year old prisoner. Nice kind of people. I don't think they are worth much. I am not surprised that this family is so friendly with the enemy; I would have been if they would not have done so. Their patriotism consists of the salvage of their possessions and on how much they could retain. I do not wish them ill but I would not care particularly if they went to the dogs. I have nothing else today to report, everything was rather quiet on our fronts.[13]

2.11.1865 Riding rather early this morning with my work detail to start the fortification lines which we selected yesterday with Gordon's division. Around noon, General Gordon came and released his troops from any further work for the day. I then went to my quarters with General Lewis to see Stevens, but I missed him; went later to Lewis' quarters and returned with him about 4 o'clock to the front since there were reports from the outpost lines that the

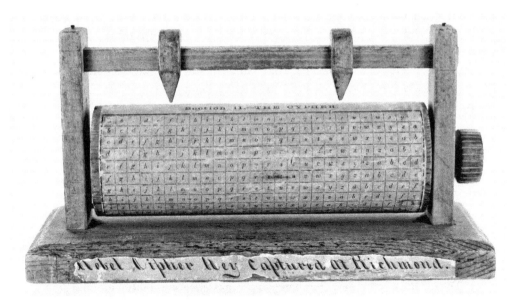

A Confederate cipher; Oscar Hinrichs burned an "undecipherable letter from Charlie Stanley" (Courtesy of Ford's Theatre National Historic Site, U.S. National Park Service)

enemy had withdrawn. We found that he had withdrawn considerably and was engaged with the building of a new line along Hatchers Run. I returned to my quarters after dark. Have nothing new to report—the whole seat of war seems to be quiet.

2.12.1865 Today is Sunday and since there is nothing to do, I am riding rather late from my quarters to our divisions quartermaster to spend the rest of the day there. No significant news as far as I know. Rumors are coming from the South that Sherman drove our troops out of Branchville. Two of our corps of the remainder of the Tennessee army are reportedly in Augusta and advancing toward Branchville. This seems possible and we could soon hear about a meeting from this area. Much will depend on whether or not Sherman will be beaten. I returned late to my quarter.

2.13.1865 Continue with my work which was started on Saturday. Pay a visit to Pegram's old brigade, and later to the camp of Johnston's brigade. We returned home around 11 o'clock at night. Received my material from Haak through Colonel [Thomas F.] Toon who brought it with him. Received a letter from Till which I will try to answer tomorrow. The newspapers report nothing of significance from either side except a few lies concerning last Monday's fighting. The enemy reports his losses to be 800; but most likely it will not be far from 2,000. Everything is quiet outside of that.[14]

2.14.1865 Following our lines today during which time I again pay a visit to Pegram's old brigade. Returned rather early and wrote a letter to my father and one to Bradford. I then started a letter to Till. Have Toon as a guest tonight. Today the newspapers confirmed that the enemy cut the railroad between Charleston and Columbia. Rumors in the camp have it that Beauregard and Sherman had a battle, but it did not materialize as it was planned, nor when or where. It could have been possible. Everything is quiet today in our lines, but it will start soon again and some will be hurt. Today the enemy lists his losses at 1,180, — one communication even says a quarter of the whole command. Nothing else of significance.

2.15.1865 Remain in my quarters today since I sent my boots out to be repaired. Concluding my letter to Till and send it out today. Have nothing to report of military importance, except that Wheeler had a little battle with Kilpatrick and defeated him not far from Columbia. He has been driven back five miles, and so ends the big battle between Beauregard and Sherman. Something might still happen within a short time. Good news from Richmond—the negroes there offer themselves voluntarily to the government. The end of the story will be that, although people still don't like the idea, 200,000 negroes will be serving in the army.

The enemy finally began the exchange of prisoners on both sides. Approximately 1,100 arrived the day before yesterday and 1,000 today. An additional 1,000 are reportedly on their way. This will help us very much, for the soldiers who remained loyal in the enemy's prisons, and refused to take an oath in spite of cruelties, will still make good soldiers. Our corps now is the smallest, and if we get our prisoners back we will be in a position to put up a good resistance in the real beginning of the campaign. Late tonight we received news from General Lee to be prepared to meet the enemy in an attack. It has been reported that enemy troops are being moved by train from the right to the left of the enemy. I believe it is rather one side, and that an attack can be expected from another side.

2.16.1865 Riding out to the front today with General Lewis and return rather late in the afternoon. Could not find out anything new there. I find on my return that orders have been issued to merge the companies and regiments; this probably will result in a great disorder, for many of our best officers are prisoners, and since it is to be done right away it is definitely a great unjustice to those men. Suggestions have been made to the troops today to find out how the previously mentioned negro question would be received. In some brigades the response was good. No news today from the South. I believe that my conjecture concerning the presumed attack on the north side was correct. Russell returned today from his leave.

2.17.1865 Since the weather is miserably bad today I am remaining in my quarters. Nothing new happened. General Johnston returned from his leave today and took over the command of the division. He is going to spend the night as our guest. The newspapers report no news of importance. Nothing of military significance happened yet in the South, although one expects it there any day. Today our inspector received a letter from the brother-in-law of our deceased General, which seems to indicate that he is a big man, although he had little to do with the General in an intimate way other than as a member of the staff. He received presents which in my opinion others should have received. So it goes in this world.

2.18.1865 Today we are going to move our headquarters from where we established it to an uninhabited house not far from Pegram's brigade. I rarely have been as totally discouraged and ill-humored as today. It might have something to do with this old gloomy, built at random house. I don't like it, and I do not think that we will spend much time here; maybe it will change for the better after we have been here for a while. The newspapers bring rumors—nothing confirmed—that Columbia is in the hands of the enemy; the telegraph lines are interrupted—it is not so impossible that there is truth in it; we don't know yet how it happened.

I read a long report from General J. E. Johnston about his campaign, after he took over Bragg's command until he reached Atlanta. It convinces me that his ideas were good, but, that as many private reports indicated, there was much discord and disagreement and he did not have the full support of his subordinates. The government also did *not* give him its full share of support. He says that he had 36,000 men infantry and artillery and circa 5,000 cavalry in the beginning of the campaign. From the state of Georgia he received once 5,000 then 10,000 men, which brought him up to 56,000 men. During the campaign he lost circa 15,000 men by various causes—which left him at the end of the campaign with 41,000 men. The enemy had 80,000 in the beginning, and his army was reinforced with circa 30,000 men—his losses have been estimated to be about 50,000 men. At the end of his report he draws a parallel between his campaign and Lee's, a little unfavorable for the latter. He should not have done this, it will harm him. All in all it is a rather good report. I wonder if he will get another command. Some seem to think that he will be given this army under the supervision of old Lee. I doubt it. Wrote to Ridgeley last night. I would like to have him with us again.

2.19.1865 Today is Sunday, and I pay a visit to Turner and McNeely, I also visit Colonel Hoffman in the hospital, return rather late to my quarters, and don't feel too well. No news to report, except some rumors, among others that our troops left Charleston. It could be possible, my idea about the whole campaign, as far as I could learn, just has not been the most brilliant, and I have more and more reason to find my earlier opinion of Beauregard justified. He is very much overrated. To confuse him about his objective, Sherman was obliged to separate his army, and all groups reached their goal without any interference to speak of. He (B) had enough men to beat anyone of these groups, if not wipe them out. He attained much fame after his defence of the port of Charleston, although I think without deserving it. Received orders this evening to investigate the bridge over Gravelly Run at Plank Road, and if possible to repair it.

2.20.1865 Riding out this morning to look at the previously mentioned bridge, but find myself feeling so unwell on my return that I did not undertake any repair work. No news. Only one of today's newspapers speaks about the departure from Charleston, the others are completely quiet about it. There seems to be no doubt that Sherman completely deluded Beauregard, and that Columbia is in his hands.[15]

2.21.1865 Feel very ill today, and therefore I will not leave my quarters today. Writing a report on the condition of the bridge I inspected yesterday, and send it off. Have nothing new to report. The newspapers bring nothing from any area. Feel too unwell to write anything further.

2.22.1865 I am still remaining in my quarters. During the night we received orders from the Corps Headquarters to prepare for an advance at daybreak, yet nothing materialized. It all was caused, I believe, by the fact that 12 men from the Videtten line defected to the enemy. This evening I had a conversation with General Johnston concerning the proposition I made General Pegram on November 29 [using the German community in New York City to create mayhem and undermine Union support for the war]. It seems he is not interested, which does not surprise me in particular, for I also have my opinion about this gentleman. I will have to look elsewhere for reasonable support. J. [James] A. Walker, Brigadier General, has been ordered to this division and Pegram's old brigade. As the oldest General he will be in command of this division. No news. Find myself very unwell today, and if my room would not be used as center of the war councel I would rather have stayed in bed today.

2.23.1865 I do not feel any better today and for that reason remain in my quarters. The weather is bad. Received a long letter from Mamie today—begin writing an answer to it, also writing to Till and Miss Kinney—a niece of Madame S [Stanley]. No news from any area. The newspapers report that the negro question concerning the 200,000 men has been turned down by the Senate, and make of course a big story out of it. But it will have to happen, if not today then tomorrow. General J. E. Johnston has to report to Lee for orders—very good—he probably will be sent to N.C., for Lee will not want to give up this army. Nothing further.[16]

2.24.1865 Remain in my quarters today, but feel much better. No definite news. There are of course always rumors; it is being heard today that we will move a line closer to Richmond or even N.C. Last night the SRR [Southside Railroad] made quite some commotion, which, however only was caused by the transportation of cotton and tobacco out of Petersburg. It is possible that the situation in the South might grow dangerous any day, so this was just a precaution in case something goes wrong, and we would be forced to leave our lines at short notice. This division received orders—earlier than usual—to send off all excess baggage of the troops, to be prepared for an early departure. There are also rumors that our corps is going to be sent south. The abandonment of Charleston reinforced the army in the field with circa 8000 bayonets, which together with Hardee's former army and the 10,000 men under [Fitzhugh] Lee and [Benjamin F.] Cheatham plus the State Militia, if necessary, ought to be enough to overthrow and repel Sherman.

I believe there only will be made a false attack to weaken Lee here, and then to attack, in which case Lee will have a beaten army, he has not enough men here to hold such a long line. Our army is spread out over a 35 mile distance—with two rivers running through. It appears at times rather disorderly to me; but I cannot tell this to anyone without being laughed at; [I] write it down, however, for my descendants. If our troops do not return before the enemy [it] could become very troublesome during this spring or summer, [and] we will be done for. But if we can hold out through the summer we will have won our game, and the damn Yanks will lose. This will probably be the last campaign of the war, and will certainly be if the matter is handled right by one or the other side.

2.25.1865 I still don't feel much better and, therefore, will remain in my quarters. No news of significance from the seat of war. The expected battle did not take place as yet, and things, as far as military matters are concerned, are coming to a standstill. I believe that we will lose if nothing is being done soon. Nothing further.

2.26.1865 Today is Sunday; remain in my quarters until about in the afternoon, when I take a little walk with New to look at the new fortification. Feel much better today, and hope I will keep on improving. There are rumors that a battle took place—Sherman reportedly has been beaten and Beauregard fatally wounded. I don't believe it to be true, or General Lee would have commented on it. Charleston is in the hands of the enemy. We only lost our heavy artillery there,—about 200 pieces. Our can[n]onboats have been blown up, and a rather large part of the city was burned with it. A large number of the most prominent inhabitants left the city.

2.27.1865 Am going out this morning to attend the work detail on the fortification. Remain there until about 3 o'clock, when I will pay a visit to Wilson and have dinner there—also something to drink, which does me very good. I also bring some back to my quarters. Tonight General Walker came to us to take over the command of the division. No news today about the war. J. E. Johnston takes over command over Beauregard in the South. Late tonight Johnston received orders to leave with his brigade for N.C. in the morning. Two regiments of Cook's brigade are also leaving.

2.28.1865 Again I am going to look after the work detail, although it is rather unpleasant and wet. General Johnston left this morning with his brigade. The northern newspapers report the enemy's capture of Wilmington. This adds 3,500 men to our field armies. I will again visit Wilson today and have dinner with him. And in the evening I will ride out with Cullen to visit a Dr. [James] Boissieux. There my rein and saddle are being stolen. Return to my quarters about 1:30 in the morning. Did not hear anything new from either side.[17]

A hilarious episode happened a few days ago in Cumberland, Md. A Lt. McNeil[l]—with circa 50 men—rode one fine evening into the nest, and takes Major General [Benjamin F.] Kelly, Commander of the Department[,] and Major General Crook of the 8th Army Corps, one of our one time friends in the campaign in the valley, with his adjutant and 2 privates into prison and brings them safely to Staunton, from where they were taken to the Hotel Libby. Mosby also had a little affair. He meets 123 enemy soldiers with 38 men, takes 64 prisoners, 92 horses, and kills and wounds 15, with the loss of one slightly wounded man.[18]

24. Lines around Petersburg

March 1, 1865–March 25, 1865

The outcome of our big attack [at Fort Stedman] was bad. . . .
Our losses, especially among the officers, were very heavy.

—Oscar Hinrichs

3.1.1865 Remain in my quarters today, since I believe our share of work on the fortification has been completed, and besides, I don't feel too well, since my splurge last night. I forgot to mention on the 25th that I wrote to Lee concerning my idea about a trip to New York [to lead a German insurrection], and sent the letter with General Gordon. He (G) was here today and spoke with him; he seemed to take on the matter without being asked to do so, and will speak with General Lee about it.

J. [John] Y. Beall C.S.N., according to the newspapers, has been hanged [at Fort Columbus on Governor's Island in New York] after much debating; I wonder if the same thing would happen to me if I were to be taken prisoner. This is all the news in the papers. Good news are promised from the South. Even though, I rather hear than see them. Johnston's brigade is stretched along the Roanoke river and part of the Weldon railroad, to catch deserters. Something which has increased considerable lately. I would like to go there for a while. Nothing further.[1]

3.2.1865 Although it is raining rather unpleasantly today I am going out to look after a work detail which is working at the fortification. In the afternoon I pay a visit to the remainder of Johnston's brigade—some officers who were serving at the court martial, and spent a pleasant afternoon. One of them, Major Divans, assured me of his friendship and promised to partake in my trip to the North. It won't materialize, because it is not customary here to befriend a foreigner and subordinate; besides it means very much to me, and I rarely have been lucky enough to accomplish anything like it. Nothing new of significance.

3.3.1865 Like yesterday I am busy with the fortification today. It rained again rather heavy and made the work unpleasant. Have no news from the southern front to report. Something is definitely happening there, because our newspapers are silent like death and let nothing slip through. The enemy did not get anything in Wilmington to make him happy—cotton and tobacco— everything was salvaged and taken out safely.[2]

3.4.1865 Since it is raining today as if the sky could collapse, I am remaining in my quarters, and dismiss my work detail for the day. New went to Richmond today on a 48 hour pass. Quite a few rumors are circulating today, from the vicinity of Staunton, which, although not confirmed by the newspapers, are not the most pleasant. Namely, that Early was attacked by the enemy with cavalry and infantry, and that the enemy occupied Staunton. I believe it is very probable—must have been with cavalry only. Early supposedly positioned himself in line of battle at Waynesboro. Many seem to doubt the truth of this, [but] I believe it.[3]

3.5.1865 Today is Sunday, for this reason I don't do anything of importance. Start a letter about the operations of the 2nd Corps, while we have been away from this army. Rumors about the Staunton affair are still circulating, which seem to confirm it more and more. From the South we had no news for a long time. The newspapers are silent about nearly all operations.

3.6.1865 The weather is nice and pleasant today. Attend to my work at the fortification. Hampton reportedly beat Kilpatrick at last and drove him completely to the enemy infantry column. If this is true, and it does not seem doubtful, Sherman will at last have to put his cards on the table. From Staunton it sounds worse. Early's whole power is supposedly strewn to the winds, and he as well as Wharton with their respective staffs taken captive. Charlottesville is said to be occupied by the enemy, and advanced to Scottsville, a little place on the James river. This would conflict with our communications via Lynchburg. Something must be going on, for our spies could find very little cavalry in Grant's lines, it supposedly has been sent to Sheridan. It looks rather gloomy everywhere. May heaven give that we get out of it at the right time and in the right way.[4]

I pay a visit to Gordon tonight where he again promises me his support for my plan. Complete later the report I mentioned yesterday, to send it off later.

I hope it will bring results, would like to see a star on my collar. Should I succeed in accomplishing my plan, I may perhaps even get three. Gave Russel $25 yesterday, and received a little bill from my friend Grymes [Maj. Gen. Bryan Grimes] today for $44.85—also a nice thing if one has no money and cannot get any. May the devil catch all friends of that kind, who take ones money out of his pocket but never put any into it. I have been promised an interview with Gordon for tomorrow concerning my plan. May heaven give that I can convince him to give me every possible support—I believe he will do it. Nothing further today.

3.7.1865 Beautiful weather today, but I remain until rather late in my quarters, go later to the fortification. When I return I find Lt. Colonel [John A.] Williams who informs me that I will get a number of slaves in the morning for labor details, which I like very much. No news, our newspapers are silent about everything that is going on. Cleared up our table accounts today. Douglas owes me $13.75. Paid my share for Dolph—$40.

3.8.1865 It is raining like mad all day, I am not going out, but stay in my quarters. During the morning I receive 94 slaves—also a nice kind. In the afternoon I receive a letter from Till, also a long letter from my parents. They did not receive a single one of all the letters I sent. Write a long letter to Gordon tonight, concerning the mentioned story. No news in the newspapers, nothing at all. Many of our soldiers again have deserted; will have to begin shooting again.[5]

3.9.1865 The weather again is rather pleasant today, but promises nothing good. Go out today to look after my work detail. In the afternoon we receive a telegram informing us that our troops under Bragg and Hoke met the enemy not far from Kinston in North Carolina, and gave him a beating, took some 1,500 prisoners and drove the enemy towards Newbern. He left his wounded on the battlefield. Our losses were few. There also comes a rumor from the valley that McNeil, Mosby, and Rosser met a number of enemies which surrounded the prisoners made by Early, and probably would have freed them. This is probable, but it seems very unlikely to me. I have no further news to report. Receive today the reports of this army, which I ordered from Smith, in two parts.[6]

3.10.1865 The government proclaimed a thanksgiving holiday. So I am not doing anything. Write a long letter to my mother and father today, and read for the rest of the day. The newspapers bring nothing new today, nor did we hear any rumors. As far as I know everything seems to be rather quiet.

3.11.1865 Go after my work detail this morning and instruct the overseer of the negroes in his duties. Receive my paints today, which I left behind in Elizabeth City three years ago, i.e. the box was damaged and the paints scattered around. Receive a telegram this afternoon, Hampton attacked Kilpatrick in his camp [at Monroe's Cross Roads] at daybreak yesterday and gave him quite a beating. His camp was captivated, many prisoners were made, artillery and wagons captured, but he could not move any of it away. Many prisoners were freed, and he left his dead and wounded behind. In my opinion Hampton is the right man in the right spot, and if the good God lets him live he will render us many more good services. May his good luck continue. No news about Sherman and his movements. Johnston is in command there, and will answer at the right time.[7]

General Lee returned to the army the previous day. I hope I will have a reply to my petition, sent through Gordon, within a short time. Yet it is hard to believe that I as a strange and unknown officer would be given such a commission. My luck definitely would have to be at a turning point. Nobody knows how much I would like to undertake it, it is my only hope for a promotion. Besides, I am getting a little bored here, and since I am now, so to speak, on foot (my horse has foot trouble, which will not permit riding it) I don't feel like mingling in a battle and cannot keep out without looking bad. Will write to Till tonight.

3.12.1865 It is Sunday again, I remain in my quarters and amuse myself as well as I can. Everyone, except the General and I, rode out. A courier from Gordon arrived last night about 12 o'clock with orders to be prepared to march out by daybreak, and, therefore, had to get up rather early. According to rumors our dear friend Sheridan from the valley is marching down along the James river, and we are supposed to hold him off. But we did not go. [Maj. Gen.] Grymes with his division marched as far as Jarratts Crossing and was called back. No other news, as far as I could learn. While we were still in the valley a rather good essay appeared in the Staunton Vindicator about old Early. I copy it here today. It is titled — Chronicles of Jubal [see appendix 2].[8]

3.13.1865 The weather is very nice today, also windy yesterday and today, which dries everything up rather fast. Continue today with my work on the fortification and remain there until late in the afternoon. Today's newspapers carry the previously received report of Hampton's victory, and seem to be making rather much fun of it. Lee also reports concerning Rosser, in the valley; he attacked the enemy not far from Harrisonburg, did not succeed too well [but] he followed the enemy, teased him very much, and in doing so made an escape for many of our prisoners, which were being led back, possible.

There is a rumor that one of the officers from our command read a bulletin in Petersburg which supposedly stated that Mexico officially recognizes us. This might have resulted from the friendliness which was exchanged between one of our generals and the commanding Mexican general across from Brownsville. The Mexican and our general exchanged visits in civilian clothes—the former came as [an] official of the emperor and is greeted by a salvo, the latter then returned the visit where our flag was saluted. At the second Mexican visit they passed our flag and saluted it. It is not at all improbable that something of the kind happened, and that our recognition will come first from that side. Mexico's recognition is France's recognition.

Early today the General [Walker] and New rode out to inspect the wagon train, but returned both rather inspected with brandy. I asked New to find out from Gordon whether he had done anything with my petition, and received the answer that it has been forwarded to Lee, but that he, Lee, would probably be much too busy to think about such things. I am beginning to lose interest, because it is being drawn out so long. It might, however, be for the best and save my neck from the rope. I wonder if I will ever get an answer to that. If so, I am very much mistaken about things here; because if one is unknown and does not have the right connections he has no chance here.

I just received notice that our corps [Gordon's Second Corps] is going to move its quarter[s], that Anderson's corps will take our place, and we [will occupy] their position at Petersburg. Also a nice area, which I don't like at all. I am in no mood to lose my headpiece in an outpost fire, which reportedly is a common practice there. May the devil catch all those fellows who run around wearing blue jackets etc. I wish this thing would come to an end, and I could take my leave, I am very tired of it.[9]

3.14.1865 Today is our last day in our present quarters. Look after my soldiers this morning, about 1 o'clock I will ride to the wagon train, exchange my horse, and proceed from there to the 3rd corps' headquarters to see Lt. Colonel Williams. He commissions me to continue with my present line [on the Confederate right flank], therefore, I have nothing to do with the lines around Petersburg; which makes me rather happy, although it might create some friction. Am remaining tonight with Turner and McNeely. Spend a pleasant evening with something to drink. Grymes marched off yesterday, Gordon today.

3.15.1865 Marching on foot to our old quarters today, since my horse is in no rideable condition. Attend to my work detail, march then back to the wagon train, where I spend the night. Our division left today for Petersburg to occupy their part of the line. The more I think about this maneuver, the less I like it, and in all probability the others don't like it any better. Nothing new to report from any side. According to rumors which seem to be true, Sheridan is with his cavalry not far from Richmond. Nothing further.

3.16.1865 Marched to our headquarters at Petersburg this morning. Truly a beautiful, clean area. We have one house across and several on both sides. Would like to know who selected this place for us. Look at part of the line occupied by our division, as well as one of our countermines. The mine is good so far, but the line does not look too good to me. I may change my mind after a closer inspection, but doubt it. Linger for some time in the streets and pay a friendly visit to [Capt. Charles H.] Dimmock in the evening. Play some chess. Could not learn anything new, nothing of significance.[10]

3.17.1865 New was nice enough today to lend me a horse, i.e. it had the shape and form of a horse, but was in reality a cow, for I rode it in terror, inasmuch as I believed to break my neck any minute; [I] ride now on this beast to my work detail on our old front, [and] lay out a new line there. On my way back I stop for a few minutes with McNeely, in the hope to get something to drink, but no luck; returned to my quarters about 7 o'clock rather tired and hungry. So ends this day—nothing new to report.

3.18.1865 Remain in the city today and "loaf about" a little. Toward evening I walk to the headquarters of General Hill and pay a visit to Williams. In the evening I go to see Dimmock and play chess; spend a very nice evening. No news from either side as far as I could learn. Lee reportedly visited Gordon today, and I would like to know very much how he received my petition, and what his decision is; I don't like to draw this out any longer. Of course, my petition will be turned down with "thank you," and I will remain here. If this is going to happen, I don't doubt it, I cannot understand our people because offers such as this are not being made every day, and maybe if the government would ask me, I would not like to undertake such a thing. For the time being I might as well regard myself stationary. Nothing else today.

3.19.1865 Today is Sunday, and I spend the best part of it writing a letter to my father. No news of military significance as far as I could learn. Movements seem to be anticipated, but for what purpose I don't know. Play a game of cards tonight.

3.20.1865 According to my promise I should have gone with Williams to attend to my work detail today, alone it was impossible to obtain a horse, and I was forced to remain in the city. I am walking around and play chess in the evening. No news of significance; according to rumors Johnston had an encounter with Sherman, but this is not official. I would not be surprised, because things happen there rather quickly, and if nothing is being done, our remaining here is only a question of time. My horse is in very bad shape, and therefore unrideable. Pay Thornton $115.39 today, my share of the provisions and other details. Give him my bills for January. Today I sold my last gold-piece for $55. Received a long letter from [John] Bradford today.[11]

3.21.1865 It is raining today, and I will remain in my quarters, again I could not obtain a horse today; otherwise I would have proceeded with my work. The newspapers confirm that Johnston met Sherman's advance guard not far from Bentonville some 40 miles from Raleigh, and beat them and a considerable part of his army. Although it was not a strong victory, it still helps us. Since the beginning of the campaign in this state the enemy lost close to 5,000 men as prisoners, besides, his other losses were far greater than ours. No further news.[12]

3.22.1865 Riding out today to attend to my work and return home about evening. Pay a visit to Dimmock. Last night Hotchkiss came to see me unexpectedly and spent the night with me. No news today; I hear that Sheridan is in command of the enemy cavalry here. Hotchkiss gave me a rather ridiculous [laughable] description of the battle at Waynesboro. As I suspected our troops just ran away. No further news today. New was a very drunk soul at his return last night with Major Carrier from Richmond.

3.23.1865 Riding out to my work today, and to lay out a new artillery work on my line. In riding out I stop at [A. P.] Hill's quarters, and play a game of cards with Williams. I don't get my work done and return rather late to my quarters. Lt. Colonel Williams rode with me. It seems that something is going to happen, since some of our Generals are riding back and forth, and a number of troops and artillery have been sent to the north side. I would not be surprised if Lee expected an attack on Longstreet, and it would be good if he would take the initiative and attack first. We shall know more about it soon.

3.24.1865 I had hoped to have an opportunity to rest my horse today, but I had to ride out. Stopped on my way to see Hill. I layed out my work, and returned home late. My ideas of yesterday seem to become reality, and the enemy is going to be attacked at 3 o'clock tomorrow [from Colquitt's Salient]. Two of B. [Bushrod] R. Johnson's brigades—[Brig. Gen. William H.] Wallace and [Brig. Gen. Matthew W.] Ransom, Heths division and our three divisions will make the attack on our front [at Fort Stedman]. Late tonight I receive orders, through Williams doing, to report to Lt. General Anderson for eventual duty at his front. I hope everything will go well for us, but I fear that something will go wrong. It is to be hoped that every opportunity will be worked out to the best advantage.[13]

———

3.25.1865 According to my orders I left my quarters shortly after 5 o'clock in the morning and reported to [Lt. Gen. Richard H.] Anderson about 7:30. Against all expectations I found everything to be quiet. Was received friendly and had a long talk with the General about things in general. Learned something from him concerning the campaign in the valley, where he met us with Kershaw. His orders were to take over the command, and to help in other ways, but he did not do it out of friendship to Early. It was the understanding that Early was to inform him about his intentions and inasfar as he could be helpful; but not to ask for advice, because in giving advice he would take over the command. When he left he advised him to concentrate more clearly, without which he would get a good beating some day. He proved to be correct.

About 1 o'clock in the afternoon [along Bushrod Johnson's position on the far western flank,] the enemy undertook some demonstrations on Cook[e]'s line, which at the time was held by Moodey [Brig. Gen. Young M. Moody], former Gracie brigadier. The enemy did not succeed [and] he was driven back within a short time, with rather heavy losses. About 5 o'clock Cook[e]'s brigade returned to its quarters [after supporting Gordon], and Moodey was moved further to the left. The enemy again tried to overtake us, but again suffered a defeat. At the first attempt approximately 200 prisoners were taken. At the second try a partial attack was made on [Brig. Gen. Henry A.] Wise's outpost brigade. At this point the resistance was not so good, and two companies reportedly were captured. The enemy proceeded to draw his attacks to the left and captured the outpost line of [Brig. Gen. Samuel] McGowan, [Brig. Gen. James H.] Lane and others and held it as well as Wise's line for the night.[14]

The outcome of our big attack [at Fort Stedman] was bad. The enemy's line was taken about 500 yards from us, but was under such heavy fire in various areas, that the attacking columns had to turn back at 9 o'clock. Our losses, especially among the officers, were very heavy. It might be close to 2,000. General Johnston's whole staff was hit. We took some 800 prisoners, one brigadier General, McLaughlin [Napoleon B. McLaughlen]. Most of our men were killed while turning back. Many were captured.[15]

Spend the night with Anderson where I am being treated very friendly. Almost all of them are from South Carolina. During the day I attend to my duties and look after the work detail I laid out yesterday. I liked General Anderson very much and would like to be on his staff. He might be able to get me a promotion, besides it would be far more pleasant to be on the staff of the corps than in a division. There is a great difference. All in all we did not gain much today, nor did we have a great loss. On Wise's front the enemy lost the captured line, but kept the others. It is possible that we will see some action here by tomorrow, but it remains to be seen. I would not be surprised.

According to rumors, Johnston had some small skirmishes with Sherman and forced him back to Goldsboro. Since this is only a distance of about 20 miles nothing much could have come of it, except to slow him down. According to the latest news Sherman was at Bentonville. Besides this there are no further news of importance to my knowledge. I think I can call myself lucky to have been spared in our attack, without shirking my duty.

25. The Last Battle of This Army

March 26, 1865–April 19, 1865

Marching this morning up to Appomat[t]ox Co. Ho. Although I am [wounded] . . .
I request my horse to give all my efforts in the last battle of this army. Our division
was arranged and I took our sharpshooters up front and attacked the enemy.

—Oscar Hinrichs

3.26.1865 Against all expectations, everything was quiet this morning on our—Anderson's—front this morning, and since it is Sunday, I spend a rather tedious morning. I did have a rather good breakfast though which in times of war means a lot. Remain until 12 o'clock with Anderson and since everything seems to be quiet I return to Petersburg. I am riding slowly, stop to see Hill for half an hour, and return to my quarters. On my return I am rather tired. My poor horse had the worst of it with his sore feet. In the afternoon I pay a visit to General Johnston and [Col. Thomas F.] Toon—the latter wounded—the first with a dislocated foot. Again I lost some friends in yesterday's activities. The whole matter does not seem to have been carried out very well, since one did not know where the enemy was active. Only a few were lost in the attack on the line. The enemy still is holding the outpost line in front of Hill's corps.[1]

I could not learn anything new about the South. Anderson promised to call me in case anything should happen there. Hope everything will remain quiet tomorrow so I can get some rest, I am very tired tonight and will go to bed as soon as I am through here. I hope to see Bradford tomorrow. This ends my third notebook about the war, I will begin a new one tomorrow. I hope that with a new book and clean pages our officers also will take on a new shine, and victory. I also like to see a few changes in my private affairs, and hope I will have the opportunity to describe them in the new book. I found much pleasure in writing [in] my diary.

3.27.1865 Remain in Petersburg today to call for my horse. During the morning I pay a visit to General Johnston and later to Toon. A little later in the day I return to Toon's quarters and make the acquaintance of a very nice young lady, who plays some musik for me, I play a little myself. Meet Harris later, take a walk with him, and drink a little too much. In the afternoon I ride to the front to send a letter to my father. But, as I said, I bent the elbow a little too often, I don't get there until the armistice is over, and I almost get killed. On returning I find Bradford, who spends the night with me. Talk with him about this and that and go to bed at a respectable time to sleep off my intoxication. I am very much ashamed about my behavior today, and hope I won't have another opportunity to write down an explanation like this. I did not hear of any news. Johnston reportedly defeated Sherman not far from Goldsboro. But since this is only a rumor I do not quite believe it. Still, it is very probable that something happened there which may lead to a battle soon.[2]

3.28.1865 March this morning with Bradford to Thornton's quarters, have breakfast there since we had nothing in the house. B. returned to Richmond this afternoon. Had a very pleasant morning with him, and had to promise to visit him soon. Find myself not in the best condition today, and am ashamed of my behavior yesterday. In the evening I first pay a visit to Dimmock's quarters and play a little chess, go later to Toon's quarters and see the ladies. Later the band of the 20th [North Carolina] regiment came, and we spent a rather nice evening, at least better than last night. I don't believe there are any news of significance. So far, the previously mentioned rumor about Johnston's battle has not been confirmed. Everyone seemed to have been prepared for a little action, and is still anticipating.[3]

3.29.1865 This morning I pay a visit to Toon, who is leaving today, to say good-bye. Ride later to my work detail and find the command there drawn in battle-array, awaiting an attack. It seems that early in the morning Sheridan moved out with his cavalry, covered by two corps. About 1:30 some Tirailleur firing took place, but with what result I don't know. After I left they had some rather heavy artillery fire. Fitz. Lee['s] cavalry division moved toward the right in the evening, also three brigades of Pickett's division. In riding back through the city I found [Major William] Carvel Hall with Mercer and took him back to my quarters. In the evening I pay a visit to Dimmock's quarters to go visiting with him, but found him feeling unwell and played chess.[4]

About 10:30 our front had heavy fire from guns and artillery, however, without causing much damage. It all originated from a little misunderstand-

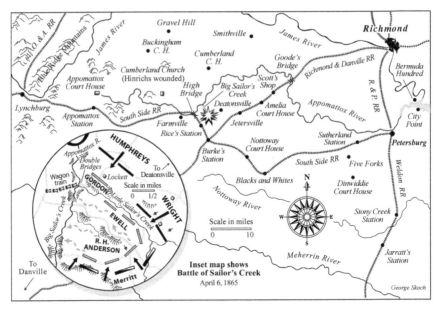

Retreat to Appomattox

ing, since both sides were waiting for an attack without making the first move. I understand, however, that attacks took place further to the right, especially on the extreme right. No definite news outside of these. It seems, however, that a major battle will take place here soon, and all preparations have been made for it.[5]

3.30.1865 Remain in the city today and pay a visit with Hall first to Dimmock, then to Mercer. During the morning a heavy fire began on our right; I would have gone there, if I did not have to have my horse reshoed, and all our trains were sent to the north side of the Appomat[t]ox [River] during the previous night, and much time would have been lost in getting there. Besides, it was raining rather hard. I hope the weather will help us in our military operations, and at least hold off the enemy cavalry. In the evening I again pay a visit to Dimmock and go out with him to make the acquaintance of a family by the name of Bannister [Banister]. Spend a nice evening.[6]

Colonel Williams came while I was with Dimmock and gave us some news about the right line. It seems that the enemy established himself in front of my line [the White Oak Road fortifications], and the whole firing was just outpost fire. Picket and three other brigades [Corse's, Steuart's, and Terry's brigades] have been sent down [to Five Forks], so that, plus cavalry, we have some 20,000 men available there. I could not learn anything new about the South, and since the newspapers did not reach us today, we remain in the dark about the happenings there. Sherman and Schofield definitely made their connection, and we can be prepared for some news from that side. I know of nothing else of significance.[7]

3.31.1865 Riding this morning rather early to the right line, and while riding heavy firing opens again. I ride a little faster and get there in time to anticipate [participate] in the pursue [pursuit] of the enemy. It seems the enemy made an attack on our outpost, we then attacked and repelled him for 1 1/2 miles. Picket[t] with his division and [Eppa] Hunton's brigade [Bushrod Johnson and three of his brigades] were detached and sent to pursue the enemy cavalry [to Dinwiddie Court House,] which seemed intent to reach the railroad. About 2 o'clock the enemy received [a] fresh supply of troops, attacked us and drove us back to our bulwarks. During our attack [at the Battle of White Oak Road], we made some 400–500 prisoners including some officers. Saw Lee and Hill with their staffs observing the operations.[8]

Stay there until dark and return rather tired to my quarters at 9 o'clock. Am going to retire soon. Again we received no newspapers today, therefore no news from the South. I would like to hear from there, but have to be patient. Would like to leave my quarters here and join Anderson, have to see if it can be done somehow. Nothing further.

4.1.1865 Riding early this morning to the right line. Make a reconnais[s]ance and find that the enemy moved to our right. In the afternoon another brigade is dispatched to Picket who was driven back to Hatcher's Run during the day. In the evening Anderson received orders to prepare himself to march out, and before I reached the front, he received the orders to depart, and he marched toward Cox Road [and Five Forks], to support Picket[t]. I believe Petersburg will have to be given up. Return rather late to my quarters, and very tired. As I go to bed the enemy again opens a terrible fire which lasts until about 1 o'clock. Find that it is nothing alarming and go to sleep quietly.[9]

4.2.1865 Before daybreak the General awakens me with the report that the enemy broke through our lines, and that everyone will have to go to the front immediately. The fighting is rather light until sunrise. The enemy broke through Gryme's [Grimes's] line and Johnston's brigade was sent to his assistance. Fort Mahone was taken by the enemy, recaptured, and again taken by the enemy. Toward evening, however, the enemy held out just about 200 paces from us, from where he could not make much progress. Four tobacco factories as well as the railroad stations were burned.[10]

Hinrichs's map within his journal entry for March 31, 1865
(Richard Brady Williams Private Collection)

At A. P. Hill's line it also went bad. A. P. Hill was killed early in the morning, and his body remained in the hands of the enemy for [some] time. During the main attack the enemy broke completely through [the] Wilcox line, and one part of this division as well as Heth's division, who had to overtake the command of the 3rd corps, were cut off from the remaining part of the army. This brought about much confusion and created much disorder. The enemy advanced until close to the south side of Southside R. Road, and remained there during the day.[11]

About noon [Longstreet's] troops of the first corps arrived [from Richmond] but could not repel the enemy. The enemy's losses were rather heavy, but our own were greater, especially prisoners. About 9 o'clock in the evening the artillery along the lines we were still holding was withdrawn. The infantry also retreated soon afterward across the Appomat[t]ox river.

I remained in our lines until about 3 o'clock in the morning, at which time I withdrew the outpost to follow the infantry, and set fire to the [Pocahontas]

The Evacuation of Petersburg (From *Harper's Pictorial History of the Great Rebellion*)

bridge. My sharpshooters covered the retreat and the bridge until it burned down. About daybreak the enemy outpost advanced with much jubilation into our lines and into the city. Our corps covered the retreat of the army. We marched all night, very slowly, since wagon and artillery could move only slowly on the bad roads, and had to be covered. Troops are in rather good spirits.[12]

4.3.1865 Continue the retreat today until 4 o'clock in the afternoon, when we rest for an hour, to await news from Longstreet, who had turned into another direction. Proceeded to march about 5 o'clock and camp about 3 o'clock near a church to await daybreak. The troops are very tired. Our animals also show a great weariness. Did not see the enemy except for some cavalry, which however, kept in the background and merely observed us.[13]

4.4.1865 Marching today on wretched roads up until Amelia Co. Ho. [after crossing the Appomattox River at Goode's Bridge] and camp for the night [at Scott's Shop, five miles east of the town]. The troops are very exhausted, many dropped out. Provisions are getting short. Had to discard many mess-kits, since the animals, lacking rest and food, could not go on with their heavy loads. Beginning to cut down artillery caissons.[14]

4.5.1865 Marching this morning to Amelia Co. Ho. where the enemy is await-ing us [at Jetersville], however, without attacking. Remain there until dark and proceed marching along the railroad towards Farmville. Today we lost about 600 wagons—among others the greatest part of the reserve trains contain-ing powder and lead. This is a hard blow for us. While we lay in battle-array I make a reconnais[s]ance, and I almost am being hit. Lose my horse during the operation, it was killed—however, I catch another one from the enemy.[15]

4.6.1865 Proceed marching today without interference until we arrive at Deatonsville about 9 o'clock, where the enemy cavalry attacks our wagon and artillery trains in several places. Have a heavy battle with [the Second Corps of] the enemy infantry; General Lewis loses almost his whole brigade. We retreat slowly, and at Deik (?) Creek [at Double Bridges over Little Sailor Creek and Big Sailor Creek]—where we had to wait to let our trains pass—we again have an even harder battle. Lose some artillery and about 500 wagons. Salvage, however, almost all animals, which were with the remainder of our artillery.[16]

Our losses, especially in my corps, are rather heavy. But we do give the enemy strong resistance [at Lockett's farm]. We are repelled by the enemy by a heavy and well executed attack, while the trains panicked. We hold the enemy until night, and proceed marching to High Bridge, where we camp for the night at about 2 o'clock. The enemy does not persue us. Meet Milton Rogers, who is performing excellent services with his section of artillery.[17]

Today the whole army is more or less involved. Our losses are heavy—especially prisoners. Take together with General Lewis a different route to High Bridge than the troops, to catch those who fled from the enemy during the last attack. Troops are becoming worthless, except the old and good soldiers. Since we lost so many wagons we have no food, which does not lift the spirit of the troops.[18]

4.7.1865 Departing this morning from High Bridge. I remain behind with about 100 of our sharpshooters to burn the railroad bridge and hold the enemy off until the bridge is unusable. The enemy made a good try to drive me away but did not succeed and lost quite a few men and horses. [Other engineers did not destroy the wagon bridge, which remained passable.][19]

Marching along the railroad to Farmville where we meet with the part of the army that had been cut off with Picket[t] on the second of the month. Form a battleline but are not being attacked. Marching along our trains for some three miles where the enemy cavalry attacked [south of Cumberland Church] and was repelled with only few losses. General Lewis was badly wounded, it is said deadly. A few minutes later I got shot and painfully hit. After some waiting I am transported away in an ambulance.[20]

4.8.1865 Last night I was being transported until 12 o'clock, we stopped and fed the animals, but had nothing for ourselves. Had also a little brush with the enemy, which did not result in anything much. Toward the afternoon I meet with our division train and remain there. Tonight we receive orders to organize the largest train and to destroy all unnecessary wagons.[21]

The Last Review (From *Harper's Pictorial History of the Great Rebellion*)

4.9.1865 Marching this morning up to Appomat[t]ox Co. Ho. Although I am [wounded and] not quite in a condition to sit on a horse I request my horse to give all my efforts in the last battle of this army. Our division was arranged and I took our sharpshooters up front and attacked the enemy. All honor and glory should be given to these troops who weak and hungry were in arms this morning, and were willing to give their lives defending honor and glory of this army and their country.[22]

Shortly after I attacked a white flag appeared in the hands of General Custar [Brigadier General George A. Custer] of the enemy with a message from Grant to Lee. The firing ceased, and after a few hours it was made known to the troops that Lee surrendered the army—8000 infantry—2,000 cavalry and a small number of artillery. I will never forget this moment. May heaven give that I never have to go through another experience of this kind. About 2 o'clock in the afternoon our troops retreated for about one mile from Appomat[t]ox Co. Ho. and camped.[23]

In the evening the enemy sent meat and bread for our troops, this were the first provisions we received in four days. Only one guard was posted on the way to the enemy camp. Every one else retired. Late in the afternoon our corps was summoned for a speech from Gordon—which, however, contained nothing of significance.[24]

4.10.1865 Today everything remained rather quiet in camp, many enemy officers came visiting our camp. I go with Col. Lee [likely Col. John W. Lea] to the headquarters of General Grant to work out a special treaty, did however, not succeed. I try to sell my horse, and get $360 in greenbacks. Don't find myself too well after being wounded. The day is wet and gloomy.[25]

———————

4.11.1865 Remain in camp today. Gordon again made a speech, which if possible, was in even poorer taste than his first. Our division received its surrender orders late in the evening. Nothing further happened today of significance. On the 9th of the month Rosser and Fitz Lee with part of their command made their way through the enemy lines and on the 10th captured an enemy train with bread etc. About 300 wagons were burned down. Take leave from many of my enemies.[26]

———————

4.12.1865 At 4 o'clock this morning the troops marched to Appomat[t]ox Co. Ho. and layed down their arms, except the officers who are permitted to keep their side-arms and private possessions. The weapons were received by the 6th[, 5th,] and 24th corps. Everything went orderly and without disturbance. Then most of the troops were marched southward with their officers. I marched some 18 miles toward Farmville. One Yankee officer made it a little easier for me in offering me a place in a wagon—gave me food in the evening and had a tent put up for me.[27]

———————

April 13th Continue my journey today up until 8 to 9 miles outside of Farmville, where I spend the night.

———————

April 14th Marching today up to 5 miles from Burksville [Burkeville Junction] and spend the night in a private home where I was received very friendly. My travelling companions were Hewat, a big tall Scot[,] and a young officer from Gloucester Co., named Dudley Barnett.

———————

April 15th Marching today the last 5 miles to Burksville Junction, lay around all day long, and am put in a train about 11 o'clock in the evening, which will take me to Petersburg, but I don't get off until about 7 o'clock in the morning.

———————

April 16th Arrive in Petersburg about 3 o'clock and after I attend to matters with the Provost Marshall I pay a short visit to my little girl friend, where I am being welcomed very friendly by her and the whole family. About 6 o'clock I travel with another train to City Pt. where we arrive at 7 o'clock. Go to bed, for I was very tired.

4.17.1865 Get my papers in order this morning and leave City Point for Washington by steamship. Have a very unpleasant night. Hewat remained at Fortress Monroe—Barnett remained in Petersburg. Find Mercer and Derneut on board.[28]

April 18th Arrive in Washington at 7 o'clock in the morning and go right away to Houghs, where I borrow some money to buy clean underwear and a civilian suit. From there I go to the Provost who delays me against all expectations, and sends me late in the afternoon to the Soldiers Rest at Baltimore station.[29]

April 19th Remain in this prison today. In the afternoon a whole negro regiment arrives, which embellishes our situation.[30]

Epilogue

Remain in this prison today.

—Oscar Hinrichs

After surrendering at Appomattox Court House, Oscar Hinrichs obtained a "Guards and Patrols Pass" in Petersburg on April 16 and traveled unhindered to Washington, D.C. From the Federal capital, he planned to take a train to Baltimore and return to his family in New York City. He arrived in Washington early during the morning of April 18 but was delayed "against all expectations" by Provost Marshal Colonel Henry H. Wells—or someone else in his department—and sent to Soldiers' Rest, a way station next to the B&O Railroad station. During the next day, Captain Oscar Hinrichs made his final journal entry, noting that he was in "this prison today."

Solemnity hung over Washington on April 19 like the black bunting and crepe draped from many of its buildings. Cannon salutes boomed all day, breaking the stillness of a national day of mourning. Six hundred family members, officials, and guests gathered at the White House for the funeral service of Abraham Lincoln. A public viewing took place later in the Capitol rotunda. As the snakelike queue inched closer, forlorn citizens wept when they gazed down upon the body of the nation's first slain president. People throughout the North remained numb, in shock.[1]

By sunset on April 19, investigators had arrested five of Booth's alleged conspirators, including Mary Surratt. Amid fever-pitched concerns about Confederate involvement in Lincoln's death, Oscar Hinrichs's former draftsman, Henry von Steinecker, implicated Oscar along with officers Edward Johnson and Henry Kyd Douglas in the conspiracy.

Major General Johnson, Oscar's commanding officer from Gettysburg to Spotsylvania, remained imprisoned at Fort Warren in Boston Harbor. He had been captured at the Battle of Nashville in December 1864. Major Douglas surrendered at Appomattox Court House with Oscar. He had not yet reached his parents' home, located on a hill near the sites where the Battle of Antietam had been fought, which looked out over the town of Shepherdstown.[2]

As one of the few rebel officers who traveled north through Washington, Oscar Hinrichs was a visible target for Unionist retaliation. According to his April 18 journal entry, he borrowed some money to buy "a civilian suit" and went from there to the provost, which means he still had on his gray uniform when he met with Federal officials. He might have received the same treatment that Douglas would soon face in Shepherdstown—arrested for wearing his rebel officer's uniform in public—or else there were concerns about his violation of the Coast Survey's oath of allegiance, which he signed in Maine prior to defecting in December 1861.

Among the exceptions to his May 29 executive order extending amnesty to Confederates, President Andrew Johnson listed people who (1) left their Northern homes to go to the South; and/or (2) violated an oath of allegiance. While interrogating Oscar, the provost marshal could have learned that he fit both of these exceptions for Confederates to receive amnesty.[3]

Confiscation of Oscar Hinrichs's journals might have been another reason he was detained. During the conspiracy trial, eyewitnesses would share how the Surrattsville tavern had been a "regular secession headquarters" and a "resort for blockade runners, spies, and parties who wanted to cross the Potomac." At the beginning of his wartime journal, Oscar made a note about John Surratt Sr., who died in August 1862: "Mr. Surrat[t] was a friend to the cause, and had been made acquainted with our intentions. He received us most cordially, giving us the use of his private parlor and prevented the numerous strangers who came into the house from intruding upon us." Being at the Surratt tavern along with Wat Bowie, known secret agent and future Mosby Ranger, would have created a major problem for Oscar if anyone knew about his unusual journey to enter the Confederacy.[4]

Federal officials brought Major Douglas to Washington, arriving on May 24 as the city honored Sherman's army during the Grand Review's second day. They put him in the Old Arsenal penitentiary, to which the Booth conspirators, and some of the witnesses, had been transferred. (Mary Surratt was in the cell next to Douglas.) On May 25, officials at Fort Warren received an order from Secretary of War Edwin Stanton to send General Johnson to Washington. According to Douglas, Edward Johnson and Oscar Hinrichs were locked up in the penitentiary with him.[5]

Judge Advocate Joseph Holt faced a daunting task as he oversaw the complex Lincoln assassination trial. During the course of two months, he allowed almost three hundred witnesses to appear. Some of them, like Henry von Steinecker, who testified at the end of the trial's first day, provided incen-

Exterior View of the Cells in which the Conspirators Are Confined
(From *Harper's Weekly*, July 8, 1865)

diary but unsubstantiated claims. Von Steinecker swore that, after Gettysburg, Booth met with officers from the Stonewall Brigade's 2nd Virginia—as well as with Oscar Hinrichs, Henry Kyd Douglas, and Edward Johnson—in the Shenandoah valley. According to von Steinecker, John Y. Beall, executed in February 1865 as a Confederate spy, also attended this alleged meeting. Purportedly they discussed plans to attack Northern cities and kill Lincoln. Several other witnesses tried to implicate Confederate officials in Richmond and Canada, but their charges, like von Steinecker's, were never proven.[6]

Captured by Union soldiers, von Steinecker had remained in prison until he brokered a deal for his freedom by lodging accusations against the three rebel officers. Hinrichs, Douglas, and Johnson prepared to discredit the sensational testimony of von Steinecker, who had deserted from the Army of Northern Virginia. In the meantime, he mysteriously disappeared—or was allowed to escape. In his postwar account, Douglas wrote that he and his comrades were treated as "semi-witnesses, semi-accused." When no other incriminating evidence emerged, the prosecutors could no longer hold the rebel officers as defendants.[7]

Hinrichs, Douglas, and Johnson nevertheless testified on May 30 as witnesses for the defense of Mary Surratt. The focus of their testimony was to impeach the credibility of von Steinecker and his claim of a plan among Confederate military officers to assassinate Lincoln. They denied knowing Booth and declared that they were unaware of any plots within the Stonewall Brigade, or elsewhere in the Army of Northern Virginia, to murder the U.S. president.[8]

Two weeks later, Federal authorities set Henry Kyd Douglas free. Edward Johnson remained in Old Capitol Prison until he signed an oath of allegiance on July 17. Federal officials released him after he received amnesty.

It is unclear as to when they freed Captain Oscar Hinrichs. He was fortunate no one found out about his early-in-the-war escapades—including his association with the rebel underground in southern Maryland, his involvement with the Surratts, and the commandeering of a Union schooner to cross the Potomac River—or his end-of-the-war schemes to destabilize the North by acting as a secret agent. That circumstantial evidence would have been devastating to his pleas of innocence and so incriminating that he could not have escaped recrimination from hyper-reactive Union leaders like Secretary of War Stanton.

Returning to New York to resume his career, Oscar would have relied on his father who had continued to prosper. In addition to serving as a German consul during the war, Carl Hinrichs further developed his importing business and established a chemical factory on Long Island, where he had lived since about 1840. In 1870 the elder Hinrichs reported on the U.S. census that he held $50,000 worth of real estate, an accumulation of assets that was significant in the postwar period.[9]

Oscar kept in touch with Mary Stanley, the wartime pen pal referred to as "Mamie" in his journals. Her father, the Reverend Harvey Stanley, officiated at their wedding on October 8, 1868, which was held at his Holy Trinity Episcopal Church in Collington, Maryland. The couple initially lived in New York City and listed Brooklyn as their place of residence in the 1870 Federal census. They had six children: Stanley, Oscar Jr., William, Sarah, Frank, and Ernest.[10]

Oscar pursued his mapmaking career in New York City until 1878. During part of that time, he worked as the principal draftsman for Colton's American Geographical Establishment and was a Fellow of the American Geographical Society of New York. In 1875 Oscar published his *Guide to Central Park*, which included a detailed map. He also produced an *Atlas of Topography*, containing a Civil War map of Confederate fortifications he helped to construct at Germanna Ford along the Rappahannock River near Chancellorsville.[11]

During the winter of 1878, Oscar Hinrichs approached George M. Wheeler in Washington, D.C., and received temporary work as a draftsman "engaged in miscellaneous work." The Wheeler Survey encountered financial difficulties,

Mary Stanley Hinrichs
(Courtesy of the Adrienne
Hessel Lissner Private
Collection)

so by the end of May 1879 he had to look for other employment. His career re-bounded when, two months later, the Federal government appointed him as Land Clerk at the General Land Office.[12]

In March 1883 Oscar received a commission to become principal clerk of the Public Surveys. His responsibilities as head of the U.S. General Land Office division included supervising all public land surveys, directing policy, and formulating technical procedures and practices. He held this post until June 1885, when President Grover A. Cleveland replaced him with another appointee. Afterward, he worked as a civil engineer. The heading on his 1891 letterhead read as follows: "Oscar Hinrichs, CE, Geographer, Surveying & Draughting, Washington, D.C." One of his projects after leaving the General Land Office was to develop a map of Mexico, which was published in 1888 as part of a North American atlas.[13]

After the war, Oscar Hinrichs continued to express himself as an artist. He designed a stained-glass window at Holy Trinity Episcopal Church, dedicating it to his wife's younger sister, Sarah, who died prematurely in 1863 at the age of eight. The stained-glass window remains intact today above the altar of the church. Additionally, he created ink drawings, including a Hinrichs coat of arms and Confederate flag.[14]

As the 1880s drew to a close, Oscar became more despondent. He had lost a prime government job and struggled to establish his next business. Stanley Hinrichs, his oldest son, passed down stories to his daughter that Oscar drank heavily, grew more resentful of other people's achievements, and had serious money problems. Oscar blamed his Confederate service for preventing him from having a more successful, lucrative career.[15]

In addition to his personal problems, Oscar faced the loss of close family members. First, his father-in-law, Reverend Stanley, died in 1885. Four years later, doctors diagnosed his wife, Mary, as having uterine cancer. His father passed away on June 29, 1890. Oscar's misery intensified as it became clear that his younger wife's illness was terminal. On August 8, 1891, he visited a friend, attorney Daniel Glassie, in Washington. Oscar gave the ex-Yankee officer a sealed letter (a "pre-suicide note"), on which he had written: "To be opened when occasion may require." Mary Stanley Hinrichs died on October 25, 1891. A year later, on September 19, 1892, Oscar shot himself in the head with his pistol.[16]

With a strong family heritage predicated on education and professional achievements, Oscar Hinrichs began his career at the U.S. Coast Survey with so much hope and promise. Yet his postwar ambitions floundered, culminating in numerous disappointments and missed opportunities.

Stanley Hinrichs, the oldest child of Oscar and Mary, graduated from law school—at what is now George Washington University—and passed the bar in 1893. He only had one child, Mary Stanley, whom he named after his mother. She married Frederick Hessel and received a doctoral degree from the University of Strasbourg in Alsace-Lorraine. She had a keen interest in American history and carefully preserved the Oscar Hinrichs journals and memorabilia, which she received from her father. At the age of eighty, she published a well-researched book on the Reverend Harvey Stanley's grandfather, whose privateering helped to fund North Carolina troops in the Revolutionary War.[17]

Oscar's only daughter, Sarah Hinrichs, shared his passion for art, culture, and personal study. She learned how to draw, paint, and sew, among many other things, from him. The prestigious Corcoran Art School in Washington, D.C., accepted her application, but she declined attending so she could help to raise her younger brothers. In 1903 Sarah married Maury H. Brown. They settled in Hyattsville, Maryland, and had three daughters: Agnes, Elizabeth, and Bobby (Barbara).

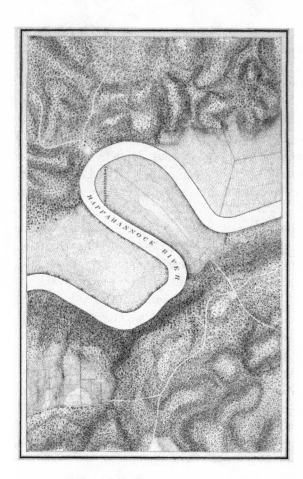

Oscar Hinrichs's postwar map of CSA fortifications along the Rappahannock River (Courtesy of the Henson Family Properties)

Sarah Hinrichs Brown fostered creative expression among her children. Having learned to appreciate music from her father (he purchased a violin and expensive piano while she was growing up), she encouraged her daughters to embrace this art form. Bobby became an accomplished pianist, playing in professional venues in the Washington, D.C., area. Betty also played the piano and organ at family gatherings. Sarah continued with her artwork, painting outdoor scenes and a beautiful watercolor rendition of her mother, Mary Stanley Hinrichs, as well as a floral-designed set of china for each of her daughters when they got married. She taught her daughters and grandchildren the value of ongoing education—"You need to keep learning something new throughout your life"—and was a voracious reader, also developing expertise in needlework, quilting, and making ceramics.[18]

Elizabeth Brown Henson's son, Jim Henson, evidently also inherited the artistic talent of his great-grandfather Oscar Hinrichs. (Barbara "Bobby"

Brown Miltenberger later became Jim Henson's stepmother.) He excelled as an innovator in children's entertainment and emerging media, combining the concept of marionette dolls and puppets to create the Muppets and other characters on Public Television's *Sesame Street*. He also applied his pioneering concepts in puppetry to the production of family-oriented movies. A 1993 biography of Jim Henson identified Sarah Hinrichs Brown as being "a major influence" in the development of his artwork. She taught Jim as a boy how "to appreciate the power of visual imagery and to value creativity" as they made drawings, painted, and sewed together. The recently published *Jim Henson: A Biography* by Brian Jay Jones also addresses the artistic heritage of Oscar Hinrichs.[19]

Despite living in many different parts of the country, descendants of Oscar Hinrichs independently saved his heirlooms, including documents, maps, ink drawings, paintings, and photographs. One of his granddaughters, Agnes Brown Jenkins, typed Oscar's postwar essay entitled "From Maine to Dixie: In the Early Days of the War," which provided more details about how he escaped from the North into the Confederacy. A great-granddaughter, Adrienne Lissner, preserved Oscar's artwork, along with memorabilia such as the diary of the Reverend Harvey Stanley. Hinrichs-related material has also been maintained as part of the Henson Family Properties in New York City.[20]

Although Oscar Hinrichs never fulfilled his grander ambitions to replicate the achievements of his father, step-grandfather, and father-in-law, he nevertheless left a strong legacy as his children built better lives for themselves and their descendants. For more than 100 years, various family members transcribed, typed, and copied his Confederate journals, sometimes preserving them in expensive binding. Thanks to them, Oscar's Civil War service has now been chronicled in *Stonewall's Prussian Mapmaker*.

Oscar Hinrichs's Immediate and Extended Family

Father and Mother
Germany and New York City
 Carl E. L. Hinrichs (1800–1890) + Fanney Bettie Klaner Hinrichs (?–1839)
  Oscar Hinrichs (1835–1892)
Father, Stepmother, and Siblings
Jamaica/Brooklyn, New York
 Carl E. L. Hinrichs Sr. (1800–1890) + Amalia M. G. Ehringhaus Hinrichs (1818–1913)
  Amelia E. Hinrichs (1841/1842–?)
  John C. E. Hinrichs (1843–1880; "Chris")
  Carl E. L. Hinrichs Jr. (1848–1901)
  James J. Hinrichs (1851/1854–?)
  Blucher E. Hinrichs (1857–1910)
Stepmother's Parents, Siblings, Nieces, and Nephews
Elizabeth City, North Carolina
 John C. Ehringhaus (1783–1865) + Matilda S. Gregory Ehringhaus (1793–1876)
  John C. B. Ehringhaus (1814–1853; "Blucher")
   Matilda Gregory Ehringhaus Bradford (1839–1916; probably "Till")
   Other children
  William F. M. Ehringhaus (ca. 1816–?)
In-Laws
Collington, Maryland
 Rev. Harvey Stanley (1809–1885) + Mary Anne Kinney Stanley (1818–1893)
  Charles H. Stanley (1842–1913; "Charlie")
  Other children
Wife, Children, and Grandchildren
 Oscar Hinrichs (1835–1892) + Mary Stanley Hinrichs (1840–1891)
  H. Stanley Hinrichs (1870–1937)
   Dr. Mary Stanley Hessel (1903–1996)
  Oscar Hinrichs Jr. (1871–1938)
  William Hinrichs (ca. 1875–ca. 1900)
  Sarah Hinrichs Brown (1876–1967)
   Mary Agnes Jenkins (1904–2001)
   Elizabeth Henson (1908–1975)
   Barbara Miltenberger Henson (1914–2012)
  Frank Hinrichs (1878–1941; "Fritz")
  Ernest Hinrichs (1882–1941)

Poetry and Songs

February 17, 1864

CONSCRIPTS

Oh weep not, conscript, weep not
Old Jeff has called for thee
A soldier Congress makes you
A soldier you must be.
Make up your mind
To stand in line
And quake not at the Yanks.
To shoot your gun
And call it fun
And for life return your thanks.

[Chorus]
Then weep not, conscript, weep not
Old Jeff has called for thee.
A soldier Congress makes you
A soldier you must be.

O weep not, conscript, weep not
If rations should be scarce
'Tis said an empty "stumic"
Will make you doubly fierce.
Then eat your crust
Your bayonet thrust
Through every Yankee heart.
And if unhurt
Your gal will sit
At home and call you smart.

Oh weep not, conscript, weep not
When marching through the mud
'Tis better far I tell you
Than spilling your lifes blood.
Then march along
And sing this song
And cuss the Yanks now and then

And when you camp
Just take a tramp
And steal a pig or hen.

O weep not, conscript, weep not
Your battling for the right.
Now, conscript let me tell you
"Don't scratch them when they bite"
But jerk your shirt
Off with a flirt
And catch them as they run
Then with your nail
The bugs assail
And "mash" them one by one.

September 15, 1864

"BURY ME ON THE FIELD, BOYS
DEATH OF MAJOR C. ROBERDEAU WHEAT
BATTLE OF GAINES' MILL, JUNE 27, 1862"

"Bury me on the field, boys," and away to the glorious fight
You may come again this way, boys, in your triumph march tonight.
But when you pass this spot, boys, I would not have you sigh
In holy cause of country, boys, who would not gladly die!

"Bury me on the field, boys," where a soldier loves to rest
And sweet shall be my sleep, boys, upon my country's breast.
For she is dearer far, boys, than aught this world can give
And I would gladly die, boys, that she may proudly live.

"Bury me on the field, boys," and there to make a stand
That shall loose the Tyrants grip, boys, from our sunny Southern land.
And teach the foul invader, boys, in Freedom's holy strife
The Southern heart will sever, boys, the fondest ties of life.

"Bury me on the field, boys," then on to meet the foe
Hands that have dug a grave, boys, shall lay their legions low.
Eyes that have wept at dawn, boys, shall smile at close of day
For Southern hearts shall triumph, boys, in the Northerner's dismay.

"Bury me on the field, boys," I do not die in vain
For Freedom's rose shall bloom, boys, from out that bloody rain.
And soon the South shall rise, boys, all glorious and fair
With sun bright rays around her, boys, and stars upon her hair.

"Bury me on the field, boys," the vision bright and sweet
Was surely sent to cheer me, boys, in this my own defeat.
Here take my trembling hand, boys, I thank you for your care
And let each soldiers heart, boys, ascend with mine in prayer.

From the battlefield of life, boys, all wounded, weary, sore
Pray that my fainting soul, boys, may reach its heavenly shore.
And in that land of peace, boys, the weary may find rest
And the poor repentant soldier, boys, finds shelter among the blest.

"Bury me on the field, boys," for life is ebbing fast
One moment more of pain, boys, and then the trial's past
I cannot see you now boys, there's a mist before my sight
But hark! I hear sweet music, boys—
Thank God
We've won the fight.

The best revenge is love—then calm
Anger with smiles, heals wounds with balm;
Give water to the thirsty foe.
The Sandal tree, as if to prove
How sweet to conquer hate by love
Perfumes the axe that lays it low.

September 16, 1864

"DAMN IT! LET IT RIP."

Come Comrades! Open wide your ears, and listen while I sing
I'll promise that you shed no tears, about the news I bring.
For all seems bright and hopeful too, in our fair Southern land
And all that *we* have now to do, is keep our gizzard full of sand.

For *we* of all the noble hosts, that strike for Southern rights
Need patience more, and suffer most, being kept away from fights.
Where Glory, Honor and our Hate would sweeten every blow
While all we do is damn the fate, that will not let us go.

For here we are and here will stay upon this island pent
With naught to do to charm away our natural discontent.
But cheer each other up with hopes, and bear the winters cold
Until good luck shall bless the ropes, thats pulled by Robert Ould.

But I for one will do my part to lighten all your hearts
I'll banish grief and laugh at care, if you will do your parts.
I'll drive blue devils from this "pen," like rats from sunken ship
If all of you will say Amen to "Damn it! Let it rip."

October 31, 1864

J. E. B. STUART'S RENDITION OF "MARYLAND"

I hear your old familiar neigh,
Maryland! My Maryland!
Asking for you corn and hay,
Maryland! My Maryland!
But you must wait till break of day,
And "Bob" will then your call obey,
And make you look so sleek and gay,
Maryland! My Maryland!

Upon your proud old back I'll sit,
Maryland! My Maryland!
When last night bivouac I quit,
Maryland! My Maryland!

To use my spurs I'll not omit,
And minding ditches not a whit,
I'll yield to you the willing bit,
Maryland, My Maryland!

Your master's heel is in your flank,
Maryland! My Maryland!
I hear his restless saber clank,
Maryland! My Maryland!
He'll ride you hard, and you may thank,
Your stars if not left lean and lank,
Without the rations due your rank,
Maryland! My Maryland!

I feel secure upon your back
Maryland! My Maryland!
When cannons roar, and rifles crack,
Maryland! My Maryland!
You bore me o'er the Pot-o-mac,
You circumvented "Little Mac,"
Oh! May I never know your lack,
Maryland! My Maryland.

March 12, 1865

"CHRONICLES OF JUBAL"

1. And it came to pass that Jubal, whose surname was Early, called together the chief of his tribes, and saith unto them: view the country around.
2. And they went forth and from a high hill of much height they viewed their enemies and all the surrounding country, and the distance they saw was exceeding great.
3. And returning they said let not all thy people go up, but let some go around our enemies, and peradventure we may scatter them.
4. So Gordon took with him several of his brethren and took a thousand and twenty and two good footmen and a thousand good horsemen, and they removed out of the camp by night that they might come upon the camp of the puritans and strike them suddenly.
5. And one of the chosen leaders was called to Jubal, and Jubal said unto him "Drive them before while my people press them behind and on both sides."
6. And there was a horseman of exceeding great name, who was in much favour with Jubal, and Jubal saith unto him "scatter my enemies on my left." And to you "Gabriel" whose surname was Wharton I say make my enemies fly in front, and to you my chosen leader Gordon, crush them on my right, and let us rejoice with exceeding great joy.
7. And when morning was nigh, Gordon went into the enemies camp dispersing them.
8. And when it was day Sheridan showed with a part of his men in the plains surrounding, but Gordon gave him no rest, but slew many of his men and leaders, and took many of his men, and chariots and horses and guns.
9. And Jubal was exceeding well pleased, and full of joy. And some he stopped to plunge into the enemy again, when behold Sheridan brought ten thousand and thirty and two fresh men. And they came like a hurricane.

10. And Jubal said unto the men that were with him and to his people fear not: fear ye not this multitude neither be ye afraid of their assault. Remember in what way we were saved at Bethel and Shiloh at Manassas and Juda[h]—and now let us stand like men and remember the covenant, and we will destroy this army before our face.

11. And all nations shall know that Sheridan is no more.

12. And the people lifted up their eyes and saw the multitude of Yankees coming against them and they fled into the plain.

13. And the trumpet sounded and Gabriel held his ground, and by degrees Gordon with his legion was pressed back by the multitude of the enemy, and then our leader Kershaw and then Ramseur and then Pegram. And Gabriel was now sorely pressed by the many horsemen of the enemy—they came against him with exceeding great noise and galloping of horses.

14. They well nigh drove him, but Gabriel drove them. But soon the trumpet sounded and then Gabriel came affront his band, and soon the whole army were running with great swiftness and were exceeding much scared.

15. They joined Battle and again fled, and most of his hindmost fell by the sword and were made prisoners. But it came to pass that very few were hindmost and they safely crossed the river.

16. Jubal then saw with pain that it was the greediness over the spoils that had cost his people so dear, and he raised his voice and saith my Lord have mercy upon me! and Harman saith amen! And he said what shall I say! seeing his people turning their back on their enemy. And as he was saying these words part of them appeared looking forth from the mountains.

17. And he said Lord have mercy on us! and one Harman, the chosen leader of horses and wagons saith amen!

18. And Jubal now saw with delight that night was nigh and he moved back calling upon his people to stop. But the spirit was gone and his people were scattered, and Sheridan and his host was coming.

19. There fell of our people on that day about two hundred killed, about six hundred and twenty and six wounded, and we lost about eight hundred prisoners.

20. And Jubal was sorely disappointed for he slew only about one thousand of the foe, wounded only about three thousand and thirty and five, and took only one thousand six hundred and twenty and six prisoners.

21. So he told his men to behold how discomfited the enemy was, and called upon them for shame not to be guilty of such a thing again.

22. Many of his people fled to the mountains and lived on locusts and wild honey and herbs. And they were hunted by the demons, but many escaped, and it came to pass that Jubal soon has as large an army as he had before.

23. And soon his people were revived and they saw that it [was] wrong to be greedy over spoils and they rent their garments and made great lamentations and put ashes on their heads, and they fell down to the ground on their faces, and they sounded the trumpets and a good counsel came unto their minds.

24. And Jubal became a better man and the Lord will soon aid his goodness. He stopped his distilleries and saith let no liquors come into camp, and his people are willing to obey him and have him for their leader.

25. And Jubal saw it was all for the best, and he saith the Lord be praised; and Harman said amen! and the judge, the patriarch, the many of many riches, said amen!

26. And his people said fight thou our battles and we will do what thou saith.

27. And Jubal contents himself and saith may we never put ourselves to flight again and Judge (the funny man and the man of great height and many riches) saith amen.
28. Here ended the first chapter.

For information on Confederate songs and poetry, see H. M. Wharton, *War Songs and Poems of the Southern Confederacy, 1861–1865* (Washington, D.C.: W. E. Scull, 1904).

Notes

Abbreviations for Commonly Used Information and Sources

ANVA   Army of Northern Virginia

AoJ   Army of the James

AoP   Army of the Potomac

AoS   Army of the Shenandoah

AoV   Army of the Valley District

AoWV   Army of West Virginia

Barrett, *Civil War NC*

> John G. Barrett, *The Civil War in North Carolina* (Chapel Hill: University of North Carolina Press, 1963)

Brandt, *Man Who Tried to Burn New York*

> Nat Brandt, *The Man Who Tried to Burn New York* (Syracuse: Syracuse University Press, 1986)

Clark, *NC Regiments*

> Walter Clark, ed., *Histories of the Several Regiments and Battalions from North Carolina in the Great War 1861–'65*, 5 vols. (1901; reprinted, Wilmington, N.C.: Broadfoot Publishing, 1996)

Clemmer, *Old Alleghany*

> Gregg S. Clemmer, *Old Alleghany: The Life and Wars of General Ed Johnson* (Staunton, Va.: Hearthside Publishing Co., 2004)

Crute, *Confederate Staff Officers*

> Joseph H. Crute Jr., *Confederate Staff Officers, 1861–1865* (Powhatan, Va.: Derwent Books, 1982)

Crute, *Units of the CSA*

> Joseph H. Crute Jr., *Units of the Confederate States Army* (Gaithersburg, Md.: Olde Soldier Books, 1987)

CSA

> Confederate States of America

Current, *Encyclopedia of the Confederacy*

> Richard N. Current, ed., *Encyclopedia of the Confederacy*, 4 vols. (New York: Simon & Schuster 1993)

Dickert, *Kershaw's Brigade*

> D. Augustus Dickert, *History of Kershaw's Brigade with Complete Roll of Companies, Biographical Sketches, Incidents, Anecdotes, etc.* (1899; reprinted, Wilmington, N.C.: Broadfoot Publishing Co., 1990)

Douglas, *I Rode with Stonewall*
    Henry Kyd Douglas, *I Rode with Stonewall* (Chapel Hill: University of North Carolina Press, 1940)
Driver, *First & Second Maryland Cavalry*
    Robert J. Driver Jr., *First & Second Maryland Cavalry, C.S.A.* (Charlottesville, Va.: Rockbridge Publishing, 1999)
Driver, *First & Second Maryland Infantry*
    Robert J. Driver Jr., *First & Second Maryland Infantry, C.S.A.* (Bowie, Md.: Willow Bend Books, 2003)
Early, *Memoir*
    Jubal A. Early, *A Memoir of the Last Year of the War for Independence, in the Confederate States of America, Containing an Account of the Operations of His Commands in the Years 1864 and 1865* (Columbia: University of South Carolina Press, 2001)
Fonvielle, *Wilmington Campaign*
    Chris E. Fonvielle Jr., *The Wilmington Campaign: Last Rays of Departing Hope* (Campbell, Calif.: Savas Publishing Co., 1997)
Foote, *Civil War*
    Shelby Foote, *The Civil War: A Narrative*, 3 vols. (New York: Random House, 1958–1974)
Freeman, *Lee's Lieutenants*
    Douglas Southall Freeman, *Lee's Lieutenants: A Study in Command*, 3 vols. (New York: Charles Scribner's Sons, 1942–1944)
Gallagher, *Ramseur*
    Gary W. Gallagher, *Stephen Dodson Ramseur: Lee's Gallant General* (Chapel Hill: University of North Carolina Press, 1985)
Gilmor, *Four Years in the Saddle*
    Harry Gilmor, *Four Years in the Saddle* (New York: Harper & Brothers, Publishers, 1866)
Gordon, *Reminiscences*
    John B. Gordon, *Reminiscences of the Civil War* (New York: Charles Scribner's Sons, 1903)
Gragg, *Confederate Goliath*
    Rod Gragg, *Confederate Goliath: The Battle of Fort Fisher* (Baton Rouge: Louisiana State University Press, 1991)
Greene, *Breaking the Rebellion*
    A. Wilson Greene, *Breaking the Back of the Rebellion: The Final Battles of the Petersburg Campaign* (Mason City, Iowa.: Savas Publishing, 2000)
Griggs, *John Pegram*
    Walter S. Griggs Jr. *General John Pegram, C.S.A.* (Lynchburg, Va.: H. E. Howard, 1993)
Hinrichs, "Maine to Dixie"
    Oscar Hinrichs, "From Maine to Dixie: In the Early Days of the War" (Henson Family Properties)
Hotchkiss, *Make Me a Map*
    Jedediah Hotchkiss, *Make Me a Map of the Valley: The Civil War Journal of Stonewall Jackson's Topographer*, ed. Archie P. McDonald (Dallas: Southern Methodist University Press, 1973)
Jackson, *First Regiment Engineer Troops*
    Harry L. Jackson, *First Regiment Engineer Troops, P.A.C.S.: Robert E. Lee's Combat Engineers* (Louisa, Va.: R. A. E. Design & Publishing, 1998)
Jones, *Rebel War Clerk's Diary*
    J. B. Jones, *A Rebel War Clerk's Diary at the Confederate States Capital*, 2 vols. (Philadelphia: J. B. Lippincott Co., 1866)

Kennedy, *Civil War Battlefield Guide*
>Frances H. Kennedy, ed., *The Civil War Battlefield Guide*, 2nd ed. (Boston: Houghton Mifflin, 1998)

KIA
>Killed in action

Klasing, *The Ehringhauses*
>Chris Klasing, *The Ehringhauses: A German-American Family in North Carolina*, http://files.usgwarchives.net/nc/pasquotank/bios/eprenhse.txt (accessed October 2013)

Krick, *Lee's Colonels*
>Robert K. Krick, *Lee's Colonels: A Biographical Register of the Field Officers of the Army of Northern Virginia*, 4th ed. (Dayton, Ohio: Morningside, 1992)

Krick, *Staff Officers*
>Robert E. L. Krick, *Staff Officers in Gray: A Biographical Register of Staff Officers in the Army of Northern Virginia* (Chapel Hill: University of North Carolina Press, 2003)

McPherson, *Battle Cry*
>McPherson, James M. *Battle Cry of Freedom: The Civil War Era* (New York: Oxford University Press, 1988)

MWIA
>Mortally wounded in action

NAMP
>National Archives Microfilm Publication

NARA I
>National Archives and Records Administration, Washington, D.C.

NARA II
>National Archives and Records Administration, College Park, Maryland

O&A RR
>Orange & Alexandria Railroad

OH
>Oscar Hinrichs

OR
>U.S. War Department, *The War of the Rebellion: A Compilation of the Official Records of the Union and Confederate Armies*, 128 vols. (Washington, D.C.: Government Printing Office, 1880–1901). All citations are from Series I of the *Official Records* unless otherwise noted.

Pfanz, *Ewell*
>Donald C. Pfanz, *Richard S. Ewell: A Soldier's Life* (Chapel Hill: University of North Carolina Press, 1998)

POW
>Prisoner of war

Robertson, *Stonewall Jackson*
>James I. Robertson Jr., *Stonewall Jackson: The Man, the Soldier, the Legend* (New York: Macmillan Publishing USA, 1997)

RR
>Railroad

SHC
>Southern Historical Collection, Wilson Library, University of North Carolina at Chapel Hill

Stephens, *Intrepid Warrior*
>Robert Grier Stephens Jr., *Intrepid Warrior: Clement Anselm Evans, Confederate General*

from Georgia, Life, Letters, and Diaries of the War Years (Dayton, Ohio: Morningside, 1992)

Tidwell, *Come Retribution*

William A. Tidwell with James O. Hall and David Winfred Gaddy, *Come Retribution: The Confederate Secret Service and the Assassination of Lincoln* (Jackson: University Press of Mississippi, 1988)

Trudeau, *Last Citadel*

Noah Andre Trudeau, *The Last Citadel: Petersburg, Virginia, June 1864–April 1865* (Boston: Little, Brown and Co., 1991)

U.S.C.S.

United States Coast Survey

Warner, *Generals in Blue*

Ezra Warner, *Generals in Blue: Lives of the Union Commanders* (Baton Rouge: Louisiana State University Press, 1964)

Warner, *Generals in Gray*

Ezra Warner, *Generals in Gray: Lives of the Confederate Commanders* (Baton Rouge: Louisiana State University Press, 1959)

Wert, *Winchester to Cedar Creek*

Jeffry D. Wert, *From Winchester to Cedar Creek: The Shenandoah Campaign of 1864* (Mechanicsburg, Pa.: Stackpole Books, 1997)

WIA

Wounded in action

Introduction

1. In 1864 Reverend Stanley appeared to abet a fellow Episcopal clergyman, the Reverend Kensey Johns Stewart, who worked on several clandestine projects for President Jefferson Davis. Tidwell, *Come Retribution*, 274–77.

2. Tidwell and his coauthors found a potential connection between Wat Bowie and Samuel Mudd. Ibid., 140–41.

3. Douglas, *I Rode with Stonewall*, 338–41; Benn Pittman, "The Assassination of President Lincoln and the Trial of the Conspirators," in *The Trial: The Assassination of President Lincoln and the Trial of the Conspirators*, ed. Edward Steers Jr. (Lexington: University Press of Kentucky, 2003), 64–66.

4. Laurie Verge, "Mary Elizabeth Surratt," in *The Trial*, ed. Steers, LIILIX.

5. In *Come Retribution*, the authors included the photo of a cipher found in John Wilkes Booth's hotel. Some of the CSA phrases used in ciphering were: "Manchester Bluff," "Complete Victory," and "Come Retribution." Tidwell, *Come Retribution*, 40.

6. See Nat Brandt's *Man Who Tried to Burn New York*.

7. OH switched from English to German in his journals starting on July 18, 1864. Was he worried about what might be contained in them? This was soon after the raid on Washington during which he wrote about the burning of buildings owned by Union leaders—as a reprisal for the Union army's torching of Lexington, Virginia—and the plan to release rebel prisoners from Pt. Lookout Prison in southern Maryland. Perhaps he was also worried about the plans and events he would be writing about in the coming months, such as his plot to wreak havoc in New York City.

8. See appendix 1 for an overview of OH's immediate and extended family. The 1840 Federal census for the Charles Hendricks [*sic*] household in Jamaica included one male between the ages of five and ten, which was Oscar Hinrichs. According to letters from his stepmother,

OH's birthday was in March. Walter D. Kamphoefner and Wolfgang Helbich, eds., *Germans in the Civil War: The Letters They Wrote Home* (Chapel Hill: University of North Carolina Press, 2006), 40; December 4, 1902, and January 11, 1903, letters from Amalia Ehringhaus Hinrichs to Stanley Hinrichs, Henson Family Properties.

9. Wolff and Hinrichs maintained an office in New York City and one in Hamburg. Later Carl Hinrichs owned a chemical factory on Long Island. Declaration of Intention and Naturalization Record of Carl E. L. Hinrichs, New York County Clerk's Office; letter from Carl Hinrichs to Bache, November 13, 1855, Correspondence of Alexander Dallas Bache, Superintendent of U.S. Coast Survey, 1843–1865 (NAMP M642, Reel 152), Records of the Coast and Geodetic Survey, Record Group 23, NARA II.

10. Amalia's oldest brother, Blucher, was also a member of the legislature and served as a general in the state militia. A great-grandson would become governor of the state. December 4, 1902, and January 11, 1903, letters from Amalia Ehringhaus Hinrichs to Stanley Hinrichs, Henson Family Properties; Klasing, *The Ehringhauses*; John Elliott Wood, ed., *Year Book: Pasquotank Historical Society, Elizabeth City, North Carolina, 1954–1957* (Elizabeth City, N.C.: Pasquotank Historical Society, n.d.), 2:155–56; Lou N. Overman and Edna M. Shannonhouse, eds., *Year Book: Pasquotank Historical Society, Elizabeth City, North Carolina* (Baltimore: Gateway Press, 1975), 3:208; J. Howard Stevens, *Albemarle: People and Places* (Elizabeth City, N.C.: M/M/T Printers, 1999), 137–38; John C. Ehringhaus advertisement, *American Beacon and Commercial Diary*, March 30, 1818; register entries for March 4, 1841; April 24, 1842; December 31, 1848; and January 15, 1854, Christ Episcopal Church.

11. Holzminden was in the Dukedom of Brunswick (Braunschweig). December 4, 1902, and January 11, 1903, letters from Amalia Ehringhaus Hinrichs to Stanley Hinrichs, Henson Family Properties.

12. With his artistic abilities, Jim Henson worked his way through college via a silk-screening business before applying his creative talents to the development of puppets for a local D.C. television station. Later based in New York City, the Jim Henson Company became recognized worldwide as a leader in the expanding television and movie media. According to Jim Henson's biographer, the name for the character "Oscar the Grouch" came from a feisty New York restaurateur whose business—Oscar's Salt of the Sea—was located near the Henson offices. Christopher Finch, *Jim Henson: The Works, the Art, the Magic, the Imagination* (New York: Random House, 1993), 4–11; Brian Jay Jones, *Jim Henson: The Biography* (New York: Ballantine Books, 2013), 6–7, 37–44, 149.

13. Congressman Robert T. Paine, Amalia's friend, helped OH to obtain a position in the Coast Survey. OH also worked on maps near Gloucester Court House in Virginia and "From Cape Fear to St. Mary's rivers, including the coast of SC and GA." Letter from Bache to OH, December 20, 1856 (NAMP M642, Reel 152), Distribution of the Parties of the Coast Survey upon the Coasts of the United States during the Surveying Season of 1859–'60, Correspondence of Alexander Dallas Bache, Superintendent of U.S. Coast Survey, 1843–1865 (NAMP M642, Reel 231), Records of the Coast and Geodetic Survey, Record Group 23, NARA II; Hinrichs, "Maine to Dixie."

14. January 11, 1903, letter from Amalia Ehringhaus Hinrichs to Stanley Hinrichs, Henson Family Properties.

15. As chief engineer of the Cape Fear area near Wilmington, Bolles oversaw construction of two sand batteries on Federal Point, one of which the Wilmington Light Infantry named "Battery Bolles" in his honor. In July 1862 he was appointed captain of artillery and put in charge of organizing the ordnance laboratory at the Fayetteville armory. Charles P. Bolles Papers, North Carolina State Archives, Raleigh, N.C.; Fonvielle, *Wilmington Campaign*, 494;

C. P. Bolles records, U.S. Coast Survey Occupations of Personnel, 1844–1870, Records of the Coast and Geodetic Survey, Record Group 23, NARA II.

16. There is no evidence that the government recovered the materials that Bolles took. Elsewhere in North Carolina, Sherman's soldiers found Coast Survey instruments and camp gear taken at Roanoke Island on April 30, 1861, when they seized the arsenal at Fayetteville near the end of the war. Albert E. Theberge, *The Coast Survey, 1807–1867*, CW1, (accessed October 2005).

17. Hinrichs, "Maine to Dixie."

18. Ibid.

19. Harvey Stanley arrived at Holy Trinity Episcopal Church in 1851, six years after the church was founded, and remained a pastor there until 1885. There was a story passed down in the Stanley family that the minister "ran a rest station of some kind in the basement [of his parsonage] for Confederates passing through the area, or through the lines," and that one of his daughters (Annie) threw stones at Union soldiers marching past the parsonage. After the war, OH designed a stained-glass window in honor of Reverend Stanley's deceased daughter, Sarah Gordon Stanley (1855–1863), which is still above the altar today in Holy Trinity Episcopal Church. Constance P. Ackerson, *Holy Trinity — Collington: Her People and Their Church* (Belair-Bowie, Md.: n.p., 1978), 123, 160–61; inscribed photo of stained-glass window at Holy Trinity Episcopal Church designed by Oscar Hinrichs, Richard Brady Williams Private Collection; Hinrichs, "Maine to Dixie."

20. Christ Episcopal Church in Elizabeth City was Reverend Stanley's first parish. John C. Ehringhaus and his family were members of his congregation. Judge Charles R. Kinney and his wife, Sarah, also attended the church, along with their daughter Mary Anne, who married Harvey Stanley on August 4, 1839. The homes of James Green and John Wright Stanly, Reverend Stanley's father and grandfather, respectively, are located on the grounds of Tryon Palace in New Bern. (The privateer and his son spelled their surname without an "e.") Mary Stanley Hessel, *Profile of a Patriot: The Story of John Wright Stanly, Revolutionary War Privateer* (New Bern, N.C.: Tryon Palace Commission, 1983), 3–4, 79–80; Christ Episcopal Church register, Elizabeth City, N.C., 248–49.

21. The Reverend Aldert Smedes and his wife started St. Mary's School in 1842. The school for young women has remained in operation continuously since then. Hinrichs, "Maine to Dixie"; the Reverend Harvey Stanley diaries, Adrienne Hessel Lissner Private Collection; William S. Powell, ed. *Encyclopedia of North Carolina* (Chapel Hill: University of North Carolina Press, 2006), 997.

22. OH did not mention the names of John and Mary Surratt in his postwar essay. It is obvious from his journal entries, however, that they were the "host" and "landlady" of the tavern. Surratt died on August 21, 1862. Hinrichs, "Maine to Dixie"; Elizabeth Steger Trindall, *Mary Surratt: An American Tragedy* (Gretna, La.: Pelican Publishing Co., 1996), 19–21, 36–45, 54–65.

23. Wat Bowie was an attorney before the war and came from a prominent family in Prince George's County, which was connected to OH's friends, such as Reverend Stanley. Bowie was an active spy; for example, he "is credited with informing General Robert E. Lee of General U. S. Grant's Wilderness Campaign in Virginia" prior to its onset in May 1864. George S. Lemmon enlisted in Company H in the 1st Maryland Infantry and was on detached duty from September 1861 to December 31, 1861. William A. Tidwell, *April '65: Confederate Covert Action in the American Civil War* (Kent, Ohio: Kent State University Press, 1995), 68–75; Donald E. Markle, *Spies and Spymasters of the Civil War* (New York: Hippocrene Books, 1994), 114–15; Driver, *First & Second Maryland Infantry*, 27–28, 460–61; Hinrichs, "Maine to Dixie."

24. Hinrichs, "Maine to Dixie."

25. Ibid.

26. Earl J. Hess, *Field Armies and Fortifications in the Civil War: The Eastern Campaigns, 1861–1865* (Chapel Hill: University of North Carolina Press, 2005), 16–24; James L. Nichols, *Confederate Engineers* (Tuscaloosa, Ala.: Confederate Publishing Co., 1957), 27–29.

27. J. Boone Bartholomees Jr., *Buff Facings and Gilt Buttons: Staff and Headquarters Operations in the Army of Northern Virginia, 1861–1865* (Columbia: University of South Carolina Press, 1998), 101–13; Krick, *Staff Officers*, 14–17; Jackson, *First Regiment Engineer Troops*, 1–13; General Orders No. 90, order book, Jeremy Francis Gilmer Papers, Number 276, SHC.

28. Ironically, Hinrichs did not find out until February 15 that the government had approved his appointment. The war clerk's other comment about OH—"He says Burnside will take Roanoke Island, and that [Brigadier General Henry] Wise and all his men will be captured"—turned out to be prophetic. Jones, *Rebel War Clerk's Diary*, 1:105.

29. OH also knew William Martin's brother, Brigadier General James G. Martin, who led the N.C. militia. Their father had been the first physician in town. Documents from the law practice of OH's uncle, Blucher Ehringhaus, as well as some of his grandfather's real estate transactions, are contained in William Martin's University of North Carolina collection. Martin continued to pay for construction of Confederate gunboats, which appears to have included Gilbert Elliott's work with the CSS *Albemarle* that was later built at Edwards Ferry on the Roanoke River. William F. Martin Papers, Number 493, SHC; John G. Barrett, *Civil War NC*, 213–31.

30. William Harwar Parker, *Recollections of a Naval Officer, 1841–1865* (Annapolis, Md.: Naval Institute Press, 1985), 257.

31. Compiled Service Records of Oscar Hinrichs, CSA Engineers (NAMP M258, Reel 106), Compiled Service Records of Confederate Soldiers Who Served in Organizations Raised Directly by the Confederate Government, War Department Collection of Confederate Records, Record Group 109, NARA I; Compiled Service Records of Oscar Hinrichs, CSA Engineers (NAMP M331A, Reel 124), Compiled Service Records of Confederate Soldiers Who Served in Organizations Raised Directly by the Confederate Government, War Department Collection of Confederate Records, Record Group 109, NARA I.

32. Hotchkiss, *Make Me a Map*, 142–47, 153–54, 167, 171–74.

33. James D. Horan, *Confederate Agent: A Discovery in History* (New York: Crown Publishers, 1954), 255–59; Brandt, *Man Who Tried to Burn New York*.

Chapter 1

1. During the war, OH transformed his journal into a contemporaneous narrative while in winter camp in 1862–63 and 1863–64. From September 15, 1863, until April 19, 1865 (when Federal authorities arrested him on his way home to New York City), he also wrote his diary entries in commercially available cloth-bound books.

2. Charles P. Bolles resigned from the U.S.C.S. on April 20, 1861, to help with the defense of Wilmington and the Cape Fear River. The rebels set up Battery Bolles as a stand-alone battery but later merged it into Fort Fisher. C. P. Bolles records, U.S. Coast Survey Occupations of Personnel, 1844–1870, Records of the Coast and Geodetic Survey, Record Group 23, NARA II; Fonvielle, *Wilmington Campaign*, 494.

3. After delegates from South Carolina met on December 20, 1860, at Institute Hall to establish "an Independent Commonwealth," there were more intense celebrations. E. Milby Burton, *The Siege of Charleston, 1861–1865* (Columbia: University of South Carolina Press, 1970), 1–3.

4. Bolles's personal records perished in a fire that destroyed his Wilmington home after the war. The Little River that OH mentioned was Little River Inlet, located at North Carolina's southernmost border along the Atlantic Ocean. Private correspondence between the author and Chris E. Fonvielle Jr.

5. McPherson, *Battle Cry*, 256–57.

6. Burton, *Siege of Charleston*, 9–11.

7. The town of Little River is now known as Calabash. During the Civil War, Lorenzo Frink was a well-respected physician who lived in Little River and owned a major plantation—Hickory Hall Plantation—located north of the Calabash River. Dr. Frink's wife came from a wealthy family in Wilmington. See www.townofcalabashnc.com; www.hchsonline.org/bio/nf.html.

8. Hull Adams was the grandson of President John Adams and a U.S.C.S. leader. Marc Friedlaender et al., eds. *Diary of Charles Francis Adams*, (Cambridge, Mass.: Belknap Press, 1986), 7:6; I. Hull Adams records, U.S. Coast Survey Occupations of Personnel, 1844–1870, Records of the Coast and Geodetic Survey, Record Group 23, NARA II.

9. NAMP M258, Reel 106; Warner, *Generals in Gray*, 297–98, 334–35; *The National Cyclopedia of American Biography, Being the History of the United States* (New York: James T. White & Co., 1894), 5:13; *Register of Officers of the Confederate States Navy, 1861–1865* (Washington, D.C.: U.S. Government Printing Office, 1931), 94.

10. NAMP M642, Reel 245.

Chapter 2

1. Lemmon enlisted in Company H in the 1st Maryland Infantry on July 1, 1861. In his service records and in McKim's regimental history, it was noted that he was on detached duty from September 1861 to December 31, 1861. McKnew served with Charles Stanley in 1861—they were on furlough from the 1st Maryland Infantry—and again later as First Lieutenant in Company B of the 1st Maryland Cavalry. OH wrote in "From Maine to Dixie" that McKnew was one of the most active Maryland blockade-runners. Hinrichs, "Maine to Dixie"; Driver, *First & Second Maryland Infantry, C.S.A.*, 27–28, 460–61; Driver, *First & Second Maryland Cavalry, C.S.A.*, 260; Randolph H. McKim, *A Soldier's Recollections: Leaves from the Diary of a Young Confederate* (New York: Longmans, Green, and Co., 1910), 36–37; American Civil War Research Database, www.civilwardata.com.

2. John Contee, a prominent citizen of Prince George's County, was a retired captain in the U.S. Navy. The DuVall plantation house—Marietta—was in Bowie, Maryland. Contee, DuVall, and their families attended Reverend Stanley's church in Collington (as did the family of Walter "Wat" Bowie). Richard Wootton lived nearby and was a member of the Maryland state legislature. John Gill, *Reminiscences of Four Years as a Private Soldier in the Confederate Army, 1861–1865* (Baltimore: Sun Printing Office, 1904), 21–22; Constance P. Ackerson, *Holy Trinity—Collington: Her People and Their Church* (Belair-Bowie, Md.: n.p., 1978), 84, 123; *Atlas of Prince George's County, Maryland, 1861* (Riverdale, Md.: Prince George's County Historical Society, 1996), 8; Harry Wright Newman, *Mareen DuVall of Middle Plantation* (self-published, 1952), 484, 525.

3. Charles H. Stanley, OH's future brother-in-law, was a private in the 1st Maryland Infantry's Company B and likely on a recruiting mission. When the regiment dissolved the following year, he would join the 1st Maryland Cavalry. Edmund Ruffin Beckwith Papers, Series 1, 1846–83, Number 3365, SHC; Effie G. Bowie, *Across the Years in Prince George's County* (Richmond: Garrett and Massie, 1947), 753.

4. John B. Brooke Jr. was among the twenty-nine Maryland legislators arrested on September 17, 1861. In 1862 he would leave his plantation and become a colonel in the Confederacy. He also served as provost marshal at Winchester. Fred Stewart and Alexander Hamilton were two other members of OH's clandestine party. The former may have been Frederick Augusta Stewart from Baltimore who enlisted on September 24, 1862, in McNeill's Partisan Rangers. There was an Alexander Hamilton from Charles County who, like Bowie, later became one of Mosby's Rangers. Daniel D. Hartzler, *Marylanders in the Confederacy* (Silver Spring, Md.: Family Line Publications, 1986), 55, 164, 280; Bowie, *Across the Years in Prince George's County*, 93; *Atlas of Prince George's County, Maryland, 1861*, 8; R. Lee Van Horn, *Out of the Past: Prince Georgians and Their Land* (Riverdale, Md.: Prince George's County Historical Society, 1976), 354; Roger U. Delauter Jr., *McNeill's Rangers* (Lynchburg, Va.: H. E. Howard, 1986), 124; Ackerson, *Holy Trinity*, 155.

5. Joseph Hooker commanded Brigadier General Daniel E. Sickles's regiments that were stationed in southern Maryland. Walter H. Hebert, *Fighting Joe Hooker* (Lincoln: University of Nebraska Press, 1999), 51–62.

6. See Hinrichs, "Maine to Dixie," for more details about the stay at the Surratt tavern. Elizabeth Steger Trindal, *Mary Surratt: An American Tragedy* (Gretna, La.: Pelican Publishing Co., 1996), 19–21, 36–45, 54–65.

7. The road south from Surrattsville led to the town of Piscataway. Fort Washington, a Union stronghold on the Potomac River, lay across from Mount Vernon and overlooked the mouth of Piscataway Creek. OH and his comrades went farther downriver toward Indian Head and Mattawoman Creek.

8. Hooker had approximately 10,000 soldiers at his disposal. Hebert, *Fighting Joe Hooker*, 51–62.

9. An 1863 U.S.C.S. map showed a road running south from Piscataway parallel to the Potomac shoreline, going beyond Indian Head and Mattawoman Creek to Port Republic. OH and his comrades traveled to a cabin on the Potomac, which was evidently situated on a ridge between the Potomac River and Mattawoman Creek. Mattawoman Creek is in Charles County and downriver from Occoquan Creek and Mason's Neck. The waterway was large enough to accommodate the schooner that OH and his friends commandeered. Dr. John W. Thomas had property next to "Market Overton," a house that is still standing today near Route 210 (Indian Head Highway) next to a Lutheran church. Hinrichs, "Maine to Dixie"; Coast Survey Map of the State of Virginia, W. L. Nicholson, Cutter Map, Boston Athenaeum; Frederick Gutheim, *The Potomac* (New York: Grosset & Dunlap, 1968), 67; private correspondence between the author and historians Elmer S. Biles, David W. Gaddy, and Laurie Verge.

10. Bowie knew a lot of Confederate sympathizers who lived in and around Port Tobacco. His alternative route was the one that Booth chose to use in crossing the Potomac after his assassination of Lincoln. William A. Tidwell, *April '65: Confederate Covert Action in the American Civil War* (Kent, Ohio: Kent State University Press, 1995), 74.

11. Hampton's legion had been transferred to Freestone Point (near the old village of Dumfries and in the vicinity of Bacon Race Church and Maple Valley) to establish the river batteries at Occoquan and Colchester. Edward G. Longacre, *Gentleman and Soldier: A Biography of Wade Hampton III* (Nashville: Rutledge Hill Press, 2003), xiii–xiv, 36–60.

12. Warner, *Generals in Gray*, 122–23.

13. B. T. Johnson, "Memoir of First Maryland Regiment," *Southern Historical Society Papers* 9, nos. 10–12 (October–December 1881): 487–88.

14. NAMP M642, Reel 249.

Chapter 3

1. Reverend Stanley and Thomas Bragg became friends when they attended an academy that was later renamed Norwich University. NAMP M258, Reel 106; Current, *Encyclopedia of the Confederacy*, 1:206–7, 4:1481; http://www.norwich.edu/about/history.html.

2. Serving as Richmond's provost marshal, Winder kept alert for Union spies who sought passports to travel within the CSA.

3. Instead of J. Adler Weston, the person OH met was probably J. Alden Weston. *OR,* Series IV, 2:735.

4. Catherine Erskine Ehringhaus, the widow of Blucher, lived in the house of OH's maternal step-grandfather along with eight of her twelve children. Among them was Matilda Gregory Ehringhaus, who may have been nicknamed "Till" and corresponded with OH during the war. Klasing, *The Ehringhauses*; 1860 Federal census of the John C. Ehringhaus household, Elizabeth City, N.C.

5. "Spies," *Richmond Examiner*, January 10, 1862; "The Case of Mr. Hinrich," *Richmond Examiner*, January 11, 1862.

6. A CSA naval officer said that the fort's four guns were poorly mounted and the ammunition magazine, looking like an "African ant hill," had a door that was exposed to an attack from the river. William Harwar Parker, *Recollections of a Naval Officer, 1841-1865* (Annapolis, Md.: Naval Institute Press, 1985), 253–54.

7. Born in Belgium, Charles F. Henningsen went to Nicaragua with William Walker, whose "filibusters," or mercenary adventurers, wanted to apply the concept of U.S. Manifest Destiny to control Latin America. Henningsen served as colonel of the 59th Virginia in Wise's Legion. Ella Lonn, *Foreigners in the Confederacy* (Chapel Hill: University of North Carolina Press, 2002), 188–90.

8. William F. Martin, an 1842 graduate of the University of North Carolina, had commanded the ground forces at Hatteras when it fell to a Union amphibious assault on August 29, 1861. Krick, *Lee's Colonels*, 265; John Elliott Wood, ed., *Year Book: Pasquotank Historical Society, Elizabeth City, North Carolina*, 1956–57 (Elizabeth City, N.C.: Pasquotank Historical Society, n.d.), 2:284; William F. Martin Papers, Number 493, SHC.

9. OH and the townspeople did not learn about the Roanoke Island defeat until February 9. Rush C. Hawkins, "Early Coast Operations in North Carolina," in *Battles and Leaders in the Civil War*, ed. R. U. Johnson and C. C. Buel (New York: Century Company, 1887), 1:640–45.

10. Foster, one of Burnsides's brigade commanders, served in the U.S.C.S. before the war. *OR,* 9:75–81.

11. Parker confirmed that the militia ran away. His naval crew joined OH in manning the fort's guns. John Ehringhaus helped to start the militia in 1842 (the Albemarle Blues, Ehringhaus Light Artillery, and Ehringhaus Light Infantry) but, at age of seventy, he could not help to protect the city. Parker, *Recollections of a Naval Officer*, 253–57; William A. Griffin, *Ante-Bellum Elizabeth City: The History of a Canal Town* (Elizabeth City, N.C.: Roanoke Press, Inc., 1970), 137–42.

12. Parker substantiated the accuracy of OH's journal entries. It is likely that OH accompanied Parker and his sailors to Norfolk. "The Burnside Expedition," *Harper's Weekly*, March 1, 1862, 135; Wood, *Year Book*, 1:23, 2:107; Parker, *Recollections of a Naval Officer*, 259–62.

13. The winter of 1861–62 was difficult for rebel soldiers. Women in Norfolk and Portsmouth organized sewing circles and "raised funds to provide them with shoes, overcoats

and blankets." John W. H. Porter, *A Record of Events in Norfolk County, Virginia, from April 19th, 1861, to May 10th, 1862* (Portsmouth, Va.: W. A. Fiske, 1892), 10, 25, 229–38.

14. NAMP M258, Reel 106.

15. Ibid.

16. John Christoph Ehringhaus became one of the most prominent citizens in Elizabeth City, with a street also being named after him. He died in August 1865 after the war ended. Klasing, *The Ehringhauses*; Wood, *Year Book*, 2:155–56; Lou N. Overman and Edna M. Shannonhouse, eds., *Year Book: Pasquotank Historical Society, Elizabeth City, North Carolina*, 3 vols. (Baltimore: Gateway Press, 1975), 3:208; J. Howard Stevens, *Albemarle: People and Places* (Elizabeth City, N.C.: M/M/T Printers, 1999), 137–38.

17. NAMP M331A, Reel 124. Regarding William N. H. Smith, see Current, *Encyclopedia of the Confederacy*, 4:1481.

18. General Blucher Ehringhaus died prematurely in 1853. One of his grandsons—John Christoph Blucher Ehringhaus—was the governor of North Carolina from 1933 to 1937. Stevens, *Albemarle*, 137–38; Klasing, *The Ehringhauses*.

19. "Spies," *Richmond Examiner*, January 10, 1862.

20. "The Case of Mr. Hinrich," *Richmond Examiner*, January 11, 1862.

21. OH arrived just in time to receive Bragg's support: the North Carolina politician resigned his position in March and returned to Petersburg. NAMP M331A, Reel 124; Current, *Encyclopedia of the Confederacy*, 1:206–7.

22. Besides being an attorney, Colonel Martin also co-owned a 760-acre plantation, mill, and about twenty-five slaves. William F. Martin and G. W. Brooks deed to Griffin plantation, May 30, 1857, Richard Brady Williams Private Collection; G. W. Brooks letter to Col. Stone, August 10, 1865, Richard Brady Williams Private Collection.

23. Dr. Rufus K. Speed, former mayor of Elizabeth City, verified what OH had communicated to Confederate authorities. NAMP M331A, Reel 124.

24. Hinrichs's half brother (probably Carl Jr.) visited Colonel Martin, who was imprisoned in Fort Columbus on Governor's Island and paroled in February 1862. He may have been a student at a boys' music school located there. Lawrence Sangston, *The Bastiles of the North by a Member of the Maryland Legislature* (Baltimore: Kelly, Hedian & Piet, 1863), 20, 64–65, 94, 131; J. H. French, *Gazetteer of the State of New York* (Syracuse: R. Pearsall Smith, 1860; reprinted two volumes in one, Baltimore: Genealogical Publishing Co., Inc., 1998), 419.

25. NAMP M331A, Reel 124.

26. Dr. Speed stated that he had "no hesitation in saying, from the evidence before me that he [OH] is fully in simpathy [*sic*] with the Confederacy in their struggle for independence and that his requirements may be made useful to the government." Ibid.

27. Carl and Amalia Hinrichs played an active role in getting OH into the U.S. Coast Survey; it is unclear what the elder Ehringhaus did other than to solicit assistance from his influential friends.

28. NAMP M642, Reel 249.

29. OH evidently wrote this letter to Bache while he was in Elizabeth City.

30. NAMP M642, Reel 249.

Chapter 4

1. A captain of engineers with three or four lieutenants—one of whom was OH—joined Joseph E. Johnston at the beginning of March 1862. As commander of the Department of Northern Virginia, Johnston instructed them to develop a retreat route to the Rappahan-

nock River. *OR*, 5:1079, 1081–82; Joseph E. Johnston, *Narrative of Military Operations, Directed during the Late War Between the States* (New York: D. Appleton & Co., 1874), 97–101.

2. Trimble was a brigade commander in Dick Ewell's division.

3. In his memoir, Johnston wrote that the engineers reported back regarding their reconnaissance to Rappahannock Station on March 6, which is also the date that OH noted in his journal. Pfanz, *Ewell*, 150–51; Johnston, *Narrative of Military Operations*, 101.

4. Johnston had to abandon supplies, including massive stores in the meat-packing facility at Thoroughfare Gap. *OR*, 5:1081, 1097–98.

5. Rogers was a civil engineer in Minnesota before the war. On March 1, 1862, he became an engineer officer under Johnston. Krick, *Staff Officers*, 257; Warner, *Generals in Gray*, 120.

6. Henry T. Douglas of Virginia was appointed lieutenant and engineer officer in February along with OH. This was likely the "Douglass" mentioned by OH and not Henry Kyd Douglas (with whom OH later became friends), who was with Stonewall Jackson at the time. "Randolph" was probably Peyton Randolph. Krick, *Staff Officers*, 115, 249.

7. Wilson Presstman, a former railroad engineer, helped to build a railroad spur from Manassas to Centreville and later served in the West. George G. Kundahl, *Alexandria Goes to War: Beyond Robert E. Lee* (Knoxville: University of Tennessee Press, 2004), 197–206.

8. The wharf along the James River connected with the main road to Yorktown and is located today within Kingsmill Resort outside Williamsburg, Virginia. Warner, *Generals in Gray*, 292. See Williamsburg and Yorktown maps in J. G. Barnard, *Report of the Engineer and Artillery Operations of the Army of the Potomac, from Its Organization to the Close of the Peninsular Campaign* (New York: D. Van Nostrand, 1863).

9. En route to the Peninsula, Pickett stopped in Richmond on April 13, 1862, for a parade. Edward G. Longacre, *Pickett, Leader of the Charge: A Biography of General George E. Pickett, C.S.A.* (Shippensburg, Pa.: White Mane Publishing Co., 1995), 64–65.

10. Prior to hearing from OH and Rogers—on April 20—Johnston sent a letter to Lee about "defects" in the defense system for Williamsburg and Yorktown. *OR*, 11(3):452; Steven H. Newton, *Joseph E. Johnston and the Defense of Richmond* (Lawrence: University Press of Kansas, 1998), 95, 103.

11. The government passed the December 1861 Bounty and Furlough Act and the April 1862 Conscription Act, which created a lot of confusion in the ranks. Kevin Conley Ruffner, "Before the Seven Days: The Reorganization of the Confederate Army in the Spring of 1862," in *The Peninsula Campaign of 1862: Yorktown to the Seven Days*, ed. William J. Miller (Campbell, Calif.: Savas Woodbury, 1995), 1:47–69.

12. Krick, *Staff Officers*, 151.

13. Jeremy Gilmer, who became head of the Engineer Bureau, concurred with OH's concerns about Harvey Hill and his lack of respect for engineers. Warner, *Generals in Gray*, 136–37; Jeremy Francis Gilmer Letter, August 17, 1862, to his wife, in Gilmer Papers, Collection No. 276, SHC.

14. On the same day—April 24, 1862—that OH was almost killed by a defective cannon, Harvey Hill wrote to Secretary of War George W. Randolph complaining about the inferior quality of his guns and how "[a]nother 24-pounder rifle burst to-day and one of Pierson's 6.4-inch guns." *OR*, 11(3):461.

15. A. P. Hill worked for the U.S.C.S. during the same time as OH. He resigned in February 1861 to join the CSA. Stephen W. Sears, *To the Gates of Richmond: The Peninsula Campaign* (New York: Ticknor & Fields, 1992), 68–82; James I. Robertson Jr. *General A. P. Hill: The Story of a Confederate Warrior* (New York: Vintage Books, 1987), 26–34.

Chapter 5

1. *OR*, 11(1):636. For details on the Battle of Drewry's Bluff, see Edwin C. Bearss, *River of Lost Opportunities: The Civil War on the James River, 1861–1862* (Lynchburg, Va.: H. E. Howard, 1995).

2. Bier resigned from the U.S. Navy on November 13, 1861, to take a lieutenant's position in the CSA Navy, later becoming Jackson's ordnance officer. Krick, *Staff Officers*, 74; Robert G. Tanner, *Stonewall in the Valley: Thomas J. "Stonewall" Jackson's Shenandoah Valley Campaign, Spring 1862* (Mechanicsburg, Pa.: Stackpole Books, 1996), 242–65.

3. During the May 23–25 action, Jackson's army captured approximately 3,000 prisoners, two rifled cannons, 9,354 small arms, and a large quantity of munitions and food stores. Robertson, *Stonewall Jackson*, 393–411.

4. Evidence of Jackson's Christian faith during the war, often manifested in the heat of battle, has been well documented. William J. Jones, *Christ in the Camp: Religion in the Confederate Army* (Richmond: B. F. Johnson & Co., 1887), 82–101.

5. Jackson's men drove 1,500 Federals out of Charlestown on May 28. Pfanz, *Ewell*, 198.

6. Tanner, *Stonewall in the Valley*, 325–43.

7. On May 30, Union troops under Generals John Geary and Abram Duryée "pushed forward" to Berryville. It is unclear how many Union soldiers remained in the Berryville area on June 1–2. In the Valley Army's rush to escape the tightening Yankee noose, OH may have confused the dates and was really in Berryville on May 31. *OR*, 12(3):293; Hotchkiss, *Make Me a Map*, 50; Tanner, *Stonewall in the Valley*, 476–83.

8. Jackson's entire army had left Strasburg by the morning of June 2. Perhaps OH rode from Berryville to Winchester on the night of May 31 and reached Strasburg on June 1.

9. OH's New Market date regarding June 4 is correct.

10. On June 2, Ashby was mortally wounded fighting another rear-guard action about two miles from Harrisonburg. Millard K. Bushong, *General Turner Ashby and Stonewall's Valley Campaign* (Verona, Va.: McClure Printing Co., 1980), 167–84.

11. Early on the morning of June 8, 1862, Jackson escaped from Port Republic during a surprise artillery attack by crossing the North River. Robert K. Krick, *Conquering the Valley: Stonewall Jackson at Port Republic* (New York: William Morrow & Co., 1996), 39–111.

12. OH reconnoitered for Ewell and mistakenly reported that "the enemy was moving a large column 2 miles" to the left. This slowed down pursuit. Jackson rode to the Cross Keys battlefield—according to the Reverend Robert Dabney—"a little after mid-day." One of Ewell's biographers also stated that Jackson offered advice to his commander on the battlefield. Ibid., 137–265; *OR*, 12(1):714, 781–82, 795–99; R. L. Dabney, *Life and Campaigns of Lieut.-Gen. Thomas J. Jackson* (New York: Blelock & Co., 1866), 418–19; Pfanz, *Ewell*, 211.

13. On June 9, Trimble's rear guard arrived in Port Republic at approximately 10:00 A.M. and set fire to the covered bridge over the North River, thus preventing Fremont from assisting Shields. Krick, *Conquering the Valley*, 446–51.

14. Jackson's troops had difficulty crossing a makeshift bridge over the South River and got a slower-than-expected start. Ibid., 291–343.

15. Union troops evidently captured OH in the woods near Ewell's initial position and held him prisoner in a house near the edge of the battlefield (perhaps the Lewiston estate). According to Shields's report, he was "10 miles beyond Conrad's Store," which means OH met another Union general, such as Brigadier General Erastus B. Tyler. *OR*, 12(1):687; Pfanz, *Ewell*, 216–18.

16. Jackson deployed his Louisiana troops to get rid of Federal artillery on the Coaling

"elevated knob." Krick, *Conquering the Valley*, 345–53, 403–31; Richard Taylor, *Destruction and Reconstruction: Personal Experiences of the Late War* (New York: D. Appleton and Co., 1879), 70–73.

17. Captain Joseph C. Clark commanded Battery E, 4th U. S. Artillery, and oversaw six guns from three batteries on the Coaling. *OR*, 12(1):693.

18. Hotchkiss, *Make Me a Map*, 55–57.

19. Bier would return to the navy in January 1863. Krick, *Staff Officers*, 74.

Chapter 6

1. Jackson's 18,500 soldiers stopped five miles short of Ashland on the night of June 25 and did not approach Mechanicsville until after 3:00 P.M. the next day. A. P. Hill had already initiated the battle on his own. Freeman, *Lee's Lieutenants*, 1:492–513; Robert K. Krick, "Sleepless in the Saddle: Stonewall Jackson in the Seven Days," in *The Richmond Campaign of 1862: The Peninsula and the Seven Days*, ed. Gary W. Gallagher (Chapel Hill: University of North Carolina Press, 2000), 66–77.

2. By the morning of June 30, McClellan's troops were in a full-scale retreat as they headed toward the James River to set up a new base of operations.

3. Many firsthand accounts described the Union stragglers and abandoned matériel captured by Jackson's army. Approximately 55,000 Federals guarded the Malvern Hill route. Brian K. Burton, *Extraordinary Circumstances: The Seven Days Battles* (Bloomington: Indiana University Press, 2001), 235–39.

4. Jackson's troops showed up late due to confusion about the location of "Cold Harbor" but turned the tide upon reaching the Gaines's Mill battlefield. Stephen W. Sears, *To the Gates of Richmond: The Peninsula Campaign* (New York: Ticknor & Fields, 1992), 210–48; John P. Dyer, *The Gallant Hood* (Indianapolis: Bobbs-Merrill Co., 1950), 85–95.

5. OH did not encounter McClellan, who was on his way from Glendale to Malvern Hill on June 30.

6. At nine thirty in the morning on June 30, Colonel Stapleton Crutchfield, in charge of Jackson's artillery, arrived at White Oak Swamp. OH was probably with him. Crutchfield chose a ridge to his right and had his men cut a swath through the dense woods to set up twenty-eight guns. He started his cannonade between 1:45 P.M. and 2 P.M. Robertson, *Stonewall Jackson*, 491–98.

7. Coup d'oeil, or "Napoleon's glance," was a concept elucidated by military historians such as Carl von Clausewitz and Antoine-Henri Jomini regarding a leader's ability to "read" situations. It has also been described as "an inner eye that permitted a general to look at a map, grasp the situation, and intuitively know how to plan, and secure victory, often employing bold and creative methods to achieve it." Jomini called "strategic coup d'oeil . . . the most valuable characteristic of a good general." In his quest to keep learning, OH studied Jomini's work during winter camp. Carol Reardon, *With a Sword in One Hand and Jomini in the Other: The Problem of Military Thought in the Civil War North* (Chapel Hill: University of North Carolina Press, 2012), 56, 78–79; Baron De Jomini, *Summary of the Art of War* (Philadelphia: Lippincott, 1879), 337; Freeman, *Lee's Lieutenants*, 1:565–69, 1:581–87.

8. Huger released the brigades of Lewis A. Armistead and Ambrose R. Wright at 3:00 A.M. on the morning of July 1. He stayed back at camp to have breakfast and did not mobilize his troops until around 9:00 A.M. Burton, *Extraordinary Circumstances*, 312–14.

9. Freeman, *Lee's Lieutenants*, 1:591–602; Burton, *Extraordinary Circumstances*, 361–64.

10. Union artillerists, with their heavier guns, had one of the most formidable positions of the war to withstand an assault. Keith S. Bohannon, "One Solid Unbroken Roar of Thunder:

Union and Confederate Artillery at the Battle of Malvern Hill," in *The Richmond Campaign of 1862: The Peninsula and the Seven Days*, ed. Gary W. Gallagher (Chapel Hill: University of North Carolina Press, 2000), 234–40.

11. As Ewell crossed Western Run and emerged from the woods along Carter's Mill Road, he became separated from Early's advance but rode forward to lead a final, desperate attack. Pfanz, *Ewell*, 232–34.

12. Major C. Roberdeau Wheat was KIA at Gaines's Mill; Scott was KIA at Glendale; and Meares was KIA at Malvern Hill. Patricia L. Faust, ed., *Historical Times Illustrated Encyclopedia of the Civil War* (New York: HarperPerennial, 1991), 818; Krick, *Lee's Colonels*, 270, 336.

Chapter 7

1. Lee sent Jackson to protect the vital Virginia Central and O&A RR crossings. Ewell left for Gordonsville on July 14. OH had to meet the challenges of a broad range of ordnance needs and, in September, would become Jackson's acting chief of ordnance. Pfanz, *Ewell*, 237–38; NAMP M258, Reel 106, and M331A, Reel 124.

2. Lee was outraged over Pope's announcements that his army would subsist off Southern farms and punish noncombatants in response for any Federal soldiers killed by guerrillas. Jones, *Rebel War Clerk's Diary*, 1:143.

3. Reinforced by A. P. Hill's division, Jackson moved his army on July 29 from Gordonsville to Green Springs valley. He hoped to reprise his 1862 Shenandoah valley strategy. Robert K. Krick, *Stonewall Jackson at Cedar Mountain* (Chapel Hill: University of North Carolina Press, 1990), 7–13.

4. Jackson ordered some of his infantry, including Colonel Douglass's Georgians, to guard the "endless lines of wagons" in his supply train. Hotchkiss noted that the enemy attacked the CSA wagon train at two points on the night of August 8 "but were met and promptly repulsed with loss at each place." Ibid., 5–9, 31, 36, 46; Krick, *Lee's Colonels*, 122; Hotchkiss, *Make Me a Map*, 67.

5. Jackson's soldiers captured Prince, a brigadier general in C. C. Augur's division, and sent him to Richmond. Taliaferro took over Winder's Stonewall Brigade. Krick, *Cedar Mountain*, 287, 357; Warner, *Generals in Blue*, 386–87; Warner, *Generals in Gray*, 340.

6. Freeman, *Lee's Lieutenants*, 2:30–47; Krick, *Cedar Mountain*, 358–59, 372, 376.

7. Jackson sent a reconnaissance in force north of Rappahannock Station, but his troops got stranded when the river rose during a torrential downpour. Engineers built a makeshift bridge, which enabled Jubal A. Early and Alexander R. Lawton to extricate their brigades. John J. Hennessy, *Return to Bull Run: The Campaign and Battle of Second Manassas* (New York: Simon & Schuster, 1993), 32–35, 71–74, 84–89.

8. Jackson also expressed concern about "the quarter-masters and the commissaries because the army was not well fed and the provisions were not brought up in time." Krick, *Lee's Colonels*, 99–100; Hotchkiss, *Make Me a Map*, 71.

9. J. E. B. Stuart complained about the lack of respect among Jackson's officers and blamed Trimble. *OR*, 12(2):650, 742–43.

10. Jackson replaced his wounded senior commanders, Ewell and Taliaferro, with Lawton and William E. Starke, respectively. *OR*, 12(2):641–45.

11. Stuart reported the prompt deployment of horse artillery by John Pelham, who helped to repulse a Federal attack on August 29. This engagement occurred at about ten in the morning. OH participated in either that same attack or in a similar one at Sudley Springs later in the day. *OR*, 12(2):646, 733–40.

12. Hennessy, *Return to Bull Run*, 339–61.

13. See David A. Welker, *Tempest at Ox Hill: The Battle of Chantilly* (Cambridge, Mass.: Da Capo Press, 2002); and Paul Taylor, *He Hath Loosed the Fateful Lightning* (Shippensburg, Pa.: White Mane Books, 2003).

14. Hotchkiss concurred with OH's account of the September 5 crossing at White's Ford. Joseph L. Harsh, *Taken at the Flood: Robert E. Lee and Confederate Strategy in the Maryland Campaign of 1862* (Kent, Ohio: Kent State University Press, 1999), 85; Hotchkiss, *Make Me a Map*, 78–80.

15. The rebels captured about 12,000 Union prisoners and a large amount of stores during Jackson's September 13–15 assault on Harpers Ferry. Chester G. Hearn, *Six Years of Hell: Harpers Ferry during the Civil War* (Baton Rouge: Louisiana State University Press, 1996), 110–12, 126–29, 186–89.

16. Members of the 27th Indiana found Harvey Hill's copy of Special Orders No. 191 wrapped around three cigars on September 13 near what would become the Monocacy battlefield. Wilbur D. Jones Jr., "Who Lost the Lost Orders? Stonewall Jackson, His Courier, and Special Orders No. 191," *Civil War Regiments* 5, no. 3 (1997): 1–26; William Allan, *Stonewall Jackson, Robert E. Lee, and the Army of Northern Virginia, 1862* (New York: Da Capo Press, 1995), 343–45.

17. More than 1,500 Union cavalrymen escaped from Harpers Ferry and rode toward Hagerstown. At dawn on September 15, they came across Longstreet's ammunition train north of Williamsport and captured eighty-five wagons. Samuel M. Blackwell Jr., *In the First Line of Battle: The 12th Illinois Cavalry in the Civil War* (DeKalb: Northern Illinois University Press, 2002), 30–35; Isaac W. Heysinger, *Antietam and the Maryland and Virginia Campaigns of 1862* (New York: Neale Publishing Co., 1912), 160–67.

18. See John Michael Priest, *Before Antietam: The Battle for South Mountain* (New York: Oxford University Press, 1992); and Brian Matthew Jordan, *Unholy Sabbath: The Battle of South Mountain in History and Memory, September 14, 1862* (New York: Savas Beatie, 2012).

19. James M. McPherson, *Crossroads of Freedom: Antietam* (New York: Oxford University Press, 2002), 116–27.

20. Straggling was a significant problem for the Confederates. One soldier wrote on September 14 that there were as many as 3,000 to 4,000 stragglers at Winchester alone. Stephen W. Sears, *Landscape Turned Red: The Battle of Antietam* (New York: Ticknor & Fields, 1983), 285–92; Joseph L. Harsh, *Sounding the Shallows: A Confederate Companion for the Maryland Campaign of 1862* (Kent, Ohio: Kent State University Press, 2000), 220–21.

21. Probably only about 30,000 Confederates remained if fighting resumed on September 18. Harsh, *Sounding the Shallows*, 201; McPherson, *Crossroads of Freedom*, 129.

22. During the night of September 18, Lee began to withdraw his army across the Potomac at Boteler's Ford near Shepherdstown. The Federals established a beachhead the next evening, but A. P. Hill's troops drove them back. Many Confederates hoped the victory at Shepherdstown would overshadow the disappointment of Antietam. Gary W. Gallagher, "'The Net Result of the Campaign Was in Our Favor': Confederate Reaction to the Maryland Campaign," in *The Antietam Campaign*, ed. Gary W. Gallagher (Chapel Hill: University of North Carolina Press, 1999), 3–7, 14. See also Thomas A. McGrath, *Shepherdstown: Last Clash of the Antietam Campaign, September 19–20, 1862* (Lynchburg, Va.: Shroeder Publications, 2007).

23. See Francis Augustin O'Reilly, *The Fredericksburg Campaign: Winter War on the Rappahannock* (Baton Rouge: Louisiana State University Press, 2003); and George C. Rable, *Fredericksburg! Fredericksburg!* (Chapel Hill: University of North Carolina Press, 2002).

Chapter 8

1. Jackson established his winter quarters at Moss Neck—located south of Fredericksburg along the Rappahannock River—and situated his headquarters in front of the Corbin family mansion. Trimble's division settled behind the house on the sprawling 1,600-acre estate. Some of Jackson's officers wrote that ANVA morale reached its peak during this interval. Robertson, *Stonewall Jackson*, 667–76; Jedediah Hotchkiss and William Allan, *Chancellorsville: Embracing the Operations of the Army of Northern Virginia, from the First Battle of Fredericksburg to the Death of Lieutenant-General Jackson* (New York: D. Van Nostrand, 1867), 13–15.

2. Taliaferro pursued a transfer to South Carolina to serve under Beauregard. OH became the chief engineer for Trimble's division. Hotchkiss, *Make Me a Map*, 110; NAMP M331A, Reel 124.

3. OH continued as chief engineer for Colston's division. On March 15, Hotchkiss made the first of sixteen journal entries about OH, writing that the engineer spent most of the day with him. Warner, *Generals in Gray*, 58–59; Hotchkiss, *Make Me a Map*, 120.

4. The initial phase of the battle—Day One—took place at Lick Run, west of Zoan Church. Hooker pulled his force back to Chancellorsville. Early on the morning of May 2, Lee and Jackson met at the crossroads of Catharine Furnace Road and the Plank Road to plan a bold strategy. Ernest B. Furgurson, *Chancellorsville 1863: The Souls of the Brave* (New York: Alfred A. Knopf, 1992), 87–130; Stephen W. Sears, *Chancellorsville* (Boston: Houghton Mifflin Co., 1996), 49–50, 234–35.

5. When Colonel T. H. Warren was wounded during Jackson's flank attack, Colston sent OH to "carry the order to take command of the brigade to the first-ranking field officer." Seeing that Warren's replacement was exhausted from the day's marching, OH gave him his horse and joined the pursuit on foot. By nine o'clock it was dark, and Colston's troops were scattered throughout the woods. OH helped to reassemble the division and later filed a detailed battle report regarding the long day of fighting. Sears, *Chancellorsville*, 264–81, 328–29; *OR*, 25(1):1003–4, 1009–10.

6. As night fell, OH rode forward "looking after some of my pioneers" and wrote in his report that the action had dwindled to desultory firing in the woods that separated the two armies. On the right, he heard "a heavy volley of musketry," which proved to be friendly fire from the North Carolina brigade of Brigadier General James H. Lane. *OR*, 25(1):1009–10; Robert K. Krick, *The Smoothbore Volley That Doomed the Confederacy: The Death of Stonewall Jackson and Other Chapters on the Army of Northern Virginia* (Baton Rouge: Louisiana State University Press, 2002), 1–41.

7. Colston had a difficult time maintaining cohesiveness among his four brigades on May 2. His problems intensified the next day as he experienced more casualties among his commanders. He commended OH, who acted as his aide-de-camp and "discharged the arduous duties of his position both during and after the battle with a zeal and ability worthy of all praise." Sears, *Chancellorsville*, 312–46; *OR*, 25(1):1005–12.

8. See Clemmer, *Old Alleghany*.

9. Ewell took over the Second Corps, with Johnson, Early, and Rodes as his division commanders. The Second Corps marched to Spotsylvania Court House and via the Orange Plank Road to Culpeper. Pfanz, *Ewell*, 273–80.

10. The Battle of Brandy Station was fought on June 9, 1863, with about 10,000 horse soldiers lined up on each side. Warner, *Generals in Blue*, 326. See Richard E. Crouch's *Brandy Station: A Battle Like None Other* (Westminster, Md.: Willow Bend Books, 2002).

11. Wilbur Sturtevant Nye, *Here Come the Rebels!* (Dayton, Ohio: Morningside, 1988), 66–74.

12. Robert E. Rodes led his division to eliminate Federal threats from Berryville and Martinsburg while keeping the Potomac fords open for the advance into Pennsylvania. Ibid., 73–75, 85–89, 124–36.

13. On June 14, Early's troops attacked Winchester's West Fort between 5:00 and 6:00 P.M. Ewell ordered Johnson to take three of his brigades to Stephenson Depot—on the Winchester & Potomac RR—to block a Union escape. Charles S. Grunder and Brandon H. Beck, *The Second Battle of Winchester, June 12–15, 1863* (Lynchburg, Va.: H. E. Howard, 1989), 28–43; *OR*, 27(2):515–17.

14. At 4:00 A.M. on June 15, Milroy's troops fled from Winchester. Walker's Stonewall Brigade joined with Johnson's reserves to stop them. Freeman, *Lee's Lieutenants*, 3:24–27.

15. Krick, *Lee's Colonels*, 191.

16. On June 21, Ewell received orders from Lee to attack Harrisburg. Reaching Carlisle on June 27, he established his headquarters at the Carlisle Barracks, where he had been stationed as a dragoon before the war. Thomas G. Tousey, *Military History of Carlisle and Carlisle Barracks* (Richmond: The Dietz Press, 1939), 160–61, 224–43.

Chapter 9

1. While Early and Rodes led their troops to Gettysburg, Johnson's men escorted the reserve artillery and wagon train back to Chambersburg. The return trip was slowed down by having to transport the results of aggressive foraging. Clemmer, *Old Alleghany*, 458–59.

2. Mosby penned one of the first books to address the controversy surrounding Stuart's circuitous ride: John S. Mosby, *Stuart's Cavalry in the Gettysburg Campaign* (New York: Moffat, Yard & Co., 1908).

3. Henry Kyd Douglas rode to see Ewell, conveying Johnson's message that his men would arrive shortly. Ewell hesitated. Walter H. Taylor wrote after the war that he transmitted a *direct* order from Lee for Ewell to seize Cemetery Hill. Douglas, *I Rode with Stonewall*, 247; Walter H. Taylor, *Four Years with General Lee* (New York: D. Appleton and Co., 1878), 94–96; Scott Bowden and Bill Warden, *Last Chance for Victory: Robert E. Lee and the Gettysburg Campaign* (Cambridge, Mass.: Da Capo Press, 2003), 199–209.

4. Johnson reached the battlefield in late afternoon when Culp's Hill was empty. Near the end of the day, Ewell belatedly sent Johnson to occupy it. The twilight probe was repulsed by the 7th Indiana. Harry W. Pfanz, *Gettysburg—Culp's Hill and Cemetery Hill* (Chapel Hill: University of North Carolina Press, 1993), 59–87; John D. Cox, *Culp's Hill: The Attack and Defense of the Union Flank, July 2, 1863* (Cambridge, Mass.: Da Capo Press, 2003), 26–43.

5. On July 2, the Second Corps started its diversionary assault at about 4:00 P.M. with a cannonade from Benner Hill. An hour later, Ewell sent in Johnson's troops. The delay enabled Union infantrymen, under Brigadier General George S. Greene, to throw up more breastworks on Culp's Hill. Meanwhile, Early sent 2,500 troops from Harry T. Hays's and Isaac E. Avery's brigades to attack East Cemetery Hill. They reached the military crest but had to retreat. Cox, *Culp's Hill*, 57–113; Pfanz, *Culp's Hill and Cemetery Hill*, 235–83.

6. Occupying either East Cemetery Hill or Culp's Hill would have jeopardized the Union's main supply line and retreat route. Porter Alexander also believed the Second Corps artillerists could have enfiladed the Union position from Culp's Hill and dispersed Meade's troops. A number of CSA leaders raised concerns about Ewell's decisions after the war. Gary W. Gallagher, "Confederate Corps Leadership on the First Day at Gettysburg: A. P. Hill and Richard S. Ewell in a Difficult Debut," in *Three Days at Gettysburg: Essays on Confeder-*

ate and Union Leadership, ed. Gary W. Gallagher (Kent, Ohio: Kent State University Press, 1999), 25–43; E. P. Alexander, *Military Memoirs of a Confederate: A Critical Narrative* (New York: Charles Scribner's Sons, 1907), 417; Edwin B. Coddington, *The Gettysburg Campaign: A Study in Command* (New York: Charles Scribner's Sons, 1968), 315–21.

7. OH's observations were fresh—he transcribed that part of his diary only five or six months later, during the 1863–64 winter quarters—and likely reflected the post-Gettysburg sentiments of his fellow officers.

8. Alexander wrote that he was unable to sustain his bombardment due to fears about ordnance shortages. The ordnance train extended all the way back to Winchester, which exacerbated the problem. Alexander, *Military Memoirs*, 431–35; Edward Porter Alexander, in *Fighting for the Confederacy: The Personal Recollections of General Edward Porter Alexander*, ed. Gary W. Gallagher (Chapel Hill: University of North Carolina Press, 1989), 245–61; *OR*, 27(2):352.

9. During the CSA retreat, the rear of Ewell's wagons passed through Monterey Pass at about 9:00 P.M. on July 4. Captain George M. Emack's Company B of the 1st Maryland Cavalry Battalion, aided by reinforcements, protected the train against 4,500 Union cavalrymen, including George Armstrong Custer. Charles Stanley, one of Emack's ninety horse soldiers, was WIA, captured, and sent to prison. Kent Masterson Brown, *Retreat from Gettysburg: Lee, Logistics, and the Pennsylvania Campaign* (Chapel Hill: University of North Carolina Press, 2005), 121–44; Driver, *First & Second Maryland Cavalry*, 56–59, 288; Eric J. Wittenberg et al., *One Continuous Fight: The Retreat from Gettysburg and the Pursuit of Lee's Army of Northern Virginia, July 4–14, 1863* (New York: Savas Beatie, 2008), 49–74.

10. Confederate engineers built a new pontoon bridge at Falling Waters using wood from torn-down buildings. Meade showed up with his army on July 12, but by the time he decided to assault on July 14, Lee's army was gone. Ewell's troops forded the Potomac north of Williamsport. Coddington, *Gettysburg Campaign*, 565–70; Brown, *Retreat from Gettysburg*, 287–330.

11. Meade's cavalry made a last-ditch charge on Henry Heth's men, who guarded the pontoon bridge. Pettigrew drew his pistol and approached a Yankee who fired from behind a barn and mortally wounded him. Earl J. Hess, *Lee's Tar Heels: The Pettigrew-Kirkland-MacRae Brigade* (Chapel Hill: University of North Carolina Press, 2002), 159–68.

12. Concerned about Meade's pursuit, Ewell decided to take his men up the Luray valley and cross the Blue Ridge farther to the south. *OR*, 27(2):449–50.

13. Kinney joined the Engineer Corps at the same time OH did, and they served together under Johnson. He "caught 'typhoid pneumonia' in recrossing the Potomac after Gettysburg" and died on July 28, 1863, at Staunton, Virginia. Krick, *Staff Officers*, 194.

Chapter 10

1. Included in an 1879 topographical atlas is a map that OH developed of the Rappahannock River at Germanna Ford based on his surveys. Oscar Hinrichs's *Atlas of Topography*, Henson Family Properties; Krick, *Lee's Colonels*, 152.

2. The Second Corps marched toward Madison Court House west of Culpeper Court House. Freeman, *Lee's Lieutenants*, 3:239.

3. On October 11, Fitzhugh Lee and two of his brigades attacked Buford's horse soldiers. Meade's cavalrymen withdrew across the Rappahannock. James L. Nichols, *General Fitzhugh Lee: A Biography* (Lynchburg, Va.: H. E. Howard, 1989), 59–60.

4. In pursuit of Meade's army, A. P. Hill led his men north toward Bristoe Station. Ewell's Corps encountered the Federal rear guard en route to Catlett Station on October

14. William D. Henderson, *The Road to Bristoe Station: Campaigning with Lee and Meade, August 1–October 20, 1863* (Lynchburg, Va.: H. E. Howard, 1987), 150–62.

5. A. P. Hill did not detect 3,000 troops in Gouverneur K. Warren's Second Corps coming up the O&A RR on his right flank. He sent forward the brigades of John R. Cooke and William W. Kirkland, which were decimated. Ibid., 163–93.

6. Meade marched his army south to engage Lee and, by November 1, his engineers had rebuilt the O&A to Warrenton Junction. Martin F. Graham and George F. Skoch, *Mine Run: A Campaign of Lost Opportunities, October 21, 1863–May 1, 1864* (Lynchburg, Va.: H. E. Howard, 1987), 2–5.

7. OH surveyed the Rapidan line as a fallback position for Lee's army. Von Steinecker had deserted from the Union army (serving under Brigadier General Louis Blenker) and sometimes also worked as a draftsman for Hotchkiss. He had entered the Confederacy via Maryland, joining the 2nd Virginia Infantry on May 15, 1863. He flip-flopped again, going back to the Federals. After the war, Von Steinecker tried to implicate OH, Henry Kyd Douglas, and Allegheny Johnson in the assassination of Lincoln. Clemmer, *Old Alleghany*, 639.

8. While Meade's left wing struck at Kelly's Ford on November 7, 30,000 soldiers under Sedgwick swept down at dusk on 2,000 unsuspecting Confederates at Rappahannock Station. (OH was not involved in establishing these inferior fortifications.) Daniel W. Barefoot, *General Robert F. Hoke: Lee's Modest Warrior* (Winston-Salem, N.C.: John F. Blair, Publisher, 1996), 96–104.

9. Lee moved his army south of the Rapidan to the thirty-mile line previously surveyed by OH. The Second Corps occupied the Confederate right flank. Lee's lookouts on Clark's Mountain announced that the AoP was on the move. Foote, *Civil War*, 2:873.

10. On November 26, French led his Third Corps across Jacob's Ford, slightly downriver from where Mine Run flowed into the Rapidan. He ordered his men to bivouac after only going a couple of miles. During the next day, he issued confusing, and sometimes contradictory, orders. Some of his officers accused him of being drunk. Ibid., 2:874; Graham and Skoch, *Mine Run*, 44–54.

11. Johnson's troops marched along Raccoon Ford Road, which cut perpendicularly across Mine Run. After passing Bartlett's Mill in midmorning, they moved south through the Wilderness. John M. Jones was in the lead, followed by Stafford and Walker. Steuart brought up the rear. Ibid., 47–53.

12. As French vacillated, Johnson turned his two-mile-long column around and confronted Prince's division. He rode to the rear of his train, which had been struck near the intersection of Raccoon Ford Road and Jacob's Ford Road, and conferred with Steuart. He established his line along a road that bordered the Payne farmsteads (there were two adjacent Payne farms). *OR*, 29(1):846–47.

13. Johnson and his 5,300 rebels confronted French's 17,000 soldiers—with another 15,000 men from Sedgwick's Sixth Corps on the way. At about four o'clock, Johnson ordered Steuart to wheel right and for all the brigades to attack. His soldiers drove the Federals through the trees to a clearing, but a lack of ammunition prevented further advancement. In his report, Johnson commended OH for gallantry and wrote that he "was wounded under heavy fire." Graham and Skoch, *Mine Run*, 53–57; *OR*, 29(1):847–48.

14. Lee united his troops on a prominent ridge west of Mine Run, and they converted "an obscure land formation into one of the strongest defensive positions of the war." Warren and Meade decided the fortifications were too difficult to breach without an extended siege. Earl J. Hess, *Field Armies and Fortifications in the Civil War: The Eastern Campaigns, 1861–1865* (Chapel Hill: University of North Carolina Press, 2005), 293–99; Graham and Skoch, *Mine Run*, 69–83.

15. At the direction of A. P. Hill, John R. Cooke advanced his North Carolinians, who were enfiladed by Warren's artillery and small-arms fire. Cooke was again wounded in the action. James I. Robertson Jr., *General A. P. Hill: The Story of a Confederate Warrior* (New York: Vintage Books, 1992), 234–39; Warner, *Generals in Gray*, 61.

16. Soon after the Battle of Chancellorsville, Hotchkiss began to write in his journal about spending more time with OH and working on maps together. Hotchkiss, *Make Me a Map*, 142–47, 153–54, 167, 171–74.

17. Hessey was a lieutenant in Company A of the new First Regiment Engineer Troops. Jackson, *First Regiment Engineer Troops*, 8, 14, 174.

18. The "Bradford" mentioned by OH was likely Captain John Bradford from the First Regiment Engineer Troops. "Till" might have been OH's stepcousin, Matilda Gregory Ehringhaus, who was about his age (she was born in 1838). "Chris" was OH's half brother, John Christoph Ehringhaus Hinrichs, who was twenty years old and served as a noncommissioned orderly sergeant on the staff of a CSA officer. Ibid., 169; War Department Collection of Confederate Records, Un-filed Slips and Papers Belonging to Confederate Service Records — March 1, 1863 & March 3, 1863 documents — Record Group 109, NARA I.

19. William N. H. Smith of Murfreesboro, North Carolina, was a CSA Congressman whose district included Elizabeth City. He had helped OH to get an appointment in the Engineer Bureau. Bolles and his brother-in-law, Chase Whiting, were evidently interested in getting OH transferred to Fort Fisher. Alfred L. Rives was assistant chief of the Engineer Department under Gilmer. W. Buck Yearns and John G. Barrett, eds., *North Carolina Civil War Documentary* (Chapel Hill: University of North Carolina Press, 1980), 8, 309–10; James L. Nichols, *Confederate Engineers* (Tuscaloosa, Ala.: Confederate Publishing Co., 1957), 19.

Chapter 11

1. The CSA was forced to use paper money or scrip. Inflation was rampant. When OH was appointed to the Engineer Corps in February 1862, a treasury note was worth about one dollar in gold. Southerners now had to exchange twenty to forty notes for one gold dollar. Current, *Encyclopedia of the Confederacy*, 1:434–36, 2:820–21; Jones, *Rebel War Clerk's Diary*, 2:140–61.

2. *Nous verrons ce que nous verrons* is a French term that means "we shall see what we shall see."

3. On December 8, 1863, Averell set out with his independent brigade on a 355-mile raid from West Virginia into western Virginia. With the return of Ewell, Lee sent Early to take command of the scattered rebel troops trying to thwart Averell. *OR*, 29(1):920–33; Jubal A. Early, *Lieutenant General Jubal Anderson Early, C.S.A.: Autobiographical Sketch and Narrative of the War Between the States* (Philadelphia: J. B. Lippincott Co., 1912), 326–31.

4. "Mercer" may have been Major George D. Mercer from southern Maryland who was a quartermaster on Johnson's staff. Krick, *Staff Officers*, 220.

5. Sedgwick commanded the AoP in place of Meade. He sent his Second Corps across the Rapidan at Morton's Ford on February 6. Ewell's troops repelled them. Gordon C. Rhea, *The Battle of the Wilderness, May 5–6, 1864* (Baton Rouge: Louisiana State University Press, 1994), 1–7.

6. Pickett left Kinston on January 30 and led his 13,000 men to New Bern. Commander John T. Wood burned a Federal side-wheeler gunboat, the *Underwriter*, on the Neuse River, but Pickett prematurely withdrew his men. Colonel Martin, OH's friend from Elizabeth City, led his regiment north from Wilmington as part of a diversionary movement commanded by his brother James. Barrett, *Civil War NC*, 202–12; William R. Trotter, *Ironclads and Colum-*

biads: The Civil War in North Carolina—The Coast (Winston-Salem, N.C.: John F. Blair, Publisher, 1989), 223–31.

7. Of the officers who escaped from Libby Prison, fifty-nine succeeded, forty-eight were recaptured, and two drowned. Ernest B. Furgurson, *Ashes of Glory: Richmond at War* (New York: Alfred A. Knopf, 1996), 242–47.

8. Virgil Carrington Jones, *Gray Ghosts and Rebel Raiders* (New York: Promontory Press, 1995), 215–16.

9. Moore served as an assistant adjutant and inspector general for Generals Taliaferro, Trimble, Colston, and Johnson. *OR*, 21, 677; 27(2):502–5; 29(1):848.

10. Doctor Coleman was the well-respected chief surgeon for the Second Corps. The week before, Lee proposed to Seddon that a medical commission be formed, with Dr. Coleman on it, to visit hospitals in the southeast to evaluate "all these patients or detailed men who are fit for field service." *OR*, 12(1):403; 12(2):191; 21:677; 25(1):1009; 29(1):848, 33:1173–74.

11. Thomas S. Taliaferro served as judge advocate for the Second Corps. Captain Warner T. Taliaferro, an ex-politician, was the assistant adjutant general for General Taliaferro (his half brother) and now served on Colston's staff. Krick, *Staff Officers*, 280.

12. Three months later, on May 24, 1864, Gouverneur Warren's men apprehended Dr. Charles J. Terrell as he tried to cross Union lines. *OR*, 36(3):157–58.

13. The cavalry raid on Richmond that OH wrote about was led by Judson Kilpatrick and Ulrich Dahlgren. After freeing Union prisoners at Belle Isle, Dahlgren and his men planned to join Kilpatrick's horse soldiers for a dash to Williamsburg. Virgil Carrington Jones, *Eight Hours before Richmond* (New York: Henry Holt and Co., 1957), 25–29.

14. On February 23, 1864, Joe Johnston's troops held back the Army of the Cumberland near Dalton, Georgia. In Florida, Joseph Finegan's rebels stopped Truman Seymour and his troops at the Battle of Olustee (or Ocean Pond) on February 20. Albert Castel, *Decision in the West: The Atlanta Campaign of 1864* (Lawrence: University Press of Kansas, 1992), 54–56; Foote, *Civil War*, 2:898–905.

Chapter 12

1. During the afternoon of February 29, Custer's cavalry struck Major Marcellus N. Moorman's artillery camp, which was composed of four batteries, including Chew's unit. The 200 rebel cannoneers resisted Custer's attack and did not lose any guns. On the other side of the state, Kilpatrick led his 3,500 horse soldiers to Beaver Dam, outside Richmond, and set fire to the railroad station. Henry B. McClellan, *The Life and Campaigns of Major General J. E. B. Stuart, Commander of the Cavalry of the Army of Northern Virginia* (Boston: Houghton Mifflin & Co., 1885), 399–401; George M. Neese, *Three Years in the Confederate Horse Artillery* (New York: Neale Publishing Co., 1911), 249–51; Krick, *Lee's Colonels*, 90, 278–80.

2. On March 1, Judson Kilpatrick's cavalrymen reached Brook Pike, five miles north of Richmond, and encountered the troops of Colonel Walter H. Stevens (Engineer Corps), who was in charge of Richmond's defenses. Kilpatrick ordered a withdrawal. Ulric Dahlgren's men got sidetracked, going to the wrong James River ford. Duane Schultz, *The Dahlgren Affair: Terror and Conspiracy in the Civil War* (New York: W. W. Norton, 1998), 117–28.

3. Krick, *Lee's Colonels*, 288.

4. Stuart arrived back in Lee's camp long enough to eat a meal before being notified that Federal cavalry had broken through Richmond's defenses. He left immediately but was too far behind to participate in the pursuit of Kilpatrick and Dahlgren. Theodore Stanford Garnett, *Riding with Stuart: Reminiscences of an Aide-de-Camp*, ed. Robert J. Trout (Shippensburg, Pa.: White Mane Publishing Co., 1994), 39–47.

5. Warner, *Generals in Gray*, 335–36.

6. When Dahlgren passed through Frederick's Hall on February 29, he discovered a rebel artillery court-martial in progress and captured a lieutenant colonel and three captains—one of the latter being Captain Dement from the 1st Maryland Battery. During his attempted escape, Dahlgren tried to use Dement as a human shield. *OR*, 29(2):688; 33:210–11; Virgil Carrington Jones, *Eight Hours before Richmond* (New York: Henry Holt and Co., 1957), 51; Schultz, *Dahlgren Affair*, 142, 251.

7. Richmond's defense consisted primarily of militia battalions from the CSA government—Armory, Arsenal, Departmental (for example, War Department), Navy, and Quartermaster. During the night of February 29, Hampton launched a surprise assault near Atlee's Station. Kilpatrick and most of his men escaped, riding to Butler's garrison at Williamsburg. *OR* 33:1301; Manly Wade Wellman, *Giant in Gray: A Biography of Wade Hampton of South Carolina* (New York: Charles Scribner's Sons, 1949), 133–35; James H. Kidd, *Personal Recollections of a Cavalryman* (Ionia, Mich.: Sentinel Printing Co., 1908), 234–60.

8. Horse soldiers from the 5th Virginia Cavalry and the 9th Virginia Cavalry, plus Home Guards, pursued and killed Dahlgren near King and Queen Court House. Officials in Richmond allegedly found papers on Dahlgren's body that advocated burning the rebel capital and killing President Davis and his cabinet. Schultz, *Dahlgren Affair*, 138–43.

9. Retaliation led to discussions about subversive countermeasures, such as freeing rebel prisoners at Camp Douglas (Chicago) and Johnson's Island (Sandusky, Ohio); the raid on St. Albans, Vermont; setting fire to New York City; and plots to kidnap Lincoln. The raid might also have been what precipitated OH's approaching of Generals Lee and Gordon a year later to sneak into New York City to foment some kind of rebellion among its German residents. Ibid., 144–60, 190–238; Tidwell, *Come Retribution*, 241–51; Jones, *Eight Hours before Richmond*, 136–48.

10. Freeman, *Lee's Lieutenants*, 3:344–49; Gordon C. Rhea, *The Battle of the Wilderness, May 5–6, 1864* (Baton Rouge: Louisiana State University Press, 1994), 34, 60–69, 79–111.

11. At dawn, Johnson's troops marched down the Orange Turnpike, fanned out on either side of Saunders Field, and threw up breastworks. The battle erupted around noon. John M. Jones's troops retreated after the death of their commander, leaving a gap in the line.

12. Battle led his brigade forward but gave ground. Stafford was mortally wounded. Gordon brought up his Georgians and stopped the Yankee momentum. In the afternoon, the brigades of Hays and Pegram from Early's division moved to Johnson's left and helped to blunt a Sixth Corps assault. Edward Steere, *The Wilderness Campaign: The Meeting of Grant and Lee* (Mechanicsburg, Pa.: Stackpole Books, 1960), 149–65, 243–58; Rhea, *Wilderness*, 140–84, 242–53, 271–73.

13. Gordon scouted out the Sixth Corps's right flank and discovered it was hanging "in the air." Lee approved his plan late in the afternoon but there was not enough daylight to take advantage of the assault. *OR*, 36(1):1037, 1040, 1085; Krick, *Lee's Colonels*, 86; Gordon, *Reminiscences*, 243–61.

14. Tallying up the Wilderness casualties was difficult since the armies immediately reengaged at Spotsylvania. Rhea concluded that there were more than 17,500 casualties for the Union (likely understated) and approximately 11,000 for the CSA. Gregory A. Mertz, "General Gouverneur K. Warren and the Fighting at Laurel Hill during the Battle of Spotsylvania Court House, May 1864," *Blue & Gray Magazine* 21, no. 4 (2004) 8–14; Rhea, *Wilderness*, 435–36, 440.

15. Ewell's Corps arrived at the battlefield during early evening, in time to prevent the Unionists from enveloping the troops of Richard H. Anderson. After dark, Ewell extended the rebel line farther east and created an irregularly shaped fortification, which became

known as the "Mule Shoe." Mertz, "Gouverneur K. Warren," 10–23, 48–52; Gordon C. Rhea, *The Battles for Spotsylvania Court House and the Road to Yellow Tavern, May 7–12, 1864* (Baton Rouge: Louisiana State University Press, 1997), 45–88.

16. Upton led a 6:00 P.M. charge and penetrated a vulnerable salient on the west side of Ewell's Mule Shoe, which Doles defended. Rebel counterattacks, bolstered by Gordon's men, drove out the Yankee attackers. Rhea, *Battles for Spotsylvania Court House*, 161–88; Gregory A. Mertz, "Upton's Attack and the Defense of Doles' Salient, Spotsylvania Court House, Va., May 10, 1864," *Blue & Gray Magazine* 18, no. 6 (2001): 6–25, 46–53; Warner, *Generals in Gray*, 74.

17. When Hancock's Second Corps—20,000 strong—struck at 4:35 A.M. on May 12, they encountered minimal artillery resistance. Witcher, commanding Jones's brigade, received a head wound, and Williams of the 2nd Louisiana was MWIA. Gordon, commanding Early's division, rallied the beleaguered Confederates. *OR*, 36(1):1072–73, 1078–80, 1086; Krick, *Lee's Colonels*, 148, 399, 404–5; Robert K. Krick, "'An Insurmountable Barrier between the Army and Ruin': The Confederate Experience at Spotsylvania's Bloody Angle," in *The Spotsylvania Campaign*, ed. Gary W. Gallagher (Chapel Hill: University of North Carolina Press, 1998), 80–126.

18. Lee directed his chief engineer to cut off the exposed Mule Shoe salient at its base by establishing new earthworks approximately "800 yards in rear of the first and constructed at night." Most of Lee's men moved into the new position during the night of May 12–13. *OR*, 36(1):1073.

19. Krick, *Staff Officers*, 108, 115, 167–68, 224, 305; Crute, *Confederate Staff Officers*, 72, 100–101.

20. Rhea projected that Grant lost over 33,000 men (28 percent of his army) after crossing the Rapidan and continuing through the Bloody Angle fight on May 12. Rhea, *Battles for Spotsylvania Court House*, 319.

21. Rhea also estimated that Lee suffered 23,000 total combat losses (35 percent) from May 5 through May 12. Ibid., 324.

22. On May 11, one of Custer's cavalrymen mortally wounded Stuart at Yellow Tavern. Freeman, *Lee's Lieutenants*, 3:424–33.

23. At the Battle of the Wilderness, John M. Jones was KIA, and Stafford was MWIA on May 5; Jenkins was killed on May 6. At Spotsylvania on May 12, Daniel was MWIA, and Perrin died instantly after being hit by seven bullets. Warner, *Generals in Gray*, 66–67, 155, 164–65, 235, 287–88.

24. Benning (May 6), Pegram (May 5), and Perry (May 6) were WIA at the Wilderness. Among general officers WIA at Spotsylvania were Hays (May 10), Johnston (May 12), McGowan (May 12), Ramseur (May 12), Henry H. Walker (May 10), and James A. Walker (May 12). Although not mentioned, Battle and J. R. Cooke were also wounded on May 10 at Spotsylvania. Rhea, *Wilderness*, 304, 400; Griggs, *John Pegram*, 96; Rhea, *Battles for Spotsylvania Court House*, 342–45.

25. Federal general officers Baxter (WIA, May 6), Getty (WIA, May 6), Hays (KIA, May 5), and Wadsworth (KIA, May 6) were casualties at the Wilderness. Among the wounded Union generals at Spotsylvania were Morris (May 9), Robinson (May 8), and Webb (May 12). At Spotsylvania, Major General Sedgwick was killed on May 9 while inspecting his lines. OH did not list Generals Stevenson or Rice, who were KIA and MWIA, respectively, on May 10 at Spotsylvania. There were no generals among the casualties at either the Wilderness or Spotsylvania by the names of Taylor, Talbot, or Carr (the latter might have been Colonel Samuel S. Carroll). Rhea, *Wilderness*, 203, 306, 310, 365, 395, 420; Rhea, *Battles for Spotsylvania Court House*, 332–39.

26. William Glenn Robertson, *Back Door to Richmond: The Bermuda Hundred Campaign, April–June 1864* (Newark: University of Delaware Press, 1987), 217.

27. With Long's twenty-nine guns in place at the truncated Mule Shoe, the Confederates resisted a surprise attack from Hancock's and Wright's troops. Grant moved his men toward Richmond to lure the rebels into an open-field fight. During the Battle of Drewry's Bluff on May 16, 1864, Beauregard's men captured Heckman. Gordon C. Rhea, *To the North Anna River: Grant and Lee, May 13–25, 1864* (Baton Rouge: Louisiana State University Press, 2000), 126–53; Krick, *Staff Officers*, 304–5; Herbert M. Schiller, *The Bermuda Hundred Campaign: "Operations on the South Side of the James River, Virginia—May, 1864"* (Dayton, Ohio: Morningside, 1988), 229–69.

28. Roger U. Delauter Jr., *McNeill's Rangers* (Lynchburg, Va.: H. E. Howard, 1986), 66–67.

29. Lee ordered Ewell on May 19 to embark on a flanking maneuver to get behind the Federal line. This led to the Battle of Harris Farm. Rhea, *North Anna River*, 164–88.

Chapter 13

1. Instead of pursuing Hancock's Second Corps, Lee sent Ewell's weakened corps south from Spotsylvania to block the Telegraph Road and protect Hanover Junction. During May 22, Hancock's troops established a foothold on the rebel side of the North Anna River. Soldiers in Warren's Corps crossed upriver at Jericho Mills and encamped. Gordon C. Rhea, *To the North Anna River: Grant and Lee, May 13–25, 1864* (Baton Rouge: Louisiana State University Press, 2000), 212–324; J. Michael Miller, *The North Anna Campaign: "Even to Hell Itself," May 21–26, 1864* (Lynchburg, Va.: H. E. Howard, 1989), 12–87.

2. Davis sent Pickett and three of his brigades, as well as Hoke's brigade, from Richmond. Breckinridge brought 2,500 men from the Shenandoah valley. Bradley Johnson's Maryland Line and Matthew C. Butler's cavalry from South Carolina were also among Lee's reinforcements. During the night of May 23–24, Lee's men constructed new fortifications whose apex was at Ox Ford, between Chesterfield Bridge and Jericho Mills. Rhea, *North Anna River*, 161, 320–24; Miller, *North Anna Campaign*, 8, 9, 24, 31.

3. Grant's troops began to entrench on May 25. Lee reorganized his army, promoting Gordon to major general with command of a permanent division. Rhea, *North Anna River*, 324–60; Miller, *North Anna Campaign*, 88–120.

4. Henry Kyd Douglas's description of what happened after Federal soldiers captured Johnson sheds some light on OH's situation. First, Douglas wrote that "at once [I] attached myself to Gordon." Second, Douglas also noted that Gordon "had brought his own staff to the division and, with members of Johnson's staff, he had a larger one than he was entitled to." OH was hesitant, however, to jockey for a position on someone else's staff. Douglas, *I Rode with Stonewall*, 282–83.

5. Butler's horse soldiers were "finely equipped, well mounted men, who never had been in action." After becoming Gordon's adjutant general, Douglas replaced the wounded Major John W. Daniel as Early's chief of staff. Freeman, *Lee's Lieutenants*, 3:499; Douglas, *I Rode with Stonewall*, 283.

6. The appendix in *Lee's Sharpshooters* includes a transcript of Hewson's eyewitness battle accounts of the Wilderness (May 18) and Spotsylvania (May 25). Hotchkiss, *Make Me a Map*, 203, 205; William S. Dunlop, *Lee's Sharpshooters; or, The Forefront of Battle: A Story of Southern Valor That Has Never Been Told* (Little Rock, Ark.: Tunnah & Pittard, Printers, 1899), 383–418, 433–75.

7. Major Thomas E. Ballard was the commissary of subsistence under Gordon and had been an assistant on Johnson's staff. Twenty-three-year-old Ned Willis, recently promoted to

brigadier general, was KIA while leading Pegram's Virginia Brigade during the Battle of Bethesda Church on May 30. *OR*, 36(3):842–43; Krick, *Staff Officers*, 66, 305; W. G. Bean, *Stonewall's Man: Sandie Pendleton* (Chapel Hill: University of North Carolina Press, 1959), 199–201.

8. Grant delayed his dawn assault on June 2 because of logistical problems. Near Bethesda Church, Heth's division joined Early's Second Corps to launch a surprise attack. Terry commanded a new Virginia Brigade, a consolidation of the Stonewall Brigade and Witcher's brigade. Early's troops drove back Burnsides's corps and a section of Warren's. During the fighting that day, a Union sharpshooter killed Doles. James I. Robertson Jr., *The Stonewall Brigade* (Baton Rouge: Louisiana State University Press, 1963), 225–28; Ernest B. Furgurson, *Not War but Murder: Cold Harbor 1864* (New York: Alfred A. Knopf, 2000), 127–31; Gordon C. Rhea, *Cold Harbor: Grant and Lee, May 26–June 3, 1864* (Baton Rouge: Louisiana State University Press, 2002), 18, 298–307, 393.

9. Hancock's troops penetrated the right side of the rebel line defended by Patton's brigade in Breckinridge's division but were repulsed by Finegan's Floridians and the 2nd Maryland Battalion. Generals Kirkland, Lane, and Law were seriously wounded; Scales was ill. There is no evidence that Battle and Finegan had major wounds. Rhea, *Cold Harbor*, 313, 318–57, 414–15; Furgurson, *Not War but Murder*, 136–80.

10. According to an analysis by Gordon Rhea, Grant probably lost about 3,500 men during the brutal June 3 charge versus Lee's 700 casualties. Rhea, *Cold Harbor*, 359–62.

11. Rhea estimated that, from the Wilderness to James River, the ANVA inflicted approximately 55,000 casualties. Lee had to replace 33,000 soldiers as well as many key commanders. Ibid., 393.

12. Nathaniel Banks was fortunate that his troops and accompanying gunboats escaped annihilation during the Red River Campaign.

13. After being captured during the ANVA's retreat from Gettysburg, Charles Stanley was transferred to Fort McHenry in Baltimore and then was transferred to the Fort Delaware prison. Driver, *First & Second Maryland Cavalry*, 288.

14. Most of OH's pencil entries for this date are faded and illegible. An officer in Kershaw's division, situated next to Field's division, wrote that "a constant fire was kept up during the day [June 4]." Meade's chief of staff recorded at 9:40 P.M. that the Confederates had "opened up a fire this evening." OH might have gotten confused about the time and date of the attack. Lilley became a brigadier general on May 31, 1864. Terry was promoted to brigadier general on May 19, 1864. Lee reassigned Ewell to the Richmond defenses. *OR*, 36(1):1065; *OR*, 36(3):571, 607, 873–74; Warner, *Generals in Gray*, 188, 302.

15. See Scott C. Patchan's *The Forgotten Fury: The Battle of Piedmont, Virginia* (Fredericksburg, Va.: Sergeant Kirkland's Museum and History Society, 1996) and Marshall Moore Brice's *Conquest of a Valley* (Charlottesville: University of Virginia Press, 1965).

16. Lee sent Breckinridge and Early to stop Hunter from destroying the western part of the Virginia Central RR. Breckinridge reached Lynchburg in the afternoon of June 8. Early, *Memoir*, 41; *OR*, 37(1):753–58; Krick, *Staff Officers*, 287.

17. Whiting commanded Wise's brigade and Martin's brigade at Port Walthall Junction near Drewry's Bluff. In June 1864 Captain John Mason became assistant quartermaster for Major William McLaughlin's artillery unit. "Cooper" may have been Lieutenant Samuel M. Cooper, who had been with the Second Corps's artillery and was serving in an "unspecified role, probably as a staff officer." Captain James Mitchel and Major G. Campbell Brown were possibly the "Mitchele and Brown" OH wrote about. William Glenn Robertson, *Back Door to Richmond: The Bermuda Hundred Campaign, April–June 1864* (Newark: University of Delaware Press, 1987), 209–15; Krick, *Staff Officers*, 84, 85, 103, 217, 222.

18. There was a Lieutenant D. H. Cockrill from the Pioneer Corps listed on an OH document in March 1863. Campbell Brown may have been the "Brown" speculating about Steinecker. Lieutenant William D. Lyons was an ordnance officer on Evans's staff. NAMP M331A, Reel 124; Campbell Brown, *Campbell Brown's Civil War: With Ewell and the Army of Northern Virginia*, ed. Terry L. Jones (Baton Rouge: Louisiana State University Press, 2001), 260–65; *OR*, 24(2):100; *OR*, 36(2):217; Krick, *Staff Officers*, 205.

19. There was no Major General Tanner. OH may have meant Major General Ramseur. Freeman, *Lee's Lieutenants*, 3:517–18.

20. Perhaps "Webb" was Lewis N. Webb who, having served as quartermaster in the First Corps, worked outside Richmond. Krick, *Staff Officers*, 298.

21. Crook had led his Federal troops to victory against Jenkins's outnumbered Confederates at the Battle of Cloyd's Mountain on May 9, 1864. Kennedy, *Civil War Battlefield Guide*, 296–97.

22. Hunter began his wave of destruction in the valley with Staunton as his first target. Soldiers set fire to public and commercial buildings (for example, the railroad station, warehouses, and workshops) and set prisoners free to riot. David Hunter Strother, *A Virginia Yankee in the Civil War: The Diaries of David Hunter Strother*, ed. Cecil D. Eby Jr. (Chapel Hill: University of North Carolina Press, 1989), 247–48.

23. Major John D. Rogers handled quartermaster duties for the Second Corps after Harman was transferred. *OR*, 36(1):1074; Krick, *Staff Officers*, 257.

24. See Eric J. Wittenberg's *Glory Enough for All: Sheridan's Second Raid and the Battle of Trevilian Station* (Washington, D.C.: Brassey's, 2001).

25. Moore was a physician—born in 1805—who had been a North Carolina legislator prior to the war. He resigned as colonel of the 29th Virginia due to health reasons but remained active in the Wythe County reserves. Krick, *Lee's Colonels*, 276.

Chapter 14

1. Lynchburg was a primary CSA supply depot and contained an arsenal and thirty-two hospitals. On June 16, Breckinridge waited in Lynchburg for Early's troops to arrive. In Charlottesville, Early forced railroad agents to help. Joseph Judge, *Season of Fire: The Confederate Strike on Washington* (Berryville, Va.: Rockbridge Publishing, Co., 1994), 94–96; *OR*, 37(1):763; Robert C. Black, *The Railroads of the Confederacy* (Chapel Hill: University of North Carolina Press, 1952), 247.

2. Early could only transport Ramseur's division and a brigade of Gordon's on June 17. The rest of his infantrymen, along with Long's artillery and the army's supply wagons, marched parallel to the railroad track. He arrived in Lynchburg at 1:00 P.M. and moved his defensive line farther away from the city. Early, *Memoir*, 42–45; H. A. Du Pont, *The Campaign of 1864 in the Valley of Virginia and the Expedition to Lynchburg* (New York: National Americana Society, 1925), 67–71.

3. Upon learning that Jackson's old corps was in front of him, and being worried about a shortage of ammunition and food, Hunter withdrew his AoWV. In Petersburg, the Union troops launched a series of disjointed attacks against Confederate defenses from June 15 to June 18. Du Pont, *The Campaign of 1864*, 75–79; Trudeau, *Last Citadel*, 3–55.

4. During the night of June 18–19, Early learned that Hunter's troops and their 200 wagons had disappeared. He led his troops to overtake the Federal rear guard at Liberty (Bedford City), which was twenty-five miles from Lynchburg. Judge, *Season of Fire*, 103–6.

5. The fleeing Yankees got to Buford's Gap first and commanded the heights there. Night

fell as the Confederates tried to dislodge them. Early and Gilmor also wrote about Hunter's mistreatment of private citizens. Early, *Memoir*, 46–51; Gilmor, *Four Years in the Saddle*, 171–83.

6. Early decided that pursuit of Hunter's army into the mountains "could only have resulted in disaster to my command from want of provisions and forage." OH was moved by the beauty of Buford's Gap and made a drawing of it in his diary. Early, *Memoir*, 48–49.

7. Early rested his troops and prepared to follow Lee's order to put pressure on Washington. Ibid., 50–51.

8. During fighting at Petersburg from June 14 to 18, the Union incurred about 10,000 casualties and the Confederates 4,000. Trudeau, *Last Citadel*, 55.

9. Hunter had ordered his men to burn VMI buildings—including the library, scientific materials, and relics from the War of 1812—in retaliation for the cadets firing on the Union army as it entered Lexington and because of the role they played at New Market. Some members of Jackson's old corps reverentially marched by the general's gravesite. Douglas, *I Rode with Stonewall*, 292; John H. Worsham, *One of Jackson's Foot Cavalry* (New York: Neale Publishing Co., 1912), 231.

10. Hotchkiss made a brief note in his diary about officers visiting Natural Bridge. Worsham wrote that some of the soldiers "were allowed to stop there an hour or two to rest and view the bridge." Douglas mentioned bands playing an impromptu concert. OH drew a picture of Natural Bridge in his diary. Hotchkiss, *Make Me a Map*, 213; Worsham, *Jackson's Foot Cavalry*, 231; Douglas, *I Rode with Stonewall*, 291; Hinrichs drawing of Natural Bridge, Richard Brady Williams Private Collection.

11. Trudeau, *Last Citadel*, 56–87.

12. Early's soldiers traveled light on June 28 with "five days rations in the waggons [*sic*] and two days in haversacks, empty waggons being left to bring the shoes when they arrived." Early, *Memoir*, 53; Krick, *Staff Officers*, 72.

13. Jubal A. Early, *Lieutenant General Jubal Anderson Early, C.S.A.: Autobiographical Sketch and Narrative of the War Between the States* (Philadelphia: J. B. Lippincott Co., 1912), 253–65.

14. Ramseur had a smaller staff, and the current AoV reorganization provided an opportune time for OH to switch staffs.

15. A. P. Hill was still with Lee defending Petersburg. After the raid on Washington, Anderson—not Hill—would help Early to defend the valley.

16. Mosby and his raiders were active around Harpers Ferry and attacked Duffield Station on the B&O RR. Gilmor operated around Winchester "to prevent all intelligence of Early's advance reaching the Federal lines." Lieutenant Ridgely was now an aide-de-camp for Ramseur. Peter A. Brown, *Mosby's Fighting Parson: The Life and Times of Sam Chapman* (Westminster, Md.: Willow Bend Books, 2001), 175–77; Gilmor, *Four Years in the Saddle*, 184; Krick, *Staff Officers*, 254.

17. Bradley Johnson would soon embark on a secret mission to free prisoners from Point Lookout. After Cold Harbor, he had also been involved in a plot to kidnap Lincoln: "I started with Hampton's permission to cross the Potomac, capture Lincoln at the Soldiers Home and bring him to Virginia. I met Early on his way to Lynchburg to head off Hunter. Early forbade me the movement and ordered me to the Valley to wait his return." Marginalia note on pages 120–21 of Johnson's personal copy of George Booth's *A Maryland Boy in Lee's Army: Personal Reminiscences of a Maryland Soldier in the War Between the States, 1861-1865*, Boston Athenaeum; Tidwell, *Come Retribution*, 235–36, 264.

18. Firing from Maryland Heights, Franz Sigel's artillerists prevented Early from leading his army on a more direct route to Washington.

19. Lee's son Robert delivered a message to Early on July 6 regarding Johnson's prisoner-release raid on Point Lookout. Early, *Memoir*, 56; Tidwell, *Come Retribution*, 143–47.

20. "Green" may have been Major Benjamin H. Greene, an engineer officer for Early. Krick, *Staff Officers*, 142.

21. Benjamin Franklin Cooling, *Monocacy: The Battle That Saved Washington* (Shippensburg, Pa.: White Mane Publishing Co., 1997), 76–85.

22. Ramseur controlled the center of Early's line, but the rebel attack stalled. Gordon's division advanced down the right bank of the river, crossed at a ford, and attacked the Union's left flank. Lew Wallace, *Lew Wallace: An Autobiography in Two Volumes* (New York: Harper & Brothers Publishers, 1906), 2:698–796; Gordon, *Reminiscences*, 309–13; Edwin C. Bearss, *The Battle of Monocacy: A Documented Report* (Frederick, Md.: Monocacy National Battlefield, 2003), 47–60.

23. Ramseur's men stayed behind to destroy the stone railroad bridge at Monocacy Junction but were unsuccessful. They caught up with the rest of Early's army near Rockville at about eleven that night. Grant sent troops to reinforce Washington's ring of forts. Gallagher, *Ramseur*, 127; Benjamin Franklin Cooling, *Jubal Early's Raid on Washington, 1864* (Baltimore: Nautical & Aviation Publishing Co. of America, 1989), 83–97, 102–5.

24. Early's infantry set out from Rockville at daylight and advanced to Seventh Street in northern Washington. Before the CSA vanguard arrived at Fort Stevens, Federal artillerists began to fire their big guns. Long's forty light cannon could not compete with them. Early, *Memoir*, 60–62; Cooling, *Early's Raid*, 107–27.

25. During the night of July 11–12, reinforcements arrived to further strengthen the Federal position. Early sent word for Bradley Johnson, on his way to Upper Marlborough, to abandon the Point Lookout raid. Cooling, *Early's Raid*, 135–55; 172.

26. Gilmor and his cavalrymen captured, and lost, Franklin, who was on his way back from the Red River Campaign. As Early's soldiers retreated, someone set fire to "Falkland," the home of Postmaster General Montgomery Blair. Francis P. Blair's house, "Silver Spring," was not burned but, as portrayed by OH, the Confederates ransacked it. In the marginalia of the Booth book, Bradley Johnson wrote on page 123 that Lee had personally asked him to set fire to Governor Bradford's country house in retaliation for Hunter's torching of Governor Letcher's home in Lexington. Johnson's personal copy of Booth, *A Maryland Boy in Lee's Army*, Boston Athenaeum; Cooling, *Early's Raid*, 164.

27. Krick, *Lee's Colonels*, 330.

Chapter 15

1. Around midday on July 16, Brigadier General Alfred N. A. Duffié's horse soldiers struck Early's wagon train near Purcellville and captured eighty-two wagons and sixty-two prisoners. Robert Ransom Jr. would soon retire, apparently due to illness. See Scott C. Patchan's *Shenandoah Summer: The 1864 Valley Campaign* (Lincoln: University of Nebraska Press, 2007) for more information on this segment of Early's campaign. Benjamin Franklin Cooling, *Jubal Early's Raid on Washington, 1864* (Baltimore: Nautical & Aviation Publishing Co. of America, 1989), 193–95; OR, 37(2):368–69; Warner, *Generals in Gray*, 254.

2. Wright led the advance through the Blue Ridge Mountains with Crook commanding the AoWV troops under him. Breckinridge's divisions (Gordon's and Echols's troops) "held the enemy in check" while Rodes's men drove the bluecoats back across the river. OR, 37(2):356–68; Joseph W. A. Whitehorne and Clarence R. Geier, "The Battle of Cool Spring, July 16–20, 1864," in *Archaeological Perspectives on the American Civil War*, ed. Clarence R. Geier and Stephen R. Potter (Gainesville: University Press of Florida, 2000), 73–93.

3. Ramseur told his wife that his "men behaved shamefully" at the Battle of Stephenson's Depot (or Rutherford's Farm). Aid-de-camp Randolph Ridgely was WIA and left behind after the Battle of Second Kernstown. Henry Kyd Douglas asked Matilda Russell, the daughter of a friend in Winchester, to help him. The other injured staff officer whom OH mentioned was probably Lieutenant William G. Callaway. Gallagher, *Ramseur*, 131–35; *OR*, 37(2):599–600; Krick, *Staff Officers*, 89, 254; Douglas, *I Rode with Stonewall*, 301–2.

4. The "Back Road" ran parallel to the Valley Pike from Winchester toward Harrisonburg. George B. Davis et al, *The Official Military Atlas of the Civil War* (New York: Fairfax Press, 1983), Plate LXXIV.

5. Less than 10,000 Yankees remained as the rear guard at Kernstown. Early's 14,000 men outnumbered them. The rebels attacked, sending the Federals in retreat down the valley to Bunker Hill. Mulligan was taken to Winchester, where he died. Kennedy, *Civil War Battlefield Guide*, 310–12; Cooling, *Early's Raid*, 210–11.

6. Thruston, a physician prior to the war, was seriously WIA at Spotsylvania and may have served a stint as provost marshal while recuperating. He would resume leadership and be WIA again at the Battle of Third Winchester. Clark, ed., *NC Regiments*, I:178, 203, 207; George Edgar Turner, *Victory Rode the Rails: The Strategic Place of the Railroads in the Civil War* (Lincoln: University of Nebraska Press, 1992), 35–36.

7. Hood initiated contact with the Yankees on July 20 (Peach Tree Creek) and July 22 (Atlanta). John P. Dyer, *The Gallant Hood* (Indianapolis: Bobbs-Merrill Co., 1950), 246–61.

8. Marmont's book contained a revised chapter (35) from Baron de Jomini's *The Art of War*. Auguste Frederic Marmont, *The Spirit of Military Institutions*, trans. by Frank Schaller (Columbia, S.C.: Evans and Cogswell, 1864); Edwin C. Bearss, *The Campaign for Vicksburg* (Dayton, Ohio: Morningside, 1986), 2:250.

9. By late July, Wright's Sixth Corps, Hunter's AoWV, and 6,000 men from Emory's Nineteenth Corps sought to contain Early's troops. Ulysses S. Grant, *Personal Memoirs of U. S. Grant in Two Volumes* (New York: Charles L. Webster & Co., 1885–1886), 2:316–22.

10. Michael A. Cavanaugh and William Marvel, *The Battle of the Crater: "The Horrid Pit,"* *June 25–August 6, 1864* (Lynchburg, Va.: H. E. Howard, 1989), 37–103.

11. Upon reaching Chambersburg at dawn on July 30, McCausland sent Gilmor to present terms to the town's leaders, which, as OH wrote, they rejected. By 8:00 A.M., fire consumed the town's business district and 550 dwellings. Ted Alexander, "McCausland's Raid and the Burning of Chambersburg," *Blue & Gray Magazine* 11, no. 6 (1994): 11–18, 46–61.

12. Douglas reported that the Confederates arrived at the College of Saint James on August 5 and that Ramseur's staff—whose "headquarter camp was on the lawn" of the school—had dinner at the home of the president. After dinner, an order came from Early to arrest Dr. Kerfoot and Professor Coit. Ramseur decided to wait until Early came the next morning. Dr. Kerfoot was the first headmaster for the College of Saint James. Douglas, *I Rode with Stonewall*, 303–4; *Saint James School Alumni Directory, 2003* (Purchase, N.Y.: Harris Publishing Co., 2003), v–vii.

13. On August 6, Early met with Kerfoot and Professor Coit to discuss an exchange for Reverend Boyd, who was arrested in April and taken from Winchester to a Wheeling prison. Douglas, *I Rode with Stonewall*, 305–6; Roger U. Delauter Jr., *Winchester in the Civil War* (Lynchburg, Va.: H. E. Howard, 1992), 64–66.

14. *OR*, 38(3):632, 689.

15. On July 17, Hunter ordered his soldiers to punish anyone in Frederick who helped Early's troops. They imprisoned the men in Wheeling, sent their wives and children to the Confederacy, confiscated their property, and sold their furniture at auctions. Editors of two secessionist newspapers were also exiled. Edward A. Miller Jr., *Lincoln's Abolitionist Gen-*

eral: *The Biography of David Hunter* (Columbia: University of South Carolina Press, 1997), 226–29, 240–42.

16. Lee sent Dick Anderson north with Fitzhugh Lee's cavalry division and Major General Joseph B. Kershaw's infantry division to harass Sheridan's army. C. Irvine Walker, *The Life of Lieutenant General Richard Heron Anderson of the Confederate States Army* (Charleston, S.C.: Art Publishing Co., 1917), 182–89.

17. Averell's cavalry caught up with McCausland and his men near Moorefield, W.Va., during the night of August 6–7. "Mudwall" Jackson was the second cousin of Stonewall Jackson and had served on his staff. *OR*, 43(1):505–6; Warner, *Generals in Gray*, 153–54.

18. Anderson's troops arrived in Front Royal from Culpeper during the night of August 14. This forced Sheridan to withdraw his force. The Atlanta rumors were erroneous. Admiral David G. Farragut led his fleet into Mobile Bay on August 5. Wert, *Winchester to Cedar Creek*, 34; Jack Friend, *West Wind, Flood Tide: The Battle of Mobile Bay* (Annapolis, Md.: Naval Institute Press, 2004), 222–43.

19. Early also wrote about the alleged spy, a private of the 54th North Carolina Regiment, whom Sheridan's men hanged on August 14 in Middletown. Early, *Memoir*, 78.

20. OH was evidently writing about an engagement that took place on August 17 south of Winchester. Jeffry D. Wert, *Custer: The Controversial Life of George Armstrong Custer* (New York: Simon & Schuster, 1996), 172–73.

Chapter 16

1. Sheridan withdrew his AoS to Halltown, which provided one of the best defensive positions in the lower Valley. Early interpreted his withdrawal as a sign of weakness. Philip Henry Sheridan, *Personal Memoirs of P. H. Sheridan, General United States Army* (New York: Charles L. Webster & Co., 1888), 1:482–84.

2. "Col. Lee" was likely John W. Lea from Caswell County, North Carolina, who was colonel of the 5th North Carolina. The infantry unit had become part of Robert D. Johnston's brigade, which he would command in the fall. OH referred to the Second Battle of Deep Bottom (or Fussell's Mill) that occurred southeast of Richmond. Clark, *NC Regiments*, 1:289–90; John Horn, *The Destruction of the Weldon Railroad: Deep Bottom, Globe Tavern, and Reams Station, August 14–25, 1864* (Lynchburg, Va.: H. E. Howard, 1991), 9–52.

3. A cavalry officer in Virginia's Laurel Brigade recounted the same "Molly Cotton-Tail" story, which he attributed to Governor Zebulon Vance from North Carolina. He added that soldiers put the reputation of their wives and children at stake if they "ran like a rabbit." Charles Triplett O'Ferrall, *Forty Years of Active Service* (New York: Neale Publishing Co., 1904), 111.

4. For the next week, OH's dates were off by one day. Instead of "August 22," he really meant "August 21," which was evident by his writing "Summit Point" through the middle of that day's entry. This revised date correlates with other sources. Hotchkiss, *Make Me a Map*, 223.

5. From Bunker Hill, Early led a column of soldiers east on August 21 to Smithfield. About three miles from Charles Town, the rebels caught up with Wright's Sixth Corps and drove it back. Sheridan's army began to set up fortifications. Rodes and Ramseur engaged in heavy skirmishing with the Federals until night fell. Early, *Memoir*, 78–79; Hotchkiss, *Make Me a Map*, 223–24.

6. Sheridan's force was almost four times larger than Early's AoV. On August 21 at Summit Point, Anderson's troops attacked those of Brigadier General James H. Wilson, whose cavalry was covering Sheridan's retrograde movement. Gary W. Gallagher, "Two Generals and

a Valley," in *The Shenandoah Valley Campaign of 1864*, ed. Gary W. Gallagher (Chapel Hill: University of North Carolina Press, 2006), 9; Wert, *Winchester to Cedar Creek*, 22, 26, 34.

7. Sheridan's army dropped back to Halltown on August 22 "under the protection of the heavy guns on Maryland Heights." Godwin commanded a North Carolina brigade in Ramseur's division. Early, *Memoir*, 79; Warner, *Generals in Gray*, 87–88, 108.

8. The 58th Virginia was now in Pegram's brigade of Virginians as part of Ramseur's division. Crute, *Units of the CSA*, 390–91; F. Ray Sibley Jr., *The Confederate Order of Battle: The Army of Northern Virginia* (Shippensburg, Pa.: White Mane Publishing, 1996), 90.

9. Early's troops "encountered a very large force of the enemy's cavalry between Leetown and Kearneysville," running into more resistance near Shepherdstown. Hotchkiss noted that "Gordon was wounded in the head, but he gallantly dashed on, the blood streaming over him." Monaghan, colonel of the 6th Louisiana Infantry, was KIA. Withers was WIA and taken prisoner. Early, *Memoir*, 79; Hotchkiss, *Make Me a Map*, 224; Krick, *Lee's Colonels*, 275, 405.

10. Hotchkiss, *Make Me a Map*, 225; Kennedy, *Civil War Battlefield Guide*, 314.

11. Heavy fighting occurred at Globe Tavern from August 18 to August 21, and the Battle of Reams Station took place on August 25. Colonel Samuel P. Spear was involved in the Weldon RR fighting, but there is no evidence that he was captured there. Horn, *Weldon Railroad*, 54–171; Roger D. Hunt and Jack. R. Brown, *Brevet Brigadier Generals in Blue* (Gaithersburg, Md.: Olde Soldier Books, 1990), 575.

12. McPherson, *Battle Cry*, 765.

13. On August 7, Lee assigned Pegram, who had recovered from his Wilderness wound, to his old brigade in the AoV. Griggs, *John Pegram*, 100.

14. Chris was OH's half brother. According to a provost marshal report, he traveled from New York City and had been in Elizabeth City for eighteen months. It appeared that Chris was trying to use subterfuge—that is, saying he was a citizen of Saxe-Coburg-Gotha—since he had been working as a noncommissioned member of a CSA officer's staff. Letters dated 4/5/1863, 8/4/1864, and 8/16/1864, J. C. E. Hinrichs File, One-Name Papers, Records of the Provost Marshal, RG 109, NARA I.

15. McPherson, *Battle Cry*, 107, 221.

16. On September 2, Early took "three divisions of infantry and part of McCausland's cavalry under Col. Ferguson, across the country towards Summit Point, on a reconnoissance [*sic*]." On the east side of Opequon Creek, Averell's horse soldiers attacked and drove back the Confederate cavalry, capturing twenty-five wagons. *OR*, 43(2):12–15; Hotchkiss, *Make Me a Map*, 226.

17. Cole's 1st Maryland Potomac Home Brigade served under Duffié. Anderson led Kershaw's division and Fitzhugh Lee's cavalry toward Richmond and ran into Crook's infantry. *OR*, 43(1):983; Dickert, *Kershaw's Brigade*, 420–22.

18. At daylight on September 4, Early led Ramseur's, Gordon's, and Wharton's divisions to assist Anderson. Upon discovering that the Federal fortifications extended from Berryville to Summit Point, Early opted not to launch a flank attack. Early, *Memoir*, 81–82; McPherson, *Battle Cry*, 772–75.

19. Early noted that the withdrawal of his men to the west side of the Opequon was made while "skirmishers were in close proximity and firing at each other." Early, *Memoir*, 82.

20. Hotchkiss wrote that Rodes's men arrived to support the rebel horse soldiers south of Stephenson's Depot and "drove Averell's cavalry some three miles, inflicting some damage." Hotchkiss, *Make Me a Map*, 227.

Chapter 17

1. Ramseur's letters to his wife reflected the same opinion articulated by OH in his journal about a CSA rebound. Gallagher, *Ramseur*, 136; Nathaniel Cheairs Hughes Jr., *General William J. Hardee: Old Reliable* (Baton Rouge: Louisiana State University Press, 1965), 235–43.

2. Douglas also wrote about Ramseur and Halsey going bird hunting. Halsey had extensive staff experience, having served under Generals Garland, Iverson, and Robert Johnston. Ridgeley was recuperating at the home of Mr. R. Y. Conrad in Winchester and needed assistance to vacate before Sheridan's soldiers arrived. Douglas, *I Rode with Stonewall*, 307–11; Krick, *Staff Officers*, 146.

3. Hardee held off Sherman's Fourth Corps at Lovejoy Station, but it was too late. Hughes, *Hardee*, 240.

4. Early recalled that on September 10, his infantry "encountered a considerable force of the enemy's cavalry, which was driven off, and then pursued by Lomax through Martinsburg across the Opequon." Early, *Memoir*, 82–83.

5. Reverend Boyd had been imprisoned during Hunter's "reign of terror" in the valley as noted in chapter 15. He arrived back in Winchester on September 11. Roger U. Delauter Jr., *Winchester in the Civil War* (Lynchburg, Va.: H. E. Howard, 1992), 77.

6. See chapter 10 regarding engagement at Rappahannock Station.

7. OH was still apprehensive about whether his half brother Chris successfully reentered the Union without disclosing his Confederate service.

8. Hotchkiss wrote that Ramseur spent the day with "Carpenter's battery on the left of the road near the Opequon." Hotchkiss, *Make Me a Map*, 228.

9. Morrison, a college classmate of Hunter McGuire, helped him to care for Stonewall Jackson after Chancellorsville. He also served as chief surgeon for Early. Robertson, *Stonewall Jackson*, 746–51; Maurice F. Shaw, *Stonewall Jackson's Surgeon, Hunter Holmes McGuire: A Biography* (Lynchburg, Va.: H. E. Howard, 1993), 23, 35.

10. Lee sent Early a message on September 2 asking him to consider returning Kershaw's division. *OR*, 43(2):862, 873–76.

11. Early, *Memoir*, 83.

12. Dick Meade served on the staffs of Generals Jackson, Taliaferro, and Ewell. Krick, *Staff Officers*, 219.

13. On August 10, 1864, Lomax was appointed major general of Early's AoV cavalry. Warner, *Generals in Gray*, 190–91.

14. Rosser took over command of Beverly H. Robertson's Laurel Brigade and performed well during the Overland Campaign. Ibid., 264–65.

15. H. M. Wharton, *War Songs and Poems of the Southern Confederacy, 1861-1865* (Washington, D.C.: W. E. Scull, 1904), 101–3.

16. Joseph F. Johnston was the younger brother of Robert D. Johnston and an aide-de-camp on his staff. Krick, *Staff Officers*, 173.

17. In the afternoon of September 17, Early led troops to Martinsburg to disrupt work on the Union RR. Douglas wrote in his diary on September 17 that "Genl Early, in these bold movements seems to rely too much upon the caution and timidity of Sheridan." Douglas, *I Rode with Stonewall*, 308–9.

18. Upon arriving in Martinsburg, Early discovered that Grant had visited Sheridan in Charles Town. He surmised that Sheridan would soon attack. Early, *Memoir*, 84–89.

Chapter 18

1. For more information on this part of Early's Campaign, see Scott C. Patchan's *The Last Battle of Winchester: Phil Sheridan, Jubal Early, and the Shenandoah Valley Campaign, August 7–September 19, 1864* (New York: Savas Beatie, 2012).

2. Mosby tried to divert Federal troops in northern Virginia. On September 13, he created a new company, which included the promotion of Wat Bowie to second lieutenant. Near Centreville—not Middletown—Union cavalrymen wounded Mosby. He convalesced in Lynchburg. Dick Anderson was on his way back to Richmond. John S. Mosby, *The Memoirs of Colonel John S. Mosby* (Boston: Little, Brown & Co., 1917), 283–96; Jeffry D. Wert, *Mosby's Rangers* (New York: Simon and Schuster, 1990), 202–9.

3. Approximately 40,000 blue-clad troops—Wright's Eighth Corps, Emory's Nineteenth Corps, and Crook's AoWV, plus Torbert's large cavalry corps—were poised near Berryville to strike at daybreak. Early scrambled and concentrated his 12,500 rebels at Winchester. Foote, *Civil War*, 3:553–54; Wert, *Winchester to Cedar Creek*, 44–45.

4. Despite Jackson's friendship with Reverend Lacy, there were staff officers, such as OH, Campbell Brown, and Dr. McGuire, who disliked the preacher. Campbell Brown, *Campbell Brown's Civil War: With Ewell and the Army of Northern Virginia*, ed. Terry L. Jones (Baton Rouge: Louisiana State University Press, 2001), 53–54; John W. Schildt, *Jackson and the Preachers* (Parsons, W.Va.: McClain Printing Co., 1982), 144–62.

5. Prussian Heros von Borcke had difficulty getting Confederate authorities to recognize his achievements. The war department sent him in May 1864 to inspect cavalry troops in southwestern Virginia. In 1866 a publisher in Scotland and England issued von Borcke's *Memoirs*, which are still regarded as "exceptionally fine recollections." Robert J. Trout, *They Followed the Plume: The Story of J. E. B. Stuart and His Staff* (Mechanicsburg, Pa.: Stackpole Books, 1993), 273–80; Richard Barksdale Harwell, *In Tall Cotton: The 200 Most Important Confederate Books for the Reader, Researcher, and Collector* (Austin, Tex.: Jenkins Publishing Co., 1978), 4.

6. On September 19 at 2:00 A.M., Wilson's cavalry division advanced on the Winchester-Berryville Road but encountered resistance from Ramseur's soldiers. The Union's Sixth Corps debouched from the canyon and attacked. A logistics problem prevented Emory's Nineteenth Corps from getting to the front and gave Early time to insert Gordon's and Rodes's men. Generals Rodes and Godwin were KIA. Wert, *Winchester to Cedar Creek*, 47–99; Roger U. Delauter and Brandon H. Beck, *The Third Battle of Winchester* (Lynchburg, Va.: H. E. Howard, 1997), 24–71; Darrell L. Collins, *Major General Robert E. Rodes of the Army of Northern Virginia: A Biography* (New York: Savas Beatie, 2008), 399–405.

7. Early led his shaken soldiers through Strasburg to Fisher's Hill. The rebel fortifications were anchored on the right against the North Fork of the Shenandoah River and extended four miles west to Little North Mountain. Early, *Memoir*, 98–99.

8. Merritt's horsemen "alone captured 775 prisoners, about 70 officers, seven battle-flags, and two pieces of artillery." Wesley Merritt, "Sheridan in the Shenandoah Valley," in *Battles and Leaders in the Civil War*, ed. R. U. Johnson and C. C. Buel (New York: Century Company, 1887), 4:509–10.

9. During the early morning attacks, Ramseur rallied his men and held off Horatio G. Wright's infantry: "Ramseur's troops never again showed any signs of breaking and were the bulwark of Early's defense through the afternoon." John W. Ellis served as governor of North Carolina at the beginning of the war but died of consumption on July 7, 1861. Gallagher, *Ramseur*, 141–46; Current, *Encyclopedia of the Confederacy*, 2:529; Krick, *Lee's Colonels*, 130.

10. Based on Grant's meeting with Sheridan at Charlestown, there was a false rumor that the Federal general in chief was on hand for the battle.

11. In 1837 the French introduced the concept of sharpshooters, or *tirailleurs*, using a carbine rifle and light-infantry tactics. Early transferred Ramseur to head Rodes's large division and moved John Pegram into his vacancy. Brigadier General Robert D. Johnston, Colonel John S. Hoffman (who replaced Pegram), and Lieutenant Colonel William S. Davis of the 12th North Carolina (who took over Godwin's unit) were Pegram's brigade commanders. Fred L. Ray, *Shock Troops of the Confederacy: The Sharpshooter Battalions of the Army of Northern Virginia* (Ashville, N.C.: CFS Press, 2006), 14–31, 181–89; Robert E. L. Krick, "'A Stampeede of Stampeeds': The Confederate Disaster at Fisher's Hill," in *Shenandoah Valley Campaign of 1864*, ed. Gary W. Gallagher (Chapel Hill: University of North Carolina Press, 2006), 162–66.

12. Breckinridge left to run the military department in southwestern Virginia. Gordon and Wharton reported directly to Early, whose command structure was shaken. Krick, "'A Stampeede of Stampeeds,'" 163.

13. Ramseur's troops manned the left side of the earthworks. Lomax's cavalry protected the Confederate far left flank near the Back Road. During the day on September 22, Crook's 5,500 troops marched through the woods around Little North Mountain and launched a surprise attack. Ibid., 161–90; Wert, *Winchester to Cedar Creek*, 117–27.

14. Early's officers bemoaned the loss of Sandie Pendleton, who had handled chief of staff duties competently for Jackson, Ewell, and Early. Brigadier General Bryan Grimes denounced Early's leadership in a letter to his wife. W. G. Bean, *Stonewall's Man: Sandie Pendleton* (Chapel Hill: University of North Carolina Press, 1959), 208–11; T. Harwell Allen, *Lee's Last Major General: Bryan Grimes of North Carolina* (Mason City, Iowa: Savas Publishing Co., 1999), 192–99.

15. Merritt, "Sheridan in the Shenandoah Valley," *Battles and Leaders in the Civil War*, 4:511.

16. Sheridan gave up pursuit on September 25 and concentrated his men around Harrisonburg. Torbert's cavalry rejoined the main Union force and focused on destroying local railroads, bridges, and military stores. Ibid., 4:511–12; Wert, *Winchester to Cedar Creek*, 133–34.

17. Kershaw's infantry and Cutshaw's artillery battalion were close enough to return to reinforce the AoV. Anderson proceeded to Richmond. Dickert, *Kershaw's Brigade*, 436–37.

18. Sheridan decided late on September 23 to replace Averell with Colonel William Powell. Wert, *Winchester to Cedar Creek*, 132–33.

19. Early, *Memoir*, 102–3.

20. Torbert's cavalrymen, after they "destroyed a large quantity of rebel Government property" in Staunton, raced to Waynesboro, where they dismantled part of the iron bridge that spanned the South River. *OR*, 43(1):29–30.

21. Grant continued to put pressure on both Richmond and Petersburg in hopes that Lee would not be able to send any more troops to the valley.

22. John Watson Morton, *The Artillery of Nathan Bedford Forrest's Cavalry: "The Wizard of the Saddle"* (Nashville: Publishing House of the M. E. Church, 1909), 222–35.

23. Merritt estimated his First Cavalry Division alone destroyed over $3 million of property in the upper valley from Port Republic to Tom's Brook. *OR*, 43(1):442–43.

Chapter 19

1. Grant launched a multipronged offensive starting on September 29 against Richmond and Petersburg to prevent Lee from sending troops to Early. See Richard J. Sommers, *Richmond Redeemed: The Siege at Petersburg* (New York: Doubleday & Co., 1981).

2. OH still served as chief engineer for Early's division, which was now commanded by Pegram. It would have been a major promotion for OH to become the engineer for the entire AoV.

3. There were high expectations for the arrival of Rosser and his Laurel Brigade, but Early resented his braggadocio. William J. Miller, "'Never Has There Been a More Complete Victory': The Cavalry Engagement at Tom's Brook, October 9, 1864," in *The Shenandoah Valley Campaign of 1864*, ed. Gary W. Gallagher (Chapel Hill: University of North Carolina Press, 2006), 135.

4. Butler's AoJ attacked the Confederate position at New Market Heights and captured Fort Harrison, reversing the latter's massive fortifications. Edward Porter Alexander, *Fighting for the Confederacy: The Personal Recollections of General Edward Porter Alexander*, ed. Gary W. Gallagher (Chapel Hill: University of North Carolina Press, 1989), 475–78.

5. OH's bad luck continued, worsened by the ongoing discontinuity in the command structure for the Second Corps and the AoV.

6. In John L. Heatwole's book on Sheridan's devastation of the valley, he combined primary and secondary documents with oral histories from relatives of people whose property was destroyed and established the "Remember Chambersburg" connection to McCausland's attack on that Pennsylvania city. Heatwole, *The Burning: Sheridan's Devastation of the Shenandoah Valley* (Charlottesville, Va.: Rockbridge Publishing, 1998), 33, 138, 200.

7. Grant wanted Sheridan to extend his army's reach to Charlottesville and Lynchburg. He ordered Halleck to repair the O&A RR to maintain an open supply and communication line. Wert, *Winchester to Cedar Creek*, 141–43.

8. Lieutenant Colonel William S. Davis of the 12th North Carolina now commanded the brigade. Ibid., 103, 110; Clark, *NC Regiments*, 1:643–47.

9. There was no large group of Confederates who escaped from Camp Chase, located four miles west of Columbus, during this period of time. Lonnie R. Speer, *Portals to Hell: Military Prisons of the Civil War* (Mechanicsburg, Pa.: Stackpole Books, 1997), 47, 222–23.

10. The long campaign adversely affected officers like OH and Douglas, who were both having new clothes made. Douglas, *I Rode with Stonewall*, 320.

11. From Arkansas, Price led 12,000 cavalrymen across the Missouri border on September 19 but was repulsed by A. J. Smith. In southwestern Virginia on October 2, Burbridge led approximately 5,000 men on an unsuccessful raid on Saltville. Foote, *Civil War*, 3:575–79; Kennedy, *Civil War Battlefield Guide*, 387.

12. Rosser directed his Laurel Brigade and Wickham's division, which Colonel Thomas T. Munford now led. Wert, *Winchester to Cedar Creek*, 144, 160, 3116.

13. Lomax's brigades dueled with Merritt's horsemen on the Union right flank—just beyond Woodstock—as Sheridan's army advanced down the Valley Pike. Along the Back Road near Little North Mountain, Rosser's men pursued Custer but misinterpreted the Federals' caution for timidity. *OR*, 43(1):431.

14. Polignac and his Texas Brigade were in Arkansas. Richard Taylor crossed the Mississippi River from western Louisiana to take command of the Department of Alabama and Mississippi. Freeman, *Lee's Lieutenants*, 3:595; Alwyn Barr, "Polignac's Texas Brigade," *Texas Gulf Coast Historical Association* 8, no. 1 (November 1864): 50–51.

15. On the morning of October 9, Merritt's men charged 800 of Lomax's ill-equipped troopers on the Valley Pike, while Custer attacked Rosser and his 1,600 men on the Back Road. OH's frustration reflected that of Early, who wrote to Lee about Lomax's cavalrymen and the "Woodstock races" episode, stating that he should "put [them] into the infantry." *OR*, 43(1):431, 559–60, 612.

16. Ibid., 520–22; Miller, "'Complete Victory,'" 142–51.

17. Miller, "'Complete Victory,'" 154–55; *OR*, 43(1):447–48.

18. Davis transferred Hardee to Charleston to command Beauregard's former department. Magruder was still in command of Texas, and Forrest had extended his raid from Alabama into Tennessee, destroying the Nashville & Decatur RR. Stanley F. Horn, *The Army of Tennessee: A Military History* (Indianapolis: Bobbs-Merrill Co., 1941), 372–74; Brian Steel Wills, *A Battle from the Start: The Life of Nathan Bedford Forrest* (New York: HarperCollins, 1992), 261.

19. Three days before—on October 7—Gregg was killed near Richmond. The commander of Hood's Texas Brigade had been one of the ANVA's most reliable brigade commanders. Warner, *Generals in Gray*, 119.

20. Current, *Encyclopedia of the Confederacy*, 3:1363.

21. Although OH received assistance from influential North Carolina leaders to procure a slot in the Engineer Corps, he was not tied to a particular locality or military unit and therefore had trouble gaining access to state resources. Officials in North Carolina tried to provide clothing for their officers and troops, aided by the state's indigenous supply of cotton. OH used the time he spent before the war in Wilmington, and with his stepmother's family in Elizabeth City, to portray himself as a temporary resident of North Carolina. Clark, *NC Regiments*, 1:34–35.

22. Sheridan hoped that most of his AoS would be transferred to the main Richmond-Petersburg front. Wright's Sixth Corps was marching to Front Royal. Wert, *Winchester to Cedar Creek*, 166.

23. On October 7, Lee tried to retake some of his lost earthworks near Fort Harrison. Freeman, *Lee's Lieutenants*, 3:508–9.

24. On October 13, Sheridan's army moved its camp from Hupp's Hill, outside Strasburg, to Cedar Creek. Early's troops initiated contact with 2,000 Yankees from one of Crook's small divisions. The outnumbered rear guard of the AoWV withdrew. Brigadier General Connor, commander of Kershaw's former brigade, suffered a severe leg injury, which required amputation. Theodore C. Mahr, *The Battle of Cedar Creek: Showdown in the Shenandoah, October 1–30, 1864* (Lynchburg, Va.: H. E. Howard, 1992), 64–69; Thomas A. Lewis, *The Guns of Cedar Creek* (New York: Harper & Row, Publishers, 1988), 107–13; Dickert, *Kershaw's Brigade*, 422, 438, 440–41.

25. Brigadier General Thomas C. Devin and his cavalry brigade captured rebel skirmishers during the morning of October 14. Federal troops remained camped behind Cedar Creek south of Middletown. Sheridan recalled the Sixth Corps from Ashby's Gap. After rejoining the main army on October 14, Wright assumed overall command. During the next evening, Sheridan departed for Front Royal and Washington. Wert, *Winchester to Cedar Creek*, 71–73, 169–71; Philip Henry Sheridan, *Personal Memoirs of P. H. Sheridan, General United States Army* (New York: Charles L. Webster & Co., 1888), 2:60–64.

26. After scrutinizing public and private CSA documents regarding Lee's army, historian Robert K. Krick came to the same viewpoint that OH espoused: many officers regarded Robert E. Rodes as the best ANVA division commander. Robert K. Krick, *The Smoothbore Volley That Doomed the Confederacy: The Death of Stonewall Jackson and Other Chapters on the Army of Northern Virginia* (Baton Rouge: Louisiana State University Press, 2002), 117–43.

27. Contrary to OH's attempt to soften Early's losses at Third Winchester and Fisher's Hill, some Richmond newspapers and government officials vilified his commanding officer. Wert, *Winchester to Cedar Creek*, 136–37.

Chapter 20

1. Twenty-one thousand rebels marched toward Cedar Creek to confront 32,000 Yankees commanded by Wright. Early, *Memoir*, 119–20; Wert, *Winchester to Cedar Creek*, 170–72.

2. While Hood's army marched through northern Georgia, Sherman reversed direction and led his "bummers" through the interior of the state. Wiley Sword, *Embrace an Angry Wind: The Confederacy's Last Hurrah — Spring Hill, Franklin, and Nashville* (New York: HarpersCollins Publishers, 1994), 57–61.

3. Pegram and OH reconnoitered along the Back Road. In his journal, Hotchkiss wrote that he and William Allan accompanied them. Hotchkiss, *Make Me a Map*, 237.

4. Pegram again took OH with him to reconnoiter the Federal right flank while Hotchkiss, Gordon, Brigadier General Clement A. Evans, and Gordon's chief of staff climbed Massanutten Mountain. Gordon conceived a plan to strike the vulnerable left flank and rear of the Yankees at dawn. Ibid., 237–38; Stephens, *Intrepid Warrior*, 475–81.

5. Pegram spent the morning at Early's headquarters and climbed up the mountain to confirm the enemy's troop dispositions. After dark, Gordon led three divisions along the base of the mountain for the surprise attack. Hotchkiss, *Make Me a Map*, 238; Gordon, *Reminiscences*, 336–37; *OR*, 43(1):561.

6. Kershaw initiated contact with the Federals at about 5:00 A.M. and Gordon's troops attacked shortly thereafter. The Union army fell back toward Middleton, trying to establish a defensive position along a ridge line. *OR*, 43(1):51–55, 158–59, 279–80, 365–66, 561–62.

7. In what became known as "Sheridan's Ride," the Union commander rode twelve miles from Winchester and led a counterattack around 4:00 P.M. Early had used the six-hour delay—often referred to as the "fatal halt"—to reorganize his troops and stop their plundering of the Federal camps. Sheridan's men drove a wedge through a gap in Gordon's thinly stretched line and Kershaw's troops. (Ramseur was on Kershaw's right, followed by Pegram and Wharton). Ibid., 52–53; Stephens, *Intrepid Warrior*, 482–92; Gordon, *Reminiscences*, 327–72; Keith S. Bohannon, "'The Fatal Halt' versus 'Bad Conduct': John B. Gordon, Jubal A. Early, and the Battle of Cedar Creek," in *The Shenandoah Valley Campaign of 1864*, ed. Gary W. Gallagher (Chapel Hill: University of North Carolina Press, 2006), 56–78.

8. Soldiers on Early's left flank, surprised by Custer's charge, frantically turned and ran. The divisions of Ramseur and Pegram held their ground but got caught up in the stampede. The rebel rear guard took flight up the Valley Pike. Taken to Sheridan's headquarters at Belle Grove, Ramseur died the next morning. *OR*, 43(1):415, 434–35, 599–600; Gallagher, *Ramseur*, 161–65.

9. OH's half brother Chris returned to New York City, where their parents lived.

10. OH was correct in his prediction that newspapers would credit Gordon for his "masterly flank attack" and blame Early for overall mismanagement of the battle. Bohannon, "'Fatal Halt,'" 71–72.

11. Accusations about Early's drinking appeared in Southern newspapers and personal correspondence, but no one produced any evidence. Early responded to the Senate Military Commission. Gary W. Gallagher, "'Two Generals and a Valley': Philip H. Sheridan and Jubal A. Early," in *The Shenandoah Valley Campaign of 1864*, ed. Gary W. Gallagher (Chapel Hill: University of North Carolina Press, 2006), 18; Charles C. Osborne, *Jubal: The Life and Times of General Jubal A. Early, CSA, Defender of the Lost Cause* (Chapel Hill: Algonquin Books of Chapel Hill, 1992), 382–83.

12. Early noted that Lomax "had been sent down the Luray Valley, was ordered to pass Front Royal, cross the river, and move across toward the Valley Pike." *OR*, 43(1):561.

13. Krick, *Staff Officers*, 292–93.

14. After serving on the staff of Stuart, Jenifer conducted inspections in 1864. Ibid., 171.

15. On October 25–26, Sheridan's horse soldiers tried to get around Early's rear, but Lomax defeated them in the Luray valley. Dearing participated in fighting near Petersburg but was not a casualty. (One of Wade Hampton's sons was KIA.) Gilmor, *Four Years in the Saddle*, 254, 271–73; Millard K. Bushong, *Old Jube: A Biography of General Jubal A. Early* (Boyce, Va.: Carr Publishing Co., 1955), 266; Freeman, *Lee's Lieutenants*, 3:615–16.

16. Early tried to shift blame to his officers and undisciplined soldiers while privately admitting to Hotchkiss he had made a mistake in not following up on the morning's successes. Early intimated that Gordon had been involved in plundering a sutler's wagon at Cedar Creek. Hotchkiss, *Make Me a Map*, 241; Osborne, *Jubal*, 381.

17. Mosby's men captured Duffié on the Winchester-Martinsburg Pike. John Scott, *Partisan Life with Col. John S. Mosby* (New York: Harper & Bros., Publishers, 1867), 350–51.

18. Trudeau, *Last Citadel*, 248, 250.

19. On October 23, the Battle of Westport was fought south of Kansas City. It was the last major battle west of the Mississippi River. Albert Castel, *General Sterling Price and the Civil War in the West* (Baton Rouge: Louisiana State University Press, 1968), 222–37.

20. On the Tennessee River, Forrest captured a Union gunboat and a transport ship.

21. NAMP M331A, Reel 124.

22. Warner, *Generals in Gray*, 230.

23. Sheridan sent his cavalry to strike the rebel flanks. Rosser brought up reinforcements on the Back Road and repelled Custer. In the Luray valley, Powell's larger force fought against McCausland's cavalry at Cedarville. *OR*, 43(1):614.

24. Charles Stanley was exchanged and released from Fort Delaware, located south of Philadelphia on Pea Patch Island, in August 1864. After being hospitalized at Richmond and Staunton, he would return for duty in December. Driver, *First & Second Maryland Cavalry*, 288; Brian Temple, *The Union Prison at Fort Delaware: A Perfect Hell on Earth* (Jefferson, N.C.: McFarland & Co., 2003), 1–18.

25. There is nothing in Gorgas's journal that provides any insights into the "French affair." Josiah Gorgas, *The Civil War Diary of General Josiah Gorgas*, ed. Frank E. Vandiver (Tuscaloosa: University of Alabama Press, 1947), 151–52.

26. Forrest lost his captured vessels but at Johnsonville destroyed gunboats, transports, and barges along with well-stocked warehouses. Foote, *Civil War*, 3:619–20.

27. The USS *Wachusetts* seized the CSS *Florida* in Bahia Harbor in Brazil on October 7. Collins returned the *Wachusetts* to Virginia with the rebel commerce raider in tow. At Hampton Roads, the *Florida* "accidentally sank." The CSS *Tallahassee*, with her name changed to CSS *Olustee*, harassed Union shipping along the Atlantic coast. Gorgas, *Civil War Diary*, 162; Current, *Encyclopedia of the Confederacy*, 4:591–92, 1567.

28. During the night of October 27, Cushing led a surprise Union raid on Plymouth, North Carolina, with a crew of twenty-five men. Barrett, *Civil War NC*, 213–31.

29. Two Union cavalry divisions advanced to Mount Jackson but were driven back by Early's infantry. Early, *Memoir*, 123.

30. Congressman Smith from North Carolina continued to help OH, probably due to his relationship with the Ehringhauses.

31. The Kilpatrick-Dahlgren raid prompted Confederate leaders to unleash a series of nonmilitary attacks, which included attempts to seize Great Lakes ships, free rebels in northern prisons, and invade St. Albans, Vt. New York City was an inviting target since it was a hotbed of Southern sympathizers. Taking advantage of his father's position as consul and alleged unrest among the city's 120,000 Germans, OH considered creating a situation similar to what happened with the Draft Riots. Brandt, *Man Who Tried to Burn New York*, 68, 82.

Chapter 21

1. Sheridan reported that, from August 10 to November 16, his AoS captured ninety-four cannons, 23,000 rounds of ordnance, more than 19,000 small arms, and 1 million rounds of small-arm ammunition, plus almost 4,000 horses. *OR*, 43(1):37.

2. On November 25, Colonel Robert M. Martin (10th Kentucky Cavalry) and a band of rebel agents unsuccessfully tried to burn down New York City hotels. Federal officials uncovered the arson plot that was planned for Election Day. Brandt, *Man Who Tried to Burn New York*, 65–124; Jane Singer, *The Confederate Dirty War: Arson, Bombings, Assassination and Plots for Chemical and Germ Attacks on the Union* (Jefferson, N.C.: McFarland & Co., 2005), 51–66.

3. OH might have written to Colonel William P. Smith, Early's engineer officer. Krick, *Staff Officers*, 255, 271.

4. George Lemmon, who had helped OH to enter the Confederacy, was captured at Gettysburg and recently released. For information on John Pegram's brother, see Peter S. Carmichael, *Lee's Young Artillerist: William R. J. Pegram* (Charlottesville: University of Virginia Press, 1995).

5. Trudeau, *Last Citadel*, 262–84. Please also see the series by Edwin C. Bearss with Bryce Suderow, *The Petersburg Campaign: The Eastern Front Battles, June–August 1864*, vol. 1 (El Dorado Hills, Calif.: Savas Beatie, 2012), and *The Petersburg Campaign: The Western Front Battles, September 1864–April 1865*, vol. 2 (El Dorado Hills, Calif.: Savas Beatie, 2013).

6. Cleburne, known as the "Stonewall of the West," died of wounds incurred during Hood's senseless charge at Franklin on November 30. Irving A. Buck, *Cleburne and His Command* (New York: Neale Publishing Co., 1908), 326–46.

7. On December 13, Sherman's soldiers overcame Fort McAllister, an earthen fort located below Savannah. E. B. Long with Barbara Long, *The Civil War Day by Day: An Almanac 1861–1865* (New York: Da Capo Press, 1985), 609–10.

8. Hood lost about 20 percent of his troops at Franklin. Five general officers, including Cleburne, were killed, mortally wounded, or captured. Thomas Robson Hay, *Hood's Tennessee Campaign* (New York: Neale Publishing, 1929), 130.

9. Two days earlier, Evans wrote to his wife describing how Gordon's troops were "stationed on the extreme right" as part of a thirty-mile-long "connected line of works." Stephens, *Intrepid Warrior*, 523–24.

10. At Nashville on December 15–16, Thomas's troops overpowered the rebels, capturing more than 4,000 prisoners and fifty-three artillery pieces. Stanley F. Horn, *The Army of Tennessee: A Military History* (Indianapolis: Bobbs-Merrill Co., 1941), 417.

11. Butler reached New Inlet, at the mouth of the Cape Fear River, on December 15, but Porter was late. Gragg, *Confederate Goliath*, 46–49.

12. On December 18, Porter's fleet of fifty-six warships belatedly rendezvoused with Butler's transport ships. The division of Major General Bushrod R. Johnson remained in the Petersburg defenses. Kirkland assumed responsibility for Martin's brigade in Hoke's division and led his soldiers to Wilmington on December 21. Fonvielle, *Wilmington Campaign*, 114–15.

13. Hetty Cary from Baltimore was considered to be one of the most beautiful women in the South. Along with her sister Jennie, she made uniforms for Maryland's rebel soldiers, smuggled contraband across Union lines, and sewed the first St. Andrew's Cross battle flag. Jennie also put the "Maryland, My Maryland" poem to music, and the sisters often sang the song at social events. While waiting to be exchanged in the spring of 1862, John Pegram

met Hetty in Richmond, where his mother lived, and they fell in love. Griggs, *John Pegram*, 39–47.

14. New had been an assistant adjutant and inspector general for Generals Hays, Early, and Ramseur. Daniel served as assistant adjutant general on the staffs of Generals Lilley, James A. Walker, and Pegram. Krick, *Staff Officers*, 109, 230; Crute, *Confederate Staff Officers*, 147.

15. Fort Branch, at Rainbow Bend on the Roanoke River, housed a 32-pound cannon and three smoothbore 24-pounders, which protected the Wilmington-Weldon RR bridge. On December 9, 1864, 1,500 soldiers under Brigadier General Innis N. Palmer unsuccessfully attacked Fort Branch. (North of Plymouth, a Union gunboat and a tugboat sank when they ran into rebel torpedoes.) Ed Johnson spent five weeks in the Fort Delaware prison. On August 5, the War Department sent him to Georgia just in time for the fall of Atlanta. At Nashville, Johnson was recaptured and sent to Fort Warren in Boston Harbor. Clint Johnson, *Touring the Carolinas' Civil War Sites* (Winston-Salem, N.C.: John F. Blair, Publisher, 1996), 80–82; Clemmer, *Old Alleghany*, 577–630.

16. Barringer, a North Carolina commander in W. H. F. "Rooney" Lee's division, was a well-respected cavalry leader. On December 21, Rosser repelled Custer's troopers near Harrisonburg, while Lomax went to Gordonsville to attack other Federal horse soldiers. After these cavalry forays were stopped, Early retired to Staunton—with Wharton's division, his artillery, and Rosser's cavalry—as the 1864 operations in the Shenandoah valley came to a close. Mary Bandy Daughtry, *Gray Cavalier: The Life and Wars of General W. H. F. "Rooney" Lee* (Cambridge, Mass.: Da Capo Press, 2002), 209–11; Early, *Memoir*, 126–27.

17. McNeely from North Carolina served under Ramseur and became assistant quartermaster for Pegram in December. Holladay worked as an ordnance officer for Robert D. Johnston. Krick, *Staff Officers*, 162, 211.

18. Gragg, *Confederate Goliath*, 40, 50–98.

19. Howard entered the Engineer Corps with OH during February of the following year. He served under A. P. Hill. Krick, *Staff Officers*, 164.

20. "Fort Fisher had withstood the greatest naval bombardment in history." Fonvielle, *Wilmington Campaign*, 178.

21. William T. Sherman, *Memoirs of General William T. Sherman, By Himself* (New York: Chas. L. Webster & Co., 1892), 2:231.

22. See George H. Miles, "God Save the South," in H. M. Wharton, *War Songs and Poems of the Southern Confederacy, 1861–1865* (Washington, D.C.: W. E. Scull, 1904), 281–83.

Chapter 22

1. The 20th North Carolina was formed in southeastern North Carolina at Smithville and Fort Caswell in June 1861. Alfred Iverson was the regiment's first colonel, followed by Thomas F. Toon. Clark, *NC Regiments*, 110–27.

2. Porter set off explosives on an expendable ship during the night of December 23–24 before Butler's transport vessels arrived back from refueling at Beaufort. Gragg, *Confederate Goliath*, 40–41, 50–53, 76–95.

3. At Edward's Ferry—located "about halfway between Hamilton and the Weldon railroad bridges"—the Confederates built the CSS *Albemarle* and sent it fifty miles downriver to Plymouth, where it harassed Union vessels until Lieutenant Cushing blew it up. John M. Coski, *Capital Navy: The Men, Ships, and Operations of the James River Squadron* (Campbell, Calif.: Savas Woodbury Publishers, 1996), 66; *OR*, 46(2):251–52.

4. Mulford from the 3rd New York Infantry was assistant agent for the exchange of prisoners at Fort Monroe. John H. Eicher and David J. Eicher, *Civil War High Commands* (Stanford, Calif.: Stanford University Press, 2001), 401.

5. Butler ordered construction of Dutch Gap Canal to cut off a long loop of the James downriver from Drewry's Bluff. *OR*, 46(2):164.

6. Douglas went to a series of weddings, which were attended by other officers, such as Longstreet, Fitzhugh Lee, and Lomax. Hetty and Jennie Cary were part of the Richmond high-society social scene. They started "Starvation Parties"—with music, dancing, and James River water but no food—to entertain officers on furlough. While Pegram was stationed outside Petersburg, he asked Hetty's mother during the Christmas holidays for her daughter's hand in marriage; the wedding date was set for January 19. Douglas, *I Rode with Stonewall*, 322–23; Griggs, *John Pegram*, 86–87, 113–14; Mary Boykin Chestnut, *A Diary from Dixie* (New York: D. Appleton & Co., 1905), 244, 260, 272–73.

7. On January 7, Grant promoted Major General Edward O. C. Ord, who served under him at Vicksburg, to replace Butler. *OR*, 46(2):61.

8. During the Tennessee Campaign, Hood lost two-thirds of his army.

9. Lincoln sent veteran politician Francis P. Blair Sr. on a flag of truce steamer up the James River to meet with Davis. *OR*, 46(2):177.

10. Porter began his second bombardment of Fort Fisher with five ironclads and fifty-four other warships (mounting a total of 627 guns) during the morning of January 13. Major General Alfred H. Terry, in charge of 9,000 AoJ soldiers, led his men ashore. Bragg had withdrawn Hoke's 6,000 soldiers to march in a parade through Wilmington. Gragg, *Confederate Goliath*, 102–37; Fonvielle, *Wilmington Campaign*, 207–33.

11. Whiting disobeyed Bragg's orders and joined Lamb in defending Fort Fisher. He bravely fought on January 15 alongside his soldiers. Fonvielle, *Wilmington Campaign*, 233–96; Gragg, *Confederate Goliath*, 138–229.

12. Bragg withdrew his men from all of the forts below the Sugar Loaf–Fort Anderson line, but it was anticlimactic since the Yankees had already sealed off the Confederacy's last major port. Fonvielle, *Wilmington Campaign*, 302.

13. Farley, from South Carolina, was on the staff of Major General Pierce M. B. Young in Hampton's Cavalry Corps. Krick, *Staff Officers*, 125.

14. The *Sentinel* article regarded "as treason the proposition before the House in secret session to open negotiations for peace." *OR*, 46(2):163.

15. The wedding of John Pegram and Hetty Cary was held at St. Paul's Episcopal Church in Richmond. Historian Peter Carmichael wrote that the bride and bridegroom celebrated their honeymoon at a "pleasant farmhouse nine miles south of Petersburg," which the general was using for his headquarters. Peter S. Carmichael, *Lee's Young Artillerist: William R. J. Pegram* (Charlottesville: University of Virginia Press, 1995), 154–55.

16. The Confederates incurred approximately 500 losses in defending Fort Fisher. The remainder of the 1,900 rebel troops became POWs. Gragg, *Confederate Goliath*, 235.

17. Davis asked Bragg to retake Fort Fisher, but the Wilmington commander refused. Fonvielle, *Wilmington Campaign*, 301.

18. Whiting was "hit twice and severely wounded in the right thigh." Lamb was shot in the hip. Gragg, *Confederate Goliath*, 192, 201; Fonvielle, *Wilmington Campaign*, 284.

19. Krick, *Staff Officers*, 139, 287.

20. "Turner" may have been Franklin P. Turner, quartermaster for Armistead Long, who had served with OH on Jackson's staff in 1862. Confederate leaders sent gunboats from their James River Squadron downriver during the night of January 23–24 to destroy Grant's supply depot at City Point. Ibid., 289; Coski, *Capital Navy*, 195–206.

21. The CSA naval offensive turned into a debacle when two of the heavy-draft ironclads got hung up and some of the other boats were damaged. Coski, *Capital Navy*, 206–11.

22. Palmer, commanding the District of North Carolina, notified Grant on January 24 that he had sent a small expedition up the Roanoke River to destroy a new ram. *OR*, 46(2):251–52.

23. Charles Bolles, OH's former Coast Survey superior who helped to start Fort Fisher, was still at Fayetteville serving as chief of the armory's ordnance laboratory and inspector of ordnance. He also commanded Child's armory battalion. Charles P. Bolles Papers, North Carolina State Archives.

24. Huston would be KIA on February 6. Colonel John W. Lea's "recuperating leave" was due to the wound he received at Third Winchester. Krick, *Lee's Colonels*, 202–4, 232; *OR*, 46(1):1270.

25. *OR*, 46(2):303; Jones, *Rebel War Clerk's Diary*, 2:385, 392; Current, *Encyclopedia of the Confederacy*, 2:599–600.

Chapter 23

1. Hetty Pegram was at the parade on February 2 when Gordon reviewed her husband's troops. Generals Lee, Longstreet, and Hill and other senior generals attended, too. Griggs, *John Pegram*, 115–16.

2. On February 18, 1865, Peck would be promoted to brigadier general. Warner, *Generals in Gray*, 231.

3. There had been previous suggestions about arming black slaves; for example, Cleburne raised the issue in January 1864. At the beginning of 1865, Lee advocated the same position. Mississippi congressman Ethelbert Barksdale would introduce a bill on February 10 that allowed acceptance of slaves for military service. The CSA Congress passed the bill on March 13, but it was too late. William C. Davis, *Look Away!* (New York: The Free Press, 2002), 157–60.

4. Meade led G. Warren's Fifth Corps and two divisions of A. A. Humphreys's Second Corps toward Hatcher's Run. The Federals set up breastworks on Lee's right flank as Pegram's division tried to keep the Boydton Plank Road open. Trudeau, *Last Citadel*, 312–14; Chris M. Calkins, *History and Tour Guide of Five Forks, Hatcher's Run and Namozine Church* (Columbus, Ohio: Blue & Gray Enterprises, 2003), 8–14.

5. Evans commanded the three brigades of Gordon's division that helped to anchor the right side of the Petersburg line. Brigades from Heth's division, including Cooke's brigade, joined them from A. P. Hill's Corps. They assaulted the Union position but were unsuccessful. Ibid., 14–16, 172–73; Greene, *Breaking the Rebellion*, 143–46.

6. Lewis's and Johnston's brigades, along with Rooney Lee's cavalry, marched toward Gravelly Run, where they encountered AoP cavalry. Federal infantry arrived, and the fighting continued until late afternoon. From OH's description, it appears that he participated in this action along Vaughan Road. Pegram reconnoitered near the defunct Dabney sawmill. Trudeau, *Last Citadel*, 318.

7. Gordon's Second Corps confronted Warren's divisions. The CSA charge led to the death of Pegram and the wounding of Hoffman. Finegan brought up Mahone's division. "The whole line now advanced to the attack," wrote Gordon in his report, "and drove the enemy in confusion to his works along the bank of the creek." Ibid., 318–21; *OR*, 46(1):390–92.

8. According to Douglas, "Pegram was shot through the body near the heart" and died in his arms. His account of Pegram's body being placed on his bed, written almost thirty-five years after the Battle of Hatcher's Run, conflicts with OH's contemporaneous diary. A deci-

sion was made to delay notifying Hetty Pegram about the death of her husband. Major New from Louisiana, one of OH's friends, informed Pegram's wife and mother-in-law the next day. Douglas, *I Rode with Stonewall*, vii, 327; Griggs, *John Pegram*, 117–20.

9. Trudeau, *Last Citadel*, 321–22.

10. On February 28, Grimes would receive his promotion to command Rodes's division, becoming the last major general to be appointed in the ANVA. The number of CSA casualties reported for the Battle of Hatcher's Run (1,000) appear to have been generated by Douglas. OH's in-the-field estimate of 200 may be more accurate. T. Harwell Allen, *Lee's Last Major General: Bryan Grimes of North Carolina* (Mason City, Iowa: Savas Publishing Co., 1999), 228–33; Douglas, *I Rode with Stonewall*, 327.

11. Schofield was not at Petersburg. Grant had assigned him to be commander of the Military Department of North Carolina. *OR*, 46(2):312–14.

12. Since August 1864, Williams had served in the field, most recently with Hill's staff at Petersburg. The "new front line," for which OH supervised construction, was most likely the fortifications along White Oak Road. Today, the Civil War Trust has protected a portion of those extant fortifications as part of a park. Krick, *Staff Officers*, 304.

13. OH's notation about burning Charles Stanley's "undecipherable letter," combined with the knowledge he gained working his way in late 1861 through the Secret Line in Southern Maryland, reinforces the impression they communicated by means of a Confederate cipher. In *Come Retribution*, the authors included the photo of a cipher found in John Wilkes Booth's hotel. Some of the CSA phrases used in ciphering were: "Manchester Bluff," "Complete Victory," and "Come Retribution." Perhaps OH or his future brother-in-law had lost track of the latest cipher-decipher phrase. Tidwell, *Come Retribution*, 40, 62.

14. Meade reported losing more than 1,500 men in the fighting between February 5 and 7. Greene, *Breaking the Rebellion*, 149.

15. North Carolina soldiers deserted to protect their families from Sherman's advancing army. Joseph T. Glatthaar, *The March to the Sea and Beyond: Sherman's Troops in the Savannah and Carolinas Campaigns* (New York: New York University Press, 1985), 136–55.

16. Mamie, OH's future wife, was the daughter of the Reverend Harvey Stanley and Mary Anne Kinney Stanley. Mary Anne had grown up in Elizabeth City with Amalia Hinrichs (OH's stepmother), and they remained close friends.

17. Bragg led his diminished army toward Goldsboro in hopes of uniting with Johnston and Hardee. "Cullen" was probably Captain George Cullen, commander of the 13th Virginia in Pegram's old brigade. Dr. Boissieux lived near the Dabney Mill site where Pegram was shot. Fonvielle, *Wilmington Campaign*, 424–33; *OR*, 46(2):1270; Calkins, *History and Tour Guide of Five Forks*, 136.

18. During the night of February 20–21, sixty of McNeill's Partisan Rangers entered a Union garrison at Cumberland, Maryland, and captured Crook and Kelly. Cavalrymen escorted the Federal officers to Richmond. During the train ride, they met Mosby, who complimented them on conducting one of the most daring raids of the war. Delauter, *McNeill's Rangers*, 95–105.

Chapter 24

1. In 1951 author James Horan discovered the papers of Captain Thomas Hines, who had been a Confederate agent with John Y. Beall. During the 1862 Shenandoah Valley Campaign, Beall served under Stonewall Jackson (his brother William was in the ANVA, too) and later became a privateer, harassing Union vessels on the Chesapeake Bay. In the fall of 1864, he hoped to commandeer the USS *Michigan*, the only Yankee gunboat on Lake Erie, and use

it to free prisoners on Johnson's Island. The plan failed, and Union detectives arrested him. During the court-martial, Beall was found guilty of being a rebel spy and hanged on February 24. James D. Horan, *Confederate Agent: A Discovery in History* (New York: Crown Publishers, 1954), 153–64, 230–31, 255–59; Tidwell, *Come Retribution*, 199–203, 336.

2. Bragg ordered most of the cotton and tobacco in Wilmington to be destroyed before leaving. Fonvielle, *Wilmington Campaign*, 421–22.

3. At the end of February 1865, Sheridan moved south with 10,000 cavalrymen—the divisions of Custer and Merritt—and confronted Early's small force at Waynesboro. Millard K. Bushong, *Old Jube: A Biography of General Jubal A. Early* (Boyce, Va.: Carr Publishing Co., 1955), 277–78.

4. On March 2, Custer's dismounted cavalrymen, with their seven-shot Spencer carbines, flanked Early's soldiers at Waynesboro. The rebels turned and ran, losing almost everything they had with them. Only Early, Wharton, Rosser, and a small number of soldiers escaped. On March 29, Lee ordered Early to return to his home in Lynchburg to await further orders—which never came. Charles C. Osborne, *Jubal: The Life and Times of General Jubal A. Early, CSA, Defender of the Lost Cause* (Chapel Hill, N.C.: Algonquin Books of Chapel Hill, 1992), 384–92.

5. In his January returns, Gordon highlighted the growing desertion problem (only a third of his 34,000 men were present for duty). OH's diary entries for the latter part of the war reflected his own weariness with the fighting. *OR*, 46(1):383; J. Tracy Power, *Lee's Miserables: Life in the Army of Northern Virginia from the Wilderness to Appomattox* (Chapel Hill: University of North Carolina Press, 1998), 307–21.

6. On March 8, approximately 6,000 soldiers in Hoke's division attacked two Yankee divisions at Wise's (or Wyse's) Fork. Bragg had overall command. The rebels captured almost 1,000 bluecoats. Barrett, *Civil War NC*, 285–90; Daniel W. Barefoot, *General Robert F. Hoke: Lee's Modest Warrior* (Winston-Salem, N.C.: John F. Blair, Publisher, 1996), 283–91.

7. On March 10, Hampton's cavalry surprised Kilpatrick and his Federal cavalry that were camped west of Fayetteville. Mark L. Bradley, *Last Stand in the Carolinas: The Battle of Bentonville* (Campbell, Calif.: Savas Woodbury Publishers, 1996), 81–104. See also Eric J. Wittenberg's *The Battle of Monroe's Crossroads and the Civil War's Final Campaign* (New York: Savas Beatie, 2006).

8. Jarratt's Station was located thirty miles south of Petersburg on the Weldon RR below the Stony Creek Station. Grimes led his men north of the Appomattox River instead of south to Jarratt's Station. Trudeau, *Last Citadel*, 89; T. Harwell Allen, *Lee's Last Major General: Bryan Grimes of North Carolina* (Mason City, Iowa: Savas Publishing Co., 1999), 235–36.

9. Lee summoned Gordon in the middle of the night on March 4 to discuss contingency strategies. Gordon developed a more-detailed plan, which he presented to Lee on March 22. Greene, *Breaking the Rebellion*, 151–57.

10. Dimmock took advantage of the social opportunities afforded by being stationed for over two years in Petersburg. Krick, *Staff Officers*, 114; A. Wilson Greene, *Civil War Petersburg: Confederate City in the Crucible of War* (Charlottesville, Va.: University of Virginia Press, 2006), 88–89, 98, 233.

11. Bradford was captain of Company H in the First Regiment Engineer Corps, which focused on maintaining Richmond's defenses. Jackson, *First Regiment Engineer Troops*, 21, 46, 108.

12. At Bentonville on March 19, Confederate generals Johnston, Hardee, and Cheatham led their troops in a valiant but disappointing attempt to stop Sherman's march through North Carolina. See also Nathaniel Cheairs Hughes Jr., *Bentonville: The Final Battle of Sherman and Johnson* (Chapel Hill: University of North Carolina Press, 1996).

13. Gordon attacked with 11,500 men and made strong initial progress, but Pickett's reinforcements did not arrive in time for support. Gordon, *Reminiscences*, 395–413.

14. Grant's troops attacked the Confederate picket line in front of Forts Gregg and Whitworth and the Boydton Plank Road. To the east, the brigades of McGowan, Lane, and Brigadier General Edward L. Thomas from Wilcox's division (Hill's corps) contended with Wright's Sixth Corps. As noted by OH, this part of the March 25 action, known as the Battle of Jones's Farm, began at about 1:00 P.M. Greene, *Breaking the Rebellion*, 160–85.

15. A current projection for CSA casualties is 2,700. McLaughlen became a brevet brigadier general of volunteers on September 30, 1864. Trudeau, *Last Citadel*, 353–54; Greene, *Breaking the Rebellion*, 156–60; Roger D. Hunt and Jack R. Brown, *Brevet Brigadier Generals in Blue* (Gaithersburg, Md.: Olde Soldier Books, 1990), 404.

Chapter 25

1. Anderson's new corps contained Bushrod Johnson's division and four artillery battalions. After Robert Johnston was wounded at Spotsylvania, Toon temporarily became a brigadier general and commanded his division until August 1864. Resuming his colonelcy, Toon led the 20th North Carolina until he was wounded—his seventh injury—at Fort Stedman. *OR*, 46(1)1274; Warner, *Generals in Gray*, 307–8.

2. Captain Richard S. Harris, Robert Johnston's quartermaster, may have been "Harris." After Bentonville, Sherman joined Lincoln and Grant on March 27 for a meeting aboard the *River Queen*. Krick, *Staff Officers*, 150.

3. OH continued his friendship with Major William W. Thornton from Walker's staff.

4. Sheridan's horsemen sidled west to Dinwiddie Court House, followed by Warren's Fifth Corps and Humphreys's Second Corps. Hall had served on the staffs of Trimble and Hoke and was now inspecting CSA troops. "Mercer" was probably Major George D. Mercer, the chief quartermaster for Gordon's Second Corps. Greene, *Breaking the Rebellion*, 207–8; Krick, *Staff Officers*, 146, 220.

5. Bushrod Johnson and his troops tried to prevent Warren's corps from controlling the intersection at the Boydton Plank and Quaker Roads, located just above Gravelly Run. Heavy fighting took place, with each side losing 300 to 400 men. This engagement is known as either the Battle of Lewis's Farm or the Battle of Quaker Road (or Gravelly Run). *OR*, 46(1)796–803, 1286–87; Greene, *Breaking the Rebellion*, 207–15.

6. Lee began to move his wagons north of the Appomattox River for a possible retrograde movement. A banker, William C. Banister, was KIA defending Petersburg in June 1864. His daughters, Anne and Molly, were among the local young women who attended social gatherings with officers such Captain Dimmock. A. Wilson Greene, *Civil War Petersburg: Confederate City in the Crucible of War* (Charlottesville: University of Virginia Press, 2006), 127, 179, 228, 233; Chris M. Calkins, *Auto Tour of Civil War Petersburg, 1861–1865* (Petersburg: City of Petersburg, 2003), 28.

7. Gouverneur Warren, a preeminent Federal engineer, believed that the White Oak Road defenses, whose construction OH had been overseeing, were well built. Lee sent Pickett with 10,000 soldiers to Five Forks. Ed Bearss and Chris Calkins, *The Battle of Five Forks* (Lynchburg, Va.: H. E. Howard, 1985), 8–10.

8. Troops on Lee's right flank attacked two Federal divisions south of White Oak Road. They drove the bluecoats back, capturing as many as 500 prisoners. Union reinforcements arrived and regained the position. Greene, *Breaking the Rebellion*, 225–33; *OR*, 46(1)677, 807–25, 1287–88; Warner, *Generals in Gray*, 146.

9. Pickett and Fitzhugh Lee rode north across Hatcher's Run to have lunch with Rosser,

infamously known as the "shad bake." By the time Pickett reached the front, his men were in disarray. Fitzhugh Lee escaped north to the railroad. Edwin C. Bearss, *Fields of Honor* (Washington, D.C.: National Geographic, 2006), 381–89; Bearss, *Five Forks*, 75–113.

10. Freeman, *Lee's Lieutenants*, 3:675–86.

11. Early on the morning of April 2, Getty's division of Wright's Sixth Corps drove their "wedge" through Lane's brigade. Lee ordered Heth to take over A. P. Hill's Third Corps. Cooke assumed his command, protecting the Southside RR until outflanked. Greene, *Breaking the Rebellion*, 293–360, 430–40; James I. Robertson Jr., *General A. P. Hill: The Story of a Confederate Warrior* (New York: Vintage Books, 1987), 314–18.

12. Lee evacuated his troops from Richmond and Petersburg and arranged for them to rendezvous at Amelia Court House. From there, the Confederates would advance south to Danville and merge with Johnston's army, possibly around Greensboro. The last of the Second Corps left Petersburg at about 1:30 A.M., after which OH supervised burning the Pocahontas Bridge. Gordon and his troops followed in the wake of Longstreet's troops; their wagon train proceeded up Woodpecker Road to Goode's Bridge. William Marvel, *Lee's Last Retreat: The Flight to Appomattox* (Chapel Hill: University of North Carolina Press, 2002), 7, 20–26.

13. Upon discovering that Bevill's Bridge was flooded, Lee, Longstreet, and Gordon were forced to cross the Appomattox at Goode's Bridge. Chris M. Calkins, *The Appomattox Campaign, March 29–April 9, 1865* (Conshohocken, Pa.: Combined Books, 1997), 58–59, 63–75; Marvel, *Lee's Last Retreat*, 27–40.

14. Lee was appalled to find that, instead of 350,000 rations for his troops, Richmond's commissaries had sent primarily ordnance stores. Marvel, *Lee's Last Retreat*, 41–52; Calkins, *Appomattox Campaign*, 75–79.

15. With the path to Danville blocked, Lee redirected his soldiers to Lynchburg. They had to make a twenty-three-mile night march to reach Farmville on the Southside RR. Freeman, *Lee's Lieutenants*, 3:691–97; Bearss, *Fields of Honor*, 393–96.

16. Gordon protected the rear guard, including a large portion of the ANVA's wagons and artillery. At Deatonville, his men withstood an aggressive attack by A. A. Humphreys's Second Corps. (This was where Lewis lost most of his brigade.) At Holt's Crossroads, Gordon's column turned right toward Lockett's Mill. Nightfall prevented a disaster. Marvel, *Lee's Last Retreat*, 67–75, 88–91.

17. Gordon's corps suffered immeasurably during the fighting at Lockett's farm, losing 1,700 men, three cannons, 270 wagons/ambulances, and thirteen battle flags. Losses at Little Sailor Creek and Marshall Crossroads were even more devastating for Lee. Ibid., 78–87, 91–94; Calkins, *Appomattox Campaign*, 97–117; Greg Eanes, *The Battles of Sailor's Creek* (Burkeville, Va.: E & H Publishing Co., 2001), 41–137.

18. Lee lost about 20 percent of his combat troops on April 6. Calkins, *Appomattox Campaign*, 114–15; Marvel, *Lee's Last Retreat*, 118–19.

19. Tracks for the Southside RR crossed the Appomattox River at High Bridge, which, with a length of 2,400 feet and an apex of 125 feet, was one of the largest bridges during that era. A wagon bridge was located underneath High Bridge. Company G of the First Engineer Regiment, commanded by Colonel Thomas M. R. Talcott, worked during the night of April 6–7, burning four of High Bridge's twenty spans. His team only started a superficial fire on the wagon bridge, which Humphreys's Second Corps extinguished. OH helped Talcott and his men to disable High Bridge, but he was gone by the time they tried to burn the wagon bridge. Jackson, *First Regiment Engineer Troops*, 146–50; Marvel, *Lee's Last Retreat*, 119–23; William Marvel, *A Place Called Appomattox* (Chapel Hill: University of North Carolina Press, 2000), 286–87.

20. Gordon's troops brought up the rear, turning north to Cumberland Church. Crook's cavalrymen struck their wagon train. Lewis and several hundred men from his depleted brigade, along with cannoneers from the famed Washington Artillery, resisted them. OH was wounded but fared better than Lewis, who was left behind. Marvel, *Lee's Last Retreat*, 126–30; William Miller Owen, *In Camp and Battle with the Washington Artillery of New Orleans* (Boston: Ticknor & Co., 1885), 378–79.

21. Grant's army converged from three directions. Before midnight, Lee met with Generals Longstreet, Gordon, and Fitzhugh Lee to develop a plan for the next day. They decided to break through the Yankee line near Appomattox Court House. Chris M. Calkins, *The Battles of Appomattox Station and Appomattox Court House, April 8–9, 1865* (Lynchburg, Va.: H. E. Howard, 1987), 7–55.

22. At sunrise on April 9, Gordon advanced his troops. Confederate sharpshooters, whom OH helped to lead despite his wound, were initially effective with their longer-range rifles against a small cavalry force but gave ground. Lee contacted Grant about surrendering. Ibid., 57–149; Stephens, *Intrepid Warrior*, 551–53; Fred L. Ray, *Shock Troops of the Confederacy: The Sharpshooter Battalions of the Army of Northern Virginia* (Ashville, N.C.: CFS Press, 2006), 268.

23. During the truce, Custer confronted Gordon's troops and demanded their surrender. Longstreet chastised him. Around 3:00 P.M., Lee rode up to the home of Wilmer McLean. Grant joined him in the parlor and offered liberal surrender terms, which Lee accepted. See Frank P. Cauble's *The Surrender Proceedings: April 9, 1865, Appomattox Court House* (Lynchburg, Va.: H. E. Howard, 1987). James Longstreet, *From Manassas to Appomattox* (Philadelphia: J. B. Lippincott Co., 1896), 627.

24. Grant instructed his soldiers to provide the rebels with food. Freeman, *Lee's Lieutenants*, 3:741; Elisha Hunt Rhodes, *All for the Union*, ed. Robert Hunt Rhodes (New York: Orion Books, 1991), 230.

25. Colonel Lea commanded at Appomattox in place of Robert Johnston. There is no evidence as to what the "special treaty" was that they wanted to address at Grant's headquarters. Krick, *Lee's Colonels*, 232; Chris M. Calkins, *The Final Bivouac: The Surrender Parade at Appomattox and the Disbanding of the Armies, April 10–May 20, 1865* (Lynchburg, Va.: H. E. Howard, 1988), 1–21.

26. Ibid., 21–30, 45; *OR*, 46(1):1304, 1322–24.

27. At dawn on April 12, Gordon and his corps led the ANVA infantry column down the Richmond-Lynchburg Stage Road to surrender at Appomattox Court House. Approximately 18,000 Confederates stacked their arms and laid down their battle flags. In the afternoon, Walker gave a final address to his division. Calkins, *Final Bivouac*, 30–46; Willie Walker Caldwell, *Stonewall Jim: A Biography of General James A. Walker, C.S.A.* (Elliston, Va.: Northcross House, Publishers, 1990), 133.

28. OH received a "Guards and Patrols Pass" from the provost marshal's office in Petersburg, permitting him to travel to City Point on the Union RR. Richard Brady Williams Private Collection.

29. Soldiers' Rest was a "way station" located next to the B&O RR station in Washington, D.C., which housed *in transit* Union soldiers.

30. Federal officials imprisoned OH on his way to New York City. Perhaps they arrested him because he was still wearing his Confederate captain's uniform, which was why his friend, Henry Kyd Douglas, was later apprehended at Shepherdstown. OH's return to New York City was further delayed when his former draftsman, Henry von Steinecker, tried to implicate him, along with Douglas and General Ed Johnson, in John Wilkes Booth's assassination of Lincoln. Douglas, *I Rode with Stonewall*, 340–41; Clemmer, *Old Alleghany*, 638.

Epilogue

1. James L. Swanson, *Manhunt: The Twelve-Day Chase for Lincoln's Killer* (New York: William Morrow, 2006), 4–6, 213–14; Michael W. Kauffman, *American Brutus: John Wilkes Booth and the Lincoln Conspiracies* (New York: Random House, 2004), 278–79.

2. Douglas, *I Rode with Stonewall*, 335–41; Clemmer, *Old Alleghany*, 638–39.

3. E. B. Long with Barbara Long, *The Civil War Day by Day: An Almanac 1861–1865* (New York: Da Capo Press, 1985), 691.

4. Louis J. Weichmann, *A True History of the Assassination of Abraham Lincoln and the Conspiracy of 1865*, ed. Floyd E. Risvold (New York: Alfred A. Knopf, 1975), 19–21.

5. Remnants of the Old Arsenal penitentiary are located today on the property of Fort McNair in Washington, D.C. Douglas, *Stonewall*, 339–41; Clemmer, *Old Alleghany*, 638.

6. Based on his journal entries, OH knew John Y. Beall (see chapter 24, note 1). James O. Hall Collection, Surratt Museum and Library; Elizabeth D. Leonard, *Lincoln's Forgotten Ally: Judge Advocate General Joseph Holt of Kentucky* (Chapel Hill: University of North Carolina Press, 2011), 209–15; William A. Tidwell, *April '65: Confederate Covert Action in the American Civil War* (Kent, Ohio: Kent State University Press, 1995), 14–29, 107–59; Kauffman, *American Brutus*, 342–50.

7. After deserting from the staff of Federal brigadier general Louis Blenker, Henry von Steinecker served as a rebel courier until Major General Johnson assigned him to work on Oscar's staff. (He also supported Jed Hotchkiss with his mapmaking.) In June 1864 von Steinecker deserted from the ANVA after being released from a Confederate guardhouse for stealing horses, which Oscar recorded in his journal. In researching his 1959 book on the Booth conspiracy, Theodore Roscoe discovered that von Steinecker's real name was Hans von Winklestein. Roscoe asserted that Judge Advocate General Holt and his team knew about the alias being used by Hinrichs's former draftsman, as well as his disreputable military record, yet tried to prevent negative information about von Steinecker from being discussed in the trial. Edward Steers, ed., *The Trial: The Assassination of President Lincoln and the Trial of the Conspirators*, (Lexington, Ky.: University Press of Kentucky, 2003), 64–66; Theodore Roscoe, *The Web of Conspiracy: The Complete Story of the Men Who Murdered Abraham Lincoln* (Englewood Cliffs, N.J.: Prentice-Hall: 1959), 454; 494–95; Douglas, *I Rode with Stonewall*, 340–41.

8. The *New York Times* covered Hinrichs's full testimony the next day. Douglas, *I Rode with Stonewall*, 348; Steers, *The Trial*, 66–69; "Trial of the Assassins," *New York Times*, May 31, 1865, 1.

9. Another sign of Carl Hinrichs's affluence is that, as recorded in several federal censuses, his household contained domestic servants from Ireland. (Carle Henrick [*sic*] household, Jamaica, N.Y., 1860; Carel E. L. Henricks [*sic*] household, Jamaica, N.Y., 1870; Charles Hinrich [*sic*] household, Jamaica, N.Y.; and Carl E. L. Hinrichs household, Brooklyn, N.Y., 1880.)

10. The Hinrichs family worshipped at Trinity Church in Brooklyn. The church listed Oscar as a lay delegate at a Protestant Episcopal Church convention held while he lived in New York City. The 1870 Federal census for Oscar Henrich [*sic*], Brooklyn, N.Y.; *Journal of the Seventh Convention of the Protestant Episcopal Church in the Diocese of Long Island Held in the Church of the Holy Trinity, Brooklyn, May 19th and 20th, 1874* (Brooklyn, N.Y.: The Convention, 1874), 14.

11. The map of the Rappahannock River area is the only known extant OH map related to his Civil War role as an engineer, which is surprising since he actively worked on maps with Hotchkiss, as noted in the latter's journals. Oscar Hinrichs, *Guide to the Central Park* (New

York: John Polhemus, Printer, 1875), 5–22; *Hinrichs' Guide Map of the Central Park* (New York: Mayer, Merkel & Ottmann, 1875), Library of Congress; *1879 Atlas of Topography*, Henson Family Properties.

12. The list of Oscar's General Land Office employment recommendations is from his single-page "Official Record" in Official Personnel Files, Records of the United States Civil Service Commission, Record Group 146, NARA, National Personnel Records Center, St. Louis, Mo.; NARA I, Record Group 77, Records of the U.S. Army Corps of Engineers, Office of U.S. Geographical Surveys West of the 100th Meridian, 1869–83, Letters Sent, 1874 – 83: letters of 10/22/78, 11/1/78, May 1879 (p. 428), and 5/13/79, from Wheeler to Hinrichs; and Register and Digests of Letters Received, 1874; 1876–82: letters from Hinrichs to Wheeler, 2/1/1879 (#143) and 4/1/79 (#742). Referenced in Wheeler's letters but not in the file are Hinrichs's letters to him of 10/15/78 and 10/26/78.

13. Charles Bolles, OH's former supervisor from the Coast Survey, surveyed the west coast of Mexico for the U.S. Navy in 1884. Perhaps he was the one who obtained the assignment for OH to produce a map of Mexico. *Official Register of the United States*, 1883, vol. 1, 549; Conover, *General Land Office*, 86; "Changes in Office," *New York Times*, June 14, 1885, 2; Oscar Hinrichs's August 8, 1891, suicide note, Probate File of Oscar Hinrichs, Office of Public Records, District of Columbia Archives; Charles P. Bolles Papers, North Carolina State Archives; Oscar Hinrichs, 1888 map of Mexico, Richard Brady Williams Private Collection.

14. An ink drawing of a Confederate flag with the saying "The Warrior's Banner Takes Its Flight to Greet the Warrior's Soul" remains as part of the OH collection passed on by his granddaughter (Mary Stanley Hessel). The quote is the last line of a poem, "Ashes of Glory," written by A. J. Requier. The original artwork appears to have been a Civil War charcoal drawing signed by "St. AG," which is preserved at Emory University. OH's memorabilia also includes other ink drawings, an extant watercolor of a riverfront city (probably Holzminden), and the translation of a French play entitled *The Prisons of Paris*. (According to Dr. Mary Stanley Hessel, Oscar spoke fluent French and Italian in addition to English and German.) Constance P. Ackerson, *Holy Trinity—Collington: Her People and Their Church* (Belair-Bowie, Md.: n.p., 1978), 160; Oscar Hinrichs coat of arms, Paul & Virginia drawing, and Confederate flag drawing, Adrienne Hessel Lissner Private Collection; Oscar Hinrichs coats of arms, Dr. Stanleigh Jenkins Private Collection; Oscar Hinrichs ink drawings, William Hinrichs Jenkins Private Collection; Wharton, *War Songs and Poems*, 187; Oscar Hinrichs watercolor painting, Cindy Lissner Hartley Private Collection; *The Prisons of Paris* transcription, Richard Brady Williams Private Collection.

15. In her notes about the Hinrichs family, Dr. Mary Stanley Hessel wrote that Oscar's grandfather—whom he was named after—was "captain of the horse" under "King William of Prussia who fought Napoleon." Because of his service, any descendant could attend the Royal Military Academy tuition free. Dr. Hessel believed that Oscar attended the military school, but there is no evidence that he did so. Summary of OH family history, Mary Stanley Hessell notes, Adrienne Hessel Lissner Private Collection.

16. Although the Holy Trinity churchyard in Bowie, Maryland, contains no markers bearing their names, Oscar and Mary Stanley Hinrichs are most likely buried at this church. The Holy Trinity burial register for the period 1885–1901 lists "Hinrichs" as being buried at the church on September 21, 1892—the burial date that is also shown on Oscar's death certificate. Mary's October 1891 death certificate states that she is buried at Holy Trinity Episcopal Church. In addition, minutes of an 1894 meeting of the church's vestry refer to "graves belonging to the Hinrichs family" as needing protection from the rector's horse to be pastured in the churchyard. Certificate of Death of Carl Ernst Ludwig Hinrichs, Department of Records and Information Services, Municipal Archives, City of New York; Mary Stanley

Hinrichs, Certificate of Death, Department of Health, Vital Records Division, Government of the District of Columbia; Oscar Hinrichs, Certificate of Death, Department of Health, Vital Records Division, Government of the District of Columbia; Oscar Hinrichs's August 8, 1891, suicide note, Probate File of Oscar Hinrichs, Office of Public Records, District of Columbia Archives; "A Strange Document," *Washington Post*, September 25, 1892, 4; vestry meeting minutes of November 18, 1894, Holy Trinity Protestant Episcopal Church Collection, Maryland State Archives SC 1226, Reel M930, 130; Burials Register, Register of Parish Records, 1885–1901, Holy Trinity Protestant Episcopal Church Collection, Maryland State Archives SC 1226-1-14, 81–82.

17. References to Stanley Hinrichs's Federal career are from his file in Official Personnel Files, Records of the United States Civil Service Commission, Record Group 146, NARA, National Personnel Records Center, St. Louis, Mo.; Adrienne Hessel Lissner, July 2006 interview with the author; Mary Stanley Hessell, *Portrait of a Patriot: The Story of John Wright Stanly, Revolutionary War Privateer* (New Bern, N.C.: Tryon Palace Commission, 1983). The Reverend Harvey Stanley added an extra "e" to his surname.

18. Sarah Hinrichs Brown watercolor painting of Mary Stanley Hinrichs, Richard Brady Williams Private Collection; Sarah Hinrichs Brown ceramic dish, Adrienne Hessel Lissner Private Collection. Purchase of a piano and violin listed in Oscar Hinrichs's August 8, 1891, suicide note, Probate File of Oscar Hinrichs, Office of Public Records, District of Columbia Archives; "A Strange Document," *Washington Post*, September 25, 1892, 4.

19. Jim Henson studied commercial art at the University of Maryland. While in college, he developed a successful local television show based on his early exploration of puppetry. Although Jim Henson died prematurely of pneumonia at the age of fifty-three, he left behind an extraordinary artistic legacy with the Muppets and his other entertainment and educational ventures. Author's interview with Barbara "Bobby" Miltenberger Henson, January 2007; Christopher Finch, *Jim Henson: The Works, the Art, the Magic, the Imagination* (New York: Random House, 1993), 2–11. See Brian Jay Jones, *Jim Henson: The Biography* (New York: Ballantine Books, 2013).

20. Hinrichs family photos, Barbara "Bobby" Miltenberger Henson Private Collection; OH coats of arms, Dr. Stanleigh Jenkins Private Collection; OH ink drawings, William Hinrichs Jenkins Private Collection; Hinrichs, "Maine to Dixie;" photos of OH, Amalia Ehringhaus Hinrichs letters, and 1879 *Atlas of Topography*, Henson Family Properties.

Selected Bibliography

Manuscripts

Boston Athenaeum, Boston, Mass.

    Map of the State of Virginia, Coast Survey Office. A. D. Bache, Supdt., compiled by W. L. Nicholson, Cutter Map Collection.

    Bradley T. Johnson's personal copy of George W. Booth, *A Maryland Boy in Lee's Army: Personal Reminiscences of a Maryland Soldier in the War Between the States, 1861–1865*. Baltimore: Privately published, 1898.

Christ Episcopal Church, Elizabeth City, N.C.

    Plat of the Elizabeth City Old Episcopal Cemetery

    Register of Parish Records

City of New York, Department of Records and Information Services, Municipal Archives, New York, N.Y.

    Certificate of Death of Carl Ernst Ludwig Hinrichs

    Certificate of Marriage of John Christophe Ehringhaus Hinrichs and Frederika Olive Sage

County Clerk's Office, New York County

    Declaration of Intention and Naturalization Record of Carl Ernst Louis Hinrichs, Cypress Hills Cemetery, Brooklyn, N.Y.

    Transcript, January 18, 2006, of Lot #1676, Section 14

Emory University, Manuscript, Archives, and Rare Book Library, Robert W. Woodruff Library, Atlanta, Ga.

    Drawing of Confederate flag by "St. AG," Picture File, B.V.

Government of the District of Columbia, Washington, D.C.

    Department of Health, Vital Records Division

        Certificate of Death of Mary Stanley Hinrichs

        Certificate of Death of Oscar Hinrichs

    Office of Public Records, District of Columbia Archives

        Probate File of Oscar Hinrichs

Cindy Lissner Hartley Private Collection

    Oscar Hinrichs watercolor painting

Henson Family Properties, New York, N.Y.

    Oscar Hinrichs, *Atlas of Topography* (1879)

    Oscar Hinrichs, *From Maine to Dixie: In the Early Days of the War*

    Amalia Ehringhaus Hinrichs Letters

    Photographs of Oscar Hinrichs

Barbara Miltenberger Henson Private Collection

    Artwork and photographs of Sarah Hinrichs Brown

    Photographs of Oscar Hinrichs, Mary Stanley Hinrichs, and Sarah Hinrichs Brown

Holy Trinity Episcopal Church, Bowie, Md.

    Photo of the Reverend Harvey Stanley

Dr. Stanleigh Jenkins Private Collection

    Oscar Hinrichs coats-of-arms

William Hinrichs Jenkins Private Collection

    Oscar Hinrichs drawings

    Non–Civil War map

    Photographs of Carl Hinrichs and Mary Anne Kinney Stanley

Adrienne Hessel Lissner Private Collection

    Sarah Hinrichs Brown ceramic dish

    Confederate flag drawing

    Mary Stanley Hessel photo

    Hinrichs family coat-of-arms

    Hinrichs family Confederate flag drawing

    H. Stanley Hinrichs photo

    Mary Stanley Hinrichs photo

    Oscar Hinrichs drawing of "Paul & Virginia"

    The Reverend Harvey Stanley diaries

    John Wright Stanly image

    Summary of Oscar Hinrichs family history, Dr. Mary Stanley Hessel

Maryland State Archives, Annapolis, Md.

    Holy Trinity Protestant Episcopal Church Collection, MSA SC 1226, Reel M930, parish register, 1845–1885; vestry minutes, 1844–1899; index, parish register, 1845–1885, and vestry minutes, 1845–1899; church records, 1826–1869; Letter of Consecration of the Chapel, signed by Bishop Whittington, March 29, 1842

    Holy Trinity Protestant Episcopal Church Collection, MSA SC 1226-1-14, register of parish records, 1885–1901

National Archives and Records Administration, National Personnel Records Center, St. Louis, Mo.

    Official Personnel File of H. Stanley Hinrichs, Record Group 146

    Official Personnel File of Oscar Hinrichs, Record Group 146

National Archives and Records Administration, Rocky Mountain Region, Denver, Colo.

    Records of the U.S. Mint, Denver, Colorado, Record Group 104

National Archives and Records Administration I, Washington, D.C.

    Compiled Service Records of Oscar Hinrichs, C.S.A. Engineers (National Archives Microfilm Publication M258, Reel 106; M331, Reel 124), Compiled Service Records of Confederate Soldiers Who Served in Organizations Raised Directly by the Confederate Government, War Department Collection of Confederate Records, Record Group 109

    Office of U.S. Geographical Surveys West of the 100th Meridian, 1869–1883, Letters Sent, 1874–1883, Record Group 77

    Office of U.S. Geographical Surveys West of the 100th Meridian, 1869–1883, Register and Digests of Letters Received, 1874, 1876–1882, Record Group 77; One-Name Papers, Records of the Provost Marshall, Record Group 109; Unfiled Slips and Papers Belonging to Confederate Service Records, Record Group 109

National Archives and Records Administration II, College Park, Md.
  Correspondence of A. D. Bache, Superintendent of U.S. Coast Survey, 1843–1865 (National Archives Microfilm Publication M258, Roll 106), Records of the Coast and Geodetic Survey, Record Group 23
  Correspondence of A. D. Bache, Superintendent of U.S. Coast Survey, 1843–1865 (National Archives Microfilm Publication M642, Roll 152), Records of the Coast and Geodetic Survey, Record Group 23
  U.S. Coast Survey Occupations of Personnel, 1844–1870, Records of the Coast and Geodetic Survey, Record Group 23
North Carolina State Archives, Raleigh, N.C.
  Charles P. Bolles Papers
Prince George's County Genealogical Society, Bowie, Md.
  "Holy Trinity Parish, Prince George's County, 1826–1869," Brigadier General Rezin Beall Chapter of D.A.R. (notes of the Reverend Harvey Stanley)
Register of Deeds for Pasquotank County, North Carolina, Elizabeth City, N.C.
  Certificate and Record of Death of A. M. G. Hinrichs
Saint Stephen and the Incarnation Episcopal Church, Washington, D.C.
  Incarnation Parish Records
Smithsonian Institution Archives, Washington, D.C.
  Salary Rolls for 1846–1904
Southern Historical Collection, University of North Carolina at Chapel Hill
  Edmund Ruffin Beckwith Papers, Series 1, 1846–1883, No. 3365
  The Lenoir Chambers Papers, 1907–1970, No. 1241, Box 22
  Jeremy Francis Gilmer Papers, 1839–1894, No. 276
  William F. Martin Papers, 1787–1865, No. 493
Surratt Museum and Library, James O. Hall Research Center, Clinton, Md.
  James O. Hall Collection
Thueringisches Staatsarchiv, Altenburg, Germany
  Geheimes Ministerium Archiv Nr. 387
U.S. Library of Congress, Geography and Map Division, Washington, D.C.
  Hinrichs' Guide Map of the Central Park. New York: Mayer, Merkel & Ottmann, 1875. G3804.N4:2C4 1875.H5.
Richard Brady Williams Private Collection
  G. W. Brooks Letter to Col. Stone, August 10, 1865
  Sarah Hinrichs Brown watercolor painting of Mary Stanley Hinrichs
  Oscar Hinrichs drawing of Buford Gap, Va.
  Oscar Hinrichs drawing of Natural Bridge, Va.
  Oscar Hinrichs "Guards and Patrols Pass," issued on April 16, 1865, for passage on the Union railroad to City Point, Va.
  Oscar Hinrichs Journal
  Oscar Hinrichs, 1888 map of Mexico
  Oscar Hinrichs transcription of "The Prisons of Paris"
  William F. Martin and G. W. Brooks deed to Griffin plantation, May 30, 1857

Databases

Ancestry.com. *1840 United States Federal Census.* Http://www.ancestry.com, accessed November 2006. Provo, Utah: The Generations Network, 2004. Original data: U.S.

Bureau of the Census. *Sixth Census of the United States, 1840.* Washington, D.C.: National Archives and Records Administration, NARA Microfilm Publication M704, 580 rolls.

———. *1850 United States Federal Census.* Http://www.ancestry.com, accessed November 2006. Provo, Utah: The Generations Network, 2005. Original data: U.S. Bureau of the Census. *Seventh Census of the United States, 1850.* Washington, D.C.: National Archives and Records Administration, National Archives Microfilm Publication M432, 1,009 rolls.

———. *1860 United States Federal Census.* Http://www.ancestry.com, accessed November 2006. Provo, Utah: The Generations Network, 2004. Original data: U.S. Bureau of the Census. *Eighth Census of the United States, 1860.* Washington, D.C.: National Archives and Records Administration, National Archives Microfilm Publication M653, 1, 438 rolls.

———. *1870 United States Federal Census.* Http://www.ancestry.com, accessed November 2006. Provo, Utah: The Generations Network, 2003. Original data: U.S. Bureau of the Census. *Ninth Census of the United States, 1870.* Washington, D.C.: National Archives and Records Administration, National Archives Microfilm Publication M593, RG 29, 1,761 rolls.

———. *1880 United States Federal Census.* H, accessed November 2006. Provo, Utah: The Generations Network, 2005. Original data: U.S. Bureau of the Census. *Tenth Census of the United States, 1880.* Washington, D.C.: National Archives and Records Administration, National Archives Microfilm Publication T9, 1,454 rolls.

———. *1900 United States Federal Census.* Http://www.ancestry.com, accessed November 2006. Provo, Utah: The Generations Network, 2004. Original data: U.S. Bureau of the Census. *Twelfth Census of the United States, 1900.* Washington, D.C.: National Archives and Records Administration, National Archives Microfilm Publication T623, 1,854 rolls.

———. *1910 United States Federal Census.* Http://www.ancestry.com, accessed November 2006. Provo, Utah: The Generations Network, 2006. Original data: U.S. Bureau of the Census. *Thirteenth Census of the United States, 1910.* Washington, D.C.: National Archives and Records Administration, National Archives Microfilm Publication T624, 1,178 rolls.

———. *1920 United States Federal Census.* Http://www.ancestry.com, accessed December 2006. Provo, Utah: The Generations Network, 2005. Original data: U.S. Bureau of the Census. *Fourteenth Census of the United States,1920.* Washington, D.C.: National Archives and Records Administration, National Archives Microfilm Publication T625, 2,076 rolls.

———. *1930 United States Federal Census.* Http://www.ancestry.com, accessed December 2006. Provo, Utah: The Generations Network, 2002. Original data: U.S. Bureau of the Census. *Fifteenth Census of the United States,1930.* Washington, D.C: National Archives and Records Administration, NARA Microfilm Publication T626, 2,667 rolls.

Brooklyn Genealogy Information Page. Http://www.bklyn-genealogy-info.com, accessed November 2006.

Family Search International Genealogical Index. IGI Individual Record—North America: "Frank Hinrichs, 09 Dec 1878 Birth Certificates, Manhattan, New York, New York." Http://www.familysearch.org, accessed October 2006.

National Cemetery Administration. *U.S. Veterans Cemeteries, ca. 1800-2006.* Http://www.ancestry.com, accessed November 2006. Provo, Utah: The Generations Network, 2006. Original data: National Cemetery Administration. *Nationwide Gravesite Locator.*

New York City Death Index. Http://www.italiangen.org/NYCDeath.stm, accessed December 2006.

Index

Callaway, William G., 316 (n. 3)

Campbell, John A., 236

Camp Chase, Ohio, 191, 322 (n. 9)

Camp Douglas, Ill., 309 (n. 9)

Canby, E. R. S., 236

Cape Hatteras, N.C., 209, 296 (n. 8)

Carlisle, Pa., 84, 85, 151, 304 (n. 16)

Carlisle Barracks, Pa., 304 (n. 16)

Carter, Thomas H., 122

Cary, Hetty, 216, 227, 326 (n. 13), 328 (nn. 6, 15), 329 (n. 1), 330 (n. 8)

Cary, Jennie, 326 (n. 13), 328 (n. 6)

Catherine Furnace, Va., 303 (n. 4)

Catlett Station, Va., 96, 103, 305 (n. 4)

Cedar Creek, Battle of, 200, 203, 219, 323 (nn. 24, 25), 324 (n. 1), 325 (n. 16)

Cedar Creek, Va., 154–56, 197

Cedar Run/Mountain, Battle of, 68

Cemetery Hill, Gettysburg, Pa., 89, 304 (n. 31)

Centreville, Va., 9, 10, 36, 96, 97, 104, 298 (n. 7), 320 (n. 2)

Chaffin's Bluff, Va., 51, 105, 187

Chambersburg, Pa., 84, 152, 155, 304 (n. 1), 316 (n. 11), 322 (n. 6)

Chancellorsville, Battle of, 10, 78–80, 98, 177, 198, 303 (n. 4)

Chancellorsville, Va., 122, 252, 274

Charleston, S.C., 6, 13–16, 109, 115, 153, 194, 209, 210, 212, 220, 225, 228, 230, 235, 245, 247–49, 323 (n. 18)

Charles Town, W.Va., 53, 113, 145, 148, 149, 159, 161, 163, 170, 177, 189, 212, 299 (n. 5), 317–20 (n. 10)

Charlottesville, Va., 58, 117, 120, 138, 217, 252, 313 (n. 1), 322 (n. 7)

Cheatham, Benjamin F., 248

Chesapeake & Ohio Canal, 175

Chester Gap, Va., 217

Chew, R. Preston, 117, 196, 308 (n. 1)

Chimborazo Hospital, Richmond, Va., 185, 187

Christ Episcopal Church, Elizabeth City, N.C., 7, 291 (n. 10), 292 (n. 20)

Ciphers, 3, 4

City Point, Va., 11, 268, 269, 334 (n. 28), 328 (n. 20)

Clark, Joseph C., 300 (n. 17)

Clark's Mountain, Va., 306 (n. 9)

Clausewitz, Carl von, 300 (n. 7)

Cleburne, Patrick, 215, 326 (nn. 6, 8), 329 (n. 3)

Cleveland, Grover, 275

Cobb's Point, N.C., 34

Cockrill, D. H., 313 (n. 18)

Cold Harbor, Battle of, 130, 132

Cole, Henry A., 163, 318 (n. 17)

Coleman, R. T., 114, 308 (n. 10)

Collington, Md., 2, 7, 8, 274, 294 (n. 2)

Collins, Napoleon, 208, 325 (n. 27)

Colston, Raleigh E., 77, 80, 114, 303 (nn. 3, 5, 7), 308 (nn. 9, 11)

Colton's American Geographical Establishment, 274

Congress Springs, Va., 140

Connor, James, 197, 323 (n. 24)

Conrad, Kate, 168

Conrad, R. Y., 319 (n. 2)

Contee, John, 21, 22, 294 (n. 2)

Cooke, John R., 75, 103, 104, 136, 240, 258, 306 (n. 5), 307 (n. 15), 310 (n. 24), 329 (n. 5), 333 (n. 11)

Cool Spring, Battle of, 149, 315 (n. 2)

Cooper, Samuel M., 312 (n. 17)

Corbin mansion, Va., 303 (n. 1)

Corcoran Art School, Washington, D.C., 276

Corley, James L., 69

Corse, Montgomery D., 262

Cosby, George B., 204

Coup d'oeil, 62, 300 (n. 7)

Covesville, Va., 138

Cox, William R., 234, 242, 243

Crook, George, 135, 136, 150, 151, 249, 313 (n. 21), 315 (n. 2), 318 (n. 17), 320 (n. 3), 321 (n. 13), 323 (n. 24), 330 (n. 18), 334 (n. 20)

Cross Keys, Battle of, 10, 54–57, 183, 184, 299 (n. 12)

Crutchfield, Stapleton, 300 (n. 6)

CSA Engineer Department/Corps, 9, 10, 12, 30, 31, 36, 39, 49, 50, 102, 113, 152, 298 (n. 13), 305 (n. 13), 307 (nn. 1, 17–19), 323 (n. 21); 327 (n. 19); First Engineer Regiment, 307 (n. 17, 18), 333 (n. 19)

CSA troops: 1st Corps, 185, 264, 313 (n. 20); 2nd Corps, 10, 91, 255, 303 (n. 9), 304 (n. 5), 305 (n. 2), 306 (n. 9), 308 (n. 10), 313 (n. 23), 322 (n. 5), 322 (n. 5), 329 (n. 7); 3rd Corps, 220, 333 (n. 11)

Cullen, George, 330 (n. 17)

Culpeper Court House, Va., 46, 47, 68, 80, 81, 95, 96, 155, 305, 317

Culp's Hill, Gettysburg, Pa., 88, 89, 304 (nn. 4–6)

Cumberland, Md., 80, 84, 155, 249, 330 (n. 18)

Cumberland Church, Va., 11, 266, 334 (n. 20)

Curlew, CSS, 33

Currency inflation, 110, 307 (n. 1)

Cushing, William B., 209, 325 (n. 28), 327 (n. 3)

Custer, George A., 156, 157, 267, 305 (n. 9), 308 (n. 1), 310 (n. 22), 317 (n. 20), 322 (nn. 13, 15), 324 (n. 8), 325 (n. 23), 327 (n. 16), 331 (nn. 3, 4), 334 (n. 23)

Cutts, Richard D., 29

Dabney, Robert, 299 (n. 12)

Dabney, Virginius, 124, 134

Dalgren, Ulrich, 118–20, 135, 308 (nn. 2, 4, 13), 309 (nn. 6, 8)

Daniel, John W., 311 (n. 5)

Daniel, Junius, 124, 310 (n. 23)

Daniel, Raleigh T., 217, 327 (n. 14)

Danville, Va., 111, 141, 173, 187, 228, 333 (nn. 12, 14)

Davis, Jefferson F., 6, 14, 19, 113, 120, 233, 290 (n. 1), 309 (n. 8), 311 (n. 2), 323 (n. 18), 328 (nn. 9, 17)

Davis, William S., 321 (n. 11), 322 (n. 8)

Deatonville, Va., 266, 333 (n. 16)

Dement, William F., 119, 309 (n. 6)

Devin, Thomas C., 323 (n. 25)

Dimmock, Charles H., 256, 257, 261, 262, 331 (n. 10), 332 (n. 6)

Dinwiddie Court House, Va., 237, 239, 263, 332 (n. 4)

Doles, George P., 123, 131, 151, 310 (n. 16), 312 (n. 8)

Double Bridges, Va., 266

Douglas, Henry Kyd: accusation against, 3, 271–73, 306 (n. 7); Spotsylvania, 124; Gordon reorganization, 129; chief of staff, 130, 311 (nn. 4, 5); 1st half Shenandoah Valley Campaign, 145, 160; 2nd half 1864 Shenandoah Valley Campaign, 174, 176, 190, 191, 314 (n. 10), 316 (nn. 3, 12), 319 (nn. 2, 17); Petersburg Campaign, 214, 216, 234, 253, 322 (n. 10), 328 (n. 6); playing chess with OH, 219; Mary Surratt's trial, 273; released from prison, 274; Pennsylvania Campaign, 304 (n. 3); Pegram's body, 329 (n. 8); casualty estimate, 330 (n. 10); arrested at Shepherdstown, 334 (n. 30)

Douglas, Henry T., 298 (n. 6)

Douglass, Marcellus, 68, 301 (n. 4)

Downsville, Md., 153

Drewry's Bluff, Va., 10, 51, 299 (n. 1), 311 (n. 27), 312 (n. 17), 328 (n. 5)

Dublin, 179

Duffié, Alfred N. A., 205, 315 (n. 1), 318 (n. 17), 325 (n. 17)

Duffield Station, 314 (n. 16)

Duryée, Abram, 299 (n. 7)

Dutch Gap Canal, Va., 189, 226, 228, 328 (n. 5)

Duvall, Edmund, 21, 22, 294 (n. 2)

Early, Jubal: 1862 Shenandoah Valley Campaign, 299 (n. 11); Second Manassas Campaign, 68, 301 (nn. 7, 11); Pennsylvania Campaign, 82, 85, 88, 303 (nn. 4, 9), 304 (nn. 1, 5, 13); after Gettysburg, 90, 91; Mine Run Campaign, 96–103; winter quarters, 115; Overland Campaign, 120–22, 123–25, 130; 1st half 1864 Shenandoah Valley Campaign, 138, 142, 307 (n. 3), 309 (n. 12), 310 (n. 17), 311 (n. 5), 312 (nn. 8, 16), 313 (nn. 1, 2, 4), 314 (nn. 6, 7, 12, 15–18), 315 (nn. 1, 19, 20, 22–26); 2nd half 1864 Shenandoah Valley Campaign, 149, 151, 156–58, 160–71, 174–78, 181–85, 197–204, 316 (nn. 5, 9, 12, 13, 15), 317 (nn. 1, 5, 6, 19), 318 (nn. 9, 16, 18, 19), 319 (nn. 4, 9, 10, 13, 17, 18), 320 (nn. 1, 3, 6, 7, 9), 321 (nn. 1, 11, 12, 14), 322 (nn. 2, 3, 15), 323 (nn. 24, 27), 324 (nn. 5, 7, 8, 10–12), 325 (nn. 14, 16, 29), 326 (n. 3), 327 (nn. 14, 16); introduction to Carl Hinrichs, 207; end of war, 252–53, 331 (nn. 3, 4); "Chronicles of Jubal," 284–86

East Cemetery Hill, Pa., 304 (nn. 3, 5, 6)

Edward's Ferry, N.C., 293 (n. 29), 327 (n. 3)

Ehringhaus, Blucher, 38, 291 (n. 10), 293 (n. 29), 296 (n. 4), 297 (n. 18)

Ehringhaus, Catherine Erskine, 296 (n. 4)

Ehringhaus, John C., 5, 37–41, 292 (n. 20), 296 (n. 11), 297 (nn. 16, 27)

Ehringhaus, John Christoph Blucher, 297 (n. 18)

Ehringhaus, Matilda Gregory (Till?), 296 (n. 4), 307 (n. 18)

Ehringhaus Light Artillery, 296 (n. 11)

Ehringhaus Light Infantry, 296 (n. 11)

Ehringhaus Street, Elizabeth City, N.C., 297 (n. 16)

Elizabeth City, N.C., 2, 5, 7, 9, 10, 30–33, 35, 37–40, 50, 211, 254, 292 (n. 20), 297 (nn. 16, 23, 29), 307 (nn. 6, 19), 318 (n. 14), 323 (n. 21), 330 (n. 16)

Elliott, Gilbert, 293 (n. 29)

Ellis, Anderson, 179

Ellis, John W., 40, 41, 320 (n. 9)

Ely's Ford, 106, 117, 119, 120

Elzey, Arnold, 29, 55

Emack, George M., 305 (n. 9)

Evans, Clement A., 215, 240–42, 313 (n. 18), 324 (n. 4), 326 (n. 9), 329 (n. 5)

Ewell, Richard S.: introduction to OH, 44–46; directed OH to reconnoiter Charles Town, 53; 1862 Shenandoah Valley Campaign, 54–58, 299 (nn. 12, 15); Seven Days Battles, 64, 301 (nn. 1, 10, 11); Cedar Run/Mountain, 67; Second Manassas Campaign, 301; 1862 Maryland Campaign, 70–71; Pennsylvania Campaign, 84, 88, 304 (nn. 3–6, 13, 16), 305 (nn. 4, 9–11); after Gettysburg, 90, 91; Mine Run Campaign, 97, 102; Overland Campaign, 123–25, 132, 169, 307 (nn. 3, 5), 309 (n. 15), 310 (n. 16), 311 (nn. 1, 29); Richmond defenses, 203, 312 (n. 14); Chancellorsville, 303 (n. 9)

Fairfield, Pa., 86

Falling Waters, W.Va., 90, 91, 305 (n. 9)

Farley, Henry S., 231, 232, 328 (n. 13)

Farmville, Va., 11, 265–68, 333 (n. 15)

Farragut, David G., 317 (n. 18)

Fauquier County, Va., 103, 104, 194

Fayetteville, N.C., 291 (n. 15), 292 (n. 16), 329 (n. 23), 331 (n. 7)

Field, Charles W., 156, 160

Finegan, Joseph, 115, 131, 241, 242, 308 (n. 14), 312 (n. 9), 329 (n. 7)

Finley's Mill, Va., 99, 100

Fisher's Hill, Va., 155, 173, 181, 183, 192, 196, 201, 207, 208, 320 (n. 7), 321 (n. 11), 323 (n. 27)

Five Forks, Battle of, 11, 262, 263; "shad bake," 332 (n. 7), 333 (n. 9)

Florida, CSS, 208, 325 (n. 27)

Foote, Henry S., 236

Forrest, Nathan Bedford, 136, 139, 185, 188, 190, 194, 206, 208, 323 (n. 18), 325 (nn. 20, 26)

Forrestville, Va., 193

Fort Branch, N.C., 217, 219, 225, 327 (n. 15)

Fort Columbus (Governor's Island), N.Y., 251, 297 (n. 24)

Fort Delaware, Pa., 132, 312 (n. 13), 325 (n. 24), 327 (n. 15)

Fort Fisher, N.C., 6, 220, 293, 307; attacks against, 220, 225, 231–33, 293 (n. 2), 307 (n. 19), 327 (n. 20), 328 (nn. 10, 11, 16, 17), 329 (n. 23)

Fort Gilmer, Va., 190, 203

Fort Gregg, Va., 332 (n. 14)

Fort Harrison Va., 187–91, 194, 203, 322 (n. 4), 323 (n. 23)

Fort Lafayette, N.Y., 16

Fort Mahone, Va., 263

Fort McRae, Va., 191

Fort Pickens, Fla., 16

Fortress Monroe, Va., 11, 92, 112, 119, 224, 269, 328 (n. 4)

Fort Stedman, Battle of, 11, 258, 332 (n. 1)

Fort Stevens, Va., 315 (n. 24)

Fort Union, Va., 81

Fort Warren, Mass., 16, 33, 271, 272, 327 (n. 15)

Fort Washington, Va., 295 (n. 7)

Fort Whitworth, Va., 332 (n. 14)

Foster, John G., 33, 34, 296 (n. 10)

Franklin, William B., 147

Frederick City, Md., 70–72, 83, 146

Fredericksburg, Battle of, 92

Fredericksburg, Va., 12, 27, 75, 78, 80, 84, 92, 93, 98, 120, 303 (n. 1)

Fredericksburg, CSS, 234, 328 (n. 20), 329 (n. 21)

Frederick's Hall, Va., 119, 309 (n. 6)

Freestone Point, Va., 295 (n. 11)

Fremont, John C., 55–58, 183

French, William H., 306 (nn. 10, 12, 13)

Frink, Dr. Lorenzo and Mrs., 15, 133, 209, 218, 243

"From Maine to Dixie" (OH postwar essay), 278, 294 (n. 1), 295 (n. 6)

Front Royal, Va., 52, 82, 91, 154–56, 201, 298, 317 (n. 18), 323 (n. 22), 324 (n. 12)

Funk, John H. S., 123, 126

Funkstown, Md., 72

Gaines's Mill, Battle of, 61, 64, 132–34, 172, 300 (n. 4), 301 (n. 12)

Garland, Samuel, 319 (n. 2)

Garrett, Thomas M., 95, 101

Geary, John, 299 (n. 7)

Georgetown Pike, Md., 146, 147

Georgia troops: 12th Infantry, 130; 13th Infantry, 68

Germanna Ford, Va., 95, 98, 99, 101, 102, 105, 106, 119, 120, 122, 274, 305 (n. 1)

Getty, George W., 124, 310 (n. 25), 333 (n. 10)

Gettysburg, Battle of, 84–86, 88, 90, 271, 304 (n. 1), 305 (n. 7), 312 (n. 13), 326 (n. 4)

Gilmer, Jeremy, F., 9, 298 (n. 13), 307 (n. 19)

Gilmor, Harry W., 113, 145, 204, 314 (nn. 5, 16), 315 (n. 26), 316 (n. 11)

Glassie, Daniel, 276

Glendale, Battle of, 62, 300 (n. 5), 301 (n. 12)

Globe Tavern, Va., 318 (n. 11)

Godwin, Archibald C., 160, 170, 172, 318 (n. 7), 320 (n. 6), 321 (n. 11)

Goldsboro, N.C., 261

Goode's Bridge, Va., 265, 333 (n. 13)

Goodwin, Claudius L., 233

Gordon, John B., 11; Maryland Campaign, 67, 68; Pennsylvania Campaign, 93; Overland Campaign, 122–26, 129–31, 133, 309 (nn. 9, 12, 13), 310 (nn. 16, 17), 311 (nn. 3–5, 7); promoted to major general, 129, 311; 1st half 1864 Shenandoah Valley Campaign, 142, 143, 146, 147, 313 (n. 2), 315 (nn. 2, 22); 2nd half 1864 Shenandoah Valley Campaign, 149, 150, 155, 156, 161–64, 167, 174, 178, 181–83, 187, 196, 197, 199, 200–204, 210, 213, 318 (nn. 9, 18), 320 (n. 6), 321 (n. 12), 324 (nn. 4–7, 9), 325 (n. 16); Petersburg Campaign, 213–15, 220–22, 226, 229, 233, 235, 238, 240, 243, 258, 326 (n. 9), 329 (nn. 1, 5, 7), 331 (nn. 5, 9), 332 (nn. 4, 13); loaned *Art of War* to OH, 228; OH New York plot, 11, 251–56; retreat to Appomattox Court House and final Army of Northern Virginia charge, 266, 267, 332 (n. 4), 333 (nn. 12, 13, 16, 19), 334 (nn. 20–24, 27); Appomattox speeches, 267, 268

Gordonsville, Va., 51, 67, 68, 93, 136, 217, 219, 301 (n. 1), 327 (n. 16)

Gorgas, Josiah, 208, 211, 230, 325 (n. 25)

Governor Island, N.Y., 40, 297 (n. 24)

Grant, U. S., 109, 120, 125, 128–30, 132–38, 140–41, 143, 145, 152, 153, 158, 162, 169, 173, 179, 185, 192, 206, 208, 213, 214, 220, 222, 229, 231, 238, 239, 243, 252, 267, 268, 292, 310 (n. 20), 311 (nn. 3, 27), 312 (nn. 8, 10), 315 (n. 23), 319 (n. 18), 320 (n. 10), 321 (nn. 1, 21), 322 (n. 7), 328 (nn. 7, 20), 329 (n. 22), 330 (n. 11), 332 (nn. 2, 14), 334 (nn. 21–25)

Gravelly Run, Va., 240, 247, 329 (n. 6), 332 (n. 5)

Green Castle, Pa., 84

Green Castle Turnpike, Pa., 83

Greene, Benjamin H., 315 (n. 20)

Greene, George S., 304 (n. 5)

Greensboro, N.C., 230, 333 (n. 12)

Green Spring Valley, Va., 67, 301 (n. 3)

Greenville, Va., 141

Greenwood Station, Va., 59

Gregg, David M., 185

Gregg, John, 194, 323

Griffith, Richard, 47

Grimes, Bryan, 155, 210, 218, 242, 243, 253–55, 263, 321 (n. 14), 330 (n. 10), 331 (n. 8)

Guard and Patrols Pass, Petersburg to City Point, 271, 334 (n. 28)

Guide to Central Park (Oscar Hinrichs), 274

Guinea Station, Va., 75

Guthrie, James, 162

Hagerstown, Md., 72, 83, 86, 89, 90, 153, 154, 302 (n. 17)

Hainesville, W.Va., 152

Hall, Carvel, 261, 332 (n. 4)

Halleck, Henry, 29, 322 (n. 7)

Hallowing Point, Mason's Neck, Va., 9, 27

Halltown, W.Va., 53, 145, 317 (n. 1), 318 (n. 7)

Halsey, Don P., 167, 168, 189, 319 (n. 2)

Hamilton, Alexander, 295 (n. 4)

Hamilton, N.C., 217

Hamilton's Crossing, Va., 80, 119, 148

Hammond's Mill, 153

Hampton, Wade, 9, 27, 119, 135, 136, 156, 173, 214, 233, 234, 252, 254, 295 (n. 11), 309 (n. 7), 314 (n. 17), 325 (n. 15), 328 (n. 13), 331 (n. 7)

Hancock, Md., 155

Hancock, Winfield S., 128, 158, 310 (n. 17), 311 (nn. 1, 27), 312 (n. 9)

Hanover Junction, Va., 128, 311 (n. 1)

Hardee, William J., 106, 125, 164, 167, 220, 248

Harman, John A., 136, 146, 313 (n. 23)

Harpers Ferry, W.Va., 71–74, 82–84, 145, 146, 152, 159, 170, 175, 197, 302 (nn. 15, 17), 314 (n. 16)

Harris, Richard S., 261, 332 (n. 2)

Harrisburg, Pa., 85, 151, 304 (n. 16)

Harris Farm, Battle of, 126, 311 (n. 29)

Harrison, William E., 49

Harrisonburg, Va., 54, 55, 143, 182, 191, 209, 211, 254, 299 (n. 10), 316 (n. 4)

Hatcher's Run, Battle of, 11, 241, 242, 329 (n. 8), 330 (n. 10)

Hatcher's Run, Va., 215, 230, 239, 240, 243, 263, 329 (n. 4), 332 (n. 9)

Hays, Alexander, 124, 310 (n. 25)

Hays, Harry T., 97, 105, 122–24, 161, 304 (n. 5), 309 (n. 12), 310 (n. 24), 327 (n. 14)

Heckman, Charles A., 125

Hedgesville, Va., 151

Heintzelman, Samuel P., 195

Henley's, Battalion, 119

Henningsen, Charles F., 32, 296 (n. 7)

Henson, Barbara Brown Miltenberger, 276–78, 337 (n. 19)

Henson, Elizabeth Brown, 276, 277

Henson, Jim, 5, 6, 277, 278, 291 (n. 12), 337 (n. 19)

Herbert, James R., 83

Hessel, Frederick, 276

Hessel, Mary Stanley, 276, 336 (nn. 14, 15), 337 (n. 17)

Hessey, David S., 104, 307 (n. 17)

Heth, Henry, 96, 97, 104, 240, 258, 264, 305 (n. 11), 312 (n. 8), 329 (n. 5), 333 (n. 11)

Hewson, Butt, 130, 311 (n. 16)

Hicks, Thomas H., 16

High Bridge, Va., 266, 333 (n. 19)

Hill, Ambrose P.: U.S. Coast Survey, 50, 298 (n. 15); Seven Days Battles, 60, 300 (n. 1); Cedar Run/Mountain, 67; 1862 Maryland Campaign, 67, 71–75, 302 (n. 22); Chancellorsville Campaign, 78, 80; Pennsylvania Campaign, 80, 84–90; after Gettysburg, 90, 91; Mine Run Campaign, 96–98, 103, 104, 115, 306 (n. 5), 307 (n. 15); 1864 winter quarters, 115; Overland Campaign, 117, 118, 120, 122, 123, 125; Petersburg Campaign, 143, 162, 214, 220, 222, 256, 257, 260, 263, 264, 314 (n. 15), 327 (n. 19), 329 (nn. 1, 5), 330 (n. 12), 332 (n. 14), 333 (n. 11); OH visited prior to death, 260; killed in action, 264

Hill, Daniel H., 47–49, 54, 106, 298 (nn. 13, 14); lost orders at Frederick City, 70, 72, 302

Hindman, Thomas, 106

Hines, Thomas, 330 (n. 1)

Hinrichs, Amalia Matilda Ehringhaus, 2, 5, 6, 202, 291 (nn. 10, 13), 297 (n. 27), 330 (n. 16)

Hinrichs, Carl, 5, 19, 37, 41, 207, 274, 276, 290 (n. 8), 291 (n. 9), 297 (n. 27), 335 (n. 9)

Hinrichs, Carl, Jr., 40, 297 (n. 24)

Hinrichs, Ernest, 274

Hinrichs, Fanney Bettie Klaner, 5

Hinrichs, Frank, 274

Hinrichs, John Christoph "Chris" Ehringhaus, 105, 162, 170, 172, 177, 184, 307 (n. 18), 318 (n. 14), 319 (n. 7), 324 (n. 9)

Hinrichs, Mary "Mamie" Stanley, 8, 202, 248, 274–77, 336 (n. 16), 337 (n. 18)

Hinrichs, Oscar: Guards and Patrols pass, 2; New York detective, 7; aided by John and Mary Surratt, 8, 24, 295 (n. 6); commandeering Union schooner, 9, 26, 27; report to Gen. Jackson, 10; pressure from Bache, 15–20; U.S. Oath of Allegiance, 16–19, 36–41; ordered to report to Cutts and Halleck in St. Louis, 29; Cobb's Point fort at Elizabeth City, 33, 296 (n. 12); CSA engineer post, 36; promoted to U.S. Coast Survey subassistant, 36; report to Gen.

312 (n. 16), 313 (nn. 3–5, 22), 314 (nn. 6, 9, 17), 315 (n. 26), 316 (nn. 9, 15), 319 (n. 5)

Hunter, Robert M. T., 236

Hunter, Robert W., 124

Hupp's Hill, Va., 156, 196–99

Huston, George, 236, 329 (n. 24)

Hutton, Eppa, 263

Hyattstown, Md., 147

Hyattsville, Md., 276

Imboden, John D., 84, 150, 194

Indiana, U.S. troops: 7th Infantry, 304 (n. 4); 27th Infantry, 302 (n. 16)

Indian Head, Va., 295 (nn. 7, 9)

Iverson, Alfred, 153, 319 (n. 2), 327 (n. 1)

Jackson, Thomas J. "Stonewall," 3, 10, 51, 54, 57, 58; leadership, 52, 197, 198; capture of Front Royal and Winchester, 52, 299 (n. 3); Christian faith, 52, 299 (n. 4); first meeting with OH, 52–53; Cross Keys and Port Republic, 54, 55, 299 (nn. 11–15), 300 (n. 16); Seven Days Battles, 60–62, 300 (nn. 1–6); Cedar Run/Mountain, 67, 68, 301 (nn. 5, 6); Second Manassas, 69; 1862 Maryland Campaign, 70–75, 302 (n. 15); Chancellorsville Campaign, 77, 78, 303 (n. 6); loss of, 82, 91, 95, 110, 147, 183, 185, 188; gravesite, 141, 314 (n. 9); Rev. Lacy, 177

Jackson, William L. "Mudwall," 150, 155, 161, 317 (n. 17)

Jacob's Ford, Va., 306 (nn. 10, 12)

James River Squadron, 328 (n. 20)

Jarratt's Station, Va., 254, 331 (n. 8)

Jeffersontown, Va., 68, 103

Jenifer, Walter H., 204, 325 (n. 14)

Jenkins, Agnes Brown, 276, 278

Jenkins, Albert G., 84

Jenkins, Micah, 124, 310 (n. 23)

Jericho Mills, Va., 311 (n. 1)

Jetersville, Va., 265

Johnson, Andrew, 272

Johnson, Bradley, 145, 147, 154–56, 163, 170–74, 311 (n. 2), 314 (n. 17), 315 (nn. 19, 25, 26)

Johnson, Bushrod R., 216, 217, 258, 263, 326 (n. 12), 332 (nn. 1, 5)

Johnson, Edward: accusation against, 3,

271–74, 306 (n. 7), 334 (n. 30); Pennsylvania Campaign, 80–90, 303 (n. 9), 304 (nn. 1, 3–5, 13, 14); after Gettysburg, 91; Mine Run Campaign, 95–106, 306 (nn. 11–13); 1864 winter quarters, 113; "Old Fencerail," 114; Overland Campaign, 120, 122–24, 309 (nn. 11, 12), 311 (n. 4); Ft. Warren Prison, 272, 327 (n. 15); Mary Surratt trial, 273; released from D.C. prison, 274; Ft. Delaware prison, 327 (n. 15); assigned von Steinecker to OH, 335 (n. 17)

Johnson's Island prison, 174, 309 (n. 9), 331 (n. 1)

Johnston, Joseph E.: introduction to OH, 46; OH to assess Yorktown defenses, 2, 10, 36, 43–50, 109, 115, 125, 126, 141, 151, 188, 194, 197, 198, 220, 232, 233, 246, 248, 249, 254, 257, 259, 261, 297 (n. 1), 298 (nn. 3–5, 10), 308 (n. 14), 330 (n. 17), 331 (n. 12), 333 (n. 12)

Johnston, Joseph F., 174, 319 (n. 16)

Johnston, Robert D., 122, 124, 174, 177, 178, 195, 200, 214–19, 224, 230–33, 236, 238, 241–49, 251, 260–63, 310 (n. 24), 319 (nn. 2, 16), 321 (n. 11), 329 (n. 6), 332 (nn. 1, 2), 334 (n. 25)

Jomini, Baron Antoine-Henri, *The Art of War*, 228, 300 (n. 7), 316 (n. 8)

Jones, Brian Jay, *Jim Henson: A Biography*, 278, 337 (n. 19)

Jones, John B., 9

Jones, John M., 95, 99–102, 118, 120–24, 145, 306 (n. 11), 309 (n. 11), 310 (nn. 17, 23)

Jones, William E., 133

Jones Farm, Battle of, 258, 332 (n. 14)

Jordan Springs, Va., 82

Kautz, August V., 185

Kearneysville, 161, 318

Kearny, Phil, 70

Kelly, Benjamin F., 249, 330 (n. 18)

Kelly's Ford, Va., 98, 306 (n. 8)

Kentucky, CSA troops: 10th Infantry, 326 (n. 2)

Kerfoot, John B., 153, 316 (nn. 12, 13)

Kernstown, Second Battle of, 150, 316 (n. 3)

Kernstown, Va., 143, 150, 156, 316 (n. 5)

Kershaw, Joseph B., 161, 171, 182–85, 187,

317, 320, 323, 332, 333; 8th Corps, 177, 203, 249, 320 (n. 3); 9th Corps, 214; 11th Corps, 78; 19th Corps, 203, 316 (n. 9), 320 (n. 6); 24th Corps, 268; Grand Review of Sherman's army, 272

University of Maryland, 337 (n. 19)

University of North Carolina, 296 (n. 8)

Upton, Emory, 123, 310 (n. 16)

Urbana, Md., 147

Valley Pike, Va., 54, 141, 150, 156, 316 (n. 4), 322 (nn. 13, 15), 324 (nn. 8, 12)

Vance, Zebulon, 215, 317 (n. 3)

Vandergriff, Supt., 138

Vaughan, John C., 150, 168, 174

Venable, Charles S., 203

Verdiersville, Va., 111, 120

Virginia, CSS, 16

Virginia II, CSS, 234, 328 (n. 20), 329 (n. 21)

Virginia Military Institute, Lexington, Va., 141, 314 (n. 9)

Virginia troops: 2nd Infantry, 3, 4, 273, 306 (n. 7); 3rd Infantry, 66; 5th Infantry, 123, 126; 13th Infantry, 330 (n. 17); 21st Infantry, 123; 25th Infantry, 99, 132; 29th, 313 (n. 25); 33rd Infantry, 236; 42nd Infantry, 161; 58th Infantry, 318 (n. 8); 59th Infantry, 296, (n. 7); 5th Cavalry, 174, 309 (n. 8); 9th Cavalry, 309 (n. 8); 19th Cavalry, 155; Stonewall Brigade, 3, 68, 83, 126, 131, 165, 174, 273, 274, 301 (n. 5), 304 (n. 14), 312 (n. 8)

Wachusetts, USS, 208, 325 (n. 27)

Wadsworth, James S., 124, 310 (n. 25)

Walker, Henry H., 124, 310 (n. 24)

Walker, James A., 82, 111, 122–24, 248, 249, 255, 304 (n. 14), 306 (n. 11), 310 (n. 24), 327 (n. 14), 332 (n. 3), 334 (n. 27)

Wallace, Lew, 147

Wallace, William H., 258

Wardensville, W.Va., 155

Warren, Gouverneur K., 143, 306 (nn. 5, 14), 307 (n. 15), 308 (n. 12), 309 (n. 14), 311 (n. 1), 312 (n. 8), 329 (nn. 4, 7), 332 (nn. 4, 5, 7)

Warren, T. H., 303 (n. 5)

Warrenton, Va., 96, 103

Warrenton Junction, Va. 306 (n. 6)

Warrenton Springs, Va., 96, 103

Washington, D.C., 2, 4, 11, 12, 14–16, 18, 24, 41, 50, 84, 101, 125, 140, 146, 147, 152, 153, 155, 175, 177, 204, 234, 236, 269, 271, 272, 274–77, 295 (n. 7), 314 (nn. 15, 18), 315 (n. 24), 323 (n. 25), 334 (n. 29), 335 (n. 5), 337 (nn. 16, 18)

Washington Artillery, 334 (n. 20)

Waynesboro, Va., 183, 209, 213, 252, 257, 321 (n. 20), 331 (nn. 3, 4)

Webb, Alexander S., 124, 310 (n. 25)

Webb, Lewis N., 313 (n. 20)

Weldon Railroad, Va., 134, 191, 214, 230, 235, 237, 239, 251, 318 (n. 11), 327 (nn. 3, 15), 331 (n. 8)

Wells, Henry H., 271

West Fort, Va., 304 (n. 13)

Weston, J. Alden, 296 (n. 3)

Westport, Battle of, 325 (n. 19)

Wharton, Gabriel C., 156, 161, 164, 178, 179, 181, 183, 187, 196, 201, 210, 213, 252, 318 (n. 18), 321 (n. 12), 324 (n. 7), 327 (n. 16), 331 (n. 4)

Wheat, C. Roberdeau, 65, 172, 301 (n. 12)

Wheeler, George M. (Wheeler Survey), 274

Wheeler, Joseph, 173, 218, 245

Wheeling, W.Va., 316 (nn. 13, 15)

White Oak Road, Battle of, 263

White Oak Road, Va., 262, 330 (n. 12), 332 (nn. 7, 8)

White Oak Swamp, Va., 61, 62, 66, 300 (n. 6)

White's Ford, Va./Md., 70, 302 (n. 14)

White Sulphur Springs, Va., 103

Whiting, Jasper, 198

Whiting, William H. C. "Chase," 19, 30, 34, 43, 61, 107, 133, 198, 216, 220, 231–33, 307 (n. 19), 312 (n. 17), 328 (nn. 11, 18)

Wickham, Williams C., 119, 157, 160, 176–78, 182, 183, 193

Wilcox, Cadmus M., 224, 264

Wilderness, Battle of, 130, 162

Wilderness Run, Va., 120

Wilderness Tavern, Va., 119

Williams, Jesse M., 123, 310 (n. 17)

Williams, John A., 243, 253, 255–57, 262, 330 (n. 12)

Williamsburg, Va., 47, 48, 112, 298 (nn. 8, 10), 308 (n. 13), 309 (n. 7)

Williamson, George, 125

Williamsport, Md., 72, 84, 90, 151, 153, 154, 302 (n. 17), 305 (n. 10)

Willis, Edward S. "Ned," 130, 311 (n. 7)

Willow Pump, Va., 187

Wilmer, Skipwith, 124

Wilmington, N.C., 6, 10, 13, 15, 16, 38, 40, 66, 109, 113, 191, 203, 209, 216, 217, 219, 220, 221, 224, 225, 229, 231–33, 235, 249, 251, 252, 291 (n. 15), 293 (n. 2), 294 (nn. 4, 7), 307 (n. 6), 323 (n. 21), 326 (n. 12), 327 (n. 15), 328 (nn. 10, 17), 331 (n. 2)

Wilmington Light Infantry, 291 (n. 15)

Wilson, James H., 317 (n. 6), 320 (n. 6)

Winchester, Second Battle of, 81, 82, 304 (n. 13)

Winchester, Third Battle of, 178, 320 (n. 3), 316 (n. 6), 323 (n. 27), 329 (n. 24)

Winchester, Va., 23, 52, 54, 58, 74, 75, 81, 82, 91, 145, 149, 150, 151, 154, 156, 157, 163–65, 167–72, 176, 178, 179, 183, 192, 196, 199, 203, 205, 206, 229, 295 (n. 4), 299, (n. 8), 302 (n. 20), 304 (nn. 13, 14), 305 (n. 8), 314 (n. 16), 316 (nn. 3, 5, 13), 317 (n. 20), 319 (nn. 2, 5), 324 (n. 7), 325 (n. 17)

Winder, Charles S., 64, 68, 301 (n. 5)

Winder, John H., 30, 31, 38, 39, 296 (n. 2)

Winklestein, Hans von (von Steinecker), 335 (n. 7)

Wise, Henry A., 32, 134, 258, 59, 293 (n. 28), 296 (n. 7), 312 (n. 17)

Witcher, William A., 123, 310 (n. 17), 312 (n. 8)

Withers, Robert W., 161, 318 (n. 9)

Wofford, William, 157

Wood, John T., 307

Woodstock, Va., 143, 192, 196, 207, 210, 322 (n. 13)

Woodstock Races, 322 (n. 15)

Wootton, Richard, 22, 23, 294 (n. 2)

Wright, Ambrose R., 111, 300 (n. 8)

Yellow Tavern, Va., 310 (n. 22)

York, Pa., 116, 143

Yorktown, Va., 112

Yorktown defenses, 47, 48, 298 (nn. 8, 10)

Young, Pierce M. B., 328 (n. 13)

Zoan Church, Va., 303 (n. 4)

Zoar Church, Va., 101, 120

CPSIA information can be obtained
at www.ICGtesting.com
Printed in the USA
LVHW100803130922
728240LV00004B/421